D1520744

ECONOMY, SOCIETY AND
POLITICS IN BENGAL:
JALPAIGURI 1869-1947

To the
People of Jalpaiguri

ECONOMY, SOCIETY AND POLITICS IN BENGAL: JALPAIGURI 1869-1947

RANAJIT DAS GUPTA

DELHI
OXFORD UNIVERSITY PRESS
BOMBAY CALCUTTA MADRAS
1992

Oxford University Press, Walton Street, Oxford OX2 6DP
New York Toronto
Delhi Bombay Calcutta Madras Karachi
Kuala Lumpur Singapore Hong Kong Tokyo
Nairobi Dar es Salaam
Melbourne Auckland

and associates in
Berlin Ibadan

SBN 0 19 562841 1

Typeset by Comprint, New Delhi 110029
Printed by Crescent Printing Works Pvt. Ltd., New Delhi 110001
and published by S.K. Mookerjee, Oxford University Press
YMCA Library Building, Jai Singh Road, New Delhi 110001

Contents

List of Tables

Acknowledgements

This work has grown out of a paper that was presented to a Rabindra Bharati University-sponsored Seminar held in early 1981. I am grateful to Sunil Kumar Sen, then Head of the Department of History in the University, who extended an invitation to me for contributing a paper to the Seminar and who originally provided stimulus for undertaking this study.

During the long period taken in the making of the work I have accumulated debts to many people and institutions and I am grateful to all of them. I must put on record my debts, first to a large number of political workers: Congressmen, Communists, Congress Socialists, Revolutionary Socialists, Forward Blocists, peasant and worker leaders and activists and also several observers of the socio-political changes who granted me interviews, some of them several times. A complete list of them has been given elsewhere. Here, however, I must make particular mention of Khagendra Nath Das Gupta, Upendra Nath Barman, Rabindranath Sikdar, Sachin Das Gupta, Madhab Datta, Bimal Hoare, Subodh Sen, Jagannath Oraon, Buni Oraon, Birendra Kumar Neogy, Samar Gangully and Bimal Das Gupta. From them I have learnt a lot. Madhab Dutta also allowed me to use his unpublished reminiscences. Interviews and discussions with Nirendranath Bagchi, Parimal Mitra, Asit Sen, Anil Mukherjee, Abul Huda, Nikhil Ghatak, Badal Sarkar, Nani Bhattacharya, Sabed Ali Ahmed and Taiyab Chaudhuri too have been very useful. Kalyani Das Gupta communicated to me some valuable information. It is a matter of lasting grief that many of them have not lived to see the completion of the work. I must also state that some of the ideas presented here had been formed in discussions with Naresh Chakrabarty and Deba Prasad (Patal) Ghosh much before the research project was undertaken.

Biswanath Mukherjee, Abdullah Rasul, Abani Lahiri and Sunil

Sen, all of whom were important district and provincial-level leaders in the late 1930s and 1940s, not only gave interviews but also spent long discussion hours in the light of their own experiences.

I am also grateful to numerous colleagues and friends. I owe much to Tanika and Sumit Sarkar who read the manuscript, offered many valuable suggestions and encouraged me to complete the work. I am also much indebted to Barun De who throughout gave me both intellectual and practical help. Gautam Chattopadhyay, Asok Sen, Nripendranath Bandyopadhyah and Sunil Munsi also went through parts of the manuscript and discussions with them helped me greatly to clarify my arguments and analysis. Debesh Roy through his perceptive writings and Paritosh Kumar Dutta through his extensive observations have deepened my understanding of some of the aspects I have dealt with.

I must also record my debts to Ravinder Kumar, Binay Bhusan Chaudhuri, Partha Chatterjee, Amalendu Guha, Gautam Bhadra, Rudrangshu Mukherjee, Sekhar Bandyopadhyay, the late Hiteshranjan Sanyal and Swaraj Basu, a young research scholar. All of them have provided useful advice and encouragement. My friend Amalendu (Fatik) Roy Chaudhuri was keenly interested in the progress of the work and gave valuable suggestions. But, sadly enough, he passed away before the work could be completed.

I also wish to thank my colleagues at the Institute especially Satyesh C. Chakraborty and Surendra Munshi for their support.

I am also greatly indebted to Kalpana Neogy, Paritosh Kumar Datta, the late Nirmal Chaudhuri, Chandidas Lahiri, Biswanath Karmakar, Manik Sanyal and Ananda Gopal Ghosh of Jalpaiguri and Gayatri Roy and Maitreya Ghatak of Calcutta for giving me access to rare books, journals and reference materials. Arun Prasad Mukerjee, while Special Inspector General, Police, West Bengal, gave me the opportunity to consult some important police records. Ranjit Das, formerly Secretary, Dooars Branch of the Indian Tea Association (Binnaguri), and its staff provided me excellent facilities for consulting their records. My friend Dipak Sanyal rendered much cooperation in making available to me certain important materials, and I also owe a special word of thanks to Ashish Gupta who supplied me with some Home Department records. I am particularly grateful to the management and staff of several institutions for providing access to source materials: the Indian Tea

Planters Association (Jalpaiguri); Nehru Memorial Museum and Library, New Delhi; National Archives of India, Delhi; West Bengal State Archives; National Library, Calcutta; West Bengal Secretariat Library; the Ananda Bazar Patrika Library; and specially to Arun Ghosh, Librarian, Kaliprasad Basu and other membes of the staff of the Library at the Centre for Studies in Social Sciences, Calcutta. I have also received excellent cooperation from the Librarian and staff of the Bidhan Chandra Roy Memorial Library, Indian Institute of Management, Calcutta. I am also grateful to late Saroj Mukherjee for giving me permission to make use of Muzaffar Ahmed Pathagar, Calcutta and also to late Gangadhar Adhikari and late Chinmohan Sehanabish for helping me to get access to the records kept at Ajoy Bhavan, New Delhi.

In Jalpaiguri town I received a great deal of help from a large number of people. Of them I would like first to mention Biman Dutta who in spite of being a busy lawyer gave valuable time to help me. Bimalendu Majumdar has helped considerably in searching for source materials and making available some of these. Bijoya Shome (née Das) compiled some necessary evidence for my enquiry. Among others, I must acknowledge my debts to Sukhamoy (Kanu) Das Gupta, Habibar Rahman, Akram Hossain and Haripda Roy. Considerable help was also provided by Banabihari Dutta and his family, Sushil Ganguly, Rana Sen and Bimal Bose in Alipur Duar, by Tusar Bandyopadhyaya and B.D. Rai in Birpara, by Bhyaram Lohar and his family in Hasimara, by Stephan Kunjuru in Kalchini, by Birendra Kumar Majumdar and the late Anil Gupta in Oodalabari, and by Mantu Saha in Chalsa. I must put on record my thanks to my hosts who provided warm hospitality during my fieldwork: in Jalpaiguri town Nirmala Mitra, Nupur and Amitaba Mitra, and Sobha Hoare, Bappaditya, Tutun and Rahul Hoare; in Mal the late Golapbasini Das Gupta; and in Delhi Maya Lahiri and her family, and Alo Bhowmik and her family.

Ajoy Sarkar went through the proofs with skill and enthusiasm. But in view of our close relationship the question of offering formal thanks to him does not arise. My thanks go to Anjushree Chakraborty who prepared the map with meticulous care, to Arun Ghosh who prepared the index, to Mamata Dutta, who helped me in collecting and processing some of the materials, to Samir Sarkar and Tapan Chakraborty who typed earlier drafts from handwritten pages and to Asit Manna, Jadav Dutta and Ashok Kr. Mondal who put the manuscript on word processor efficiently and cheerfully.

Initial research and writing were partly financed and supported by Centre for Studies in Social Sciences, Calcutta. But without the generous funds and assistance from the Centre for Management Development Studies (CMDS), Indian Institute of Management, Calcutta, this work would not have been completed. The study also received support from City College, Calcutta. I am grateful to the authorities of these institutions.

I have presented and discussed parts of the book in seminars at Nehru Memorial Museum and Library, New Delhi, Jadavpur University, Centre for Studies in Social Sciences, Calcutta and North Bengal University. My thanks to all particupants in those seminars.

Earlier versions of parts of this book have appeared in Amit Kumar Gupta (ed.), *Myth and Reality: The Struggle for Freedom in India, 1945-47*, (Manohar, New Delhi, 1987) and *Economic and Political Weekly* (22 November 1986 and 30 September 1989). I am grateful to the editors and publishers of these volumes for giving me permission for reproducing materials previously published.

I owe special thanks to the Oxford University Press, New Delhi for the trouble and care they have taken to publish this work.

I am aware that there are many shortcomings in the book and I alone am responsible for these. Any failure to mention my debt is inadvertent and is regretted.

A final few words. My mother Shrimati Asru Bala Das Gupta, a doctor by profession, had an innate compassion for suffering people and was an ardent patriot and friend of the Communist movement. She had given her unstinted support to my work among the peasants and workers in Jalpaiguri in the 1950s which contributed to the formation of my early notions about the society and politics in the district. It is an everlasting grief that she did not see the beginning of the research. My father Shri Indu Bhusan Das Gupta inculcated an inquisitiveness in my boyhood days. But he did not live to see even my involvement in academic work.

Although Chhaya despaired at the long time—more than a decade now—taken by the work and wondered at times whether it would ever be completed, the book would not have taken its present form without her unflagging support, understanding and encouragement over the years. Abhijit, Soma and Anirban have in their own ways lightened some of the stresses and strains of writing the book. I cannot but wonder whether I have done justice to them.

Ranajit Das Gupta
Indian Institute of Management, Calcutta

Abbreviations

BAR	*Report on the Administration of Bengal* (Bengal Administration Report), annual
BLAP	Bengal Legislative Assembly Proceedings
BLCP	Bengal Legislative Council Proceedings
BLRC	*Report of the Land Revenue Commission, Bengal, 1940*
COI 1891 Report	*Census of India, 1891*, Vol 3, *Report of the Census of Bengal*
COI 1901 Report	*Census of India, 1901*, Vol. 6, *The Lower Provinces of Bengal and their Feudatories*, Pt. 1, *Report*
COI 1911 Report	*Census of India 1911*, Vol. 5, *Bengal, Bihar and Orissa and Sikkim, Pts. 1 and 2, Report and Tables*
COI 1921 Report	*Census of India, 1921*, Vol. 5, *Bengal*, Pt. 1, *Report*
Centenary Souvenir	*Jalpaiguri Jela Satabarshikee Smarak Grantha*, Jalpaiguri, 1970
DBITA	Duars Branch of Indian Tea Association
DPA	Duars Planters Association
Dinajpur SSR	*Final Report on the Survey and Settlement Operations in the District of Dinajpur, 1934-40*
Duars SSR	*Survey and Settlement of theWestern Duars in the District of Jalpaiguri, 1889-95*
EPW	*Economic and Political Weekly*
FCR 1 and 2	Bengal. Home. Political. Divisional Commissioner's Fortnightly Confidential Report. 1 refers to the 1st half of a month and 2 to the 2nd half

FR 1 and 2	NAI. Home. Political. Confidential. Fortnightly Report on the Political Situation in Bengal. 1 refers to the 1st half of a month and 2 to the 2nd half
GOB	Government of Bengal ·
GOI	Government of India
GOWB	Government of West Bengal
IESHR	*Indian Economic and Social History Review*
IHR	*The Indian Historical Review*
ITA	Indian Tea Association
ITPA	Indian Tea Planters Association
Jalpaiguri DH	*West Bengal: District Handbooks: Jalpaiguri*
Jalpaiguri DG	*Eastern Bengal and Assam District Gazetteers: Jalpaiguri*
Jalpiaguri SSR	*Final Report on the Survey and Settlement Operations in the Jalpaiguri District, 1906-16*
NAI	National Archives of India, New Delhi
Rangpur SSR	*Final Report on the Rangpur Survey and Settlement Operations, 1931-38*
SAB	*A Statistical Account of Bengal*
WBSA	West Bengal State Archives, Calcutta

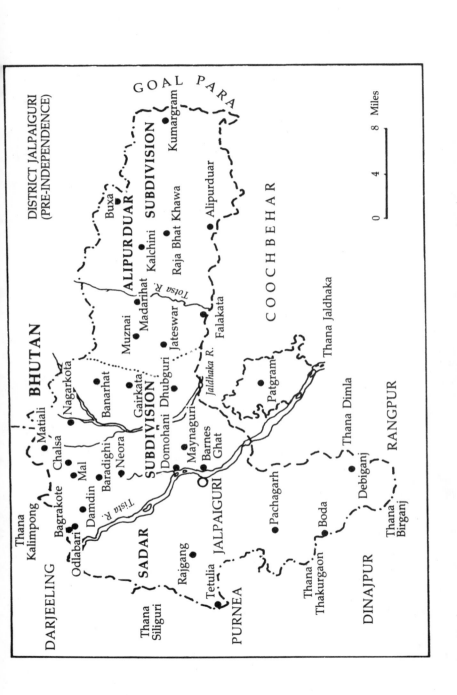

DISTRICT JALPAIGURI
(PRE-INDEPENDENCE)

GOAL PARA

BHUTAN

ALIPURDUAR SUBDIVISION

Buxa

Kalchini

Kumargram

Raja Bhat Khawa

Alipurduar

Muznai

Madarihat

Jateswar

Falakata

Totsa R.

COOCH BEHAR

Nagarkota

Banarhat

Gairkata

Domohani Dhubguri

Jaldhaka R.

Thana Jaldhaka

Matiali

Chalsa

Neora

Baradighi

Maynaguri

Barnes Ghat

SUBDIVISION

Patgram

Mal

Damdin

Bagrakote

Tista R.

JALPAIGURI

Pachagarh

Thana Dimla

Debigani

RANGPUR

Thana Kalimpong

Odlabari

SADAR

Rajgang

Boda

Thana Birgani

DARJEELING

Tetulia

Thana Siliguri

PURNEA

Thana Thakurgaon

DINAJPUR

0   4   8   Miles

1 Introduction

The present work is a study on the historical process of economic, social and political changes in the district of Jalpaiguri (in north Bengal) in late colonial period. The starting point is 1869, the year the district was formed, and the terminal point is the year of Independence and Partition.

The work is one more addition to the burgeoning literature on regional-local history in India. One major factor behind the recent interest in local history has been the awareness among a large body of historians that all-India or even provincial studies of the highly variegated and complex historical processes in a vast and complex country like India often leave many crucial gaps in our knowledge. It is felt that case studies at the regional, local or micro-level will be of help in bringing to light many dark corners of the history of our recent past and that local case studies will contribute towards a better comprehension and deeper understanding of the unfolding of diverse historical processes, their coexistence and complex inter-connexions at the all-India level. It is out of such a belief that this work has been undertaken. It should, however, be added such regional local histories can only be complementaries to all-India and provincial histories and not substitutes for the latter.

One may ask why of all the districts in Bengal, Jalpaiguri has been chosen. Several explanations may be offered. One is personal. The author belongs to Jalpaiguri district and has the advantage of knowing certain aspects of the district from close quarters. But there is something more than the personal consideration. Jalpaiguri, which was the northern-most plain district in undivided Bengal, had a number of distinctive ecological, demographic and socio-economic features. The district, formally constituted in 1869, had two different arrangements for administration. The population consisted overwhelmingly of Hinduized and Islamized autochthons and immigrant tribals like Oraons, Mundas and Santals. They constituted the basic producers, while Bengali Hindus and Muslims immigrating from east Bengal dominated services and professions and Marwaris, wholesale and retail trade. Thus, the society in Jalpaiguri was a plural society marked by considerable socio-cultural differentiations.

As regards the economy, the most distinguishing feature was the introduction and consolidation of the European-owned and controlled tea plantation economy—a typical form of colonial economic penetration and exploitation. The economy came to be characterized by diverse forms of subjugation and systematic methods of coercion, even terrorization against labour. The agrarian structure came to be marked, as in most other frontier districts of Bengal, by the evolution of the *jotedar-adhiar* relationship marked by multiple forms of surplus extraction and dependency. One of the aims of this work is to study the working of the plantation system and agrarian class structure of Jalpaiguri district in the late nineteenth and early twentieth centuries within the broader dimensions of colonial political economy.

The specificities of the economy and society of Jalpaiguri affected various social groups and social classes in significant ways and had their imprints on the various socio-political activities and movements that unfolded in the district, for example, the social mobility movement among the Rajbansi Hindus which had its own peculiarities and the short-lived Tana Bhagat movement among the Oraon workers in the Jalpaiguri Duars. A distinctive feature of the Rajbansi movement was that it was neither subsumed into Congress nationalism like the Mahisyas of Midnapore, nor developed into a separatist force like the Namasudras. It is also remarkable that throughout the period under consideration Jalpaiguri remained free from any overt Hindu-Muslim conflict, though tensions were not entirely absent. A study of such a district, it is hoped, will be of help in bringing out the differences as well as the similarities of the local pattern with the pattern of socio-political changes that took place at the national and provincial levels.

One more major consideration behind the choice has been the nature and particularities of the popular movements that the district witnessed in the closing decade of the period under study: a quick shift in the Krishak Samiti's activities towards a focus on *adhiars* or share-croppers several years before the *tebhaga* struggle, the role of unionized railway labour in mobilizing plantation labour and tribal *adhiars* in parts of Duars, the beginning of Duars plantation labour organization and movement, the *tebhaga* movement in Debiganj-Pachagar-Boda in 1946-7, the combination of railway labour-plantation labour-*adhiar* peasant-tribal interaction producing a popular upsurge in parts of Duars in early 1947, and the creation of parallel political authority in areas of struggle. An examination of these movements is important on its own merit and may also be of help in exploring popular movements in other regions and areas.

While the above considerations have led the author to opt for a district study and choose Jalpaiguri for such a study, the broad focus is on the unfolding of a number of social and political movements—movements that at times overlapped and also reinforced each other as well as those that remained distanced from each other or even worked at cross-purposes. A major focus is, however, on the nationalist politics at various levels and also on the complex connexions and interactions between it and popular movements at the base level and also the process and extent of transformation of nationalist politics into a radical, left politics involving worker and peasant mobilization. As regards the left politics, the origin and progress of peasant and worker movements led by the Communist Party are considered in some details. It is hoped that the findings of this study will be of more than historical significance.

Finally, a few words may be added about the sources. I have tried to utilize a wide range of primary and secondary sources and the select bibliography gives an indication of the materials—both official and unofficial—which have been consulted. But most of the unpublished materials were consulted either in Calcutta or New Delhi. Being a study on the district of Jalpaiguri, an important source should have been the materials available there. But I had to face an almost insuperable difficulty in getting source materials in Jalpaiguri. The devastating flood that occurred in Jalpaiguri in 1968 played havoc with a major part of local materials such as the records that had been preserved at the Collectorate Record Room and Divisional Commissioner's Office in Jalpaiguri, the files of weeklies and journals published from Jalpaiguri, and records of business organizations like Indian Tea Planters Association, Jal-paiguri. I was nevertheless able to locate some such materials and have made considerable use of these. But I could not locate even a single issue of *Nishan*, the weekly mouthpiece of Muslim League politics in Jalpaiguri. To make up for the problems with regard to local materials, I have met and interviewed as many people as possible who were either active in or close witnesses to the social and political life from 1920 to 1947. Their memory has constituted a source for important and interesting information and social and political perceptions. Interviewing people—political leaders and workers at the district level, peasant and labour activists at the grassroots and observers with sensitivities—who have lived and experienced the period under study, has been a most exciting part of this study.

2 The Land and the People

ADMINISTRATIVE HISTORY

Jalpaiguri was the northern-most district in pre-1947 Bengal[1]. It was bounded on the west by the Purnea district of Bihar and Darjeeling district, on the north by the Himalayan kingdom of Bhutan and also Darjeeling district, on the south by the districts of Rangpur and Dinajpur and the Princely State of Koch Bihar and on the east by Goalpara district of Assam. In 1947, under the Radcliffe Award the five police stations of Patgram, Tetulia, Pachagar, Boda and Debiganj went to East Pakistan (now Bangladesh).

The district consisted of two well-defined tracts which differed in physical features, history, administrative arrangement, types of economic activities, tenurial arrangement and production systems. One tract which lay to the west of the Tista river and also Patgram to the east of the river (see Map) came under British rule after the East India Company received the Dewani in 1765. The total area of this tract in 1931 was 879 sq. miles. The other tract lying to the east of Tista, known as Western Duars or in common parlance Duars[2], having an area of 2053 sq. miles, was taken away from Bhutan at the end of the Anglo-Bhutan War of 1864-5[3]. It deserves mention that till the 1940s people of local origin not only in Jalpaiguri but in neighbouring Rangpur district too referred to Duars as 'Bhotan'[4].

In the perspective of administrative history of the Bengal Presidency, the district of Jalpaiguri was most recent. It came into being in January 1869 by the amalgamation of the Tetulia subdivision of Rangpur district with the recently annexed Duars. The district headquarters came to be located in Jalpaiguri, a village which was the residence of the Zamindar of the Baikunthapur estate. Hooker who visited 'Jalpaigoree' in early 1849 described it as a 'large straggling village'[5].The place also had a military cantonment even before it was selected as the district headquarters. Some time later it was also chosen as the headquarters of the Commissioner for Rajshahi Division.

Political history prior to British conquest

Part of the older tract, specifically speaking the *chaklas* of Boda and Patgram, was under the Zamindari estate of the Koch Bihar Raj[6]. Accounts differ about the rise of Koch kings. According to one account, the kingdom was founded by Vishu or Visvasimha, who was born most probably in a Mech family, sometime in the closing decade of the fifteenth century(1496-1553?). On assuming power he got himself anointed as king, according to Hindu rites. Available accounts suggest that it was during his rule that the Koches became semi-Hinduized and adopted the name of Rajbansis, that is, of the royal race[7]. It deserves mention that the Koch Bihar Raj was the only ruling princely house in the whole of Bengal which retained the status of independent rulers during the Mughal period and continued as protected native princedom under British rule. But in the *chaklas* mentioned above the Koch Bihar rulers had the status of Zamindars even in the pre-British days.

The rest of the older tract was under the Zamindari of Baikunthapur. It was held by the Raikats (Rai-Kot, that is, chief of the fort), a collateral branch of the Koch Bihar Raj, Sishu or Sisyasimha, the step-brother of Visva, being the first Raikat. In the early years the Raikats acknowledged the suzerainty of the Koch Bihar Raj. But from about 1588 till 1770s, that is, for nearly two centuries Baikunthapur was in reality an autonomous semi-feudatory kingdom paying tribute to the Mughal Government. However, probably because of help given by Darpadev Raikat, Raja of Baikunthapur, to the Sannyasi rebels, sometime in 1770s it was reduced to the position of a Zamindari. After 1793, the Baikunthapur Zamindari was settled in perpetuity[8].

Administrative arrangement under the British

Administratively, the two tracts came to have different arrangements. The portion separated from Rangpur district was known as the Regulation tract, as it was administered under the ordinary laws and regulations in force in Bengal. The Duars or the non-Regulation tract was administered under the Scheduled Districts Act of 1874. This meant that no Act passed by any legislature was automatically applicable to the non-Regulation tract unless the Governor-General or the Governor directed so. Under this Act the head of the district administration or Collector-Magistrate, known as Deputy Commissioner, came to enjoy and exercise much greater power and authority than the District Magistrates of the non-scheduled or regulated districts[9]. One major implication was that in the non-regulation tract any activity considered prejudicial to the British Raj was virtually ruled out. In his work of administration the Deputy Commissioner was assisted by two Subdivisional Officers (SDO)[10] and Superintendent of Police, the officer in charge of the district police administration. Till early 1940s all these officials were British and they supervised a large body of Indian assistants and clerks.

The late nineteenth and early twentieth centuries witnessed a steady and systematic extension of British administration and control. The colonial authority assumed the responsibility for the maintenance of law and order and intervened vigorously whenever it considered that there was any threat to the existing order, introduced important changes in the agrarian system prevailing in the tract annexed from Bhutan (the area separated from Rangpur district was already under the purview of the Permanent Settlement), resorted to periodic measurements of land and re-assessment of revenue, actively promoted the expansion of the tea plantation system which was launched under the aegis of the British planters and helped the planters to organize migration of labour and also to keep it under firm control. The growing intervention of the colonial state came to have a deep and far-reaching impact on the economy and society in Jalpaiguri district.

While the administrative set-up indicated above was a crucial component of the power-structure that emerged during British rule, there were several other important elements. In the tea plantation areas, the European planters and their assistants in combination with their Indian counterparts exercised power and control. There were, as well, *chowkidars*, *dafadars*, *sardars* and *baidars*. In the rural society in the Regulation tract, the two Zamindars and their *amlas*, the *jotedars* or the chief tenants, the *dewanias*

and the moneylenders, grain-dealers and traders were parts of the
hierarchy. In the rural areas of Duars all the latter elements except
the Zamindars and their *amlas* were present. Under British rule,
they consolidated their position.

ECOLOGICAL ASPECTS

The physical and climatic features of the tract that earlier belonged
to Rangpur district differed little from those of the latter district
and the adjoining portion of the Dinajpur district. That part of
Jalpaiguri district presented a picture of a slightly undulating
expanse of level paddy fields and scrub jungles, broken only by
groves of bamboos, betelnut palms and fruit trees and the home-
steads of the *jotedars* surrounded by the houses of relations and
under-tenants. This physical feature was diversified only by the
Baikunthapur forest in the north. The land was a relatively old
settled tract with comparatively large population and was generally fertile.

The larger part of the Duars was, on the other hand, a submon-
tane tract cut up by numerous rivers and streams, which in the
rainy season became raging torrents, and covered for the most part
by almost impenetrable forests and reed jungles, giving shelter to
wild animals, and had a very scanty population. The geo-physical
and environmental features resulted in poor communications,
which were made extremely difficult in the rainy months, and
dispersed pattern of small settlements. By the early twentieth
century the entire tract, except for intervals of patches of ordinary
cultivation and large patches of reserved forests, came to be stud-
ded with tea gardens all over[11].

DEMOGRAPHIC AND SOCIAL BACKGROUND

The population size of Jalpaiguri district was never large. At the
time of the 1921 Census, the total population of the district was
9,36,269 with a density of just 319 per square mile. Only Khulna, of
all the plain districts in Bengal, had a scantier population. It will be
found from Table 1.1 that the earlier censuses reported much
smaller population. In fact, most part of the district, except the old

settled tracts of Boda, Patgram and Jalpaiguri—the tracts which earlier formed part of Rangpur district—was extremely sparsely populated.

The table shows that, in the last three decades of the nineteenth century and the first decade of the twentieth century, there was a remarkable increase of population, but this was confined entirely to the Duars. In the Regulation portion or the permanently settled area there was virtually no increase in the 50-year period between 1872 and 1921. This portion was already relatively densely populated and had almost reached the physical limits of expansion and cultivation. In fact, there was a steady drift of population from that part into the Duars where land was fertile and the rent rates low and, to a lesser extent, into the Siliguri subdivision of the Darjeeling district[12].

In the Duars there was a phenomenal, six times, increase of population between 1872 and 1921. This growth was primarily due to the massive migration of labour into the tea gardens. Besides that, peasant cultivators too were attracted not only from the western tract of the district but also from Rangpur district and Koch Bihar State. Census figures show that after Calcutta and Darjeeling district, it was in Jalpaiguri district that the greatest proportion of the population came to be composed of immigrants. Thus, the number of immigrants per thousand of actual population was 664 in Calcutta, 390 in Darjeeling and 287 in Jalpaiguri[13].

Table 2.1
Population Growth in Jalpaiguri District, 1872-1931

Census Year	Jalpaiguri District		Western Duars	
	Population	% Increase	Population	%Increase
1872	4 17 855	–	90 668	–
1881	5 80 570	26.97	1 82 687	101.49
1891	6 80 736	28.30	2 96 348	62.21
1901	7 87 380	15.66	4 10 606	38.55
1911	9 02 660	14.64	5 19 372	26.49
1921	9 36 269	3.72	5 58 971	7.62
1931	9 83 357	5.00	6 61 068	18.26

SOURCE: Census Reports for the relevant years.

Table 2.2
Population in Jalpaiguri District by Selected Social Groups, 1921

	Population	Per cent
High Castes		
Brahman	7 269	0.77
Vaidya	758	0.08
Kayastha	4 871	0.52
Rajput(Chhetri)	7 430	0.79
Intermediate & Low Castes		
Artisan Castes[a]	41 501	4.43
Service Castes[b]	7 575	0.80
Trading Castes[c]	1 319	0.14
Hinduized Autochthonous Social Groups[d]		
Khen(Khyan)	3 830	0.40
Koch	1 380	0.14
Mech	10 777	1.15
Rajbansi	3 10 545	33.16
Immigrant Tribals		
Munda	34 601	3.69
Oraon	1 15 350	12.32
Santal	23 988	2.56
Himalayan Groups		
Nepalis	19 023	2.03
Bhutia	4 997	0.53
Other Indian Social Groups		
Muslim	2 31 683	24.74
Sheikh[e]	2 26 767	
Saiyad	771	
Indian Christian	8 324	0.88
Foreign and Related Groups		
European	288	0.04
Anglo-Indian	114	
Others	1 04 476	11.18
Total	9 36 269	100

SOURCE: *Census of India*, 1921, *Bengal*, Pt.II, Table XIII, Pts. A, B and Appendix; Table XV

NOTES: [a]Artisan castes include Chamar, Dom, Jugi, Tanti, Kolu, Kamar, Kumhar, Lohar, Muchi, Sutradhar, Sonar, Sunri and Teli.

At this stage it needs to be mentioned that the population of the district was not a homogenous one. The society was composed of numerous and diverse social groups, of several historically evolved and even evolving social collectivities. As indicated in Table 1.2, the population belonged to different ethnic, linguistic and cultural groups, to various castes and religious communities.

Jalpaiguri is the land of several autochthonous groups: Meches, Rajbansis, Garos, Rabhas and Totos. All these groups perhaps barring the last one went through important social, religious and economic changes during the last few centuries.

Meches[14]

The Meches were one of the original and numerous inhabitants of the Duars and adjacent tracts and exercised control over fairly large areas in earlier centuries. According to a Persian chronicle, the *Tabakat-i-Nasori*, a Mech chief who embraced Islam and took the name of Ali Mech helped Muhammed Bakhtiar Khalji in his expedition in early thirteenth century. Several accounts state that the Koch Bihar Raj family is descended from a Mech leader Haria *alias* Haridas Mandal. Since the thirteenth century the Meches experienced a process of both Hinduization and Islamization.

In later centuries, however, their power suffered considerable decline. Following the British annexation, the process of decline became particularly marked and rapid. The Meches were originally accustomed to shifting cultivation. But finding themselves displaced from their lands by extension of tea plantation, by Rajbansi Hindus and Rajbansi Muslims who were habituated to cultivation by making use of ploughs and through exploitation by moneylenders and speculators, they were compelled to move to the more thinly-populated areas in the east of the district. By 1921 their number was greatly reduced.

---

[b]Service castes include Dhoba, Napit and Hari.
[c]Trading castes include Gandhabanik, Saha, Subarnabanik and Tambulibanik. The Census Tables do not give figures for Marwari traders.
[d]No figure is available for Islamized autochthonous groups like Rajbansis and Meches which were quite large. Figures for small groups like Rabhas and Garos are also not given in the Census Tables.
[e]Most of the Sheikhs were probably of local origin, that is, Islamized Rajbansis and Meches. See text below.

Rajbansi Hindus

The Rajbansis constituting the most numerous group among the autochthons of the district went through the parallel processes of Hinduization and Islamization. It is, however, curious that usually Rajbansis are only Hindus and all Muslims referred to as local Muslims are non-Rajbansis. But in the present work such a view is rejected and the position is taken that there are Rajbansi Hindus and Rajbansi Muslims[15]. In this sub-section our discussion is mainly confined to the former.

In this connexion it is relevant to note that the Hinduized Rajbansis constituted the single largest Hinduized social group in the population of the north Bengal districts of Jalpaiguri, Rangpur, Dinajpur and Koch Bihar. The Rajbansis along with the Paliyas and Deshis of Dinajpur and the Koches, the last three having little significant differences with the former, were almost entirely found in the wide stretch of the country extending from the districts of Malda and Purnea to Goalpara in Assam. They as well as the Muslims of local, that is, north Bengal origin, the bulk of whom were most probably 'Islamized' Rajbansis or Koches or their subdivisions spoke, a dialect which according to Grierson, 'is called Rajbangsi, and while undoubtedly belonging to the eastern branch [of Bengali language], has still points of difference which entitle it to be called as a separate dialect'[16].

Rajbansi intelligentsia, political leaders and social reformers, however, by and large strongly disagree with what has been stated above and emphatically deny any affinity between the Rajbansis on the one hand and the Koches, Paliyas and Bodos on the other. Difficulties arise because of the fact that though the Rajbansis have a rich and complex history, it is yet to be written and constructed properly. Their history includes the history of the people of the north Bengal districts mentioned above and also of part of Assam. They were once a regionally dominant political power and founded several powerful kingdoms[17]. Their precise origin, status and folk history remain obscure. Existing history is largely based on the accounts left by the colonial administrators and colonial ethnographers and what follows below is drawn to a considerable extent from such accounts.

From various accounts, though not always consistent and very clear, it appears that when the British conquered the Rajbansis they belonged to a semi-tribal community who for a considerable

period were settled agriculturists, with regional diversities, raising crops mainly using a plough drawn by bullocks, though retaining traces of slash-and-burn practices or hunting and gathering
methods. Even at that point of time, as discussed in the next
chapter, the Rajbansis formed a considerably differentiated peasant society.

Buchanan-Hamilton who visited eastern India in the early
nineteenth century considered the Rajbansis to be the 'aboriginals
of Kamrup and be strongly characterized by their features as
belonging to the great eastern race of mankind'[18]. He also noted
that they were called indiscriminately Koch and Rajbansi, although
they had introduced numerous distinctions amongst themselves.
At that time they appeared to have been recognized as true Sudras
by Maithili and Kamrupi Brahmans but not by the Bengali
Brahmans[19]. In 1872, Dalton considered that the physical appearance of the Koches showed that they were non-Aryans and belonged to a Dravidian stock[20]. Writing in 1891 Risley stated:

> Koch, Koch-mandai, Rajbansi, Paliya, Desi constituted a large
> Dravidian tribe of North-Eastern or Eastern Bengal, among whom
> there are grounds for suspecting some admixture of Mongoloid
> blood[21].

Giving support to the thesis of fusion of different races, in 1951
and again in 1974 Suniti Kumar Chatterjee observed:

> The masses of North Bengal are very largely of Bodo origin or mixed
> Austric-Dravidian-Mongoloid, where groups of peoples from lower
> Bengal (*Bhati-des*) and Bihar have penetrated among them. They can
> now mainly be described as *Koch* i.e. Hinduised or Semi-Hinduised
> Bodo who had abandoned their original Tibeto-Burman speech and
> have adopted the Northern dialect of Bengali ... they are proud to
> call themselves *Raj-bansi* and to claim to be called Kshatriyas ...[22].

Some historians and anthropologists have questioned the idea
of Dravidian-Mongoloid admixture and have stressed the Mon-
goloid element.[23]. Charu Chandra Sanyal, the noted anthropolo-
gist of Jalpaiguri, in his massive work on the Rajbansis observes
that the 'Koches are non-Aryan in origin. Some of them adopted
Hinduism and became Rajbansis'. Thus, while the ethnic origin of
the Koches and Rajbansis is somewhat uncertain and the issue is

perhaps not of much relevance for the present study, it may be tentatively observed that these groups can be considered as an extension of the Bodos of Assam and East Bengal. They were subject to a process of Hinduization and claimed themselves to be Rajbansis, that is, kindred of the royal family[24].

It deserves particular mention that, as early as the nineteenth century, the Koch or Rajbansi chiefs basing themselves on Hindu Scripture and Epics were setting up their claim to be considered as Kshatriya. Their arguments were that in the hoary past (*c.* 2550-2350 BC) they were known as Haihaya Kshatriyas who being attacked by Parasuram and Sagar of the Bhrigu dynasty fled to places outside the Aryan territories (according to some accounts, to Paundra Desh in Bengal and Bihar and, according to other accounts, Kamrup), took shelter among the non-Aryans, remained incognito and in the course of time lost their Kshatriya characteristics and identity[25]. The claim received a fillip, as discussed in a subsequent chapter, in later years, particularly in the early decades of the twentieth century and came to be associated with a social reform movement.

The colonial rulers considered the Rajbansis an uncivilized people. Writing in the early nineteenth century Buchanan-Hamilton observed that the Rajbansis, Koches etc. were 'generally looked upon as low and impure'[26]. And in the 1870s Hunter, the colonial scholar-administrator, referred to them as 'semi-aboriginal tribes'[27].

Not only the British rulers but the high caste Hindus too treated the Rajbansis contemptuously. As the District Census Report for Jalpaiguri for 1891 put it, the social status of the Rajbansis 'was extremely low, and no high caste Hindu could be induced to take cooked food from their hands or smoke in their *hookas*'[28].

The Rajbansi Hindus and also the Rajbansi Muslims—'the lowest classes of Hindus and Muhammedans'—were viewed as 'indolent and superstitious'[29]. As late as 1930s, the Rajbansis of the adjacent district of Rangpur were considered to be 'lazy cultivators'. But the reason for the alleged indolence was not an ethnic or racial or community characteristic. One major reason was the fact that land was plentiful and fertile, rainfall abundant and hence crops were sufficient for adequate living. Sunder, the Settlement Officer for the 1889-95 Survey and Settlement in the Western Duars, touching on this aspect remarked:

...the exuberant fertility of the soil engenders indolence, little nour-
ishment sufficing for the natives, and a sufficiency being procurable
without much exertion[30].

The indolence and extreme lassitude were also engendered by
the humidity of climate and severity of malarious fever. Jalpaiguri
was among the six districts in Bengal which had the highest fever
mortality figure in eight out of the ten years ending in 1901, and
epidemic cholera was an annual scourge. All this adversely affected the vitality of the people. Inequalities, poverty and malnutrition referred to below further impaired the health of the people.
Such a condition lowered their physical resistance.

The bulk of the three lakh Hinduized Rajbansis and Koches and
of the two lakh thirty thousand Muslims, particularly the Nasyas[31]
and Sheikhs of Jalpaiguri district, constituted peasants of different
categories. A striking feature was the low division of labour in the
rural society. The social life of the Rajbansi Hindus and also of the
Rajbansi Muslims, that is, the local Muslims in Jalpaiguri and
adjacent districts came to be marked by the absence of distinct
occupational and specialized service, artisan and trading groups.
There were no village servants such as barbers, washermen and
scavengers. Virtually all the artisans like potters, blacksmiths and
carpenters were from outside the local communities. For example,
cartwheels were made by carpenters who came from Bihar. There
were, however, spinners and weavers among the local population,
but their work was of a crude nature[32].

Virtual absence of roads and consequent difficulties in trans-
portation narrowed down the range of social and economic contact with the outside world. Purchase and sale of artisan products
and surplus of crops used to take place in the weekly or bi-weekly
hats and also the annual month-long *mela* or fair at Jalpesh in
February-March.

Mainly because of the geo-physical features the rural population did not live in large villages of the kind which were found in
eastern, southern and western Bengal. They lived in tiny and
scattered clusters of a few houses—usually not more than ten to
fifteen houses—called a *tari*. Several *taris* constituted a village or a
settlement. In the Duars such a settlement was often named after
the *jotedar* or landholder who had organized the reclamation of
land and who had leased in the *jote* or holding[33].

The process of Hinduization

It is appropriate to mention here that the Hinduized Rajbansis formed a loosely differentiated and amorphous community with very loose adherence to *Puranic* Hindu faith[34]. Over time, particularly since about the late fifteenth century, they were increasin̹ 'v being exposed to Brahmanical religion; for quite a long time, as mentioned above, they had been claiming that they represented the traditional Kshatriya caste; and, further, by the late nineteenth century they came to be recognized as a distinct Hindu caste or *jati*.

However, even in the early twentieth century the impact of orthodox Hindu religion and of caste-based social practices and rituals remained very much partial and in many respects superficial. And the religious beliefs and practices of the Hinduized Rajbansis were to a large extent non-Brahmanical. By the late nineteenth century, a sort of syncretism between non-Brahmanical faith and *Puranic* Hinduism seems to have been taking place. However, their religious beliefs and rituals, marriage customs, funeral ceremonies and various social practices show that the process of Hinduization was (and is) marked by considerable tension and even conflict.

The Hinduized Rajbansis believed that nature was controlled by various deities and good or evil spirits, and ceremonial rites were performed to propitiate these supernatural forces. They worshipped such gods, goddesses and spirits such as Shiva in different forms, Mahakal representing the principal form, *Bisohari Thakurani* or the localized form of Manasa (the snake goddess) being the most widely worshipped female divinity, Tista Buri or the goddess of the sacred river Tista, Bhandani or *dang dhari mao*—a female figure seated on a tiger representing the mother who fought the demons with *dang* or weapons, Bormo Thakur or the fire god, Bisti Thakur or the rain god, Paban Thakur or the wind god, Saleswari or Goddess of forest and Kali in her various forms. Garam Thakur was a curious combination of several deities forming an omnibus village deity and was enshrined in a meagre temple created on the outskirts of a village, usually inside a bamboo grove. Almost all of these gods and goddesses were non-Vedic, non-Smriti and non-Brahman in origin. It was Bhandani and not Durga which was worshipped with great festivity. It was Tista and not Ganga which was of importance in Rajbansi social and religious life. Offerings were made to Muslim saints like Satya Pir.

Many of the ceremonies were magico-religious in nature. The *Hudum deo puja* performed in case of severe drought was a conspicuous example of this. It was a sort of fertility rite in which women of a village went during a dark night into a distant paddy field and danced in the nude and sang (mostly obscene) songs abusing the rain god.

Although some of the *pujas* were performed by Kamrupi and Maithili Brahmans, most of them were done by non-Brahmans, that is, Rajbansi priests called Odhikaries. Ojhas or exorcists belonging to Rajbansi community or Hadi caste, an *antyaja* caste, performed rituals to appease or ward off evil spirits. All this shows that the Rajbansi Hindus while being drawn into the Hindu fold, continued to retain many non-Brahmanical practices and rituals.

Bisua, or Bisuba, was a spring-hunt festival in which all able-bodied males went out for a hunt and had to kill an edible animal and consume its meat either roasted or cooked in the forest. It was clearly a relic of pre-agricultural hunting social life.

Marriage customs

From the marriage customs prevalent among the Rajbansi Hindus till the early twentieth century and even much later it is apparent that the influence of Shastric Hindu practices and rituals were limited[35]. The *phul bio* or marriage with a virgin settled by the elders and presided over by a Brahman (mostly Kamrupi) priest or a Rajbansi Odhikari was the form usually accepted by the society and the marriage ceremony closely resembled that of the caste Hindus.

But there were several types of marriages, quite widely prevalent, which were not permissible in orthodox Hindu households. Divorce was allowed and a loose form of widow remarriage took place. In many cases marriage was merely a matter of mutual consent to live together as man and wife and such union was not objected to by the society. A feature of the regular marriage was that the bridegroom had to pay a bride-price. One consequence of this custom was that many of the young men of poor families could not pay the bride-price. Hence, they either had to remain unmarried or had to enter into a marriage form other than the *phul bio*. One form was that a widow in want of a man to look after her property kept a *dangua* or an unmarried man who lived with her as her husband but who could be turned out any time she liked.

Status of women

The Rajbansi Hindu family was patrilinear and patrilocal. However, in Rajbansi Hindu society the position of women was better in many respects than in 'clean' Hindu caste families. That they were allowed to divorce, re-marry and live with a man without any formal marriage ceremony has already been noted. They also participated in social and economic life. A major part of their daily life consisted of activities centring around the husking of paddy, fetching water, cooking food for the family, looking after children, that is, work within the home. But they also did a major part of labour in the field and forest. While women belonging to 'clean' Hindu castes did not work outside the home, in Jalpaiguri and also Rangpur, Dinajpur, Koch Bihar and other adjacent districts the Rajbansi women took part in some of the major agricultural operations, such as weeding, transplanting of paddy or reaping it, and retting of jute. They however, did not take part in ploughing. They did not observe any *purdah* or seclusion, collected forest produce, moved freely in the countryside and attended the *hats* to sell produce and make purchases[36]. Thus, they had major role in work outside the home. This, however, did not necessarily ensure autonomy within the family.

The dress of the Rajbansi Hindu women was a *sari* or wrapper called *phota-kapor* which was folded across the body and extended from just above the breasts to the knees. Men, particularly the poor, used to wear a small cloth, called a *nengte* (loin cloth), just sufficient to cover the private parts[37].

In every homestead of a *jotedar* family there were five or more huts including a *dari-ghar* or outer room. The huts were made of bamboo-matting or grass reeds covered over with earth mixed with cowdung, and roofs were thatched with *chhan* grass. That the undertenants and *adhiars* of such a family used to live in houses consisting of one or two huts clustered around the house of the *jotedar* has already been mentioned.

Islam and the local people

The second largest component in the population of the district was composed of Muslims. Taking the district as a whole, Muslims constituted a minority—just one-fourth of the total population. This was in marked contrast to the religious community-wise composition of population in most of the districts in east and north Bengal including neighbouring Rangpur and Dinajpur in all of which Muslims formed a large majority. In Jalpaiguri district the Muslims were in majority only in Boda, Pachagar and Tetulia—the *thana* areas adjacent to the districts of Rangpur and Dinajpur—and had large concentration in two more *thana* areas, Debiganj and Patgram.

The Muslims of Jalpaiguri, however, did not constitute a homogenous community or group. They had two major segments : (a) the local Muslims the bulk of whom was composed of converted Rajbansis, Koches and Meches[38], and (b) the Muslims who had migrated mainly from the east Bengal districts of Noakhali and Comilla. It should be mentioned here that the local Muslims include those who originally came from Jalpaiguri district as well as those belonging to other north Bengal districts, particularly Rangpur, Dinajpur and Malda, the adjacent areas of Purnea district and the Koch Bihar State. Though no precise estimate is available, it may safely be stated that the local Muslims were preponderant among the Muslim population in Jalpaiguri district and particularly in the rural areas. Further, the overwhelming majority of the local Muslims belonged to a differentiated cultivating or peasant society, *adhiars* forming a large proportion of that society. Muslims who came from east Bengal, particularly from Noakhali and Comilla districts, were very few in the countryside and most of them were found in Jalpaiguri town.

Like the early history of the Rajbansi Hindus, that of the local Muslims too is uncertain. In the 1911 *District Gazeteer*, Gruning stated that Sheikhs and Nasyas forming more than 99 per cent of the Muslim population were 'native to the district'[39]. This suggests that the bulk of the local Muslims were converted or Islamized autochthons like Rajbansis, Koches, Paliyas and Meches. However, a fair number of the district's Muslims came originally from Dinajpur, Rangpur and Purnea districts and from the Koch Bihar State[40]. The Baikunthapur zamindars encouraged migration of Muslims from Dinajpur and nearby districts to facilitate extension of cultivation. Colonel Hedayet Ali of Patna, who took an important part in the Anglo-Bhutan War, also helped migration and settlement of some Bihari Muslims in the scantily populated Duars. Some accounts also suggest that many of the Muslims of the district were most probably a mixed group with converts and the immigrant Muslim soldiers and colonizers, who came in the wake of the Pathan and Mughal conquests, living side by side and intermarrying[41]. It seems that Islamization could make notable progress because Hinduism was not deeply rooted among the autochthons. The simplicity of the Islamic faith also made it particularly attractive[42].

Process of Syncretization

With regard to the religious beliefs and practices, it needs to be observed that the Islamized Rajbansis, Koches or Meches were not very strict in adhering to orthodox Islamic faith and tradition. Many of their observances had a folk-form characterized by worship of Pirs and Mursheds and contained elements of nature worship and of non-orthodox Hinduism. They participated in many of the religious ceremonies and social festivals of the Rajbansi Hindus, such as Tista Buri and Biso Hari *pujas* or festivals like Bisua. Participation of Rajbansi Hindus in Muslim ceremonies like Muharram too were widely prevalent[43]. What A.C. Hartley, the Rangpur Settlement Officer, wrote in 1932, was very much true for Jalpaiguri in the late nineteenth and early twentieth centuries too. He narrated:

> Ballads in honour of Bishohari and Satya Pir (sometimes known as Satya Narayan) are preserved and sung by people of both the faiths. The worship of Jakha, also a Rajbansi deity, was noted in some thanas and the use of a white flag on the burial ground is very reminiscent of the white canopy used by the Rajbansis on their cremation ground ... the regular attendance of men of both the faiths at 'Jatra' and 'Kirtan' parties is common[44].

In many other aspects too there were important similarities between the Hinduized and Islamized local people in their socio-cultural traditions and practices. There were also instances of Rajbansi Hindus and Rajbansi Muslims living in the same hamlets and in some cases even in the same homestead, though in separate houses[45]. Food habits were same except that the Muslims did not take pork. In appearence, dress and language and speech bulk of the local Muslims differed little from the Rajbansi Hindus. First names of the local Muslims were often indistinguishable from those of the Rajbansi Hindus[46]. Muslim women, generally speaking, did not use *burkhas* and participated in agricultural operations. Married women often used vermillon on their forehead. Many customs were common to both the groups.

It may be observed that these two social groups formed the core of the landholders of various categories as well as of the poor peasants and *adhiars* of the district. Later on some of the tribals who immigrated into the district from Chhotanagpur and Santal Parganas in the wake of the growth of the plantation system came to form a sizeable proportion of the peasant masses and rural poor in the Duars.

A significant feature of the social life was the absence of any tension and rivalry between the Hinduized autochthons and Islamized autochthons. Thus a peaceful mingling and a cultural syncretization had been taking place.

Minor autochthon groups

In the Duars a few other local groups were found. These were the Rabhas and Garos[47] who were considered to be the western branch of the Kachhari or Bodo tribe. As these groups were numerically very small and did not have any significant role in the broader socio-economic life of the district, any elaborate discussion is not being attempted here.

Immigrant population groups

That some Brahmans—Bengalis, Maithilis of north Bihar, Pandas from Orissa and Kamrupis who were actually from Sylhet—as well as a few other higher caste Bengali Hindus were found in the Regulation portion of the district as early as the early nineteenth century is learnt from several accounts. But their number was miniscule. Further, there is no evidence to indicate any presence of higher caste Bengali Hindus in the Duars before its annexation by the British. It was only since the formation of the district in 1869 that they began to move into the district including its Duars part as government servants and professionals such as lawyers and doctors. The Sahas, a Bengali caste group, came as trading people.

'Noakhali Muslims'

Among the various immigrant population groups, a particularly important one was the segment of Muslims which came from the districts of Noakhali and Tipperah(Comilla) in south-eastern Bengal as service-holders, professionals and *maulvis*. Rahim Baksh, the *peshkar* or head assistant in the Deputy Commissioner's office in the 1870s, was a resourceful and enterprising person who emerged as one of the pioneers of the Indian-owned sector of the tea plantation enterprise. He and his son-in-law Musharraff Hossain came to have a very important place in that sector, acquired large landed property in the *jotedari* form and wielded wide influence in the economic, political and social life of the district. They hailed from the Noakhali-Comilla districts and made use of their influence and contacts to encourage Muslim migration from the two districts to Jalpaiguri and provide jobs and various occupational opportunities to aspiring Muslim migrants.

Because of their Noakhali connexions these migrants came to be known as Noakhali Muslims. In contrast to local Muslims most of whom were rural people and agriculturists, the bulk of the former group settled in Jalpaiguri town and were engaged in a variety of non-agricultural occupations. Their social traditions and practices differed in many ways from those of the Muslims of local origin. In their religious belief and social mores they were much more orthodox than the local Muslims and usually kept away from Hindu religious ceremonies and festivals[48]. Their mode of dressing (the *pajama* and *lungi*), differed from that of the locals. Though social and cultural interaction, including intermarriage between the two segments were not altogether absent, the Noakhali Muslims were very particular about their distinctive identity.

Other Immigrant Groups

The immigrant Bengalis—both Hindus and Muslims—coming from outside the district came to be known in the local parlance as *bhatias*, people who came from the direction of *bhati* or ebbtide. The district also came to be traversed by Marwari merchants and traders, in local parlance called *kayas*, and some Muslim traders from Bihar and the United Provinces (U.P.). Many of the *bhatias* or eastern Bengalis—Hindus and Muslims—were officials in the colonial administration, lawyers, petty traders and *jotedars*. They, along with the *kayas*, very often cheated, harassed and exploited the local people in numerous and diverse ways. Besides that, they treated the latter in a most contemptuous manner referring to them as *bahes* in the sense of rural idiots. The Rajbansi Hindus were considered by the upper caste Hindus as an unclean social group from whose hands water could not be taken[49]. Naturally enough, the *bhatias* and *kayas*, irrespective of their occupation and economic position, were regarded by the local Hindus and Muslims with fear and resentment as well as deference.

Large numbers of people came from Bihar and U.P. as unskilled labourers, earthworkers, domestic hands, washermen etc.[50] All of them were mainly temporary male migrants retaining their links with their village homes and periodically going back there.

Immigrant tribal peasants

With the launching of the tea plantations in the Duars in the mid-1870s and its subsequent rapid growth, a new element was introduced into the demographic composition, social life and economy of the district. The change took the form of large-scale migration of tribal peasants—particularly Oraon, Munda and Santal peasants—from Chhotanagpur and Santal Parganas to the tea gardens.[51]

In their homelands these tribal people belonged to peasant communities differentiation among whom was of limited extent. Their agriculture was, however, closely linked with magico-religious practices. It is noteworthy that despite considerable differences between the different tribal groups, these communities had social customs, cultural traditions and religious beliefs which were similar in many respects. Further, each of these groups had a powerful community bond.

Since the seventeenth century these tribal groups were in a state of turmoil as a consequence of massive social, political and economic influences emanating from their Hinduized neighbours. Following the penetration of British rule in the second half of the eighteenth century and consequent socio-economic changes, their economy, livelihood and social life came to be severely dislocated. One inevitable result was a series of tribal risings against the British and also the Indian exploiting and oppressing interests who were in league with them. At the same time, the impoverished tribal peasants tended to be pushed out of their traditional habitat.

This took the form of huge migration fostered and organized by the tea planters of Assam and the two northern districts of Bengal under the direct protection of the colonial state. The movement to the Duars was a part of this historical process. Of the various tribal peasant communities which moved to the Duars, numerically the largest group consisted of the Oraons whose number increased from just 210 in 1881 to 62,844 in 1901 and, further, to 1,15,350 in 1921. The Mundas, the second largest immigrant tribal group, numbered only 1,855 in 1891, but by 1901 rose to 11,672 and by 1921 to 34,601. The Santals numbered 10,857 in 1901 and about 24,000 in 1921. Of these groups while the Oraons spoke a dialect belonging to the Dravidian family of languages, the Mundas, Santals and several other small immigrant tribal groups used speeches affiliated to the Mundari family. In course of time in the Duars a new dialect known as *Sadri*—a mixed form of Mundari, Kurukh, Hindi and Bengali—evolved from communication among themselves and with others[52].

It deserves notice that, in the early decades, many of the immigrant tribal peasants-turned-tea garden workers used to return to their homeland after one or two tea seasons and come back to the gardens after some time and, thus, constituted a sort of circulating population. In course of time the majority, though often retaining links with their village homes, settled permanently in the Duars[53]. Further, a sizeable number of those who settled permanently and worked as wage labour in the tea gardens, later on, for a variety of reasons, withdrew from plantation work as their chief occupation and switched over to peasant agriculture primarily as poor peasants and *adhiars*.

Over the years as a result of diverse influences, their customs and culture came to be modified in important ways. A very large section was subjected to the impact of Hindu religion and Hindu social practices, while another section embraced Christianity. However, both the segments retained their traditional religious beliefs and social practices to a very substantial extent[54].

It has been indicated earlier that in various spheres of social life there was an intermingling of Rajbansi Hindus and local Muslims creating condition for the growth of a composite culture with elements of syncretism at the base level. In contrast to that, because of the deliberate policy, pursued by the planters as discussed in a later chapter, the immigrant tribals, particularly the plantation workers, had to lead practically a life of segregated existence and their points of contact with the other population groups remained minimal. However, by the second and third generations the settlement patterns led to the development of at least some working relationship. *Hats* and other market places became meeting points for economic and social intercourse between the local people and the immigrant tribals. But the Bengali middle class belonging to higher castes as well as the Marwaris with their widespread social network bypassed and indeed looked down upon the indigenous population groups and the immigrant tribals.

Nepalis[55]

In connexion with the demographic composition it should also be mentioned that the hilly tract of the district came to be inhabited by, among others, a sizeable group composed of several Nepali castes. In 1921 they numbered nearly 20,000. A very large proportion of them were employed on tea gardens as labourers and also as junior supervisors such as *baidars, chowkidars*, etc.

European groups

So far the focus of discussion has been on the Indian society of Jalpaiguri. It is, however, time to take a brief look at the Europeans and Anglo-Indians. As in all districts of Bengal, Jalpaiguri had a small core of European administrators. But the district also came to have a body of non-official Europeans which was larger than that found in most of the mofussil districts. They moved into the district or, to be more specific, into the Duars as tea planters soon after the annexation of the latter tract and alongwith the launching of the plantation agriculture. The place and role of the Europeans—of both official and non-official Europeans—are discussed in a subsequent chapter.

Concluding Observations

It follows from what has been stated in this chapter above, that the district's population came to have an 'extraordinary admixture' of diverse social collectivities. The society as it stood in the late nineteenth and early twentieth centuries was characterized by frag-

mentation into various castes, religious communities, ethnic groups
and linguistic-cultural groups. The society, however, was not
divided into watertight compartments or niches and there was
considerable interaction between the different social groups. Along
with other factors—particularly the economic aspects discussed in
the following two chapters—the demographic composition and
socio-cultural dimensions came to influence social and political
movements in the district in significant ways. These are considered later in the book.

3 The Socio-Economic Setting I: Process of Agrarian Changes, 1870-1920

LAND REVENUE ARRANGEMENTS

Annexed in two phases, Jalpaiguri district came to have two distinct tenurial and land revenue arrangements. The tracts lying on the west of the river Tista and also a small tract in the east, as shown in the preceding chapter, were covered by the Permanent Settlement and these two tracts consisted of two large estates. The Bengal Tenancy Act (B T Act) of 1885 and all other laws in force throughout Bengal applied fully to these tracts[1].

The Duars part was, however, not brought under the Permanent Settlement. It was divided into 180 grants or temporarily settled estates leased for tea cultivation and five *khas mahals* or 'government estates'. These estates included all of the Western Duars outside the tea gardens and reserved forests divided into four *tahsils* (revenue collection areas) of Mainaguri, Falakata, Alipur and Bhalka and also the *tahsil* of Ambari Falakata situated on the west of Tista. In the *khas mahal* area the objective of the government was to maximize revenue collection and with that objective in view the government dealt directly with the tenants, settled or leased out cultivable land for definite periods and made periodic revision of revenue. The tenants or lessees came to enjoy heritable and transferable rights subject to certain conditions[2].

But whatever might have been the original tenurial arrangements in the two tracts and the difference between them, the structure of agrarian society that evolved over time and the manner in which land came to be held and operated in practice was, with some variations in details, in important respects the same throughout the district. To be more specific, from the angle of forms and methods of generation, appropriation and use of surplus and from that of class there was no significant difference between the systems prevailing in the two tracts. In this connexion it may additionally be observed that the systems found to be existing in Jalpaiguri, resembled to a considerable extent the system found in large parts of the two adjoining districts of Rangpur and Dinajpur and also the Terai portion of Darjeeling district. Throughout the district there were, as stated in the 1911 *Jalpaiguri District Gazetteer*, primarily three categories of tenants. First, there were the *jotedars* or tenants-in-chief. In the permanently settled tract they held land or *jotes* (holdings) immediately under the two zamindars. A large number of them ranked as *raiyats* under the provisions of the Bengal Tenancy Act and some others as proprietors and tenure-holders[3]. In the *khas mahal* areas of Duars they held *jotes* under the Government. Some of the *jotedars* were of giant-size and held hundreds of acres of land. Second, there were cash rent-paying sub-tenants like *chukanidars* and *mulandars* with derivative subgrades like *dar-chukanidars* or *dar-dar-chukanidars* differing only in degree. Finally, there were the produce rent-paying *adhiar* or *prajas* holding land under *jotedars* or *chukanidars*[4]. While cultivation with own and family labour was and remained a significant feature, the form of control over land and labour that emerged and grew as the critical one was the *jotedar-adhiar* system or the *barga* system based on sharing of crops usually on a 50:50 basis. The system was not something totally new. That some form of *jotedar-adhiar* system was in existence in late eighteenth century Bengal is evident from Colebrook's 1794 treatise *Remarks on the Husbandary and Internal Commerce of Bengal*[5]. In Patgram and Boda *parganas* and Dinajpur the extent of the *adhiar* system, as found by Buchanan-Hamilton in 1808-10, was quite large[6]. But the emergence of the *jotedar-adhiar* system and share-cropping was induced mainly by the subsistence requirements of the large landholders and *jotedars*. The distinctiveness of the system in the closing decades of the nineteenth and early decades of the twentieth centuries lay in its rapid spread in the north Bengal districts and the Sunderban areas in south Bengal largely in response to the working of a process of switch from a subsistence economy to a market economy. A related feature was that the system grew as an integral part of a wider economy—to colonial economy[7].

THE JOTEDAR-ADHIAR SYSTEM

Little is known about the genesis of the *jotedar-adhiar* system in the
Jalpaiguri district. But, as indicated above, the system was prevalent in the tract that came to be permanently settled from the late
eighteenth century and in the Western Duars under Bhutia rule[8].

Early 1870s

Drawing upon an account prepared in 1870 by J. Tweedie (the first
Deputy Commissioner of Jalpaiguri district), of the agrarian set-
up, particularly of the *jotedar-adhiar* system prevailing in the
permanently settled tract in the early 1870s, Hunter stated:

> Almost every man in the District tills a plot of ground for himself.
> Several of the smaller husbandmen, however, in addition to culti-
> vating their own small patches, also till the field of others, receiving
> in return for their labour one-half of the share of the crop[9].

Describing the prevailing arrangement he wrote:

> These men are called *adhiari* cultivators; the holders of the land pays
> the zamindar's or landlord's rent; and also supplies the seed-grain,
> the cultivators having to find the plough cattle, agricultural imple-
> ments, and labour. This, however, applies only to the Regulation
> part of the District west of Tista[10].

Thus, in the zamindari area the *adhiars* supplied the main inputs.

What was the position in the Duars? The agrarian relations that
had evolved during the rule by Bhutan needs to be researched. But
on the basis of the accounts which are available the following may
be observed. Tweedie considered that the *jotedars* represented the
original reclaimers of the soil, had hereditary rights, could sell the
land, and were in the habit of temporarily alienating it by usufruc-
tuary mortgage. Beneath the *jotedar*, Tweedie found three
categories—the *chukanidars* who held farms for a fixed term being
more than one year and paid the *jotedar* an ascertained money rent,
the *raiyats* described as tenants by the year and paying to the
jotedar a yearly money rent, and the *prajas*, or tenants-at-will, often
receiving from the *jotedar* the ploughs, animal power and seed-
grain needed for and giving to the *jotedar* half the produce.

Thus, while the *adhiars'* share of the crop was the same in both the tracts, in the zamindari areas the *adhiar* peasants had to supply most of the inputs and in the Duars the *jotedars* took the responsibility of supplying these. Explaining this variation Hunter observed:

> The reason for this is that in the tract to the west of the Tista almost the whole of the land is taken up and cultivated; while in the western Duars ... there is still a great deal of available uncultivated jungle land, and the tenure holders have to offer additional inducements to the husbandman[12].

Thus, in the labour-scarce Duars with vast uncultivated areas *adhiars* had to be induced by the landholders on *jotedars* to reclaim waste lands and take up cultivation. With regard to the *praja*, 'the most general of the actual cultivators', it was stated:

> [The praja] is called *adhiari* praja, as his rent consists of half the yield of his crops ... [There are two classes of *prajas*. In the first case] he supplies his own cattle and plough, but receives from the *jotedar*, *chukanidar*, or *dar-chukanidar* who employs him, the seed necessary for the cultivation of his fields; at harvest time he makes over to his landlord half the crop. [In Mainaguri and some other places] the *praja* is provided by his landlord with seed-grain, cattle, and plough, and, in addition, when first engaged, a certain amount of rice for food, which is not to be returned until he leaves the jot, and then without interest. Should he at any time require more food, it is advanced by the landlord, to be repaid out of the year's crop, with interest at fifty to hundred per cent ...
> It will be seen ... that the actual cultivators are mainly the *prajas*, who till the land for *jotedars*, *chukanidars*, or *dar-chukanidars* but that the latter also till some portion of their holdings with their own hand[13].

To sum up, in the early 1870s the agrarian society in Jalpaiguri consisted of, besides the two big zamindars, three categories of agricultural population : (a) the big *jotedars*, considered to be the initial organizers of reclamation of uncultivated wastes and jungle land, (i) holding their *jotes* at an easy rent, (ii) leasing out land to under-*raiyats* on high cash rent and/or (iii) cultivating mainly by engaging *adhiars* at rack-rent; (b) small *jotedars*, *chukanidars* and *dar-chukanidars* cultivating mainly with their own labour and family labour; and (c) *adhiars* of various types, perhaps all of whom had physically cleared jungles and reclaimed land for cultivation.

Relevantly, it may be mentioned that available accounts relating to the early 1870s suggest that wage-earning labourers were rare in the district[14].

In this set-up the *jotedars*, particularly those having large-sized *jotes*, resorted to extraction of surplus in the form of appropriation of half of the gross produce as rent based on *adhi* cultivation. The *jotedars* also took to grain-lending as food or money-lending at usurious rates of interest[15]. Often the *jotedars* were also involved in trade in agricultural produce, particularly paddy and jute, and obtained a large margin through manipulation of market mechanisms. This combination of large landholding with money-lending and grain dealing and also trading activities made the big *jotedars* a formidable power in the social and economic life in the countryside of Jalpaiguri.

This power of the large *jotedars* and their allied interests on the one hand and, on the other hand, the dependence of the *adhiars* on the former in various ways along with the insecure rights of the latter in land, reduced them to the position of near-serfs, of tied and dependent peasants.

Growth of tea plantations and its impact

The first penetration of capitalist enterprise in the Western Duars in the form of tea plantations took place in 1874. Subsequent years of the nineteenth century saw rapid expansion of the tea plantations and large growth of tea garden labour force. Those years also witnessed the extension of roads, railway and communications. All this helped to open up markets for agricultural produce—rice, jute, tobacco, mustard, etc. All this provided stimulus for commercialization of Jalpaiguri's subsistence-oriented agriculture and for extension of cultivation and reclamation of land[16]. In consequence, in late 1870s and throughout the 1880s and 1890s clearing of jungles and reclamation of land for ordinary cultivation, that is, peasant agriculture (in addition to that for plantation agriculture) made rapid progress. By the turn of the century large parts of the Duars changed from jungle wastelands with little human habitation into cultivated area and growing settlements. Thus, Jalpaiguri's subsistence-oriented agricultural economy and society became increasingly integrated with the British Indian market and wider colonial economy.

Immigration into Duars

The closing decades of the century saw a constant stream of immigration from the neighbouring Koch Bihar State and Rangpur district. Peasants resorted to migration partly because of high rent and oppression in those two territories. This migration amounted to a sort of protest. In addition, Rangpur suffered from demographic pressure. All this operated as what may be considered as 'push' factors. At the Western Duars end, 'pull' factors operated in the form of low rent, easy availability of land and fertility of soil[17]. Those migrants who had necessary resources settled as *jotedars* and *chukanidars*. But most of the immigrants were impoverished and were absorbed as *adhiars*. Further, peasant labour of local origin was not sufficient in number. Under the circumstances, part of the new cultivation began to be undertaken through tribal peasants from Chhotanagpur and Santal Parganas[18] whose migration into the district was organized by the tea planters. Some ex-tea garden labourers settled as cultivators—perhaps a very limited number as small *jotedars* or *chukanidars*, but mostly as *adhiars*. The total number of such tribal peasants could not, however, have been large in those days. For, according to the 1891 Census, the total number of Oraons in the district including those engaged in plantation work was just around 20,000 and numerically the Oraons were the most important among the immigrant tribals. Those engaged in agriculture must have had constituted a small fraction of them. However, these tribals were considered by the district officials as eminently suitable for clearing of wild animal-infested jungles, reclamation of waste lands and extension of cultivation in the Duars. They were considered as persevering and industrious and supposed to have possessed the capacity to withstand the notoriously bad climate much better than the original inhabitants like the Hinduized and Islamized Rajbansis[19].

Increasing differentiation

That the agrarian society of Jalpaiguri was already in the 1870s a differentiated one has been noted earlier. The subsequent decades saw growing differentiation. With the rapid progress of cultivation, raising of crops for sale in markets and extension of exchange economy, the *jotedars* and *chukanidars*, particularly the larger ones among them, prospered. Further, the fact that Duars was an area of recent reclamation and new settlement facilitated the process of differentiation. For, the big *jotedars* and substantial peasants had the resources to resort to large scale reclamation of waste lands and clearing of jungles. In the 1891 *District Census Report* the majority of the *jotedars* were enumerated as 'actual cultivators', but the bigger *jotedars* both in the permanently settled area and Duars were already described as 'mere collectors of rent'[20]. The Deputy Commissioner noted that many *jotedars* were resorting to various types of 'unscrupulous' and 'unfair exactions'[21]. In all this a tendency towards dissociation of the big *jotedars* from the process of production was distinctly noticeable. In the Regulation or permanently settled portion there was another tendency. While many of the *jotedars* had been holding lands for generations, a tendency of passing of some lands to Marwaris and Bengali *bhadraloks* was already discernible[22]. Evidently, there was alienation of land from Rajbansi Hindu and Muslim peasants and *jotedars* too to non-agriculturalists engaged in other occupations.

At the same time, as shown below, the number of *adhiars* was on the increase. Indicating their immiserization Lowis, Commissioner of Rajshahi Division, stated in 1888 that, in addition to the obligation of paying half share to their respective *jotedars*, the *adhiars* had to bear the burden of debt to the former and also that of usurious interest rates[23]. Thus, the *adhiars* were subjected to multiple forms of surplus extraction.

Describing the degraded condition and insecurity of *adhiars* in Western Duars as well as their utter dependence on the *jotedars* for their subsistence and means needed for carrying on cultivation, Sunder, the Settlement Officer during the Settlement Operations in the years 1989-95, observed[24].

> This tenant has no rights. He pays rent in kind, namely, half of all crops he may grow on land which is allowed to him. He is in a chronic state of debt, and does little or nothing to improve his position. On entering a jote the adhiar or praja receives from the jotedar an advance of 2 bis of paddy (about 12 maunds) as bhuta or bhutali to enable him to tide over the time until he reaps a crop. Some adhiars also receive an advance of Rs.5 to Rs.10.

These advances did not carry any interest. However, all loans were not interest-free. Sunder reported :

If the adhiar's supply of bhuta be exhausted, the jotedar has to lend him more paddy ... this loan carries interest at 50 per cent; in jungle land no interest is paid.

With regard to the division of crops he stated that the reaping and threshing was always done in the *jotedar's* compound. After that was done, the latter first took his half share and then recovered, with interest the paddy he had lent the *adhiar*. If the whole of the *praja's* or *adhiar's* share was used in liquidating the debt and a part of the debt still remained uncovered, the unpaid portion was allowed to stand over and the *jotedar* recovered it when the next crop was reaped. If necessary, he also advanced more paddy.

Socio-economic ties

Evidently enough, a close socio-economic tie existed between the *jotedars* and *adhiars*. The *jotedars* took some trouble and made expenses to bring the wastes and jungles under cultivation. They inducted landless cultivators from elsewhere and supplied them necessary agricultural inputs. They also provided them with consumption loans to enable them to survive. Thus, these *jotedars* had some role in the organization of production. But too much should not be made of this role, for throughout the nineteenth century and also the early twentieth century the technique of production including use of seeds, manure and animal power remained more or less unchanged. Consequently, there was also no change in production efficiency. What happened was that because of the stimulus provided by opening of new markets, the *jotedars*, particularly the bigger ones with substantial resources, showed readiness to take up clearing of jungle land, extension of cultivation and growing of cash crops. Another aspect is that in a labour-scarce situation, the *jotedars* spent a sum of money to keep the *adhiars* tied to them. They also knew that many of the *adhiars* were so impoverished that they lacked the wherewithal to reclaim and cultivate the lands. These were supplied, as noted earlier, also as inducements. Indicating this McAlpin, the Officiating Director of Land Records in 1914, wrote that both in the zamindari tract and government estates 'there are areas on the margins of cultivation where the landlords supply everything in order to attract cultivators'[25].

The latter aspect actually enabled the *jotedars* to exercise considerable control and have a patronage position over the life situation of the *adhiars*. The latter were caught in a 'web of dependency' on the former[26]. Further, as soon as the land began to produce crops through the labour of the *adhiars*, they had to pay rent as high as half of the gross produce. In addition to the half share rent, they were also subjected to other exactions, that is, *abwabs*. Though, not enumerated or detailed, these were considered as 'unfair' by the Deputy Commissioner in 1881.

Various forms of non-economic domination, often hidden by an appearance of benevolence and paternalism constituted one more crucial aspect of the *jotedar-adhiar* relationship. But behind such an appearence the *adhiars* were always treated by the *jotedars* as socially inferior in status, even when the two belonged to the same socio-religious group. Such treatment and unequal relationship were symbolized by the form of address and various unwritten dos and don'ts for the *adhiars*. While passing by the *jotedar's* house, the *adhiars* were prohibited from wearing shoes or carrying umbrellas. In the presence of the *jotedar*, the *adhiar* had to remain standing or sit on the ground. Such a relationship tended to reinforce the economic power and domination by the *jotedars*. Further, physical coercion was often used to enforce the social and economic power of the *jotedars*[27].

Official attitude

At times British civilians admitted some of the inequities of the *jotedar-adhiar* arrangement and the middle-man character of many *jotedars*. Nolan, Commissioner of Rajshahi Division in early 1890s, noted that 'on the large jotes ... the owner is practically a middle man'[28]. But, generally speaking, they adopted a supportive attitude towards the *jotedars* as well as the *adhi* system. An 1884 communication shows that the Bengal Government considered that the *adhiari* system was the only possible one in a newly-settled country[29]. Nolan in his remarks on Sundar's Settlement Report observed:

In regard to different classes of cultivators in the Duars, I may observe that the jotedari system has on the whole worked well. It has not interfered with the enhancement of the revenue ... The absentee jotédars, an element of the presence of which much was at one time made, are less than eight per cent, and they include many persons who live near their jotes, though not on them ...

He further observed :

The system of dividing crops has always seemed to me an objectionable method of taking the rent of land, inasmuch as it deprives the farmer of one-half of the usual motive for industry. But it is not a bad way of paying a labourer, as it gives him an interest in his work, inferior no doubt to that of the owner working his own field, but superior to that of the ordinary farm-hand. Mr. Sunder's description of the *adhiar* ... shows that ... he receives shelter, food by way of advances, and all the instruments of industry, contributing only his work[30].

Nolan considered that most of the *jotedars* were residents and physically participated in the process of cultivation. In stressing these aspects he exhibited a belief in the entrepreneurial role of the *jotedars*. And this was not his personal belief. He represented the prevailing government opinion[31].

With the sort of attitude expressed by Nolan, it is not surprising that in the closing years of the nineteenth century and early decades of the twentieth century there took place an extension and consolidation of the *jotedar-adhiar* system with 'remarkable rapidity'. But his expectation about the role of *jotedars* was belied by subsequent developments. As a matter of fact, the character of the *jotedars*, as found and described by Nolan—physically taking part in the act of cultivation—considerably changed. Milligan's observation 'that the position stated by Mr. Nolan was entirely reversed'[32] brought out the harsh reality.

Factors facilitating extension and consolidation of the jotedar-adhiar system

While the official attitude of support to the *jotedars* was one factor that encouraged the growth of the *adhi* system, too much importance should not be attached to it. No less important, if not more, were the objective, that is, agro-economic factors which brought about significant and, in fact, far-reaching changes in the structure of control over land and labour and also the social existence form of peasant labour in Jalpaiguri.

Structure of land-holdings

In the first place, as noted earlier, the structure of *jotes* or *jotedari* land holdings was extremely inequitous, with a few big and even giant-sized *jotes* at one end and a large number of small *jotedari* interests at the other. For example, one *jote* in the *taluka* of Godairkuti in Duars was as large as 2,781 acres[33]. And this was not an isolated instance. While some of the *jotedars* were non-residents, many were residents and took some part in the process of cultivation. But the Dinajpur Settlement Officer's observation, that many holdings were so large that it was not feasible on the part of the big *jotedars* to cultivate the entire holding themselves or with the help of their family members even if they intended to do so[34], was no less relevant for Jalpaiguri in the early twentieth century. Because of the size it was also not possible for them even to superintend the work on all their lands[35]. So in all such cases considerable amounts of land were given out for *adhi* cultivation.

Commercialization of agriculture

One crucial factor contributing towards the rapid growth of the *jotedar-adhiar* system was the process of transition from a near-natural, subsistence economy having limited market transactions to a market-oriented economy[36]. The later years of the nineteenth and early years of the twentieth centuries constituted a period of cultivation of crops for sale in the market. For example, in the Duars the area under jute, a cash crop, increased from 59,800 acres in 1901-02 to 125,500 acres in 1907-08[37]. These were also years of expanding trade in rice, jute, tobacco and other agricultural produce and, further, almost continuous and general rise in prices. Thus, during the 1880s there was a 50 per cent rise in prices of staple crops[38]. The price of common rice, rose from about Re1 as 8 a maund to about Rs 3 a maund during the period 1893 to 1902. After remaining at the same level it went up to Rs 5 a maund in 1908[39]. This trend, with some variations, remained in operation in the next decade and, among other effects, led to the rapid intrusion and spread of money economy.

One important factor behind the commercialization of agriculture as mentioned already, as well as a major component of the process was the growth of the tea plantation enterprise. This and also the associated changes like the springing up of markets in the neighbourhood of the tea gardens acted as stimulants for expansion of cultivation and trade in paddy and other agricultural produce. As the local supply of rice was inadequate to meet the increased demand of the large and growing tea garden population, it had to be imported in considerable quantities from Dinajpur[40]. In the wake of the launching of the plantation enterprise the district of Jalpaiguri came to be provided with railway communication. Jalpaiguri town was connected by railways in 1878 and the Bengal Duars Railway was launched in the 1890s in order to facilitate the opening up of Duars and the promotion of the tea industry. These facilitated disposal of the produce of the soil and provided impetus to trade[41]. All these developments stimulated the process of differentiation in the rural society in Jalpaiguri district. In such a situation, large holdings helped the big *jotedars* and substantial peasants to enrich themselves. The situation was also conducive to their enrichment through exploitation of produce rents, usurious money and grain lending and transfer of holdings of small *jotedars*, *chukanidars* and peasants.

The process of differentiation and consolidation of large *jotedari* interests was associated with the increasing cultivation of cash crops in general and jute in particular. That the cultivators were particularly keen on cultivation of jute is shown by the rapid increase in area under jute, in some parts of the district even at the expense of *aus* or *bhadoi* rice cultivation. But the jute trade was characterized by sudden and wide fluctuations because of uncertainties of international demand[42]. Small *jotedars* and small peasants who constituted the bulk of the landowning rural population had to bear the major brunt of such fluctuations. The typical problem of the peasant growers in Jalpaiguri is stated in the *District Gazetteer:* 'In 1906-07 the price of jute ruled very high and in the following year cultivators grew large quantities of it; prices, however, fell and they did not make as much profit as they had expected to do[43]'. Such fluctuations often meant impoverishment of the poorer sections which in its turn strengthened the position of the large landed interests. The latter were the only sections to derive some sustained benefits from the jute economy[44].

Land speculation and land alienation

It deserves to be mentioned here that since the early years of the present century, if not still earlier, a land boom had also set in

Duars. Perhaps the single most important factor was the expanding tea cultivation. Milligan stressed the process of absorption of a considerable extent of *jotes* by expanding tea cultivation and its consequences. This 'turned adrift a number of cultivators ...'[45]. Continuing he stated, 'A regular land boom occurred, the general tendency being for small jotedars to sell off their developed jotes at ever increasing prices ...'[46]. Elaborating this aspect he reported, 'A few years before the inception of the present settlement a wave of land speculation swept over the Duars, and it seemed that the character of the *jotedari* interest would soon be entirely changed. Non-resident capitalists of every description bought up *jotes* right and left'. In support of his contention he presented some data: 'Out of 5,542 transfers which came to the notice of the Settlement Officer, the purchaser in 3,444 was *jotedars* already in possession of other *jotes*, in 637 cases he was *mahajan*, in 83 cases a pleader, in 100 cases a tea garden or its representative, while in 1,298 cases the purchaser was a *chukanidar* and presumably a resident cultivator. In 1912 it was ascertained that out of 9,910 mal *jotes* as many as 3,996 were held by non-resident *jotedars*'[47]. Thus, considerable alienation of peasant holdings to various categories of non-cultivating interests took place. Table 3.1 gives an indication of the nature of alienation.

Indebtedness as an instrument of land alienation

Besides land speculation, indebtedness was a major mechanism behind land transfer. Contemporary reports indicate that there were two groups of creditors: (a) *jotedars* and substantial peasants and (b) non-agriculturist professional money-lenders or *mahajans* and traders. But whoever might have been the creditors, the indebted cultivators were burdened with heavy interest payment. According to an enquiry made in 1905, the rate of interest in different areas of the Duars varied from 12 per cent to 75 per cent. But Gruning commented, 'It is doubtful if a cultivator is ever able to borrow at such a low rate of interest as 12 per cent, and it is probable that he has often to pay more than 37 per cent'[48]. Obviously enough, a large chunk of income of the peasants was eaten up by interest payment and this made repayment of loans difficult.

   That the money-lenders were getting hold of the land was noted both in the *District Gazetteer* and Milligan's *Settlement Report*. Gruning considered that the money-lenders were getting on the

Table 3.1

Classification of Alienation of Jotes in Falakata Tahsil, 1905

Class of people	Number of jotes	Percentage of jotes	Area in acres	Percentage of total area transferred
Rajbansi	1,638	39.80	58 665.23	33.80
Muhammedan	1,092	26.50	40 739.47	23.50
Mech	381	9.20	7 599.52	4.37
Jaldha	19	0.46	577.16	0.33
Garo	17	0.41	302.28	0.17
Santhal	2	0.04	24.52	0.01
Oraon	263	6.40	6 182.99	3.56
Nepali	140	3.40	4 990.49	2.87
Marwari	115	2.80	6 551.13	3.77
Up-countrymen	272	6.60	14 097.20	8.12
Kabuli	14	0.34	381.41	0.22
Assamese	18	0.40	1 132.65	0.65
European	7	0.17	1 036.19	0.59
All others including Bengali middle class	136	3.30	5 074.22	2.92
Total	4,114	99.78	1,73,523.46	99.08

SOURCE: Gruning, *Jalpaiguri District Gazetteer*, p. 99.

land probably to a much greater extent in the permanently settled portion than in the Duars. Though the sources do not always indicate who the money-lenders were, agriculturists or non-agriculturists, some observations make it quite clear that many of them belonged to the latter category. Thus, by the end of the first decade of the twentieth century in the Baikunthapur estate many of the *jotes* were held by middlemen. In the Koch Bihar Zamindari 'nearly all the lands in the vicinity of Saldanga had passed into the possession of a Marwari firm locally known as Saldanga Kaya'[49]. In Falakata *tahsil* in the Duars, according to enquiries made in 1905, about 15 per cent of the settled area were in the hands of Marwaris, upcountrymen, kabulis, and other persons many of whom were Bengali *babus*[50]. 'Out of 227 *jots* comprised in the *taluks* of Tatgaon, Udlabari and Saoga Fulbari in the Mainaguri *tahsil*, 102 or 45 per cent were transferred in 1904-05 and the *tahsildar* reported that many of them had passed into the hands of professional money-lenders. During the same year the *tahsildar* of Falakata gave a list of 71 *jots*, covering 1,882 acres, which had been sold to known money-lenders ...'. Further, '*chukanidars* appear to mortgage and sell their holdings freely to money-lenders'[51]. Though Milligan does not give detailed data, his observations and also his 1912 finding about land transfers indicate that the process continued during the period of settlements operations.

Revenue increase and land alienation

Enhancement of revenue at each successive settlements in the Duars on the ground of increase in land value[52] has been another factor behind land transfers. The first settlement in 1871 raised the revenue of the area settled from Rs 39,526 to Rs 86,330[53]. (This excluded the *parganas* of South Mainaguri). The general result of the second settlement taking effect from April 1880 for Duars as a whole excluding the South Mainaguri *parganas* was to enhance the revenue from Rs 88,618 to Rs 1,51,862. The assessment pressed too heavily on the *jotedars*, resulting in considerable default in collections, relinquishments and desertions[54]. In the third settlement known as Sunder's settlement made in 1889-95, the revenue was raised by 60 per cent due to (a) increase in the area under cultivation and (b) enhancement of the rates[55].

The enhanced revenue demand came to be associated with an increase in the rent burden on the small *jotedars* and *chukanidars*. Thus, during 1880s the rent was increased by 50 per cent. As the Duars SSR stated, '... *jotedars* were obtaining a profit from their *chukanidars* ...'[56]. This must have adversely affected the position of the latter.

It would not be inappropriate to mention here that *jote* lands were taken also by some ex-tea garden labourers, most probably the *sardars*, *baidars*, *chaprasis* etc., that is, those workers who had somewhat higher earnings than the ordinary labourers or coolies and were thus in a position to make some saving. According to figures collected by Milligan in 1910, 64,281 acres of *jote* lands were in the possession of ex-tea garden workers excluding the Paharias for whom no estimate could be made[57].

Out of whose hands was land passing out ? In the permanently settled area land was being lost by small *jotedars* and *chukanidars* presumably most of them being Rajbansi Hindus and Rajbansi Muslims. In the Duars too much land was going out of the hands of peasants belonging to the same social groups. There the Meches too suffered greatly.

Force as a factor behind land alienation

Land alienation took place through force too. Investigations conducted at the time of the settlement operations disclosed that in many cases outright force was applied to degrade tenants. It was found that 'the *giri* [the local term for the landlord immediately superior to the tenant] was forcibly converting a cash-paying tenant into an *adhiar*—a common tendency throughout the district'[58]. The specific form of the force is not indicated in the source. It, however, appears that many of the peasants who were inducted to clear the forests and bring land under cultivation were initially settled as cash-paying tenants under the *jotedars*, but once the land was made fit for cultivation these peasants were forcibly reduced to the position of *adhiars*.

Implication of land alienation

What were the implications of this land alienation for the agrarian structure? Three separate but interrelated tendencies were noticeable. The first tendency was in relation to the 'land-controlling interests'. Here, again, there were two sub-tendencies. One was the strengthening of the position of the original big *jotedars* and substantial peasants, the 'old land-controlling interests', rooted in the rural society. The second was the emergence of 'new land-controlling interests', the majority deriving strength from liquid capital accumulated through grain and money-lending, trading operations and land speculation. Pleaders, *muktears*, service holders and tea planters too came to form an important constituent of the 'new land-controlling imterests'. Many of these 'new' interests or *jotedars* were non-residents, that is, absentees. At the time of Sunder's Settlement non-residents constituted only 8 per cent of all the *jotedars*. But Milligan reported that the number and proportion of such *jotedars*, though not precisely given, rapidly increased in the two and half decades following the earlier settlement[59].

Evidently enough, all this contributed towards the spread of *adhiari* cultivation.

Secondly, a distinct process of differentiation and degradation, through land transfer caused by increasing burdens of debt and rent and even use of sheer force, was in operation. But it deserves particular notice in the case of Jalpaiguri district that land alienation and degradation, whether in the permanently settled portion or in the Duars, did not result in 'proletarianization'. Many officials specifically mentioned that in Jalpaiguri district there was no distinct category of wage-earning labourers other than that of the tea garden labourers. The 1911 *District Gazetteer* reported that the demand for labour was large, but there was practically no local supply[60].

The third tendency closely linked to the above one was the rapid growth of an unprotected tenancy-structure in the form of the *adhiari* system. Gruning noted, 'In some cases the sellers sink to the position of *adhiars* and at the mercy of the new *jotedars*, who can turn them at any time'[61]. Milligan reported 'the almost entire disappearence of the lower grades of cash-paying tenants and a marked proportional decrease even of the *chukanidars* ...'[62]. A point that needs to be emphasized here is that the spread of the *adhiari* form as an integral part of the colonial commercialization of agriculture gave a distinctively new imprint to the *adhiari* system. In the conditions prevailing in north Bengal, and Jalpaiguri in particular, the *adhiari* system turned out to be a mechanism for the spread of cultivation, the raising of crops required by the colonial economy and enrichment and consolidation of the *jotedars* and elements having close links with them who proved to be of support-base of the colonial rule.

Extent of adhi *cultivation*

What were the size and extent of *adhi* cultivation? Available data show a large increase in *adhi* cultivation during the period under consideration. It has been suggested that before the First World War, the share-cropping form of tenancy was 'more of an exception' in the north and east Bengal districts[63]. But this was not true for at least Jalpaiguri and also the districts of Rangpur and Dinajpur. In the Western Duars Sunder found that 22,170 *adhiars* were in occupation of 71,366 acres. In the settlement operations conducted by Milligan, names of 32,408 *adhiars* were recorded and were found to be in occupation of 1,34,355 acres[64]. And Milligan considered that this was an underestimate. For some reason or other, names of many *adhiars* were not recorded. Regarding the permanently settled portion Milligan observed, 'Whatever may have been the extent of the system in the past, I calculated in 1912 that 2/3 of the cultivation in the zamindary area was done in this way'[65]. Figures collected by McAlpin show that in 1914, 49 per cent of a test area in Jalpaiguri was under share-cropping[66]. According to Milligan's Settlement Report, in the district as a whole more than 30 per cent of the total settled area was cultivated by share-croppers[67]. All this suggests that crop-sharing was becoming an increasingly important element in the pre-war agrarian system of Jalpaiguri.

Position of adhiars by 1920

What was the customary, legal and economic position of the *adhiars*? It was by and large similar to the one described by Sunder. Milligan described the position of the *adhiars* in the zamindari area in the following terms:

> *Adhiars* or *projas* have been customarily regarded as labourers cultivating the land of proprietors, jotdars or chukanidars on a half-share basis. They were not considered to have any right or title but liable to be ejected at the will of their employer. They are sometimes found to have lived for many years in the same place and cultivated the same land and to be independent of their *giri*, as the immediate landlord of an *adhiar* is called, in the matter of ploughs and cattle and even seed[68].

He further noted:

> The great majority however move from field to field, from *giri* to *giri*, from locality to locality and have to be supplied with all the implements of agriculture, with seed and often subsistence. Between these extremes many differences in degree occur but local custom has never recognized any difference in kind. To complete the tale of the *adhiar's* position, as we found it, his *giri* supplies him with a free house and prescribes the crops he has to grow; while in addition to growing that crop the *adhiar* works as a general labourer for hire on the lands of his *giri* or on those of his neighbours. In the jute steeping

season and at the seasons of ploughing and reaping the *adhiar* can make a substantial income in cash besides being fed free by his employer for the day[69].

In the Duars the *adhiars'* position was not much different from the above description.

From this description it must not be concluded that the position of an *adhiar* was that of a labourer. With reference to this question McAlpin observed:

in Jalpaiguri Mr. Sunder did not contend that the *adhiar* was a labourer, but that he was a tenant without any rights[70].

Milligan too considered that the *adhiar* cannot be considered a labourer. Expressing his concern over the lack of tenancy rights of the share-croppers he wrote in 1919:

It was felt to be intolerable that an agricultural system, which was extending and establishing itself with such remarkable rapidity as the *adhiari* system has done during the last quarter of a century, should deny all rights in the land to the class which forms the basis and backbone of any community carrying on agriculture under its auspices. It was resolved that this settlement must at least make a beginning in the eradication of this gross injustice[71].

Continuing he observed:

[But] such was the unanimity and rigidity of local [*jotedars'*] opinion on the question that ... all *adhiars* were at first merely recorded in the *khatians* of *jotedars* and *chukanidars* in the column of subordinate interests in the occupation of plots ... It further transpired that in many cases written agreements were drawn up ... It appeared that in most cases where such a document was executed the *giri* was forcibly converting a cash paying tenant into an *adhiar*—a common tendency throughout the district. The essential features of these *kabuliyats* were that the *adhiar* bound himself to repay advances, deliver half the crop, obey orders, properly cultivate the land, and vacate it at the end of the contract, ... the fact that such *kabuliyats* were by no means uncommon went far to contradict the popular definition of an *adhiar* as a mere labourer[72].

Thus, a very large proportion, if not the majority, of the peasant producers came to be constituted of what may be characterized as dependent peasantry[73]. The *adhiars* constituting the vast bulk of the peasantry had no tenancy right and fixity of tenure. They could not even take the fruits of the trees planted on the land on which their huts stood. Surplus labour from them was extracted through a multiplicity of forms: high produce rent, usurious interest charges and a variety of other exactions. As a consequence of all such extractions the *adhiars* could not meet even their minimum consumption requirements from labour exerted on the plot of land rented from their *jotedars* or *giris*. Not infrequently the entire amount of the *adhiars'* share was absorbed in meeting the claims of their *jotedars* and they had nothing to take back home. Large sections of *adhiars* and rural poor were so impoverished that they were not even in a position to procure salt and they cooked vegetable curry with *cheka*[74]. Often they had to subsist on fruits, all kinds of wild roots and leaves.

Under such circumstances and with no other sources of livelihood open to them, the *adhiars* became inextricably bound to the *jotedars* for their very survival. They had to take consumption loan and borrow seeds and even draught animal ploughs to cultivate their lands from the *jotedars*. Thus, the vast mass of *adhiars* were reduced to a state of dependency and subjugation to the *jotedars*.

Agrarian structure in the early twentieth century

It is appropriate to give here a summary view of the agrarian structure as it stood by the end of the second decade of the twentieth century. In the permanently settled portion of the district there were two big zamindars who possessed a good deal of land and lived almost completely on rents, various cesses and tolls. In the Duars the Government itself was the proprietor. In both the tracts there was a large number of landholders who held fairly substantial and secure holdings or *jotes* as *jotedars*. These *jotedars* were recruited, and continued to be recruited, through a process of differentiation within the peasantry on the one hand, and from among non-agriculturists who made an attempt to have a share in surplus appropriation on the other. They either rented out land to the *chukanindars* or got their land cultivated with the help of *adhiars*. Some of the *chukanidars* too had very large land holdings.

In the permanently settled area, a *jotedar* held land immediately under a zamindar, his rent being liable to enhancement. Having originally acquired a right either to cultivate it himself or to sublet it to others, his title therein was permanent and heritable but not transferable without the consent of the proprietor obtained by payment of a *salami*. While some of the *jotedars* ranked as tenureholders, others were considered as *raiyats* under the provisions of the Bengal Tenancy Act. Below a *jotedar* was the *chukanidar* or *mulandar* holding land on a money rent, which was liable to enhancement. His title was permanent and heritable, but not transferable without his *jotedar's* consent. Most of these subtenants had by early twentieth century acquired a right of occupancy under the provisions of the B T Act[75].

The tenancies in the Duars were with some variations similar to those in the permanently settled part of the district. The *jotes* as permanent, heritable and transferable tenancies were under various restrictions. These were liable to sale, if the rent due was not paid. The *chukanidars* held land under the *jotedars* and by early years of the twentieth century they came to have occupancy rights. The big ones among them got a large part of their land cultivated with the help of *adhiars*. The big *jotedars* (and *chukanidars*), as seen earlier, became the principal suppliers of agricultural credit and were, in many cases, also involved in trade in paddy and jute. Thus, there developed a process of complex interweaving of trade, usury and *jotedari* property[76].

It is the *jotedars*, particularly the big ones among them, and substantial peasants who came to exercise very great economic and social power and authority in the village society. Along with their economic power derived from landed property and usury and trade, many of them functioned as *dewanias*. A *dewania* was a resourceful person who was known for his ready wit and who acted on behalf of villagers, particularly poorer ones, attached to him in their dealings with various agencies outside the village. They occupied a crucial position as intermediaries *vis-à-vis* the higher level legal, administrative and political system[77].

Below the big *jotedars* and other categories of substantial landholders were the petty *jotedars* and *chukanidars*, who lived primarily on the produce of their lands and engaged share-croppers to cultivate that portion of their land which they could not cultivate themselves. Then there were the poor peasants and landless peasants who carried on a subsistence existence through share-cropping.

Place of share-cropping in Jalpaiguri

In this connexion what needs to be particularly noted is the place and importance of share-cropping in Jalpaiguri. Share-cropping or *adhiari* with certain variations was found to be prevalent in many other parts of Bengal. But only in a few districts and areas was it so important as in Jalpaiguri and Dinajpur, Rangpur and Terai in Darjeeling. The *barga* or share-cropping was common in the western Bengal districts of Midnapore and Bankura, but it became so only in the 1920s and 1930s. In some other districts of west Bengal, namely Birbhum, Howrah and Burdwan, it was merely an adjunct to other forms of agricultural enterprise[78]. In central Bengal the differentiation within the peasantry took mainly the form of 'proliferation of cash-paying underryotee tenancies and the continued prevalence of forms such as *utbandi*'[79]. In eastern Bengal by and large an undifferentiated peasant economy prevailed till the late 1930s. But in Jalpaiguri and parts of north Bengal the *jotedar-adhiar* system became firmly, extensively and prominently established by the late nineteenth century. The first two decades of the twentieth century saw rapid and further extension and strengthening of the system and its evolution as the predominant form of agricultural economy and pre-eminent mechanism of surplus appropriation from agriculture[80]. This mechanism linked the land-poor and landless peasants and the *jotedars* rather than peasants and zamindars as in east Bengal districts. The *adhiari*, the local term for the *barga* form of share-cropping, was the typical social existence form of labour in the district. For the bulk of *adhiars* this mechanism involved varying degrees of *unfreedom*, particularly in the form of debt-bondage. All this constituted integral and specific aspects of the process of colonialization of Jalpaiguri's agrarian economy.

The inefficiency and inequities of the *jotedar-adhiar* system were, however, viewed in some official circles with considerable concern. Voicing this concern Milligan wrote :

> It should be clearly stated that the rapid growth of the *Adhiari* system is viewed with alarm and disapproval by Government, and

that the deliberate aim of the policy now inaugurated is to check the further spread of a system which is so economically unsound—in the zamindary areas, by replacing the helpless *Adhiar* of today by an *Adhiar* who has recognized tenant rights in the Western Duars by discouraging cultivation by *Adhiars*, by reducing the size of *jotes* so as to eliminate the necessity for sub-infeudation, by increasing the area held by small resident cultivators, and lastly, as in the zamindary area, by converting the *Adhiar*, who has no recognized rights, into a tenant[81].

It was out of such concern that certain measures were taken to give some protection to sections of *adhiars*. It was decided that in Duars the *adhiars* who cultivated with their own ploughs and cattle would be deemed as tenants who could not be evicted 'except by their own consent or under order of a Civil Court'[82]. In the permanently settled area, *adhiars* having their own ploughs and cattle were classified as tenants where their landlords were considered as tenure-holders and not tenants and as under-*raiyats* where their landlords were classed as *raiyats*[83].

But given the process of agro-economic changes which had already set in Jalpaiguri and indeed in Bengal as a whole, it was almost impossible to arrest the process of differentiation through sole reliance on legal and administrative measures. It is instructive to note that the move made in 1923 by the John Kerr Committee, appointed by the Bengal Legislative Council, to recognize as tenants those produce-paying cultivators who supplied their own cattle and seeds and chose their crops, aroused such a formidable opposition among the *jotedars* and middle class landholders that the move had to be abandoned[84].

Structural change

It has sometimes been argued that there has been little change in the agrarian structure of Bengal under British rule[85]. This appears to be reasonable. But available accounts clearly show that by 1920 and, in fact, by the turn of the century very significant changes had occurred in the agrarian structure of Jalpaiguri in the form of transformation of cultivating and resident *jotedars* into non-cultivating and even non-resident *jotedars*, the intrusion of non-agriculturist *mahajans*, traders and professional people into the rural society, the increasing concentration of landholdings in the hands of the *jotedars*, and the impoverishment and loss of land by small landholders and small peasants resulting in the swelling of rural poor, and landless *adhiars* or *adhiars* owning tiny plots. These changes were brought about by the extension of communication network, the rise in prices of agricultural produce, the intrusion of money, the commercialization of agriculture, the enrichment of substantial peasantry and the process of differentiation among the peasantry and cultivating *jotedars*. While all these factors were in operation also in the neighbouring north Bengal districts, one additional factor in the case of Jalpaiguri district, particularly the Duars, was the growth of the plantation system and the associated influx of a huge tea garden labouring population. Thus, there were far-reaching social changes as critical elements in the process of colonialization of Jalpaiguri's economy and society.

Consequences for the production process

A point that needs to be stressed here is that the agrarian relations that evolved in Jalpaiguri were not only extremely inequitous but also stood in the way of any significant improvement and transformation of agriculture and, in fact, led to a semi-stagnant agriculture characterized by unchanged productivity, unchanged technique of production and unchanged organization of production. The two big zamindars were pure rentiers spending a major part of their time in Calcutta in luxurious living and merry-making. The Raikats were also involved in highly expensive litigation[86]. They did virtually nothing for the improvement of agriculture and remained by and large divorced from the world of social production.

The process of economic changes both within the agrarian economy and outside it resulted in increasing differentiation within the peasantry, enrichment and consolidation of the substantial peasants and the 'old' *jotedars* as well as intrusion of exogenous elements—professional money-lenders, traders and professional and service-holding groups who together may be termed as the 'new' *jotedars*. All this, in turn led to the growing hold of the *jotedars* over land, labour and produce and an increasing separation between actual cultivation and land rights. That by early years of the present century many of them were turned into mere rent receivers was noted in the *Jalpaiguri District Gazetteer*[87] Even the resident and non-absentee *jotedars* found as late as the closing decades of the nineteenth century became increasingly dissociated from the actual process of production. While the share-cropping itself entailed such a process of dissociation, this was accelerated through the expanding opportunities for making large gains through usury and trade.

But very little of the surplus appropriated through the extraction of produce rent-cum-trade-cum-usury was used for improvement of cultivation. Nor was their savings invested in the growing tea industry of the district. Major part of the surplus appropriated by the *jotedars* and allied interests were put into all sorts of unproductive and wasteful expenditure. While the rural poor and *adhiars* lived in a state of hunger, misery and social degradation, the *jotedars*, particularly the big ones, maintained ostentatious style of living. They lived in sprawling, large, often two-storied wooden houses. Their wealth came to be displayed mainly in the form of land, cattle, plough, number of *adhiars* and *golas* or granaries. Many of them made a show of their wealth by having at least one elephant. Needless to say that the food habits and dress of the *jotedars* and rural rich differed markedly from those of the peasant masses, particularly the *adhiars*[88].

Under such circumstances, it is no wonder that agriculture remained in a state of semi-stagnation. As Milligan observed:

> The backwardness of agriculture throughout the district is remarkable, the more so as the climate is so favourable. Not only is the variety and in some cases the quality of the crops grown exceedingly meagre, but the implements of agriculture are absolutely primitive and agricultural livestock are of the poorest quality. No attempt is made to explore the possibilities which the soil and climate hold out, but the cultivators go on doggedly growing rice and jute, rice and jute. It matters not that the situation of his land is much better suited for the growth of other crops, the cultivator pins his faith on rice and jute. In places excellent tobacco is grown, notably in Falakata tehsil and in Patgram; mustard is grown a good deal in the Duars; sugar-cane in Baikunthapur and Boda to a small extent very little in the Duars. These with a few miscellaneous seed crops and a moderate quantity of the poorest varieties of potatoes, vegetable and fruit make up the total of produce[89].

It was a picture of unchanged technique of cultivation and pattern of land use, and agricultural stagnation. Even where some changes took place, these were made in such a way that adverse consequences followed. There was an increase in the area under jute. This helped to reduce to some extent the sole dependence of the peasants on rice production. But the increase in jute cultivation took place at the expense of the *bhadoi* or *aus* rice crop which was the peasants' food[90]. The peasants also resorted to selling a large proportion of the rice crop raised by them. The latter two changes had the effect of reducing the subsistence element in the peasant economy and extending monetization. But these changes took place not because the peasants had any surplus grain but because they were forced to raise jute and sell even part of their food crop in order to pay rents and interests on loan and to get hold of some cash to enable them to purchase oil, salt, cloth and such other goods. Thus the agrarian structure marked by the predominance of *jotedar-adhiar* relations evolved as a constraint on agricultural production and peasant economy. By mid-1910s it became evident that serious problems were accumulating within Jalpaiguri's agrarian economy. Both the *District Gazetteer* and Milligan's Settlement Report contain enough evidence of the working of such a process.

Inter-community relationships

Before concluding this chapter, it is pertinent and important to take a brief note of a few other specificities and longrun features of the agrarian society in Jalpaiguri district. One of these was that in the district there was no religious community-wise and caste-wise divide between the *jotedars* and their allies on the one hand and the mass of peasantry and rural poor including the *adhiars* on the other. The *jotedars* were overwhelmingly both Hinduized and Islamized Rajbansis and Meches and the peasants and rural poor too had similar affiliation. This was in sharp contrast to the agrarian society of many of the east and north Bengal districts which was marked by the predominance of caste Hindu zamindars and intermediate tenure-holders on the one hand and the predominance of Muslim and in some districts also of lower caste Hindu tenants on the other[91].

It is also noteworthy that neither of the two major zamindar families of the district belonged to the upper caste Hindu category[92]. The Raikats in particular were not significantly different from the Rajbansi Hindu and Rajbansi Muslim peasantry in terms of linguistic, cultural, social and ethnic attributes. The Raikats belonged to a Hinduized autochthonous group Rajbansi/Koch and rose to the position of a feudal power on the basis of certain privileges historically acquired by them. In consequence, the sort of tension and contradiction found in most of the eastern and northern Bengal districts between exploitative landowning interests culturally, socially and ethnically different from the peasant masses[93] was almost entirely absent in Jalpaiguri. Related to this was the feature that oppression by petty zamindari officials or *amlas* belonging to the caste Hindus was also not very pronounced in Jalpaiguri.

Yet one more feature was that in Jalpaiguri a large proportion of the *jotedars* belonged to the category of either tenure-holders at enhanceable rent or *mokarari raiyats*, that is, *raiyats* at fixed rent and thus were much more privileged than occupancy and non-occupancy *raiyats* who constituted the bulk of tenants in most of the eastern and northern Bengal districts. In such a structural context the points of conflict between the tenure-holders and *raiyats* among whom Muslims constituted a large proportion in the zamindari area of the district with the two zamindars, were not so sharp as in eastern and other northern Bengal districts. Excessive *abwabs*, enhancement of rent and maltreatment by the zamindar and his officials were also not much marked in Jalpaiguri. The question of honourable treatment of the Muslims *jotedars* and substantial cultivators in the zamindar's *kachhari*, which was a major point of conflict in other districts, was never an issue in Jalpaiguri.

Local Muslim *jotedars* and substantial cultivators letting out large part of their holdings to *bargadars* were socially and culturally part of what may be considered as a peasant community[94]. The local Rajbansi Hindu *jotedars* too belonged to the same category. They had common economic interests, and the socio-cultural relationship between the Rajbansi Muslim and Rajbansi Hindu *jotedars* by and large did not have elements of strain and tension. Appropriately it may be noted that there was also no religious community-wise divide among the grain-dealers and money-lenders having local origin.

In many districts the operations of exploitative outsiders, mostly Marwari traders and moneylenders in the countryside and their relationship with the Muslim tenantry, had been a major source of aggravation of communal tension and growth of communalism[95].

The extent and nature of operations of non-Bengali and non-local immigrant Bengali mercantile and usurious elements in the countryside of Jalpaiguri district, particularly in the areas which had concentrations of Muslim peasants, and their impact on inter-community relationship, requires further investigation. Available evidence, however, does not indicate that this had any particular adverse impact.

All these had a critical bearing on politics in Jalpaiguri. This aspect is considered in the later chapters of this work.

4 The Socio-Economic Setting II : Growth of Plantation Enterprise, Urban Structure and some Longrun Tendencies, 1870-1920

INTRODUCTION AND GROWTH OF TEA PLANTATION ECONOMY

While the *jotedar-adhiar* system constituted one of the distinctive features of Jalpaiguri's economy and society, the most significant one was the growth of a 'capitalist' enterprise in the form of the tea plantation system. What was the nature of this plantation enterprise? The introduction and growth of the tea plantation enterprise in the district, as in Assam and elsewhere in India, took place with the active assistance of the colonial state and, further, were not the products of operation of indigenous economic forces but of exogenous development and requirements of the imperial order. It was geared to a demand abroad for an exotic drink. Earnings from tea export along with those from other major Indian exports played a critical role in Britain's international trade and capital flow relations and in the maintenance of the British imperial system.[1] Capital, enterprise and management were imported into the district, even the unskilled labour needed by the industry was brought from a considerable distance and the involvement of the local people of the district was only marginal. The late nineteenth and early twentieth centuries saw phenomenal growth of tea plantation enterprise but this was essentially in the nature of creation and consolidation of an enclave economy which failed to generate any broad-based and dynamic transformation process. This was, however, not a unique feature of the Jalpaiguri tea plantation system but typical of all plantation economies and systems.

The introduction of the tea plantation enterprise in the district was an extension of the cultivation and manufacture of tea in other places of north-east India. That the Duars had considerable potential as a tea growing area was noted as early as 1859, that is, several years before the annexation of the Duars.[2] The first tea garden was opened by Dr Brougham, an old-hand in tea plantation at Gazaldoba[3] on the left bank of Tista in the western portion of the Duars in 1874 and he employed as his manager one Richard Houghton whom the *District Gazetteer* describes as the pioneer of tea in the Jalpaiguri district.[4] By 1876, 13 gardens were started. In 1878, just four years after the beginning of tea cultivation in the district the Duars Planters Association (DPA), a body composed of European planters, that is, European Managers, Assistant Managers, Supervisors etc. was formed.

Without going into details it may be observed that the history of the Duars tea plantation enterprise, which cannot be separated from that of the Assam enterprise and the international economic network, can for the period up to 1929 be broadly divided into four phases. The entire period from 1874 to 1896 was one of remarkable expansion in terms of acreage under tea and production. However in 1897 the industry faced a severe depression caused partly by the speculative mentality that had seized it. The depression lasted for several years. A recovery began only after 1907 or so, and the spur continued till the outbreak of the World War. There was once more a slowing down during the war years, but activities again revived from 1917. This phase which eventually turned out as the last phase of expansion continued till the end of the 1920s. In 1931 the number of tea estates in Jalpaiguri district reached 151.[5] Of these 143 gardens were situated in the Duars and the remaining 8 were located on western side of the river Tista near the town of Jalpaiguri.

A few words on the level of prosperity of the industry may be made here. There were years of low prices, low profits and low dividends. But on the whole the industry went through considerable prosperity and in some years just minted money. In the opening years of the century the dividends of the Duars gardens were moderate. But in 1909 the average dividends reached 17 per cent. In the second decade, particularly in the war years the expansion was very limited. But the industry reaped high profits. In 1915 the dividends averaged as high as 47 per cent and many of

Table 4.1
Statistics of Tea in Jalpaiguri, 1874-1951

Year	No. of gardens	Total under tea (in acres)	Approximate production (in lbs.)	Average in lbs. per acre of mature plants	Number of labourers employed		
					Permanent	Temporary	Total
(1)	(2)	(3)	(4)	(5)	(6)	(7)	(8)
1874	1	...	...	...	...	...	...
1876	13	818	29 520	...	...	...	...
1881	55	6 230	1 027 116	...	...	...	...
1892	182	38 583	18 278 628	...	...	...	...
1901	235	76 403	31 087 537	441	47 365	21 254	68 619
1907	180	81 338	45 196 894	...	...	...	...
1911	191	90 859	48 820 637	583	56 693	18 622	75 315
1921	131	1 12 688	43 287 187	426	86 693	1 871	88 564
1931	151	1 32 074	66 447 715	534	1 12 591	4 262	1 16 583
1941	189	1 31 770	94 604 450	765	1 36 491	4 896	1 41 387
1951	158	1 34 473	137 194 660	1020	...	...	1 78 009

SOURCES: For the years 1874 to 1892 and 1907 *Jalpaiguri DG*, p.103, and for the remaining years *Jalpaiguri District Handbook*, p.lii.

these dividends were tax-free. After some decline in profits and dividends in the last years of the decade, a recovery took place in the 1920s and for most part of the third decade the profits and dividends remained quite high.[6]

Role of the colonial state

Behind the rapid growth and prosperity of the Duars tea enterprise the colonial state had a very important role. As in the case of the Assam enterprise, the British Indian government or its provincial and district-level officials provided direct as well as indirect help and protection to the Duars planters. Administration of law and order, allotment of land, labour recruitment and control methods, promotion of transport and communication, forest policy, policy with regard to setting up of *hats* or weekly tea garden and village markets, taxation measures or administration of institutions like District Board—all were explicitly designed to help the European owned and European controlled tea plantation enterprise[7].

While some of the relevant evidence and examples are given later in this chapter, here the salient aspects of the land settlement policy are noted. Land was one of the two most important assets of the tea enterprise (the other one being the tea bushes with 50 to 60 years of life) and evidence shows that the government leased out lands—categorized as waste lands—to the intending planters on specially favourable terms. Under the Waste Land Rules introduced in 1896, a preliminary lease was made for a term of five years, the land being rent-free for the first year and after that on a rental of 3 annas an acre for the second year and an additional 3 annas for each successive year upto 12 annas an acre. Such rents were much lower than the rates in the backward areas of the district. Each grant was to be a compact one and to be capable of being enclosed in a ring-fence. If it was found by inspection that during the currency of the lease not less than 15 per cent of the total area of the grant had been brought under cultivation, and actually bore tea plants, the lessee was entitled to the renewal of the lease for a further period of 30 years, and to renewals for similar periods in perpetuity. The government reserved the right to fix rents subject to certain lower and upper limits[8]. Perhaps it would not be wrong to suggest that without such a land policy the tea plantations would not have got started at all. The planters usually grabbed more lands than were needed or could be managed by them. The tea grants contained materials required for house construction and, in many cases, also valuable timber. Surplus lands of the plantations were used for settling labourers as tenants[9]. Much of the land under tea grants was also in excess of all the requirements taken together. It was this sort of control over land along with several other political, economic and social aspects which was one of the critical factors contributing towards the prosperity and high profits of the Duars industry.

Entrepreneurship in Duars plantations

At this stage some characteristics of the entrepreneurship in the Duars tea deserves to be noted. That in the initial years the tea plantation enterprise in Jalpaiguri was, as elsewhere in north east India, under firm British control is well-known. While quite a large number of rupee companies were registered in India, the majority were sterling companies. But that did not mean that all of their capital was brought from Britain. Irrespective of the place of registration, the bulk of capital of the European tea companies including the Duars companies, was raised in India out of the earnings of firms owned and managed by British citizens or of British individuals who had made money out of various activities[10]. For example, Ellenbarrie and Manabarrie, two early Duars gardens were opened by a Calcutta bank manager, a Darjeeling planter and a sub-manager of the Land Mortgage Bank and later came to be managed by Duncan Brothers. Hope was started by the manager of a Darjeeling garden[11]. Further, all the European companies had their management entrusted to one or other of the British-owned managing agency houses of Calcutta (such as Duncan Brothers, Williamson Magor and Co. or Davenport and Co.) which had interlocking interests in diverse activities. Thus, Duncan Brothers which was very prominent in the Duars plantations had also substantial interests in jute manufacturing, insurance and several other activities[12] and Andrew Yule & Co. had in addition to Duars tea interests in coal, jute, copper, insurance, steamships, power, etc.[13].

Along with the extensive British control of the tea plantation enterprise, a distinctive feature of the Duars enterprise was the emergence of a small but growing core of Indian entrepreneurship, mainly Bengali entrepreneurship. This feature was not present in the Darjeeling or Assam plantations. Much has been written on the aversion of the Bengali middle class to business and industry. But it is remarkable that within just four years of the launching of the tea plantation enterprise in the Duars, in the year 1877, Munshi Rahim Baksh, a Bengali Muslim hailing from Noakhali district and working as *a peshkar* or head assistant at the Deputy Commissioner's office in Jalpaiguri town, took a tea grant of 728 acres and launched the first Indian tea garden, the Jaldhacca Tea Estate, as a proprietory concern[14]. Under the advice of Bhagaban Chandra Bose, a Deputy Magistrate posted in Jalpaiguri, and at the initiative of several immigrant Bengali lawyers and persons of resource who had settled in Jalpaiguri town, the first Indian joint stock tea company, Jalpaiguri Tea Co. Ltd., was started in 1879[15]. However, in the early decades the growth of Indian entrepreneurship which has been chronicled by Birendra Chandra Ghosh, who himself belonged to a leading planter family, and also analysed by Shib Sankar Mukherjee[16] was slow and in the 31 years between 1879 and 1910 only eleven companies were started. The major reason was, as shown below, unfavourable political and economic environment. The high watermark of Indian entrepreneurship in the Duars was a period which roughly stretched from 1910 till about 1930[17]. By the latter year the Indian entrepreneurs came to own 47 gardens in Jalpaiguri district and about 37 per cent of the total capital (Rs 73,88,029 out of Rs 2,00,67,579) invested in the tea industry in the district[18]. Most of the Indian-owned companies had their offices in Jalpaiguri town, some outside Jalpaiguri town and a few outside the district[19].

Some characteristics of Indian entrepreneurship

With regard to the Indian entrepreneurship several points need to be made. First, in the Jalpaiguri tea plantation enterprise the early Indian entrepreneurship was in a sense a local one. Among the Indian entrepreneurs, Bengali Hindus and Bengali Muslims residing in Jalpaiguri town were the earliest to make entry into the industry and constituted the largest single group. It was, however, local entrepreneurship not in the sense of entrepreneurship thrown up by the 'sons of the soil' like the Rajbansi Hindus or the local Muslims but in the sense that most of the early entrepreneurs were Bengalis. But all of these Bengali entrepreneurs were immigrant Bengalis settled in Jalpaiguri town. They were generally lawyers, legal practioners and similar professional people, contractors, merchants and service-holders. The majority of them such as the families of Gopal Chandra Ghosh and his son-in-law Tarini Prosad Roy, Rahim Baksh and his son-in-law Musharruff Hossian, Joy Chandra Sanyal or Sashi Kumar Neogi or Bhabani Charan Ghatak came from east Bengal and north Bengal districts like Dacca, Noakhali and Pabna. Of course quite early, that is, in the 1890s two zamindar families of Nadia district in central Bengal—Sahas and Pal Chaudhuries—made an entry into the industry[20]. In the second decade of the present century P.D. Raikat, the Jalpaiguri zamindar, started several gardens within his Baikunthapur zamindari area[21]. In the third and early fourth decades a number of gardens were established by Rajbansi Hindus and Muslims who had a *jotedari* background, for example, Laxmikanta Das, Bhojnarayan Singh and Nepucha Mohammad as promoter directors[22]. In the 1920s the Rahuts, a *jotedar* family originally hailing from Dacca, entered the industry. It should be mentioned that usually the *jotedar* promoters did not make much investment, but in lieu of the price of the land kept corresponding shares[23]. It was also during the second and third decades that the Dagas, a Marwari family which had been active in trade and finance since the 1870s, joined many tea enterprises.

Secondly, a list of some of these entrepreneurs show that the Indian entrepreneurship was as much a Muslim entrepreneurship as a Hindu entrepreneurship. There was no particular religious or sectarian community component in this entrepreneurship. Many of the Indian ventures, such as the Anjuman Tea Co. Ltd. (1889) or Ramjhora Tea Co. (1907) were sponsored jointly by some of the leading Hindu and Muslim planters[24].

Thirdly, the major source of capital invested by these people in the tea industry were the savings made out of their income from legal practice and various professional activities, service or trade and commerce[25].

Fourthly, those among the Jalpaiguri's middle class who had savings adequate enough to start a tea garden did not hesitate to enter into the hitherto untried and unexplored area of tea enterprise and take risks. It seems that the early Bengali entrepreneurs were in a sense spurred by a sort of adventurousness. Some of them were also motivated by the nationalist spirit. The interest shown by Bhagaban Bose reflected that spirit. At the same time, the connections that they had with the British officials and British planters in their capacity of government employees and of lawyers and legal advisers facilitated their entry into the plantation enterprise. Success and experience of the early Indian planters prompted others to move into the enterprise. Fifthly, the Bengali entrepreneurship of Jalpaiguri town did not remain confined within Jalpaiguri district only. From 1911 onwards it spread out to Terai in Darjeeling district and Assam. In 1933 the total number of Indian-owned tea companies in the entire north-east India stood at 163, and of these 88 were owned and controlled by the Bengalis of Jalpaiguri district[26]. A last and a general point that emerges from what has been stated above is that given appropriate opportunities Indians including Bengalis with resource were not reluctant to undertake entrepreneurial risk and enterprise. But the fact that virtually all of them were immigrants raises the question: did their venture have any connexion with immigration? This is an aspect that needs exploration.

Problems faced by Indian planters

The growth of the Indian sector of the Jalpaiguri tea industry had, however, to face serious hurdles. As noted by a foremost historian of private enterprise in India, 'The dominance of modern industry by European business houses before the First World War was supported and reinforced by a whole set of administrative, political, and financial arrangement within India. The European businessmen very consciously set themselves apart from 'native' businessmen, they claimed a cultural and racial affinity with the British rulers of India which was denied to the Indians who might compete with them'. All this 'afforded European businessmen a substantial and systematic advantage over their Indian rivals in India'[27]. This was also the position in the Jalpaiguri tea enterprise. There was overt racial prejudice and systematic discrimination on the part of the well-entrenched European planters. Till 1915 the commercial association, the Dooars Planters Association (DPA), was an exclusively European affair, the membership being open to only European gardens. Even after 1915, when representation within the Association was allowed to Indian-owned gardens, the DPA remained a predominantly European association primarily looking after the interests of the European planters. The 1915 move itself was largely motivated by the need to bring the Indian gardens within the purview of the Dooars Labour Code, a labour control measure designed to serve the European planter interests[28]. The management of European gardens was entirely in the hands of Europeans and Anglo-Indians and it was only in 1946 that for the first time an Indian was appointed as an assistant manager. Throughout the Duars many clubs were organized by the planters for social gathering, but these were open only to Europeans[29].

Discrimination, however, did not remain confined to the areas mentioned above. In fact, an entire series of administrative, financial and economic policies and measures were introduced and maintained over the years to prevent and impede the growth of the Indian entrepreneurship. A formidable hurdle faced by the Indians was the difficulty in getting lands for the plantation. As noted earlier, rapid expansion of Indian plantation enterprise was a post-1910 phenomenon. But by 1910 all the available waste lands were leased out and most of these were leased out to the European planters. Under the circumstances, the new entrepreneurs, largely Indians, had to seek *jote* lands for plantation. These lands, once earmarked for ordinary peasant cultivation, had been left uncultivated because of unsuitability for paddy or jute cultivation. But in 1914, presumably under pressure from the European planters, through an administrative order the provincial government prohibited clubbing of *jote* lands in a ring fence for the purpose of tea plantation. It meant that no land was available to enterprising Bengalis and other Indians for opening new tea gardens. It was only after much lobbying and demonstration of loyalist attitude on the part of the Indian planters and the Indian Tea Planters Association (ITPA), which was formed in 1915 to look after the interests of the Indian planters of Jalpaiguri, that the ban was lifted in 1924[30]. Even after that, the European planters and managers remained jealous of the growth of the Indian sector and often used their influence and connexions with the European officials to prevent the sale of *jote* lands to prospective Indian planters. In his address to the DPA's annual general meeting held in early 1927 the DPA Chairman deprecated any further conversion of *jote* lands into tea lands[31].

Another major hurdle was that under the European-controlled financial and banking system and practice, institutional finance was not available to the Indian planters. Under the circumstances, the Indian planters had to procure finance from Marwari businessmen and money-lenders against promissory notes executed by the concerned Directors. There were moments of crisis when money had to be obtained by pawning family ornaments. Borrowing from friends and relatives was also not an uncommon practice. The family-centred management of the Indian companies was often of help in tiding over difficulties. Along with these, in 1888 the Indian entrepreneurs of Jalpaiguri started their own financial institution, the Jalpaiguri Banking and Trading Corporation, and some time later the Bengal Dooars Bank[32].

The difficulties faced by the Indian planters were compounded by the tight control that the British had over practically all the vital areas of tea industry and business, such as labour supply, allotment of railway wagons, coal supply, stores movement, carriage of tea, auctions, warehousing, tea tasting and broking, procurement of machinery and supply of tea chests. In all these areas systematic discrimination was practised against the Indian planters as a result of which the latter were placed in an enormously disadvantageous position. Not infrequently labour engaged in Indian gardens were enticed away by the European gardens and various obstacles were put in the way of transport and movement of men and materials through European gardens. The policy with regard to statutory cess introduced by the Government in the early years of the century for tea propaganda purposes also bore the marks of discrimination.

In short, the political, social and economic environment was highly unfavourable, if not hostile, for the growth of Indian entrepreneurship in the Jalpaiguri plantation enterprise. It was in such a situation that in 1915 at the initiative of Tarini Prosad Roy, Aminur Rahman, Jyotish Chandra Sanyal, Jogesh Chandra Ghose and several others, the Indian planters organized the Indian Tea Planters' Association (ITPA) with the aims of safeguarding their interests and ventilating their grievances to the government. However, despite the fact of discrimination and existence of tension the Indian planters as well as the ITPA refrained from entering into any open or total conflict with the planters. One major reason was their heavy dependence on British officials and British businessmen and planters in many respects. It may also be mentioned here that for many years a group of Indian planters led by Musharruff Hossian maintained a distance from the ITPA, though later on they joined it[33]. These relationships had, as noticed elsewhere, had important bearing on the political trends and movements in the district.

Labour in Duars plantations and its specificities

In the first few years of the tea plantation enterprise in the Duars, the labour employed was almost entirely Nepali. But it was soon found that the supply of Nepali labour was not sufficient to meet the growing requirements of the tea plantations. Further, the local inhabitants were reluctant to work in the gardens. Under the circumstances, the planters had to look elsewhere for securing labour and the experience of the Assam plantations indicated the areas from which labour could be procured. Within seven years of the launching of the first garden, a trickle of Chhotanagpur labour started arriving in the Duars. The 1881 census recorded 210 Oraons and smaller numbers of other immigrant tribal groups. The number grew rapidly in subsequent years and by 1901 a sizeable labour force was built up (Table 3.1). While Nepali immigrants from the Darjeeling district continued to constitute a fair proportion of the labour force in the gardens located in the hilly areas of the Duars, the overwhelming majority was recruited from distant Chhotanagpur and the Santal Parganas. According to the 1901 Census Report, there were 188,223 immigrants in the district as a whole. The bulk of them were enumerated in the Duars and 'about half of the immigrants [were] tea garden coolies from Chhotanagpur and Santal Parganas'. The Migration Statement showed that 80,436 immigrants were from Ranchi district and 10,562 from Santal Parganas[34]. The 1911 Census reported that the number of persons born in Ranchi and enumerated in Jalpaiguri district was no less than 126,214[35].

The method of recruitment for the Duars gardens differed from that adopted by the planters in Assam. The Duars labourers were 'free' in the sense that they were not indentured labourers subject to penal measures. Perhaps one reason for this difference was that by the early 1880s migration from Chhotanagpur and nearby areas for work in tea gardens was an established social process. More-over, by the time the tea industry came to be started in Jalpaiguri district, because of certain inconveniences of the indentured sys-tem experienced by the Assam planters and increasing labour protests in diverse forms, even the latter had given up their exclusive dependence on that system and had been introducing non-indentured recruitment through garden *sardars*. An additional reason, as suggested by Griffiths, might have been the fact that 'the Duars was much nearer than Assam to its principal recruiting grounds'[36] and so the planters did not resort to such overt acts of coercion which were found in Assam.

But from this, it must not be considered that the Duars tea garden labour was free from coercive methods of labour control. There is enough evidence to show that considerable coercion, direct as well as indirect, and sometimes outright terrorization techniques were used by the planters and their agents in (i) procuring labour, (ii) putting them to work and (iii) keeping them under control. It was partly due to considerable involvement of Indians in the Duars tea enterprise that the system of recruitment of labour and their conditions did not receive much public attention and governmental enquiry. Hence, it is difficult to provide detailed documentary evidence in support of the above. But even the limited materials available for the late nineteenth and early twentieth centuries and somewhat detailed account of conditions of labour as late as the early 1940s[37] make it abundantly clear that the Duars plantation labour was wage labour put under various types of non-economic constraints which severely restricted the mobility of labour and it turned out as 'labour held in bondage in a free market'[38]

Methods of recruitment of labour[39] involved all sorts of unscrupulous methods, deceptions and not infrequently even outright violence to recruit men, women and children. Moreover, the destitution and precarious conditions of existence of the tribal peasants in Chhotanagpur and Santal Parganas made them fall easy prey to the alluring prospect in the tea gardens held out before them as well as various enticements offered to them by the recruiters. The recruits were kept in prison-like transit depots and sent to the gardens under heavy guard.

At the time of recruitment they were given an advance, partly refundable and partly non-refundable. This advance was given to the recruits to pay off debts in their country and to enable them to meet road and sundry expenses[40]. This practice gave them the impression that they were not free to move. This impression was strengthened by the further practice by which every new recruit was required to put his thumb impression on an agreement bond for work for a period of at least six months in the tea estate which brought him from his native place bearing all the incidental expenses[41].

On their arrival at the gardens, the labourers were put in a concentration camp-like situation. The managers enjoying the explicit or implicit support of the colonial authority and the *mystique* of the *sahib* were law unto themselves. Physical coercion, beatings, flogging—all these were quite common. Incidents of death from physical torture were not unknown. There are unrecorded accounts of troublesome workers being thrown into furnaces of garden factories[42].

The very fact that thousands of tribal peasants were wrenched from their habitat and moved to work-sites far from their homes and that these distant migrants were herded together in totally unfamiliar surroundings itself put a restriction on their movement and freedom. This labour system—the recruitment from a long distance, the separation of workers from their known environment, their total isolation from the proximate surroundings because of geographical location, ethnic, social, cultural and language distances and barriers, and various forms of open as well as concealed compulsion in organizing migration—made the workers particularly vulnerable to violence and coercion. That the Duars plantation area was a non-Regulation tract meant that many of the ordinary laws and regulations were not in force in the area. This administrative feature gave virtually unlimited power to the sahibs.

Along with this, various other devices were also resorted to by the planters to keep the labour under control. In most of the gardens plots of land were given to the labourers for the purpose of cultivation, either free or at a nominal rent as an enticement to land-hungry dispossessed tribal peasants as well as a means of binding them to the garden as cottars on the plantations. *Hats* (weekly/bi-weekly markets) too were arranged in a manner that control could be maintained over the labourers. In order to keep the labourers of a garden confined within the garden and to reduce their contact with the outside world including labourers from other gardens and neighbouring villagers to the minimum, the planters by mutual arrangement among themselves introduced the practice of 'universal Sunday *hat*'[43]. In case there was a move on the part of any quarter to hold a *hat* on a day other than Sunday, the planters put pressure on the government to prevent this[44].

The Labour Rules turned out to be another method of having control over labour. It was in 1905 that the DPA worked out a set of Labour Rules which laid down that gardens enticing labourers from other gardens were bound to reimburse the losing gardens the expenses it had incurred on bringing a worker to the Duars and the money it had advanced to him. Though the labourer was legally free to move from one garden to another, the implementation of the Labour Rules effectively curbed this freedom. Moreover, to deal with any recalcitrance and unrest on the part of the labourers and to keep them under firm control the European planters organized and maintained a private coercive machinery, the North Bengal Mounted Rifles (NBMR)[45]. Thus, though the Duars labourers were formally and juridically free, the planters devised various direct and indirect methods to keep them on the garden and to hold them virtually in a state of captivity.

The conditions of work and living constituted a vital aspect. There was no law and no government supervision in the matter of emigration to the Duars, wages, tasks, and general management of the estates. In 1912 the Dooars Labour Act was passed, but it was concerned with government inspection only in the matters of sanitation and public health. The enactment was prompted by the high incidence of sickness resulting in absenteeism and heavy death toll among the workers due to various diseases, particularly malaria and black water fever. The *sahibs* too often fell prey to these scourges and acutely felt the need for some measures to control these[46].

The labourers had to do the most back-breaking work outdoors under conditions of intense heat, heavy downpour and severe cold. As reported by Sunder, in the cold weather and rains plucking work was done from 7 a.m. till about 6 p.m. with two hours leave[47]. The labourers had to do a variety of most arduous tasks ranging from hoeing, pruning etc. to plucking under the close supervision of a whole array of an Indian subordinate staff—*sardar, dafadar, chaprasi*, head *dafadar* or *baidar* employed to act as a check on the *sardar* and *dafadar*, and *munshi* or outdoor native assistant engaged to keep watch over the entire operation[48]. All of them, however, worked under the supervision of the *sahib*. Unlike in Assam where the *sardar's* work usually ended once the recruitment work was over, in the Duars gardens the *sardar* was in a sense the key element in putting the labourers to work and exercising discipline over them. Because of abysmally low wages and also because of abuses of payment through the *sardars* the labourers became indebted to the *sardars* or their men and in some cases to the garden management[49]. Under the circumstances, 'the sardars in the Duars may be said', as an official Committee observed, 'to own the coolies who have been recruited by themselves or by their nominees'[50]. Thus, in addition to other methods, extensive indebtedness and relations of personal domination and dependency were used to keep labour firmly under control[51]. .

The power of the *sardars* and other members of the subordinate staff was derived from the *sahibs*. They kept close watch on the work of the labour force as well as lower supervising staff. In contrast to Assam, the *sahibs* were not armed with legal power. Yet they were the *only* authority for the labourers. Any 'indiscipline' and 'laxity' resulted in severe punishment. Coolie women fell victim to their lust. Much more important than actual assaults was the threat and fear of assaults.

Along with the labour system which itself was an extra-economic method, certain other non-market practices, such as housing tied to employment, allotment of tiny plots of land, garden or *kaya*-owned shops, part payment in rice, ties of indebtedness and personal dependency relations put severe restrictions on the mobility of labour. In many respects the labourers were reduced to a semi-servile status and the labour market came to be infested with various methods of coercion. Further, labour was under the control of planters and other elements allied with them not only just during the working hours but even during their non-working hours.

Such a structure of the labour market enabled the planters to discard market mechanisms in the determination of wages. The wage rate came to be fixed at a level that would provide subsistence at most to a single worker. So to procure subsistence for the family, the female and child members of the family had to join the labour force and make earnings. Further, even the earnings of the entire family remained at an abysmally low level and the family had to procure part of the means of subsistence by working outside the plantation, that is, by cultivating its staple food like rice on the tiny plot allotted to it. And this involved a lengthening of the working hour and, what is more, a part re-peasantization of wage labour in the plantations.

In connexion with wages the method of payment needs to be briefly touched on. In the early decades and later on too the practice was to fix a *hazira* for the daily task, while the worker, if he wanted, could in addition earn overtime, which was known as *doubli*. In the earlier decades in all the gardens the amount earned for the *hazira* was paid monthly, while the *doubli* was paid weekly[52].

With regard to actual remuneration the following may be stated. In the early 1890s on the tea gardens the average wage rates were Rs 6 a month for men, Rs 4.8 to Rs 5 for women, and Rs 2.8 to Rs 3 for children[53]. In a report written in 1900 the Deputy Commissioner of Jalpaiguri estimated that the average earnings of the most industrious male labour was not more than Rs 60 a year. Moreover, though the children, often just toddlers, had to do the plucking, usually they were not paid a separate wage and their pluckings went into the mother's basket[54]. Official reports show that in the years between 1893 and 1908 there was a 66 per cent rise in the price of rice, the staple food of the tea garden labourers, and more than that in that of wheat, but the wage rates remained unchanged[55]. Because of such meagre earnings they became indebted to the *sardars* and in some cases to the garden management[56]. Sunder had reported, '... they [the labourers] are comfortably housed, good drinking water is supplied to them .... they are regularly looked after by a Native doctor, often by a qualified European doctor on a high pay ....'[57]. But official reports of as late as 1946 or 1948 admitted that the houses made of bamboos with thatched roofs and sides were nothing but hovels with insufficient light and air[58], and sanitations had no standard worth mentioning[59]. Indian 'doctors' were not qualified, and European doctors, Arbuthnot reported, were not available for treating the 'coolies', and any regular hospital did not exist[60].

In short, the labourers were strictly controlled, poorly paid, illiterate, malnourished and diseased. It should be added that all this—the involuntary nature of work, the hard toil, the meagre wages and the sub-human living conditions—deterred local people from seeking work in the tea gardens.

Tea industry and its spread effects

The introduction of the tea plantation enterprise in Jalpaiguri was certainly a major innovation. But looking at the impact of the tea industry on technological and economic growth, it must be noted that, as in other areas of the Indian tea industry, the Jalpaiguri industry operated at a low level of technology, showed little technological innovation, and only a few tasks involved any level of skill beyond what could be acquired quickly on the job. This meant that employment could fluctuate rapidly to meet changes in demand and problems caused by variations in the weather.

As regards the impact of the tea plantation on the economy of North Bengal as a whole and the Duars in particular, the tea plantation system being essentially a superimposed one had very tenuous links with the hinterland and extremely limited spread effects. A great deal of the income generated was leaked abroad, and the growth of the industry did not lead to the setting up of any manufacturing industry, not even of any tea chest or timber industry, though timber was available in abundance. The extent of dependence of the industry on foreign supplies even as late as in 1918 was graphically described by J.C.K. Peterson, then Controller of Munitions, Bengal. He wrote :

> Much of the Indian tea crop was, and still is, packed in boxes obtained from foreign countries. Patent chests are imported from Russia, Canada or Japan and the metal fittings required from England or America. Hoop iron, rails, clips for fastening the patent chests also came from foreign countries. Without these supplies it would be impossible to pack tea ... The pruning knives, hoes, forks, and kodallies used in the gardens and practically all the machinery required for the manufacture of tea are also imported[61]

The *District Gazetteer* reported that apart from the manufacture of tea, the other industries of the district were of little importance and were mainly directed to supplying the simple needs of a rural population. While indigenous enterprise and capital located primarily in Jalpaiguri town obtained some access to the industry, the bulk of the local people had a kind of peripheral coexistence with the industry, and this kind of coexistence continued till the attainment of independence in 1947 without any basic change in the relationship.

It is not that the tea industry did not generate any secondary or tertiary economic activity. It played a role in the clearing of forests and setting up of settlements on forest-cleared lands centring around plantation. But its transformative impact did not go much beyond this. The industry's own contribution to the building up of infrastructure in the Duars was of very limited extent. The European planters organized in the Dooars Planters Association were keen on the creation of infrastructure needed by the plantations in the form of railways, roads and bridges and prevailed upon the administration to take up the responsibility of doing so. The Jalpaiguri town was linked to Calcutta and Siliguri by what was called in the 1870s the Northern Bengal State Railways (later known as the Eastern Bengal State Railways) as far back as 1878. With the growth of the tea industry the planters pressed the government for introducing railways in the Duars to assist them in developing the tea industry and in opening up the Duars. It was as a result of this that railways were constructed by the Bengal Dooars Railway (BDR) under a contract between the Secretary of State for India and the Octavius Steel and Co. of London and Calcutta entered into in 1891 and also the Cooch Behar State Railways. Liberal government assistance was provided to the BDR in the form of free grants of land and free supply of timber from the reserved forests. The contract also provided that the District Board was to pay, if necessary, a certain sum to raise the net profits of the undertaking[62]. Along with this, the government and the District Board constructed and maintained not only all the major roads and bridges but also many of the smaller roads connecting tea gardens with the major highways. Though the financial contribution of the planters in the extension of local communications was almost negligible, it was they who along with the ex-officio European members came to constitute the majority of members of the Jalpaiguri District Board. Thus, out of the seventeen members, all of them either ex-officio or nominated ones, of the first District Board of Jalpaiguri constituted in 1887 six were European officials and five were European planters. By and large this remained the pattern of composition of the District Board for a number of decades[63]. These European members, particularly the planters, exercised a most powerful influence on the functioning of and decision-making in the District Board, and under their influence most of the expenditure and activities were directed towards meeting the infrastructural requirements of the planters[64].

A totally roundabout way in which the tea industry could be said to have contributed to the growth of the economy in the Duars was that the rapidly growing food requirements for the tea garden labour force and the extension of communication provided some stimulus to agriculture. Jungle lands were cleared, area under cultivation increased, people came from adjoining areas to settle down as agriculturists, rice cultivation was intensified, cash crops like jute and tobacco were grown, and the economy became increasingly monetized. All this came to be associated, as noted in the preceding chapter, with the extension and consolidation of the *jotedar-adhiar* system.

SMALL TOWN GROWTH IN COLONIAL CONTEXT

The extremely limited impact of the growth of the tea plantation enterprise and colonialized commercialization is also indicated by the very restricted extent and character of urban growth in the district[65]. Throughout the period of British rule it remained essentially a rural and plantation district. Till 1951 Jalpaiguri, the district headquarters, was the only settlement in the district which was considered to be a town by the census authority. In 1921 its population constituted a meagre 1.6 per cent of the district's population. It did not have any electricity before 1933 and no waterworks before 1935. Alipurduars, the headquarters of the subdivision of the same name and the second largest settlement, acquired the status of a non-municipal town as late as 1951. Several market centres—called *bandars* by Bengalis immigrating from east Bengal—dealing in jute, paddy, tobacco, vegetables and *sal* timber grew. But the 1911 *District Gazetteer* listed only six chief trading centres in the Duars : Jorpakri, Mainaguri, Falakata, Madarihat, Buxa and Alipurduars. In the Regulation portion the number of trading centres were only five : Jalpaiguri town, Tetulia, Rajnagar, Saldanga, Debiganj and Baura, the principal river mart of the district[65]. These apart, Domohoni on the left bank of the Tista, almost to the opposite of Jalpaiguri town, grew as a railway settlement with a small locoshop of the Bengal Duars railway.

Among these settlements, Jalpaiguri town deserves somewhat detailed consideration. The place had been the headquarters of the Raikats since the second decade of the eighteenth century. But it grew and gained in importance during the period of British rule primarily as the centre of political and administrative domination over the district and also, perhaps to no less extent, as a centre of trade and commerce. Its growth and relative prosperity also partly stemmed from the fact that the Bengali entrepreneurship in the tea plantation enterprise was mainly based in that town and registered offices of most of the Indian tea concerns came to be located there. In 1878 the town came to be connected with Calcutta, the centre of political and commercial power in the Bengal Presidency. It was connected with Duars through Barnes *ghat* on the east bank of Tista by ferry. The town provided the channel through which cotton cloth, corrugated iron and various consumer goods reached to the interior trading centres and villages and also the channel for mobilizing and siphoning off tea, jute, tobacco, timber etc.

Social and economic relations in the town emerged out of expanding services, professional and economic interests within the framework of colonial administrative, political and economic institutions. Even the physical features bore the imprint of a colonial town. Built on the right bank of river Tista, it had a nucleus of government offices, courts, Jalpaiguri Club or the Planters' Club commonly known as the European Club and residential bungalows for European officers with beautifully laid gardens and lawns. Away from the river and to the west was the sprawling native town consisting of scattered houses, all except the brick-built palace of the Raikats(Rajbari), with wooden flooring, bamboo mat walls and straw or a few with wooden roofings and large compounds[67] and a market place (Dinbazar) and large jute godowns owned by the Ralli Brothers and Landel Clarke Cos. located on the outskirts of the native town. The native town was divided into localities or *paras* usually named after an occupation such as Babu *para*, Ukil *para*, Muhuri *para*, Teli *para* etc. and residences in the bazar area. The setting had many rural features[68].

The growth of the town is indicated by figures of population changes presented in Table 4.2. The population increase was primarily due to immigration from other places. It was essentially a settlers' town and came to be overwhelmingly inhabited by Bengali Hindus and Muslims coming from east Bengal and also from the north Bengal districts of Pabna and Rajshahi, the former constituting the majority community. Immigrant Bengalis came as government clerks, lawyers, teachers, contractors etc. Later on the successful and more affluent among them, particularly the law-

Table 4.2
Growth of Jalpaiguri Town

Year	Persons	Decadal variation	Decadal percentage variation
1872	6,598		
1881	7,936	+ 1,338	+ 20.27
1891	9,682	+ 1,746	+ 22.00
1901	9,708	+ .26	+ .26
1911	11,469	+ 1,761	+ 18.14
1921	14,520	+ 3,051	+ 26.60
1931	18,962	+ 4,442	+ 30.59
1941	27,766	+ 8,804	+ 46.43

SOURCE: Census Reports for the relevant years.

yers who usually had high income[69], turned to tea plantation. Muslim Sowdagars from Dacca district and Marwaris came as traders and merchants[70]. While the Sowdagars were mainly retail traders, Marwaris were engaged in both retail and wholesale business. Major Bengali families, both Hindus and Muslims, as well as the Marwaris retained links with their kin in ancestral places and made periodic visits. Earthworkers, unskilled day labourers and domestic servants came mainly from north Bihar districts. As there was no functional division among the Rajbansi Hindus, washermen, barbers, sweepers etc. too came from Bihar. The autochthons of the districts, the Rajbansi Hindus and local Muslims, formed a minuscule fraction of the town population and the former were considered by the caste Hindus as virtually outcastes. Similarly, the Muslims of local origin were looked down upon by the Noakhali Muslims. In course of time some of the autochthonous Hindus and Muslims, particularly who had substantial landed and *jotedari* interests, turned to English education, legal professions and government service and the more successful and affluent among them came to reside in the town, while usually maintaining their main household establishments in the villages.

In considering the social and economic situation in Jalpaiguri town it is instructive to take note of the occupational pattern of the population. Though we do not have any data with regard to this aspect, on the basis of qualitative evidence we may hazard to observe that government servants and tea office employees, lawyers and other professional groups, traders, merchants and contractors constituted an unusually large proportion of the town population. In contrast to most of the urban and semi-urban centres in Bengal including those in north Bengal districts like Rangpur and Dinajpur, in Jalpaiguri town landed interests and agriculturists comprised a much smaller proportion.

Another remarkable feature was with regard to the place and influence of different religious communities and caste groups. The social and economic situation in the urban and semi-urban centres in eastern and most of the northern Bengal districts was marked by domination of upper caste Bengali Hindu zamindars and intermediary tenureholders and also Hindu trading and money-lending interests. Further, the Hindu-dominated urban and semi-urban centres were surrounded by villages in which Muslims and in some districts Muslims together with lower caste Hindus, for example, Namasudras, were preponderant. Jalpaiguri town was a contrast to this type of urban centres. It was essentially, as mentioned above, a settlers' town of recent origin, a town in which immigrants formed the bulk of the population. Numerically speaking, according to the 1921 Census, the proportion of Muslims and that of Hindus in the town population were equal[70]. The town was built and developed as much by Hindu lawyers, professional people, service-holders and merchants as by their Muslim counterparts. That in the growth of the Indian plantation enterprise both Bengali Hindu and Muslim entrepreneurs made significant contributions and that many tea companies were floated and run jointly have been noted above. Unlike most of the eastern and northern Bengal urban centres, Jalpaiguri town was not a seat of Hindu feudal and commercial exploitation of a predominantly Muslim tenantry[71].

In some recent writings it has been suggested that the share of Muslims in government services, the legal profession, municipal institution and economic activities like plantation entrepreneurship and business was disproportionate to their numerical strength in the district's population[72]. But even a cursory examination of relevant evidence reveals that the suggestion is, to say the least, not reasonable. One thing is that it is totally wrong to lump together all Hindus on the one side and all Muslims on the other side disregarding significant divisions within each of these two communities. There cannot be any denial of the fact that the immigrant Bengali caste Hindus constituting a meagre 1.37 per cent of the district's total population had a disproportionately large, if not the dominant, share in all the areas mentioned above, while Rajbansi Hindus, forming 33 per cent of the district's total population, had a marginalized existence. Muslims who were prominent in various areas of urban life and activities were overwhelmingly Noakhali Muslims, while the share of Muslims of local origin was negligible. Another important aspect is that the immigrant tribals forming nearly 19 per cent of the district population did not have any place in or entry to any sector of Jalpaiguri's urban life. It is misleading to gloss over such details and complexities.

Yet one more feature was that the relationship between the two major communities was at least till the end of the second decade, by and large, free from any tension and conflict. Rather, it was marked by considerable friendly social intercourse. Muslims used to enthusiastically take part in Hindu religious and social festivals like Durga *puja* and *holi* (the spring festival of sprinkling of coloured water and *abir*) and women members of respected Hindu *bhadralok* families used to distribute *sarbat* and sweets to tired Muharram processionists[73]. There were instances of Muslims acting as organizers of Hindu festivals. For example, Ismail Huq Chaudhuri acted as secretary of a Dol puja or spring festival committee for several years[74].

In discussing the social, administrative, political and economic life of the town the place of the Europeans deserves notice. Numerically, the Europeans constituted a negligible fraction of the town population. They also remained an alien part of Jalpaiguri society and were exclusive to a high degree. Yet for several decades they played a most influential role in the social and political life.

As in other Bengal districts, in Jalpaiguri too the European civil servants were for all practical purposes leaders of institutionalized political life as well as arbiters of all revenue, public works and criminal affairs. But in Jalpaiguri town as well as in the district the physical presence and role of the Europeans were much more widely and strongly felt than in most of the Bengal districts and mofussil towns. The most important reason for this was the growth of the European-controlled plantation enterprise. The European community composed of civil servants, a fairly large body of tea garden managers, assistant managers and supervisors and a few associated with the jute trading companies occupied strategic positions in the organized social affairs, administration and economy of the district. Even such local bodies as the Road Cess Committee (which was in existence till 1887), the District Board (established in 1887) and the Alipur Duars Local Board (formed in 1899) were virtually run by and for the benefit of planters' interests. In the municipal affairs (the municipality coming into existence in 1885) planters' interests were not directly involved, and the Bengal Municipal Act of 1884 provided for slow introduction of elective principle in small towns. Yet the government chose to proceed cautiously. Till 1916 the Deputy Commissioner continued to function as the Chairman and all the municipal commissioners were nominated. Thus, the alien rulers were the real masters at the helm of municipal affairs too[75]. The extent of European domination in various public affairs is also indicated by the fact that even the Managing Committee of the Jalpaiguri Hospital was heavily loaded with European officials and planters.

The European community itself was divided in terms of occupation and status, the civil servants occupying the most prestigious and important position. But in their relation with the Indians all of them exhibited a racist attitude. The European Club which acted as a meeting ground for all categories of Europeans was an exclusive social organization and no Indian, except one or two actively collaborating with the Europeans, was admitted into the club. The racial discrimination being observed in the town was indicated also by the fact that for several years Indians had no access to a bridge over Karla river (flowing through the town) constructed near the court in 1916. The European presence was very much felt at the time of month-long exercise and function of the North Bengal Mounted Rifes—drill, shooting, polo, hockey and races—held every year on the race course ground, an occasion which was at times graced by the presence of the Governor. Indians were allowed to have a view of all this, but from a considerable distance[76].

With the passage of time, slow but significant changes began to take place in the leadership pattern. Though deprived of any important share in the administrative and political structure, almost from the very inception of the town, leading Bengalis—pleaders, teachers, service-holders, traders, landowners, etc.—functioned as active leaders of their neighbourhood communities and of the town through religious, cultural and social service organizations and/or the municipality. For a variety of reasons, within the Bengali middle class those belonging to the legal profession took the most active part in the process of socio-economic changes. They, followed by the service-holders, not only provided the social leadership, but also acted as pioneers in the economic field and launched the Indian sector of the plantation industry. This leadership was provided by both Hindu and Muslim families. The families of Gopal Chandra Ghosh and his son Jogesh Chandra, Joy Chandra Sanyal, Tarini Prasad Roy, Shashi Kumar Neogy[77], Rahim Baksh and his son-in-law Musharraff Hossain and Mohammed Sonaullah, a local Muslim well-known for his philanthrophy[78], provide some typical examples of this leadership pattern. Jagadindra Dev Raikat, the adopted son of the Baikunthapur Zamindar Jogendra Dev Raikat, also took active role in the public affairs of the town.

It should, however, be mentioned that despite the relative prosperity and affluence of important sections of the Bengali middle class and flow of considerable amount of money obtained from the Indian sector of the plantation enterprise and other sources like the legal profession, the social and cultural institutions of the town remained weak. *Trisrota*, a monthly magazine launched in 1901, had to be discontinued after a few years[79] and the next attempt to bring out a periodical in any form was made as late as 1924. Arya Natya Samaj, established in 1904, functioned mainly as a drama club and except for a few years during the period of Swadeshi Movement did not have any wider role in the socio-cultural life[80]. There were some moves for spread of education including girls' education[81], but on the whole, these remained limited. Upto 1920, the town had only one High School, the government-run Jalpaiguri Zilla School. Till 1942 there was no college in the town, and those aspiring for college education had to go to Rangpur or Koch Bihar or Rajshahi or even as far as Calcutta. Under the circumstances only the students hailing from affluent families could afford to have college and higher education. It is difficult to explain the feeble nature of socio-cultural efforts. One can not but wonder whether this had anything to do with the scope

for making easy money through activities connected with plantation enterprise. Perhaps a more important reason was the lack of
any organic relationship of the immigrant Bengalis of Jalpaiguri
town with the vast masses of the district—both the Hindu and
Muslim peasants of autochthonous origin and the immigrant plantation labour.

The next important population settlement in the district was
Alipur Duar. It too grew as a seat of British administration. Like
Jalpaiguri town, Alipur Duar too was a settlers' settlement inhabited mostly by upper caste lawyers, service-holders, traders and
merchants who came mainly from east Bengal. The Muslim presence in Alipur Duar was markedly less than in Jalpaiguri town and
the Rajbansi Hindu presence was negligible. For many decades it
exhibited features of rural settlement and did not even have a
regular daily market[82].

In view of the features of the growth of these two small towns
one can hardly speak of any urbanization process.

A SUMMING-UP AND PERSPECTIVE

The period from 1869 to 1920 saw the rapid transformation of
Jalpaiguri's natural or subsistence economy and society into their
colonial capitalist phase and also the consolidation of the latter.
Jalpaiguri came to provide a paradigm of maldevelopment caused
by colonial commercialization and capitalism. The process of
change was characterized by the growth of the plantation system
which was a particular manifestation of colonial capitalism along
with the extension and consolidation of the *jotedar-adhiar* relation.
The two were two interrelated sub-systems of the colonial socio-
economic order and these two did not allow for any dynamic and
transformative economic and social development and had a stul-
tifying impact on regional development. Further, both the systems
grew and thrived on the basis of forms of labour which were
essentially of an unfree nature. The agrarian system was based on
varying degrees of exploitation and oppression of the working
peasantry including captivity of poor and *adhiar* peasants by the
zamindars and *jotedars*. The plantation system too flourished on
the basis of labour which was under various forms of compulsion.
The two forms of social labour were also two sub-systems of

employment of labour within the colonial system for working and administering the system and for establishing market networks and nodes of communication. These in their turn led to the growth of a social chain of subordinate officials, serviceholders, lawyers, teachers and collaborating traders and merchants—all adding up to the growth of a large and heterogeneous body of petty bourgeoisie. The contradictions of colonialism also gave rise to indigenous capitalist entrepreneurship which, as in other areas of Indian entrepreneurship, had a second-class status within the European controlled plantation system and administrative framework. The petty bourgeoisie as well as the Indian, mostly Bengali Hindu and Muslim, entrepreneurs had their own contradictions—some openly exhibiting their collaborating and loyalist tendencies, some others holding an ambivalent attitude, and still others, particularly the lower middle classes resenting the alien rule as well as the *herrenvolk* attitude of the rulers and planters. The principal contradictions were considerably complicated and also blurred to a certain extent by the presence of a host of variegated socio-economic features and processes such as domination in various spheres by the immigrant Bengalis or those referred to as *bhatias*—both Hindu and Muslim—over the autochthons and immigrant tribals and labour and socio-cultural differentiation in a plural society. In consequence of all this, by the early twentieth century diverse elements of tension and conflict had accumulated in the social and political life of Jalpaiguri town and district and soon these found varied and complex manifestations.

5   Emergence and Growth of Socio-Political Movements, 1905-20

In the colonial context of British India nationalist politics has often been viewed, if not solely, at least basically as a reflection of the concern of Western educated élite for constitutional reforms and competition and conflict among what have been considered as élite groups for having on increasing share in the formal political institutions under the Raj[1]. But politics is viewed here as an endeavour on the part of the people to bring about a transformation in their social, economic and political situation. It is from this standpoint that the emergence and growth of socio-political movements including nationalist politics in Jalpaiguri is considered in this volume.

SWADESHI MOVEMENT AND ITS IMPACT

In Jalpaiguri district nationalist stirrings emerged in the first decade of the twentieth century. Imperialist policy of 'divide-and-rule' as expressed by Curzon's initiative to downgrade Bengali predominance in the spheres of higher education, government services and nationalist politics, and the 1905 partition of Bengal Presidency led to a political and cultural ferment among Bengalis throughout the former imperial Presidency. Bengalis, both Hindus and Muslims in western Bengal and mainly Hindus in east Bengal, came out against the imperial policy and developed the ideology of Swadeshi nationalism[2]. Even in east Bengal initial Muslim reaction to Curzon's proposals was quite adverse. The Muslim opposition, however, did not last long[3].

In the nationalist perspective Jalpaiguri was till then torpid.

Political consciousness remained at a low level both in the localist context and in the context of the mainstream of the national movement[4]. However, the Swadeshi and anti-partition movement had its reverberations in the district and Jalpaiguri town in particular. The district itself was included in the newly created province of Eastern Bengal and Assam. It began as an urban middle class movement in which leadership and inspiration were provided by legal practioners, teachers and Bengali planters. Students and young men from these families were active participants in this movement.The day on which partition took effect, 16 October, 1905, *rakhi-bandhan* was observed by all Bengalis as a symbol of brotherhood and unity of the people of Bengal. In Jalpaiguri town too the day was observed. A large crowd led by Jogesh Chandra Ghose, a leading tea planter, walked barefoot (the traditional Hindu sign of mourning) through the town. A campaign was launched to boycott foreign goods. At Dinbazar, the market place of the town, propaganda for the boycott led to the arrest of three young men. Two of them were sentenced to imprisonment for two weeks[5].

Nationalist feeling was sometimes expressed by individual action. Sometime in September—October of 1907 a sixty-year old pleader, Durga Charan Sanyal, was sentenced to four years imprisonment for assaulting two Europeans. According to available accounts, though Sanyal had a valid railway ticket he was forcibly obstructed by two European passengers from boarding a train compartment at Hili station in Dinajpur district, and this provoked him to assault the Europeans involved[6].

While this incident dramatically revealed the mood of the period, much more significant were various other expressions of nationalist feeling. Available accounts show that large number of students in Jalpaiguri town boycotted schools and some of them were punished for that[7]. One of them was Birendra Nath Das Gupta, a well-known revolutionary terrorist in his later life. In 1905 he boycotted the final examination at the Jalpaiguri Zilla School and joined the Rangpur National School[8]. In 1907 a national school was founded in Jalpaiguri town itself and located at the ground of the Arya Natya Samaj, a drama-cum-cultural organization established in 1904. Jogesh Chandra Ghose, Tariniprasad Roy, a lawyer-turned-planter, Shashi Kumar Neogi, a leading lawyer well-known for his social work, Taraprasad Biswas, Umagati Roy,

Trailokya Nath Moulik, (all of them too lawyers) and some other gentlemen took the initiative in setting up the school. Bipin Chandra Pal came to Jalpaiguri to inaugurate the school. A large number of boys, many of whom in later years turned out as prominent persons of the town, joined the school[9]. It remained in existence for several years[10].

In the meanwhile some of the nationalist-minded people of the town decided to open a Swadeshi Textile concern at Jalpaiguri town. In early 1907 the Jalpaiguri Pioneer Weaving Mill was established with a nominal capital of Rs 50,000 and production commenced in December of that year. Jajneswar Sanyal was sent to Japan for training in textile technology. Some weavers were brought from Madras to work in the Mill. But like many other Swadeshi enterprises in Bengal it ran at a loss and was eventually bought by the Mohini Mills of Kushtia[11]. A Swadeshi Shilpa Bhandar and Yubak Bhandar were also set up to sell products of Swadeshi industry and handicrafts[12]. Sarat Chandra Sen, a nationalist-minded service-holder, took initiative in founding a library named Union Club and also a gymnasium. Both the organizations were used to inculcate patriotism and discipline among the students and youth[13].

As elsewhere in Bengal, in Jalpaiguri and other north Bengal districts secret extremist groups were formed. A group known as the North Bengal group was formed to organize and co-ordinate extremist activists in the north Bengal districts and a unit of the group was formed in Jalpaiguri town[14]. Several incidents of arson and theft of gunpowder took place in the town. There were also reports about a band of 'armed bhadralog' moving in Jalpaiguri district including the tea garden areas 'for the purpose of committing political dacoities'[15]. In 1911 Birendra Nath Datta Gupta who had earlier resided in Jalpaiguri and was a student of Jalpaiguri Zilla School for some years, in a daring action killed Samsul Alam, a DIG of Police who had been entrusted with the responsibility of conducting the Alipur Bomb Case, within the premises of Calcutta High Court[16]. Within the district itself there were several incidents of theft of arms. In 1916 young activists were sent to the Duars to find out safe place for keeping arms and also help revolutionary activities[17]. But the extremist group of Jalpaiguri failed to maintain their activities for long and by the end of the First World War the extremists ceased to have any regular functioning within the district. (Earlier in 1911 the partition was annulled and the district was placed in the newly created province of Bengal).

To sum up, the period of Swadeshi Movement in Bengal saw the sprouting of nationalism in Jalpaiguri and the nationalist activities had several dimensions. But these had serious limitations. Some of the activities undertaken by sections of nationalists such as regular readings of the *Gita*, holding of *kirtan* with the objective of camouflaging revolutionary activities or oath-taking before the goddess Kali, bore the imprint of Hindu religion. Further, Muslims were not enrolled as members of the Arya Natya Samaj, the hall of which was the venue of many nationalist activities and in the construction of which a Muslim (Md Sonaullah) had contributed liberally. Another basic weakness was that the nationalist activities remained confined among Jalpaiguri town-based nationalist-minded sections of upper caste Hindu middle class. Available accounts suggest that the rural population constituted overwhelmingly of Hinduized and Islamized Rajbansis remained entirely untouched by the nationalist stir. The large and growing body of the tea garden labour force too was totally unaffected. The Noakhali Muslims and the tiny group of educated Rajbansi Hindus residing in Jalpaiguri town did not have any link with the nationalist stirrings. The attitude of immigrant Muslims of course fitted in with the apathy and, by and large, outright opposition of the east Bengal Muslims towards the Swadeshi Movement. Even the nationalist-minded Hindu middle class or *bhadraloks* failec' to build up any regular, stable nationalist organization. All these indicate the limitations of the first phase of nationalist activities in Jalpaiguri.

MUSLIM ATTITUDE AND ACTIVITIES

It is appropriate to mention here that the period witnessed the formation of an incipient sectional politics among the Muslims and, in fact, almost solely among the immigrant Bengali Muslims, that is, Noakhali Muslims. However, a Muslim religious-cum-social-cum-semi-political association Anjuman-i-Islamia had been established in Jalpaiguri as far back as 1892[18]. But no further information is available on its early career.

As a matter of fact, sectional attitudes and activities of an assertive nature came to be manifested in the early years of the century. While these were partly related to the reaction to the Swadeshi Movement, in Jalpaiguri's context particularly important were the activities in relation to plantation entrepreneurship. Till the Swadeshi years the Indian entrepreneurship in Jalpaiguri's tea plantations was characterized by what has been termed as 'open group' activity in the sense that most of the Indian-owned gardens were launched and managed jointly by both Bengali Hindus and Muslims, all being immigrants. But the post-Swadeshi years came to be marked by 'closed group' activity. While in the earlier phase entry into an entrepreneurial group was made on the basis of merit and qualification, in the later phase this came to be determined by community identity[19].

In this connexion the early career and role of Musharraff Hossain (1871-1966) deserve mention. Born at Cheora in Tipperah (Comilla) district he was a law graduate of the Calcutta University. He settled in Jalpaiguri town after marrying the elder daughter of Khan Bahadur Rahim Baksh, who enjoyed considerable wealth and prestige, and began legal practice there. Soon he established himself as a leading tea planter and also acquired big *jotedari* holdings. Jalpaiguri was at that time one of the districts in the newly constituted province of Eastern Bengal and Assam and the changed political situation created a socio-political environment in which this energetic young Muslim entrepreneur came to represent the latent aspirations of his community, particularly the immigrant Bengali Muslims. By the end of the first decade he rose to a leading position among the latter and became the central figure in the 'closed group' Muslim entrepreneurial activity. Around mid-1910s Musharraff Hossain became Vice-Chairman of the Jalpaiguri Municipality and in late 1910s was appointed a Honorary Magistrate. His achievement gave a new confidence to the Noakhali Muslims and generated a growing awareness about sectional community identity.

But, as shown in earlier chapters, Muslim society in Jalpaiguri district was a fragmented one, and the social, cultural and political integration of the Noakhali Muslims with the Muslims of autochthonous origin remained weak. This found reflection, as discussed later in this work, in the manifestation of divergent political attitudes and tendencies during the subsequent decades.

THE RAJBANSI KSHATRIYA MOVEMENT

In dealing with the socio-political stirrings of the period it is important to take account of a movement that emerged and spread among the Rajbansi Hindus of Jalpaiguri district and also other districts of north Bengal, particularly Rangpur and Dinajpur, the princely State of Koch Bihar and Goalpara district in Assam. The movement came to be called the Rajbansi Kshatriya movement by its leaders and participants[20].

The background to the movement was provided by the social, political and economic changes that took place under British rule. The fact for over several centuries social mobility involving various autochthonous groups of north Bengal, particularly the Rajbansis and Koches, had been taking place has been noticed in an earlier chapter. The British rule brought about major dislocation in the socio-economic life of the rural population resulting in narrowing down of opportunities and increased pressure on available resources. In Jalpaiguri district a major disrupting factor was the launching of the tea plantation enterprise. Further, services and professions came to be monopolized by upper caste Hindus and Noakhali Muslims. At the same time, new opportunities for social mobility were opened up through commercialization of agriculture, improvement of communications and spread of education, though to a very limited extent. These contrary processes generated new social tensions and strivings which partly found expression through the Rajbansi Kshatriya movement. Certain moves by the colonial government, particularly the census operations which since 1891 tried to classify each Hindu social group or caste on the basis of social hierarchy recognized by Hindu public opinion directly contributed to the growth of the movement.

The movement centred around the claim that the Rajbansi Hindus were Kshatriyas of Aryan origin, a claim which, as mentioned in a previous chapter, could be traced at least as far back as the beginning of the nineteenth century. The claim began to take the shape of a movement at the time of the census of 1891[21]. The census authority gave instructions to the effect that the `Rajbansi is the same as Koch'[22]. Several leading Rajbansi zamindars and *jotedars* of Rangpur, Haramohan Khajanchi being one of them, took initiative in voicing protest against this and in forming a `Rangpur Bratya Kshatriya Jatir Unnati Bidhayani Sabha'. They urged F.M. Skrine, then District Magistrate of Rangpur, to recognize Rajbansis as a caste separate from the Koch and to allow them to be enumerated as Kshatriyas in the census. Skrine sought the opinion of the Rangpur Dharma Sabha, an association of Brahman pundits. The Dharma Sabha in its turn, according to the Rajbansi Kshatriya scholar U.N. Barman, after consultation with representatives of different schools of Pandit Samaj, important personalities of Hindu society and prominent 'Rajbansi Kshatriyas', gave the opinion that the Rajbansis and the Koches were two entirely different castes, that the former were of Kshatriya origin and that they had been degraded to a Bratya state due to non-observance of Vedic practices. They might be recognized as Bratya Kshatriyas or members of the warrior caste who had temporarily fallen from their high caste. The District Magistrate made a recommendation to the Census Superintendent to allow Rajbansis to be enrolled as Bratya Kshatriyas against their caste status and also issued a general circular to the effect that the Rajbansis might write their caste as Bratya Kshatriyas in all official correspondence. This pacified the Rajbansis and for the time being the movement subsided.[23]

The movement gathered momentum again during the census of 1901. Following the recommendation made by Skrine, the Rajbansis had expected that their Kshatriya status would be recorded in the census report and that they would be returned as a caste separate from the Koch. But they were greatly disappointed to find that they were returned under the general head, Koch, a term very much despised by the Rajbansis claiming Kshatriya status, implying that they were the same as Koch. It was also learnt by them that in the 1901 census operations then going on they were to be enrolled as mere Rajbansi and not as Rajbansi Kshatriya. This generated considerable discontent and they urged the concerned authority to accord them the status of Kshatriya caste. But this demand failed to get any positive response and in the 1901 census the Rajbansis were once more bracketed with the Koch[24]. It seems that opposition from sections of high caste Hindus was an important factor behind the rejection of the demand.

This caused much resentment and led by Panchanan Sarkar (1865-1935; more well-known as Barman as he took this, a Kshatriya-like surname), the Rajbansi Kshatriya movement spread throughout north Bengal including Jalpaiguri[25]. Barman was originally an inhabitant of the Koch Bihar State and was the first lawyer with a post-graduate degree in Arts among the Rajbansis. But he was driven out from the State for his opposition to some affairs in the Raj family[26]. In 1901 he joined the Rangpur Bar. The late nineteenth and early twentieth century decades constituted a period of change and social tension. The socio-economic backwardness of the Rajbansi Hindus and the repeated refusal to accord Kshatriya status to them hurt him. He himself had to suffer humiliating treatment from upper caste Hindus. Thus, once while going from the Bar Library to a court he, by mistake took the toga of a Brahman lawyer. Later on after realizing his mistake he wanted to return it, but the Brahman lawyer threw it away and burst out, 'I hate to use a toga used by a Rajbansi'. There were also instances of discrimination being practised by caste Hindus with regard to Rajbansi students staying in hostels[27].

It was in this background that Panchanan Barman took the initiative in mobilizing Rajbansi Hindus in striving for a proud Kshatriya identity. Already zealous attempts were being made by some Rajbansi scholars and pandits to compile materials of history, folk tales and folk songs, proverbs and sayings to establish the claim to Kshatriya status. Basing themselves on the Hindu shastras and *Puranas* they sought to strengthen their claim[28]. At the same time, Panchanan Barman highlighted the need for social reform. Among the measures emphasized by the leaders of the Rajbansi Kshatriya movement were the wearing of the sacred thread, reduction of the days of mourning on the death of either parent from thirty days to twelve days which was the mourning period for high caste Hindus, and change of surname from Das to Barman, Singha and Roy. For his role in awakening the Rajbansis Panchanan Barman emerged as the most popular and respected leader of the community. It was under his leadership that prior to the 1911 census the movement gathered momentum. In May 1910 several hundred Rajbansis, mostly landholders, *jotedars* and substantial peasants, from different districts of north Bengal, Goalpara in Assam and Koch Behar State assembled in a conference in Rangpur town. From the conference, the Kshatriya Samiti, an organization of Rajbansi Kshatriyas, was formed with Madhusudan Roy, a lawyer from Jalpaiguri, as President and Panchanan Barman as Secretary. The conference formulated the aims and objectives of the Samiti and laid down the organizational structure[29]. The structure consisted of (i) an Executive Committee which was to formulate and implement the Samiti's policies, (ii) a Finance Committee which was to look after the financial matters, and (iii) a Publication and Publicity Committee. The constitution provided for members of three categories :(i) *Sadharan* or ordinary members, (ii) *Pracharak* or *Ganya* (distinguished) members, the members who would deveote all their time for the work of the Samiti, and (iii) *Manya* ir respectable members[30]. Following the setting up of the Samiti, in the words of L.S.S. O'Malley, the Superintendent of the 1911 census operations in Bengal, 'a most persistent agitation was carried on by the Rajbansis'[31]. They pressed that they be recorded separately from the Koch and be recognized as Kshatriyas by descent. The former demand was conceded, while the other one was turned down.

The movement with particular emphasis on *upanayana sanskara* or the wearing of the sacred thread and on the basis of that readmission to Kshatriya status. In February 1912 (27 Magh 1319 B.S.) several thousand Rajbansis from different districts of north Bengal congregated at Debiganj on the bank of Karatoya, a river sacred to the Rajbansis (in Jalpaiguri district) and took sacred thread[32]. In the subsequent years a large number of similar congregations were organized in different places. Guided by a small group of Rajbansi lawyers and educated persons, the Samiti worked for the spread of education among members of the community. The Samiti which included many *jotedars* and prosperous peasants raised community funds for providing loans to Rajbansi agriculturists, urged the latter to improve their agricultural practices and called upon them to organize co-operative credit societies[33]. It condemned in strong terms any move to emulate the caste Hindu practice of giving dowry by the parents of a bride[34]. It brought out a monthly journal *Kshatriya*[35] which dealt with various socio-economic problems facing the Rajbansis and published several booklets on Hindu shastras. It is interesting that in its attempt to secure wider recognition for the Rajbansis as Rajput Kshatriyas the Samiti soon after its formation tried to develop links with the Bharatiya Kshatriya Mahasabha, an association of Rajput thakurs in northern and western India[36].

The Samiti called upon the Rajbansi youth to take training in physical exercise and learn the use of *lathis*, daggers etc. The outbreak of the First World War prompted the Samiti leaders to give a call to the young men of the community to show their Kshatriya, that is, martial abilities by joining the British army and issued appeal to the government for raising two battalions composed exclusively of Rajbansis. Responding to the call, several hundred Rajbansi youth from Jalpaiguri, Rangpur, Dinajpur and Goalpara joined the army and went to the war front. In recognition of the service rendered by Panchanan Barman in the war effort, in 1919 he was conferred the titles Rai Saheb and M.B.E (Member of the British Empire)[37].

The Samiti described itself as a 'non-political' association aiming at the 'intellectual, social, moral and religious progress of the Community'[38]. However, on several occasions it took a political position. The fourth annual conference held at Debiganj in Jalpaiguri in June 1913 declared that the Rajbansi Kshatriyas were 'loyal subjects' and expressed 'great indignation at the most heinous bomb-outrage upon Viceroy [Hardinge]'[39] at the time of his entry into the new capital of Delhi in December 1912. The tenth conference held in 1919 expressed great rejoicing at the British victory in the war with loud cheers for the King Emperor[40]. In the background of nationalist agitation and activities around constitutional reforms in the War years and immediate post-War years, in a representation to the Bengal Government in November 1917 the Samiti spoke of its 'apprehensions of tendencies ... of discontent and even disrespect for law and order '[41], and urged for separate representation in future constitutional reforms[42].

It should be stated here that the movement had to face some opposition from certain sections within the community[43]. Many *bhatias* or Bengali immigrants into north Bengal and caste Hindus opposed the move to gain Kshatriya status. The Koch Bihar State officials too, many of whom were immigrant upper caste Bengalis, tried to create difficulties in the way of the movement[44]. Perhaps one major reason was the contempt with which the Rajbansi leaders viewed the Koch.

On the whole, the Rajbansi Kshatriya movement represented an endeavour to find social identity and status for the Rajbansi Hindus in a situation of considerable flux and contained significant elements of dissent and opposition to upper caste domination. But the movement was not without its anomalies and internal tension. It exhibited Sanskritizing tendencies with an assertion of Aryan origin and striving for the higher social status of Kshatriyas by borrowing higher caste customs and rituals (like wearing of sacred thread and reduction of days of mourning at the death of any one of the parents). They emphatically rejected any suggestion to the effect that the Rajbansis and the Koches had a common tribal or semi-tribal past and totally dissociated themselves from the latter. Thus the movement was a conservative one with claim to a higher status within the existing caste hierarchy and there was no attack on or even a critique of the caste system. In contrast to some of the caste movements with a radical potential (for example, the Satyashodak Samaj in Maharashtra[45]) which rejected Brahman religious authority, the Rajbansi Kshatriya movement attempted to get recognition from Brahman pandits and *shastric* sanction. It kept away from the nationalist movement, sought opportunities for more jobs, education and political favours from the government, looked forward to a period of benevolent rule of the British and openly displayed its loyalty to the Raj. It did not have any programme for the poor peasants and *adhiars* who constituted the bulk of the Rajbansi Hindu peasantry. The movement remained confined, in the main, among the large landholders, *jotedars* and better off peasants. However, it would not be incorrect to view it as 'a distorted but important'[46] manifestation of socio-economic tensions and conflicts.

SPARKS OF LABOUR PROTEST

Before proceeding further, it is important to take note of what may be considered as early labour protests. As noted in the preceding chapter, the tea garden labourers were terribly exploited and oppressed. In some writings they have been considered as passive victims of exploitation and oppression. But available official accounts indicate a different picture. There were sparks of labour unrest from the early days of the formation of the plantation labour force. Thus, Sunder in his Settlement Report of 1895 complained, '... they often show a spirit of independence and insubordination which tries the patience and goodwill of the managers of gardens very considerably. Frequently the coolies are masters of the situation'. Even combinations and strikes were not unknown. He observed, 'Those among them who have the least influence instigate and combine and sometimes give great trouble by causing the labour force to remain within the lines instead of attending to work'[47].

There were also reports of labour troubles in the early twentieth century. An official enquiry conducted in 1904 disclosed that the manager of a tea garden in the Alipur Duars subdivision reported a riot that had occurred at his garden in September 1903. The coolies, who were working overtime, threw away the leaf and broke the glass doors of the godown. Police assistance had to be sought for, and the case was 'declared to be a true case of rioting'[48]. It was also reported that occasionally strikes took place. Sometimes strikes were of a prolonged and serious nature. In such cases assistance was 'obtained from other gardens to carry on the work, a similar accommodation being given in similar circumstances'. At times, the demands made by labourers had to be conceded. Sometimes labour protest took the form of mass desertion of an estate[49]. The *District Gazetteer* reported that in cases of attempts to impose very heavy tasks, coolies struck work or went to other gardens where the tasks were less heavy[50].

The *District Gazetteer* also mentioned a 'most serious disturbance' in the form of a riot in 1906. The price of rice was high throughout the year and, after the damage done to the communications by floods in August of that year, it rose to famine rates. This made the labourers restive. The *District Gazetteer* reported that the Santal labourers belonging to the gardens in the vicinity of Dam Dim and Chalsa in the western part of Duars united to raid the markets and looted the big *hat* at Bataigol near Mal and a few shops near Chalsa railway station. According to the official account, 'some of the Chhotanagpur people also joined in when they saw what was going on, but the disturbance was planned and started by the Santhals'. The rioters were quickly suppressed with the aid of the armed police, and the ringleaders arrested and punished. The North Bengal Mounted Rifles were also called out to prevent the spread and recrudescence of the disturbance[51].

It is true that these early protest actions on the part of the workers were of a sporadic and shortlived nature. Except for the riot over the issue of price, perhaps all the other actions took place at the individual garden levels. They also lacked any modern ideology. It is possible that they often acted from a sense of tribal solidarity and tribal social institutions were used in channelizing their discontent. But all these were embryonic forms of protest and struggle against incorporation into the plantation system which constituted a specific form of colonial exploitation and oppression as well as of bargaining over conditions of work.

Oraon labour agitation

Related to the above protests but of a different nature in many respects was a widespread agitation among the Duars plantation labour. Starting in several gardens in November 1915, it spread rapidly to a large number of gardens stretching over the extensive Duars plantation tract and continued till mid-1916. Although the movement was a short-lived one, it had several distinctive and significant features[52].

The agitation was, in fact, an extension of the Tana Bhagat movement that had originated among the Oraon peasants in the Ranchi district of Chhotanagpur in April 1914[53]. Initially, the Ranchi movement had the character of a religious and social reform movement. But eventually it also came to have important economic and political dimensions. The movement was based on aspirations of Oraon peasants for deliverance from the exploitation and oppression of the *zamindars, mahajans* and *sarkar*.

In its origin the Tana Bhagat movement was a messianic movement[54]. It was believed that a Messiah would come to redeem the Oraons from their plight. They were called upon to 'pull out' (*tana*) ghosts and evil spirits which were held responsible for their misery. They were asked to purify and reform their lives. They were also told to give up ploughing their fields which entailed cruelty to cows and oxen but failed to protect them from poverty and famine. In this a yearning for going back to a pre-settled form of agriculture and a protest against exploitation by the landlords and the government could be discerned. Some of the *tana bhagats* even stopped payment of rent to their landlords and ploughing. They were, moreover, called upon to do no work as coolies and labourers under men of other castes and tribes. The latter aspect referred to labour in the tea gardens as well as in the fields of large landholders in many districts of Bengal and Bihar[55]. The movement soon assumed forms that were considered dangerous by the colonial government.

Soon reverberations of the Ranchi movement came to be felt in the distant Duars. But the Duars movement was not just a replication of the movement in Ranchi. The specificity of its locale, particularly the British-dominated plantation economy and the exploitation and oppression of plantation labour in the Duars, had its distinctive imprints on the movement.

The year 1916 was a war year and the stir came to be viewed by the planters and the colonial government as well with considerable alarm. In his address to the Annual General Meeting of the Dooars Planters Association (DPA) held in January 1917, W.L. Travers, the DPA Chairman, spoke of the 'great anxiety' caused to the European planters by the outbreak of what was considered by them as 'a new and dangerous movement amongst the Oraons' in the early months of 1916[56]. In the Bengal Government's *Report on the Administration of Bengal* for 1916-17 it was stated that the labourers of several gardens were 'said to be eschewing meat and strong drink and singing songs containing references to a German Victory'[57].

The agitation consisted of two phases, though these were never clearly demarcated. In the first phase, it was primarily a socioreligious reform movement. There was an initiation ceremony, and those who passed through this ceremony called themselves *bhagats* or devouts. Those Oraons who refused to go through the ceremony seem to have been excommunicated and the fear of excommunication perhaps persuaded many Oraons to join the movement[58]. At the initial stage, the stir was viewed by the planters as an expression of aspiration for social and spiritual improvement and, hence, the planters and the district administration were not much perturbed. But there was a swift transition to the second phase characterized by an anti-British and anti-planter content and direction, and these came to be infused with Oraon religiosity. It was this latter aspect which was one of the factors that gave the agitation a wide appeal. According to the official version, the movement in the Duars had a political orientation from the very beginning and with the unfolding of the movement this became increasingly pronounced. In the trial of Bania Oraon, Laudha Oraon and Mangra Oraon, all tea garden workers, for their allegedly leading role in the movement the prosecution case was that since November 1915 Oraon tea garden workers had been

holding meetings at nights and singing hymns to the 'German Father', whom they invoke[d] as if he was a god, calling on him to come and drive out the English, whom they compare[d] to devils, and give an independent raj to the Oraons[59].

Another feature was that, though throughout its course the movement, by and large, remained peaceful, it was in the second phase that it came to exhibit a relatively militant tone. Inter-tribal solidarity was another distinctive feature that came to be manifested. Though the movement was predominantly a movement of the Oraon workers, it did not remain confined to them alone. It came to involve, as shown later, several non-Oraon tribal and semi-tribal groups too.

The incident that first brought the movement to the notice of the district administration indicated the political dimension unmistakably. The official account of the incident is given below:

'A man named Charua Oraon cut his wife's throat and then tried to cut his son. He told the police that the villagers had asked him to 'sing the name of the Germans' and had threatened that, if he did not, a devil named Logo would kill him. He and his wife resolved to kill themselves rather than be killed by a devil... He said that an unknown man was always telling him to recite something, and that as he refused, every one abused him and his wife, so they resolved to commit suicide....'[60] Charua was too badly wounded to explain what he refused to recite and died in the jail hospital.

The event was reported to the police on 25 January 1916. Subsequently, P.T. Monckton, Superintendent of Police(SP) made enquiries to find out what the 'mysterious recitations' were. On 25 February he received a letter from the manager of the Tasati Tea Estate, containing a list of eight Oraon men and six Oraon women who were holding seditious meetings and calling to the 'German Father' to come and save them[61].

On 1 March the DPA Chairman informed the police that a meeting of garden managers was held to discuss the Oraon unrest, but they could only discover that 'mysterious meetings' were being held at night and that trouble at the Fagua puja (18 to 21 March) was apprehended. On 2 March the Manager of Sarugaon Tea Estate intimated the police that Hasru, a *sardar* in that garden, was involved in the movement and 'was adopting a threatening attitude towards the garden staff...'[62]. On 1 March the SP went to the Tasati Tea Estate, interrogated some Oraon labourers and made some arrests.

On 4 March, an informal meeting of the DPA Committee was held and this was attended by the Deputy Commissioner of Jalpaiguri and also the SP. From what they heard, the latter considered that in one garden the movement had gone very far, and that 'there was a distinct seditious element in connection with the German Raj'. In another garden he was informed that 'the coolies had refused to do work, saying that they had no allegiance to the British Raj'. He found that 'the coolies were almost in mutiny saying that the German Raj was coming in to govern the country'[63].

The meeting was told by one member of the committee:

> ... the idea was held that the Germans would take possession of the Raj, and that those who helped the Germans would be rewarded by gifts of land in [Chhoto] Nagpur, their ancient country[64].

The managers reported acts of open defiance of authority. In Sarugaon T.E. Hasru and Kandru refused to work. When told by the manager to report themselves to the office, they threw down their hoes and ran away[65]. In the trial of three Oraon workers of the Gurjangjhoha T.E. (western Duars) the prosecution referred to another instance of collective defiance. The estate manager was informed by the *chowkidar* that the Oraon workers of the garden were having meetings and songs in lonely places. This information alarmed the manager and he sent for two Oraon leaders. They came accompanied by forty Oraon workers. The leaders were asked to leave the garden and go elsewhere. But they refused to be separated from others. Later on they left the manager and while they were leaving they were 'heard to mutter something in the Oraon language which the garden officers did not understand'. But the manager's servant interpreted it to mean, 'If we beat him, what will happen?'[66]

These instances of course need to be considered with caution. With reference to the Gurjangjhora incident *Amrita Bazar Patrika* of 10 May 1916 editorially observed, 'There is no evidence to show if the servant interpreted the coolies correctly or not'. As pointed out in the same editorial,'... among so large a population not a single act of violence or rowdyism... was reported.'[67] Yet it is evident that the movement had a distinct anti-British political overtone. The agitation, it may be reiterated, had a tribal religious dimension too. All this came to be articulated *inter alia* in the collective singing, often continuing till midnight. Despite its ambiguity, the following song composed by Letho, a *sardar* in the Tasati T.E., and cited during the trial of Oraon workers as evidence of sedition shows the Oraon political attitude:

> German Baba is coming,
> Is slowly slowly coming;
> Drive away the devils Manaldanal;
> Cast them adrift in the sea.
> Suruj Baba (the sun) is coming;
> The devils of the Oven will be driven away
> And cast adrift in the sea.
> Tarijan (the stars) is coming,
> Is slowly slowly coming,
> Is coming to our very courtyard
> The chigri devils will be driven away
> And cast adrift in the sea[68].

One prosecution witness, Birsai, told the Special Tribunal appointed to try the arrested tribal workers, mainly Oraons and a few non-Oraons, who were alleged to have taken a leading role in the movement :

> ... Yes, he had heard it [the song], and it meant that the Germans were coming to make war, and the Government people would be thrown into the sea. He said that new school always speak of the Germans as Suruj Baba (the sun)... and that Tarijan Baba also meant the Germans, while the devils Manaldanal meant the English, and the devils of the Oraons or hearth meant those Oraons who did not join the new movement[69].

The Special Tribunal in its 'Judgement in the Oraon Case' accepted this interpretation:

> Now it is certain that the Oraons are not under any mistaken notion as to who and what the Germans are. Two or three witnesses have told us that the export of tea from the garden was stopped for a time in December [1915], and they heard from the manager that it was because there was war between the English and the Germans. And when the price of salt and foodgrains rose in the markets the *modis* [grocers] and *mahajans* also told them that it was due to the war with

the Germans. So it appears that the new Oraons are deliberately invoking the head of the King's enemies as if he were a God and calling on him to come and cast certain devils into the sea[70].

The Special Tribunal further stated:

The devils cannot be spiritual devils, and it is highly probable that they represent the English. Manaldanal is a particularly exacting devil ... such a devil might well be chosen to represent the Government.

While the details of this interpretation may not be correct, that the song had an anti-imperialist content is unmistakable. And, further, this was informed with tribal religious consciousness.

At this stage it is appropriate to raise several questions: How did the movement start in the Duars? How was it organized? How did its message spread? Available accounts suggest that some Oraons coming from Chhotanagpur first brought the message of the movement to the Duars. Travers reported that the 'disseminators were often young intelligent boys' who appeared 'to have learnt the part of a preacher of the new faith'. Once the message reached the Duars, some of the *sardars*, though certainly not all, played a crucial role in organizing the network[71].

What were the mechanisms of transmission of the message of the movement? There must have been, to borrow the language from a major work on peasant insurgency, 'a variety of means which were all specific to a pre-literate culture...'[72]. As Child, one DPA Committee member reported: '... six weeks ago a message—a letter with a few rupees and some rice—had come from Manabari [T.E.] and had been passed from hand to hand among his sirdar and then sent on to Hope [T.E.] and other gardens'[73].

It is not surprising that the British planters found all this incomprehensible. The managers and the British administrators repeatedly referred to 'mysterious meetings', 'mysterious recitations', 'unknown messages', and so on. In fact, such meetings and songs were among the important 'instruments of transmission' and mobilization of the Oraon workers. Travers in the address referred to above stated:

... mysterious meetings were held at night, in lonely places where interference by other was improbable. The Oraons attended armed with bows and arrows, axes and spears, and sentries were posted who threatened to kill any stranger who approached. He know that at these meetings songs were sung in which the aid of the German Baba was invoked. They were taught and believed that the British Raj was coming to an end, and that if they aided the Germans the latter would give them land in their ancient country where a subsidiary Oraon Raj would be established. Not only were the British Sahibs to be driven out, but also the Mundas and Moham-medans[74].

The spread of the movement with its pronounced anti-British and pro-German tone and aspiration for a Oraon raj caused great alarm in the minds of the planters as well as the government officials. Though there was no report of any overt acts of violence such as physical assaults, riot or murder, the collective mobiliza-tion of discontented and agitated tribal workers and several incidents of open defiance of the garden management amounted to a frontal confrontation with the authority. In the prevailing atmosphere these came to be regarded as a threat to the existing order in the Duars plantation tract. The March meeting of the DPA Committee attended, among others, by the Deputy Commissioner and the SP worked out in details measures for suppressing the agitation. Loyal *sardars* were made special constables, responsible for maintenance of discipline in the garden, and armed police pickets and police camps were set up in different parts of the Duars to keep watch on the restive Oraons[75]. Many arrests were made and a Special Tribunal was appointed under the Defence of India Act to try the 'ringleaders'. Some of the arrested Oraons were sentenced to rigorous imprisonment for varying periods[76]. The Fagua puja passed off without any disturbance and by late 1916 the agitation petered out.

But the planters remained in a state of apprehension about the recrudescence of the movement. Thus, when Ghura alias Somra, who was considered as 'one of the instigators in the Oraon unrest' and had been sentenced to six months' imprisonment, returned to the Duars in March 1917 after his release from jail, there was a consternation among the planters and they pressed the district police authority for taking action against him. In reponse to this, the SP forwarded to the DPA Chairman a list of 29 Oraons who had been convicted for their alleged subversive role in the agitation and advised the garden managers not to give any jobs to the released persons and, further, to withdraw all land that might have been given to them or even their relations[77].

In May 1917 in the neighbouring Terai Plantation area in the Darjeeling district there was a limited outbreak of a similar agitation[78]. In Jalpaiguri district, however, there was no fresh outbreak of the movement.

Nature of the movement

Any analysis of the nature of this short-lived ferment is full of complexities. The movement had three distinct strands: religious, social and political. However, the three strands which were present through its course interacted and interpenetrated with each other giving a considerably complex complexion to the movement. It is because of this aspect that to many of the colonial officials the movement represented largely 'superstition and demonology'. Many of them were not in a position to understand the language, idiom and 'code' of the struggle of the tribal workers. J.W. Nelson of the Criminal Intelligence Office, however, showed somewhat greater perception. He mentioned three aspects of the movement:

(1) Economic unrest due to the rise in prices, which was attributed to evil spirits and witches—hence attempts to drive evil spirits out of the villages and the murder of supposed witches.

(2) A religious revival of a highly emotional type with secret all-night meetings and the singing of *mantras*.

(3) A social movement, closely connected with the religious movement, directed towards elevation of the caste. Hence the prohibition of animal food and intoxicating drink, resolution not to work as palki-bearers, & c. As in all such movements the influence of Hindu ideas is obvious[79].

In this observation one finds indication of an awareness of a complex inter-relationship between religious fervour, social reform efforts and concern about economic issues. Nelson, however, failed to note the issue of political power underlying the agitation among the tribal workers.

But on the basis of an analysis of an Oraon song sung in the Duars another official hinted at the political dimensions:

Some portions of the song suggest that the movement is an attempt to purify the tribal religion and to cast off superstitions and to get rid of corruption of ancient faith... It appears probable that the restriction of flesh food to white goats and white fowls is based on their being the proper offerings to Dharmesh and is connected with a scheme for driving out foreign devils[80].

The socio-religious aspect mentioned above was a common feature of many of the tribal protest movements in India under British rule. But, in addition to that, the Duars movement had a distinct political orientation. The Oraon songs sung in the Duars repeatedly and emphatically spoke of driving out the British and the establishment of an independent Oraon raj, where all land alienated from the tribal peasants would be restored to them.

In their vision for an independent Oraon raj the Oraon workers came to look upon the Germans as their emancipators. This led the British planters and some colonial officials to suspect German hands behind the Oraon agitation[81]. It should be added the the British rulers and their associates had always tried to explain anti-imperialism and any popular mobilization in terms of manipulation by an external agency such as German or Russian power and disgruntled Indians. But, despite much efforts made by the prosecution, no foreign, that is, German manipulation could be established[82].

But how one is to explain the Oraon view of the Germans and even the Kaiser? The explanation lies basically in the specific historical context. The immediate international background was one of victories won by the Germans in the early years of the War. The dislocating impact of the War on the tea export, tea industry and employment in the industry was experienced by the Oraon workers. They were told by the *mudis* (grocers), *kayas* (Marwari traders in the Duars) and money-lenders that the sharp rise in the prices of salt and foodgrains were due to the war. The reverses suffered by the British gave rise to the rumour that the British raj was not only in crisis but was also coming to an end. Here was a rumour about the weakening of the authority structure eventually leading to the breakdown of authority. It was against such a background that the enemy's enemy came to be viewed by the Oraons as friends and, indeed, even as their emancipators. In all this the anti-British, anti-imperialist dimension of the movement is manifest.

One additional dimension was the anti-planter or anti-capitalist one. The Oraons and other tribals involved in the Duars agitation also acted as workers. In their 'defiance of garden management' and 'refusal to work', about which the planters and DPA showed great concern, there was evidence of class conflict, though of an incipient nature. The latter dimension came to be *subsumed* under manifestations of anti-imperialism.

The anti-imperialist and anti-capitalist affinities in the Duars, however, did not exclude community and, in this case, tribal affinity. In fact, the responses to foreign rule and planter domination came to be encapsulated in tribal religious consciousness, a dimension which made many aspects and expressions of the Duars agitation largely incomprehensible to the planters and colonial officialdom. It was also this tribal-cultural identity which inevitably gave rise to some ambiguities. But while one can hardly ignore the importance of this identity, it needs to be stressed that it did not lead to displacement of anti-imperialist and anti-planter dimensions[83].

The Duars agitation, as noted above, began as a continuation of the Chhotanagpur Tana Bhagat movement among the Oraons of Duars and was initially an example of vertical mobilization embracing Oraon plantation workers. But, as mentioned earlier, the Duars agitation soon came to involve non-Oraon tribal, semi-tribal and even a few non-tribal workers, although the Oraons constituted the predominant element. The most clear evidence of participation of the non-Oraons is an incomplete list of convicted workers[84]. Besides the names of 23 Oraons, it contained names of 2 Mundas, 2 Mahalis, 1 Goala (milkman, cowherd) and 1 Teli(oilman), all of whom had been sentenced to rigorous imprisonment for taking part in the movement. This testifies also to the feature of horizontal mobilization. Thus here was solidarity at the level of Oraon workers and also solidarity between Oraon and non-Oraon workers which was more than just tribal or ethnic solidarity. These also signified an awareness among sections of Duars workers about the exploitation and oppression experienced by them and entailed anti-imperialist as well as worker solidarities.

What were the actual mechanics of achieving, maintaining and consolidating these solidarities? The account of the genesis and unfolding of the tribal worker movement presented earlier shows that various mechanisms were combined in varying degrees.

These were, among others, the pull of tribal ties and tradition, the parleys and assemblies such as meetings held in the 'coolie' lines and also lonely places, the collective chanting of *mantras* or incantations, the use of community or tribal idioms and 'codes', the reforms in social and religious practices (e.g. eschewing of meat and strong drinks and prohibition of community dances and songs), the rumour about imminent British defeat and German victory, the vision of an independent Oraon raj, the promise of land, and the power of religious, political and community commitment to 'exterminate the Sahibs' sanctified through 'the vow sworn by God, Germany and blood'. The experience of rise in prices of salt and foodgrains and the information about fall in tea exports were put to intelligent use to spread the rumour of British raj in crisis. It appears that a roving band of young 'volunteers' or cadres' carried the message of the movement initially from Chhotanagpur to the Duars and later on from garden to garden and helped to forge and strengthen the solidarities mentioned above. Taking various relevant aspects into consideration, it can be stated that in its origin, direction and content the movement was an instance of self-mobilization based on tribal solidarities and its roots lay in the miserable social existence condition of the tribal workers in the Duars plantation area and also the tribal peasants in general in Chhotanagpur. Further, it was an autonomous movement—autonomous in relation to non-tribal or any outsider leadership and organization.

The Duars tribal labour agitation, as in the case of any popular movement, had its share of fence-sitters, vacillators and collaborators. The flow of information to the managers illustrates the extent of collaboration. The authorities too encouraged dissidence and betrayal.

In view of all this, the solidarity of the workers involved in the movement found expression in the exercise of collective authority against the non-committed, vacillators and workers loyal to the authorities. The major instrument to get support from those who were undecided and also to deal with dissidence from the movement was social boycott or excommunication which was often accompanied by abuse and threat. This is what appears to have happened in the case of Charua and his wife.

A distinctive feature that deserves to be mentioned was the

movement's democratic character. Most of the tribal movements in colonial India were centred around a supreme leader having prophetic power[85]. But the Duars movement, though an extension of the well-known Ranchi movement, did not have any such leader. Available records highlight the role of garden *sardars* and also that of collective consultations through assemblies and gatherings.

Despite the presence of many significant dimensions, this particular variant of protest and struggle of tribal peasants turned into plantation workers soon ran its course. The impact of the movement on the subsequent socio-political life of the tribal and particularly Oraon workers remained ambivalent.

Before concluding this section, one more observation needs to be made. That one is in relation to the nationalist attitude towards the Duars tribal labour agitation which was, in fact, the earliest instance of popular anti-imperialist protest and struggle not only in the Duars but in the district of Jalpaiguri as a whole. It is found that, may be because of patriotic consideration and/or some other reasons, the nationalist daily *Amrita Bazar Patrika* took a sympathetic view of this protest and struggle. But the nationalists of Jalpaiguri district itself, however, appear to have remained totally indifferent to it. That the Oraon agitation came to the notice of some of the nationalists of the district has been put on record[86]. But there was no awareness of its significance and the need for having any links with it. A major part of the explanation lies in the wide socio-cultural gap that the *bhadralok* (upper-caste educated Bengali middle class) nationalists of Jalpaiguri had with the 'coolies'. Thus, tribal anti-imperialism and *bhadralok* nationalism remained distanced from each other.

PEASANTS

That the bulk of the peasant masses were subjected to multiple forms of exploitation and oppression has been discussed in a previous chapter. How did the peasants, particularly the poor peasants and *adhiars* respond to this? It has been suggested in this chapter that the agrarian society was ridden with contradictions and strains. But we do not have till now much evidence to show the response and behaviour of the peasants during the period considered in this chapter. To conclude, the survey made in this chapter shows that the varied and complex tensions that were present in Jalpaiguri's economy, society and politics began to find interesting manifestations through a variety of political and social activities.

6 Nationalist Politics—Advance and Problems, 1921-29

During 1921 and early 1922 new possibilities for truly significant advance in nationalist politics in Jalpaiguri district could be discerned. But in the years 1921 to 1929 the political life and trends came to be marked by many complex and contradictory developments.

IMPACT OF THE NON-COOPERATION MOVEMENT 1921-22

It may be observed that till early 1921, nationalist organization in the district as well as the town was haphazard and virtually non-existent. It was only in the years 1921 and 1922 that nationalist organizations sprang up in several parts of the district.

The background and stimulus to this revival and growth of nationalist politics in Jalpaiguri were provided by the entry of Gandhi in the political life of the country and his message and style of functioning, the considerable spread of nationalist politics and the vastly enhanced range of popular movements in the years following the First World War[1]. It is all these which snowballed into the Non-Cooperation-Khilafat movements of the years of 1921 and 1922[2]. Jalpaiguri too came to be involved in it and a large number of people from a variety of social backgrounds became involved in it.

The immediate post-war years saw an anti-imperialist upsurge. The specificities of the overall post-War socio-economic conjuncture of circumstances—profound social changes, and increase in strains and stresses, the phenomenon of Gandhi and the filtering ın of vague reports of world-wide revolutionary changes—led to what Sumit Sarkar calls 'crucial shifts in collective mentalities'[3]. The situation was such that people from various classes and strata were ready to respond to the nationalist message as well as often to act autonomously, that is, independent of any elite leadership. The unfolding of the nationalist movement in Jalpaiguri illustrates the operation of both the processes. But there were several features which were specific to the district.

It may be noted that the special Calcutta Congress session held in September 1920 which drew up a Non-Cooperation programme was attended, among others, by a young man from Jalpaiguri. He was Khagendra Nath Das Gupta (1898-1985), one of the brothers of Birendra Nath Das Gupta, a well-known revolutionary. Earlier Khagendra Nath was associated with secret revolutionary societies, but by 1920 along with many other revolutionary terrorists he had became somewhat disenchanted with extremist activity and was in search of a new path. He became tremendously impressed by Gandhi's speech at the Calcutta Congress session and the call for Non-Cooperation[4]. In fact, many members of the North Bengal group with which he was associated agreed to suspend their revolutionary activities and resolved to plunge themselves into the Non-Cooperation movement for which preparations were being made.

In November 1920, Khagendra Nath went back to Jalpaiguri and several of his former revolutionary associates extended support to him[5]. Well-known revolutionary leaders like Bipin Bihari Ganguly, Surendra Mohan Ghosh and Jatindra Mohan Roy, a leader of the North Bengal group, also encouraged his activity. As in most of the districts of Bengal, Jalpaiguri had no Congress organization. By mid-April 1921, a District Congress Committee was formed with Jagadindra Deb Raikat as the first President. He was the adopted son of the Baikunthapur zamindar, the late Jogindra Deb Raikat, and was highly respected by both immigrant Bengalis and Rajbansis[6]. Jyotish Chandra Sanyal, a *muktear* well-known for his public spirit and son of Durga Chandra Sanyal, was chosen as the Secretary[7]. Jyotish Chandra was also elected to the Bengal Provincial Congress Committee(BPCC). Among other prominent Congressmen of Jalpaiguri town were Kiran Chandra Sikdar, Charu Chandra Sanyal (1897-1980), a talented young doctor who gave up his research work at the Medical College, Sreenath Hore and Pritinidhan Roy, both lawyers and Tarapada Sanyal, a doctor. A District Khilafat Committee was also formed with Md. Sonaullah, a large-hearted rich *jotedar* of local origin residing in Jalpaiguri town, as a leading figure of the said Committee[8]. Little is known about the composition and subsequent activity of the District Khilafat Committee. It is noteworthy that most of the educated and prominent Muslims of the town who came from east Bengal districts, that is, the 'Noakhali Muslims' like Musharaff Hossain and Waliur Rahman, kept away from the nationalist and Khilafat politics. Available reports, however, indicate that local level Khilafat committees were formed in a number of places including quite far-off ones like Matiali[9], and in certain areas participation of local Muslims in the Non-Cooperation-Khilafat movements in the district was quite large.

However, Khagendra Nath Das Gupta and a batch of dedicated young Congress workers like Byomkesh Majumdar and Makhan Sanyal plunged themselves into work in the rural areas. They became involved in propagating the message of 'Swaraj within a year' and in building up a network of Congress organizations in the district. Soon a subdivisional Congress Committee was formed in Alipur Duars Subdivision with Rasiklal Ganguly, a *muktear* and old resident of that town, as President and Sibdayal Pal as Secretary[10]. What is more, being vaguely aware of the need for getting the support of the rural masses, the Congress workers began to go out of the district town to the market and distributing centres, locally known as *bandars*, like Boda, Patgram, Falakata, Madarihat and Mainaguri which had sprung up along the main roads and also to remote villages and *taris* or tiny settlements. They used all forms of transport to reach these places, going by trains if the railway line passed near the market centres and villages, but usually by bullock carts or cycles or just a pair of legs, as in most parts there was no road[11].

The progress of the Non-Cooperation movement in different parts of the country and in Calcutta and other districts of Bengal, Gandhi's message and political style, popular images about Gandhi[12] as well as the work on the part of the Congress workers of Jalpaiguri drew considerable response from the small-town petty bourgeoisie of Jalpaiguri and Alipur Duar. In both the towns, lawyers, traders, students and unemployed youth turned out as ardent nationalists. *The Mussalman* of 22 April 1921 reported that Jalpaiguri town, 'a most dully and sleepy place', became 'animated.... through the great influence of Mahatma Gandhi'. It mentioned that several meetings of Swaraj were held and even prostitutes participated in these meetings, and that use of intoxicants like wine, ganja, cigarette and all foreign goods was given up. The 6 and 13 April 1921 were observed as complete *hartal* days not only in the town but in some of the *mufassil* places also. A huge meeting attended by thousands of people, according to *The Mussalman's* report, 10,000 people, was held on 13 April.

As part of the organizational programme of the Congress, the BPCC was given the quota of collecting Rs 1 crore for the Tilak Swaraj Fund, enrolling of 1 crore Congress members and introduction of 20 lakh *charkhas* in villages and homes. In this, Jalpaiguri's quota was fixed at Rs 30,000 for the Tilak Swaraj Fund, 30 thousand Congress members and 6 thousand *charkhas*. The quotas were to be fulfilled by 30 June 1921[13].

In late May, Chitta Ranjan Das, a Khilafatist leader Maulana Samsuddin, Das' wife Basanti Debi and several other leaders visited Jalpaiguri. On the arrival of Das and his party on 26 May they were received by a huge crowd at the station. Almost all the leading persons of the town were present. The town resounded with shouts of 'Gandhiji Ki Jai', 'Chitta Ranjan Das Ki jai', 'Bande Mataram', 'Allah Ho Akbar' and such other slogans. In the afternoon, according to a newspaper account, 'a monster meeting' was held. An address on behalf of the local municipality was read out by the municipality Vice-Chairman Ganesh Chandra Sanyal. Das and Samsuddin explained the situation with special stress on the wrongs of Khilafat and Punjab and gave a call for making the Non-Cooperation movement a success. A women's meeting was held in the Arya Natya Samaj Hall. Apart from women from middle class families, prostitutes attended the meeting in large numbers. In the next two days Das met various people and discussed the Non-Cooperation programme[14].

In response to Das' call, Ganesh Chandra Sanyal suspended his law practice and Jagadindra Deb Raikat resigned from the post of Honorary Magistrate. Some students came out of the government school. Many prominent persons of the town including some tea planters like Jogesh Chandra Ghose and Tarini Prasad Roy contributed to the Tilak Swaraj Fund. Md. Sonaullah made the largest individual contribution of Rs 10 thousand and Das gave him the honorific title 'Amir-ul-Mulk'. Many women contributed gold and ornaments[15].

In the rural areas the Congress workers at first contacted the *jotedars* and substantial peasants and sought their help to draw in the rural masses into the movement. Initially the response was not favourable. Further, the Congress workers had to contend with the tremendous social, economic and political influence of the Baikunthapur zamindar Raja Prasanna Deb Raikat who took an avowedly loyalist and anti-Congress position. The attitude of the Kshatriya Samiti too was unfavourable. But soon sections of both Rajbansi Hindu and Rajbansi Muslim rural population including several big *jotedars* came to hear the Congress leaders, responded with enthusiasm, gave food, money and shelter to Congress workers and enrolled themselves as Congress members and volunteers[16]. Tying up of Khilafat with Non-Cooperation helped to get the support of sections of Muslim *jotedars* and masses.

In course of the movement many local and village-level leaders were thrown up[17]. While most of the district and sub-division leaders had independent professional backgrounds or came from town middle class families, the former came from rural backgrounds. Many of them belonged to relatively well off groups. Some belonged to *jotedar* families, a few of them (for example, Mahendra Basunia and Tarini Basunia of Mainaguri and Chhainuddin of Nagrakata) being quite big ones. They were men who had economic independence, literacy, some leisure and links with the district and subdivisional towns and market centres. Many of the *thana* and village-level Congress workers and volunteers, however, came from less better off rural groups.

Scores of meetings were held in Jalpaiguri and Alipurduar towns and at market centres and *hats* in different parts of the district. These meetings were addressed by district as well as local and village-level leaders. They spoke on (1) government repression as exemplified by the Jalianwala Bagh massacre and violation of modesty of women and merciless repression on tea garden coolies at Chandpur, (2) economic grievances such as impounding of cattle and imposition of fines, enhancement of rent and extortions like court fees, road cess etc., (3) harmful effects of liquor and the revenue earned by the government from extensive consumption of liquor, and (4) even such subjects as oppression on Indian 'coolies' in Fiji and other European colonies. 'We want self-government through non-cooperation, the only means to have it', urged the speakers[18].

It is through such meetings that ideas of nationalism and non-cooperation filtered down to the lower levels. A major source of the spread of anti-Raj and nationalist feeling were the contacts and gossips at the market places and *hats*. Gossips or rumour had a particular role to play in a society where the bulk of the rural population was illiterate. As in many areas in different parts of India, particularly in semi-tribal and low caste inhabited or relatively cut-off areas, Gandhi came to be viewed as a demi-god and Puja offerings were made to him by the rural folk[19]. Gandhi was a messiah—an *avtar*—for them, and they as well as the tribal tea garden workers indulged in all sorts of myth-making. Words went round that an apocalyptic Gandhi Raj was soon to come[20].

The Congress activity took other forms too. The law courts were viewed by the peasants as disastrous traps for them. In consequence the call for the boycott of British courts had a good response. Congress arbitration courts were set up in many places and large number of disputes were settled in these courts. There was a marked decline in the number of legal suits in the official courts in Jalpaiguri and Alipur Duar towns[21]. In the latter town this form of activity was particularly successful and a number of pleaders, *muktears* and their clerks suspended their practice[22]. As a part of the programme to boycott government schools, a number of primary and upper primary national schools were also started[23]. Picketing continued in Jalpaiguri town to enforce boycott of foreign cloth and yarn. In October 1921, the Marwari dealers in foreign piece goods agreed not to sell foreign cloth and kept the agreement for eight months. At several market centres in rural areas too, peaceful picketing of excise and foreign cloth shops were resorted to. In meetings held at various places of the district, bonfires of foreign cloth were made in a demonstrative manner before hundreds and even thousands of enthusiastic supporters[24].

Along with all this, constructive activities along Gandhian lines were taken up. Between September 1921 and April 1922 1,000 *charkhas* were distributed. Of these, 500 *charkhas* were in operation in April 1922[25]. Two weaving schools, one in Jalpaiguri town and another one at Patgram Bazar, were established[26].

Despite all these varied forms of the Non-Cooperation movement, which were in conformity with the Gandhian programme and spread of the Congress organizations, there cannot be any denying of the fact that in large parts of the district, Congress organization was either weak or non-existent. But the impact of the Non-Cooperation-Khilafat movements went far beyond the limited influence of the Congress organizational network and far surpassed the concrete activities or intentions of the Congress leaders[27]. Rumour had a particular role to play in such a development. It is possible to cite several fascinating examples of this sort of popular movement in Jalpaiguri.

In Jalpaiguri district as well as in the neighbouring Darjeeling district British rule meant, as seen in the preceding chapter, very largely the rule of the European planters. Yet the Congress leaders in Jalpaiguri did little to launch any struggle against these planters and to involve the large body of tea garden labourers. One major reason was the formidable difficulty in approaching the plantation workers. The way they were kept, almost insulated them from all outside influences and away from close contacts with not only the peasant population but even from labourers of other gardens. There was no freedom of movement on the plantations and the presence of *khadi*-capped Congress volunteers and villagers was not tolerated within a planter's domain. The non-Regulated status of the Duars itself was an impediment. But in addition to these obstacles, the close social and familial links that many of the Jalpaiguri Congress leaders had with Jalpaiguri-based Bengali planters had a restraining influence on the former. This was indicated in no uncertain language by the Chairman of the Dooars Planters Association, the association of the European planters, in his *Report* for the year 1921. He observed, 'The quiet influence of our Indian friends both in Jalpaiguri [town] and in the district helped greatly to preserve the peace and I am sure I express my feelings when I say that we are deeply grateful to them for their help ...'[28].

Yet there were rumblings of labour discontent in the tea-belt of North-east India including the Duars in Jalpaiguri. Persistent economic hardship was certainly a factor behind their discontent. But that was not something new. What made them restive was the apocalyptic rumour of the coming Gandhi raj in place of the British raj. Despite many obstacles in the way of contact between the labouring population of the tea gardens and outsiders, it was not possible to exclude all contacts. Rural Congress volunteers came into contacts with the sprawling labour population in the *hats* and bazars. They built their own images about the power and personality of Gandhi.

All this found expression in the stir among the plantation labour, though of a sporadic and uncoordinated nature. It was officially reported that in July 1921 'there was ... disquieting evidence of unrest among the tea garden coolies in the Duars and the Darjeeling district. Non-cooperators had been quick to take advantage of a certain amount of genuine discontent to the extent of urging the coolies to take over the land and managements. Several strikes occurred and, in one case, where the Manager and Assistant Manager of a tea garden had been chased to their bungalow and confined there, an attempt to arrest the ringleaders failed'. With direct reference to the role of rumour and its apocalyptic nature the same report stated, 'A widespred rumour to the effect that on a certain date, which was put conveniently forward from time to time, a terrible storm would destroy all those who had then not declared for Gandhi, was in part responsible for temporary stoppages'[29]. The DPA Chairman too in his address referred to above observed, 'A bold attempt to cause trouble by such an appeal [to superstition] was made by a self-styled Holy Man, who at one time gained a considerable following amongst garden labour especially Paharias ...'[30]. Though these troubles proved to be of a sporadic and shortlived nature, these indicated the impact of Non-Cooperation movement on tea garden labourers. There were also instances of open confrontation between the peasant masses and Congress volunteers on the one hand and the European planters on the other (see below).

In the province as a whole there was a lull in the movement from July to October 1921. But in October the campaign for boycott of foreign goods was intensified and by the end of the year there was a fresh spurt throughout Bengal. In early January it was officially reported that the situation was 'volcanic' and that there was 'a strong undercurrent of disorderly elements'[31]. The Fortnightly Political Report for the first half of February clearly indicated that the Non-Cooperation movement was spreading to relatively backward areas of the sprawling Presidency[32]. The Report for the second half made pointed reference to several incidents in the

Jalpaiguri Duars. It was reported that in January serious attempts
were made by the Jalpaiguri DCC 'to enlist the aid of hill-men,
including Gurkhas, presumably with the object of tampering with
the loyalty of the armed police'[33].

Available official and non-official accounts also reveal that
there was an underlying current of seething peasant discontent
which took militant forms and broke into violence, especially in
February 1922, that were not perhaps planned and intended by the
district Congress leaders. That any movement for not paying rent
or even government revenue was, generally speaking, discour-
aged by Gandhi and the Congress leadership is well-established.
Yet such campaigns took place in different areas of the country. In
Jalpaiguri too no-revenue move took concrete shape. An official
account reported that 'throughout the district [of Jalpaiguri] the
payment of *kists* [revenue instalments] is very backward, and
fishing rents, grazing fees and tolls of government *hats* have been
largely withheld'[34]. Though such forms of movement were not on
the agenda of either the provincial Congress or the district Congress, local-level Congress leaders and volunteers on their own
campaigned in the rural areas and *hats* for non-payment of revenue for the *khas mahal* estates and tolls in *khas mahal hats*. The
movement became fairly widespread in parts of Alipur Duars
subdivision and particularly in certain areas under the border and
remote police station of Kumargram in that subdivision[35]. There
was a noticeable decline in the collection of land revenue in the
district. Thus, the percentage of total land revenue demand actually collected declined from 97.31 in 1921-2 to 86.72 in 1922-3[36].

The Fortnightly Political Report also reported one incident in
which a *tahsildar*, grazing *muharar* and several peons were assaulted when driving buffaloes to the pound from government
khas lands[37]. The issue that was involved here was perhaps that of
the grazing rights.

In the same month an incident of a more serious nature took
place at Madarihat, a flourishing market centre inhabited by
Rajbansis, Muslims and tribals, in the Duars. On 12 February 1922,
which was a *hat* day, an altercation took place between a Marwari
shopkeeper and a Santal labourer (or peasant ?) over the price of
two gunny bags, and the latter was assaulted. Following this, the
Santal collected some men of his tribe, and the Marwari's shop was
looted. Thereupon a case was instituted, and on 21 February, a

police officer attached to the Madarihat *thana* went with an armed force to village Salkumar, searched some houses and arrested four Santals who were identified as having participated in the looting on 21 February.

A large crowd consisting of Muslims, Santals and Oraons, variously estimated at between 15 to 400 and wearing Gandhi caps, collected there and demanded the release of the arrested persons. As the police party refused to meet the demand, the party was surrounded and the crowd tried to forcibly rescue the prisoners. A scuffle took place in which the police officer was knocked over, one constable's *pugri* (headgear) was taken away and an attempt was made to snatch away a rifle. At the same time, some persons in the crowd began to pull the arrested persons away. Fire was opened and after 14 rounds of buckshot and one of ball had been expended, the crowd was dispersed. In the incident 3 men were killed and 4 severely wounded, while another 8 or 9 were slightly wounded. One of the dead persons was, significantly enough, found wearing a Gandhi cap with the inscription 'Falakata Swaraj No.141' on it. No less significant is the following account: 'The crowd which consisted of Muhammedans, Santals and Oraons before attacking the police proclaimed the fact, of which they were apparently fully convinced, that they were immune from bullet wounds because they were wearing Gandhi Maharaja's caps'[38].

Another form that the movement took was the boycott of tea garden *hats* and setting up of rival *hats*. Many of the *hats* in Duars where the peasants brought their produce for sale were owned and managed by the tea estates. The peasants were subjected to various exactions and oppression and these remained as points of serious grievances and discontent. Further, in the days of Non-Cooperation the Congress volunteers were prohibited from propagating *swadeshi* and the message of the Gandhian movement not only in the cooly lines but also in these *hats*. Under the circumstances, the Congress volunteers and the rural masses on their own initiative and most probably without any guidance from the district organization took steps for boycotting tea garden *hats* and establishment of new *hats* under popular control. In early February 1922 government officials reported several such attempts to set up rival *hats* and the planters were apprehensive that propaganda was spreading from Assam[39].

This form of movement became particularly noticeable in cer-

tain remote parts of Alipur Duars Subdivision. Of several such
incidents, the most well-known was the boycott of Kulkuli *hat* near
Kumargram in March. As in other tea garden *hats*, in Kulkuli *hat*
too the European manager and his men had the last say in all
affairs. But Congress volunteers held a *hat* meeting and organized
picketing of foreign cloth and excise shops in the *hats*. Among
those who took a prominent part in it was Magha Roy, also known
as Magha Dewania, a village-level popular leader. The *hat* authority took objection to all this. In protest against this a rival *hat* was
started on a plot of land owned by a nationalist-minded *jotedar*.
Magha Dewania and a large number of volunteers were arrested
and brought to Alipur Duar town for trial. Hundreds of village
and town people assembled in the court compound and demanded release of Magha and other arrested persons. As the Sub-
Divisional Officer (SDO) was not present in his office, they marched
to his bungalow. To pacify the large gathering, the SDO had to
release the arrested Congress workers. But sometimes later Magha
Roy, Chandradip Singh, a popular Bihari Congress worker of
Alipur Duars, and a few others were tried and sentenced to
imprisonment[40]. The incident provides a striking example of reaction of the villagers to the oppressive attitude and practices of the
European planters and their insulting behaviour to the Congress
volunteers, the followers of Gandhi, and of popular initiative at
the grass-roots level.

It is interesting that most of the incidents of *hat* boycott took
place after the Non-Cooperation movement was called off by the
Congress Working Committee by its resolution of 12 February
1922. It is also interesting that even in early March the Deputy
Commissioner of Jalpaiguri found that the people living in the
eastern part of the district 'actually believed that swaraj had come
and that they would pay no rent or taxes'[41].

In fact, despite the formal withdrawal of the all-India movement, anti-government agitation continued to take place in different parts of the country until early 1923. At various places of the
Jalpaiguri district too picketing of foreign cloth and liquor shops
and settling of disputes through Congress arbitration courts continued[42]. Local leaders of such activities were being arrested and
sentenced to imprisonment for varying terms. For example,
Manmatha Datta, Secretary, Boda Thana Congress Committee
and Munshi Elahi Baksh and Darajuddin Ahmed, President and

Secretary, respectively, of the Khilafat Committee and two other workers were arrested on 5 July 1922. Hundreds of people from the rural areas assembled in Jalpaiguri town to witness their trial. The slogans 'Bande Mataram', 'Alla Ho Akbar' and 'Mahatma Gandhi Ki Jai' reverberated throughout the town[43]. Sporadic incidents of picketing and agitation too were reported from time to time. Even as late as March 1923 there was a serious disturbance arising out of picketing of Marwari shops selling foreign cloth and salt at Ziranganja *hat*, some four miles away from Mainaguri, a thriving market centre, in the Duars. According to available newspaper accounts, one Congress volunteer picketing such shops was caught by a Marwari shopkeeper and kept confined. Following this, a large and excited crowd gathered, and fell on the Marwaris, beat them up severely and looted all the Marwari shops. Later on the police came, searched the houses of neighbouring villages and arrested about 60 villagers. Badges and Gandhi caps were taken away from the volunteers at the time of their arrests. In order to terrorize the local people, the police resorted to indiscriminate arrests of persons known to have any sympathy for the Congress[44].

To sum up, the course of the Non-Cooperation movement in Jalpaiguri district aroused nationalist political conciousness in the minds of thousands of people of widely varying social backgrounds, particularly Rajbansi peasants—both Hindus and Muslims—and plantation labour, and brought them into the vortex of nationalist movement. This movement, however, had two interconnected but distinctly separate currents. One was the forms and issues which had the approval of Gandhi and the formal Congress leadership. The other one was that of popular politics, initiative and self-mobilization at the grass roots level. The unrest among Nepali and tribal tea garden workers, non-payment of revenue and rents, boycott of tea-garden *hats*, incidents of popular violence at Madarihat and Mainaguri—all were examples of the second current. All these reflected the existence of widespread discontent at the popular level. This current also had an element of 'popular messianism' and demonstrated the impact of Gandhi on the minds of peasants and labourers who had a sort of marginalized existence. Gandhi, Non-Cooperation and anger against the Raj and its collaborators, and not the constitutional changes introduced by the Montford reforms, captured the imagination of the masses.

urther, this current was not constrained by legalism or constitu-
onalism and exhibited a certain degree of militancy on the part of
ie labouring masses. The two currents influenced each other but
id not merge together. The district Congress leadership, how-
ver, did not show much of awareness of these aspects. These
ere, however, features of the nationalist movement not only in
ie district of Jalpaiguri but in Bengal and, in fact, in the country
s a whole[45].

ATIONALIST ACTIVITIES 1923-29

he years between the withdrawal of the Non-Cooperation move-
ient and the launching of the Civil Disobedience movement came
 be marked, among other things, by intense controversies among
ie nationalists around three issues, that is, those around Council
itry, Hindu-Muslim relationship and the 1928 Amendments to
ie Bengal Tenancy Act. After C.R. Das' death in 1925, the
rganizational life of the Bengal Congress was characterized by
itter factional squabbles between Subhas Chandra Bose and
itindra Mohan Sen Gupta and their respective followers. There
as also a band of Gandhian Congress workers carrying on quiet,
onstructive activities and social work in the rural areas.

What impact did all this have on the political life of Jalpaiguri?
n the issue of Council entry the Jalpaiguri Congress workers
ded with the 'No-changers'. Jyotish Chandra Sanyal was perhaps
ie only prominent Congress worker to support Chittaranjan on
ie issue of Council entry. But there was little reflection of other
sues among the Jalpaiguri nationalists.

Some of them resorted to various types of constructive work. A
oinning and weaving school was opened in 1922 to train people
 self-sufficiency and discipline. It was followed by the opening of
weaving centre at Jalpaiguri town in the same year. Among those
ho took prominent part in this type of activity were Charu
handra Sanyal, Kiran Chandra Sikdar, Heramba Kumar Bose
id Shiben Bhattacharya. Kumudini Kanta Chakravarty tried to
rganize a match factory and Manoranjan Das Gupta's effort was
 run an oil-pressing concern. Some of the Jalpaiguri nationalists
irned to social reform too. For example, Kaviraj Satish Chandra
ahiri established a night school for the Doms (scavengers)[46]. But

there was nothing comparable to the emergence of groups of rura
Gandhian workers in a number of Bengal districts and the networl
of *khadi* centres, *ashrams* and other constructive organizations tha
were set up by them[47]. In fact, most of the varied efforts made by
the Congress leaders and workers of Jalpaiguri soon came tc
nought.

It had been mentioned above that with the progress of the Non
Cooperation movement Congress organizations came to be set uţ
in many parts of the district. In Jalpaiguri town prominent person
like Sreenath Hoare, Pritinidhan Ray, Trailokya Nath Moulik anc
Nirendra Binode Sen, all lawyers, Jyotish Chandra Sanyal, ɛ
muktear, Tarapada Sanyal, a medical practioner, and Tariniprasac
Roy, a leading tea planter, had joined the Congress[48]. But, as iı
many other districts, by the end of 1923 the Jalpaiguri Distric
Congress Committee was in a state of decline. Khagendra Nath'
arrest in October 1924 under the Bengal Ordinance removed fron
the political life of district a leading organizer. In the absence o
effective guidance from above and faced with government repres
sion, the *thana* and local-level Congress committees too virtuall
ceased to exist.

But nationalist ideas remained in circulation among variou
sections of the population. There were several sources. In the firs
place, from time to time nationalist leaders visited Jalpaigurī
addressed meetings and spoke about nationalism and swaraj. Oı
10 February 1923, Congress workers from the North Bengal dis
trict, except Darjeeling and Malda, assembled at Jalpaiguri t
discuss how to carry on most effectively the programme laid dowı
by the Gaya Congress. Das attended the meeting, stayed in Jał
paiguri for a few days and held discussions with local Congres
leaders and workers. In late April 1923, Acharya Prafulla Chandr
Roy accompanied by Dr Sundari Mohan Das and Kiran Sanka
Roy visited Jalpaiguri and addressed two meetings[49].

Gandhi visited Jalpaiguri on 9 and 10 June 1925. Elaborat
preparations were made to give him a befitting reception. Fror
the early morning of the day of his arrival people poured in fror
far away parts of the district to have a *darshan* of Gandhi. Accord
ing to a newspaper account, 'the seething mass of human heads.
stood on both sides of the road leading from the station t
Gopalpur Bhavan', the residence of a leading tea planter Joges
Ghose, where Gandhi stayed. In the afternoon a meeting of moı

:han 10,000 people was held. Addresses were presented to him on
oehalf of the Jalpaiguri Municipality, the Reception Committee,
:he ITPA, Hindu Sabha, Students Association and a number of
other bodies. He mainly dwelt on *khaddar*, exhorted the rich to
:ontribute their mite, the educated to improve *charkha* and the
ooor to popularize *khaddar*. He emphasized the need for
Hindu-Muslim unity, castigated untouchability as a blot on Hinduism and pointed out the growing vice of drinking and laxity of
morality[50].

In the winter of 1926 Sarojini Naidu visited Jalpaiguri and
addressed a large meeting. In April 1928 Subhas Chandra Bose
visited Jalpaiguri and addressed two meetings. In September 1929
. M. Sen Gupta and several other leaders came to Jalpaiguri on the
occasion of a youth conference (see below). These visits of the
nationalist leaders helped to keep in circulation the ideas of
nationalism and social reforms.

Another important source was the daily newspapers published
rom Calcutta as well as the local weeklies. *Janamat* was brought
out in January 1924 with Jyotish Chandra Sanyal as the editor[51]. In
1925 another weekly, *Trisrota*, was launched under the editorship
of Suresh Chandra Pal. After his release in late 1927/early 1928
Khagendra Nath brought out one more periodical *Muktibani*[52]. All
hese local papers helped to spread the message of nationalism.

The third major source of nationalism was education outside
alpaiguri. The district did not have any college. The Jackson
Medical School was established only in 1931. So those who wanted
o continue their study after the completion of school education
usually went to Rangpur Carmichael College, Rajshahi Government College, Coochbehar Victoria College, or one of the Calcutta
Colleges. A large number of students got ideas of nationalism
here. Particularly significant was the impact of revolutionary
errorism on them. The disenchantment with Gandhian ideas and
methods, the ineffectiveness of the Bengal Congress leadership
and, above all, an urge for launching a militant struggle for making
he country free provided fertile ground for breeding of revolu-
ionary terrorism[53]. These were also the years in which the political
ife in Bengal came to be marked by outbursts of peasant agita-
ion[54], massive working class struggles in industrial centres of
Bengal[55] and growth of militant youth and student movement[56].
All this, particularly revolutionary terrorism and growth of youth

and student movements, had considerable impact on the minds o
students and youth of those days[57].

The various revolutionary terrorist groups tried to establis
contacts with students and youth in different mufassil town:
Jalpaiguri was no exception to such effort[58]. At the same tim
some of the Jalpaiguri students studying in colleges outside Ja
paiguri came into contact with such revolutionary groups and als
with youth and student associations. When such revolutionary
minded students went back to their home town Jalpaiguri durin
vacation or after completing their studies, they tried to draw i
students and youth of the town into the fold of their activity. Fo
example, Birendra Nath Datta (1903-76), son of a tea garden docto
in the Duars and closely related to the Hore family, had joine
Rajshahi Government College after passing his Matriculatio
Examination. Soon he came under the influence of revolutionar
terrorism and within a short time developed into an organizer o
remarkable ability. During his vacations he spent his time i
Jalpaiguri making contact with and organizing like-minded stu
dents and youth[59].

It was at the initiative of these students and youth that
gymnasium was organized ostensibly to give training in physic
exercise and use of *lathis* and daggers. In secret they also practise
use of fire arms. A study circle too was organized[60]. In continu
ation of these activities and in order to give more organized an
coordinated shape to all this, on 21 September 1929 Jalpaigu
District Youth Conference was held at the Arya Natya Samaj Ha
J.M. Sen Gupta accompanied by Dr Bhupendra Nath Datta, Pr
fessor Nripendra Chandra Banerjee, Jnanjan Neogy and Prata
Chandra Guha Roy attended and addressed the Conference. Th
Conference gave a call to the youth of Bengal to join the freedo
struggle, organize rural population, undertake the work of sprea
ing education and making the youth aware of social problems
Birendra Nath was elected as Secretary of the District You
Organization. While one ostensible purpose of the Conference w
to consolidate and give formal organizational shape to the you
activities going on for several years, its other major purpose,
in the case of all such conferences in those days, was to provide
cover for secret meetings of revolutionary activists. The Beng
Government viewed the Conference as something specially da
gerous[62].

Almost immediately after the District Youth Conference an incident took place that created a considerable stir. In Jalpaiguri town on the Vijaya Dashami day the custom was to take the Durga images on decorated and illuminated boats before immersing these in the Karla river flowing through the town. On that occasion a *mela* was held on the river sites and thousands of people, many of them from remote villages, used to visit the *mela* and congregate on the banks of the river to have a view of the immersion ceremony which had a beauty of its own. On the Vijaya Dashami day in October 1929, several youths demonstratively took out a boat, decorated it with national flags and banners on which nationalist messages were inscribed and raised revolutionary nationalist slogans. For this act Birendra Nath Datta, Swaprakash Datta, Bijoy K. Hoare, Chunilal Bose, Sasadhar Kar, a relatively senior revolutionary activist, and several other students were arrested, prosecuted and convicted[63]. This action, however, failed to cow down militant sections of the youth and they carried on various forms of activity ranging from physical training to holding of debates and study circles[64].

Taking an overall view of the political life in the district in the years between 1923 and 1929, one finds that it was not devoid of political activity or even excitement. But the Congress failed to carry forward and consolidate the advance made during 1921 and early 1922, mobilize the mass forces and draw in the varied social forces of the district. The period came to be marked by serious limitations and many complexities.

AMBIGUITIES AND FRAGMENTATION

For convenience of analysis, the years from 1921 to 1929 may be taken as a whole. It may be observed that a major part of the root of the decline of the Congress in Jalpaiguri lay in the incapacity of the district Congress leadership to work out any cohesive, meaningful socio-economic programme, and plan activities keeping in view the specific context and specific problems of Jalpaiguri district. The DCC leadership composed entirely of town-based caste Hindu *bhadraloks*, many of them having close links wth the planters, failed to address any one of the major problems which were specific to Jalpaiguri district—problems like the exploitation of plantation labour, the *jotedar-adhiar* system and its consequences, government policies in the *khas mahal* areas and the Rajbansi Kshatriya movement—or make use of the opportunity provided by the amicable nature of Hindu-Muslim relations prevailing in the countryside. It did not show even any awareness of such problems or opportunity. The constructive activities undertaken by the Congress leaders, for example, the setting up of a weaving centre or the opening of a match factory or welfare work for the low castes were also not component of any broad programme. Those engaged in constructive work failed to build up any sustained and stable network of such activities.

Coordinated political activity was built up to a certain extent only along the stream of revolutionary terrorism. But by its very nature it had to be secretive and could not have any mass dimension. In the particular context of Jalpaiguri a serious limitation of the revolutionary youth activity was its failure to draw in Rajbansi Hindu and local Muslim students and youth. Such activity remained confined to upper caste young men from the *bhadralok* background. In fact, a basic limitation of the political life in the district in the mid and late 1920s was the absence of any mass-based politics. The district Congress leadership did little to develop any substantial link with plantation labour and peasant masses.

Contradictory tendencies

Contradictory tendencies within the nationalist forces themselves could be discerned even during the days of the Non-Cooperation movement. That the Indian tea planters of Jalpaiguri had conflicts with the entrenched European plantation interests has been noticed earlier. Many of the leading Bengali Hindu planters, for example, Jogesh Chandra Ghosh and Tariniprasad Roy supported the Non-Cooperation movement and contributed to the Swaraj Fund. Throughout the 1920s they had some sort of involvement in the nationalist politics.

Yet their support was never unequivocal. It was also not uniform. The structure of the plantation economy and organization made the Indian planters considerably dependent on government support and European economic interests. When during the early phase of the Non-Cooperation movement Ronaldshay (later

Lord Zetland), then Governor of Bengal, visited Jalpaiguri in February 1921, Jogesh Ghosh took considerable pains in showing him the manufacture of tea, in all its phases, at a time of the year which was not the season for tea manufacture in a bid to please the Governor and get help from the government not just for himself but also for other Indian planters. In fact, it was soon after this that the ban on cultivation of tea on *jote* land was lifted[65].

There are other instances of ambiguities. The planters professing nationalism had apprehension about the impact that the Non-Cooperation-Khilafat movements could have on the plantation labour and, further, that such apprehension had a constraining effect on the spread of the movement. The fear of labour agitation, as shown below, continued to have an inhibiting effect on the spread of the nationalist movement in later years too.

Thus, in discussing the state of nationalist politics in the district in the late 1920s the Deputy Commissioner in a report submitted in September 1929 stated:

> The district is non-political because all the politically minded people in it are deeply concerned financially with tea and they do not want the labour force upset[66].

He reported that his 'personal relations with the Congress officials here' including Khagendra Nath Das Gupta who was the DCC Secretary at that time were 'friendly'. Giving his assessment the Deputy Commissioner observed, 'As far as can be gauged there is not enough ferment within the district to spread very far or to do much damage and the people are very backward and are not reached by newspaper'.

Reverting back to the situation in the plantation area about which the Bengal Government was very worried he further reported, 'I should regard the tea garden area as quite safe... There is sufficient control by the managers and staff to make it unlikely that agitators could make much headway, before being discovered and turned out ...' He remarked:

> ...no interference with labour on tea gardens is likely. The Congress leaders and every Indian of means in Jalpaiguri are deeply involved in the tea industry and the last thing they desire is any trouble which affect the dividends. Possibly they would not mind creating trouble in British-owned gardens but would be afraid of it spreading to Indian gardens[67].

The assessment made by this district official was not too wide off the mark.

Rajbansi Kshatriya movement

Another expression of the complexity and divergent tendencies in the socio-political life of the district lay in the fact that the educated upper caste *bhadralok* leaders of the Congress did not accord any significance to the Rajbansi Kshatriya movement which had emerged earlier and which had been growing during the 1920s under the leadership of Panchanan Barman. In Jalpaiguri the movement which had been continuing under Madhusudan Roy was joined by younger leaders like Upendra Nath Barman (1898-1987), a Rajbansi lawyer of imagination and dynamism[68].

Large sections of Rajbansi Hindus had joined the Non-Cooperation movement, but the Congress leadership failed to commit the Kshatriya Samiti movement to any political opposition to the British Raj. As a matter of fact, the Kshatriya movement kept away from Non-Cooperation politics. The movement representing the aspirations of the incipient Rajbansi middle class and also Rajbansi zamindars and *jotedars* had its beginnings in striving for upward mobility and for recognition of a distinct socio-cultural identity. But the movement which in 1917 had asked for special representation in the legislatures, had been developing, during the 1920s also as a political movement and looking upon the British government as the patron of the Rajbansi Kshatriya movement.

One official report mentions that the Rajbansi Kshatriya movement became temporarily involved in the Non-Cooperation movement in July 1921[69]; but it is quite possible that this report emanating from the Intelligence Branch reflected an exaggerated view of the sweep of the Non-Cooperation movement. In fact, all accounts left by the Kshatriya Samiti leaders show that the Samiti not only distanced itself from the Non-Cooperation movement but also opposed it. Upendranath who had in his early youth connexion with the revolutionary terrorist association, Anushilan Samiti, later on under the influence of the Kshatriya Samiti cut off all relations with it and refused to participate in the Non-Cooperation movement[70]. In fact, Kshatriya Samiti was committed to a success of the Dyarchy introduced under the Montford reforms. It participated in all the four elections held in the Bengal Legislative

Council in 1920, 1923, 1926 and 1929 under the 1919 Act and achieved striking electoral success. It is particularly significant that in the 1923 election, in which the Swarajists took part with the declared aim of wrecking the Dyarchy from within and succeeded in capturing majority of the elected general Hindu and Muslim seats, the Kshatriya Samiti defeated the Swarajists in the two seats contested by the Samiti. Panchanan Barman and Nagendra Narayan Roy were the two victorious candidates[71].

In its annual conferences held during the 1920s the Samiti regularly reiterated its firm loyalty to the British Government[72]. In its various resolutions it concentrated on the demands for formation of a Rajbansi Kshatriya batallion, nomination of adequate number of Rajbansi Kshatriyas to the District Board, Union Boards, Municipalities etc., that is, local self-government institutions, suitable measures for spread of education and increased job opportunities for the educated Rajbansi Kshatriya youth. Old issues like the importance of strict adherence to the *shastric* rituals and rousing of social awareness against the introduction of dowry in the Rajbansi society were also stressed[73]. In essence, the Samiti sought to enhance the social, economic and political position of the Rajbansi community in general and of a counter-elite in particular through greater patronage from the colonial regime. In the view of the Samiti leaders the colonial government was an improvement over the earlier rulers in many respects and was considered by them to have introduced an egalitarian rule without any caste, community or language discrimination[74]. It is out of such an understanding that the Kshatriya Samiti leaders pursued a loyalist political strategy.

Three other important aspects of the movement deserve mention here. One, it has been noted earlier that as a part of the movement's quest for wider social recognition of a high caste status, the Samiti had established contact with the Bharatiya Kshatriya Mahasabha in 1920. Later on formal organizational links were forged and Panchanan Barman was elected an office-bearer of the all India body[75]. It, however, appears that this was essentially of symbolic value.

Two, the movement's appeal contained a mixture of evocation of the past glory of the Rajbansi Kshatriya and Hindu revivalism with at times explicit anti-Muslim tones. *Nari niryatan* or outrage of sexual purity of Rajbansi and other Hindu women by Muslims became a recurrent issue. The ideal of *dangdhari mao* or weapon-wielding Hindu women was put forward[76]. The Samiti developed a close relationship with the Hindu Sabha and sent representative to the latter's provincial conferences[77]. It is interesting that at least in one or two years a few Muslims took part in the Samiti's conferences[78]. The eighteenth conference even referred to the need for developing unity of Hindus and Muslims of local origin against the *bhatias*, that is, immigrant Bengalis. But Hindu revivalism predominated and precluded any common programme and common organization for the Rajbansi Hindus and Rajbansi Muslims.

The third aspect that needs to be mentioned is the agrarian issue. Rajbansi landholders, *jotedars* and substantial peasants were among the supporters of the movement. It is no wonder that the movement never raised any agrarian issues at its own initiative. But on two occasions the Samiti's representatives in the Bengal Legislative Council had to take a stand on moves to amend the B.T. Act of 1885. In 1922 Panchanan Barman was made a member of the Committee to consider such amendments. While on the question of relations between landlords and *jotedars* who were either tenure-holders or *raiyats* he was keen to further the interests of these two groups against the zamindars, on the question of giving recognition to the *adhiar* or sharecropper his position was decidedly against the *adhiar*[79]. In the 1928 Bengal Legislative Council debate on the amendment of the B.T. Act, Nagendra Narayan Ray, the only Council member representing the Samiti, on the whole, once more took a similar position[80]. This attitude towards agrarian relations kept the potential of the movement considerably limited.

Muslim politics

Yet one more major dimension of the varied contradictions in the socio-political life of the district was the further growth of a feeling of Muslim sectional identity which had made its appearence in the Swadeshi and post-Swadeshi years. The Khilafat-Non-Cooperation movements brought large sections of Muslim rural and peasant masses into nationalist politics. But it was perhaps exclusively the affair of Muslims of local origin. Certainly they constituted the bulk of the Muslims of Jalpaiguri. However, the town-based 'Noakhali Muslims' who were active in the legal profession, promotion of tea companies and acquisition of *jotedari* interests remained totally indifferent, if not hostile, to these movements.

It may be recalled here that in Jalpaiguri's context the 'closed group' entrepreneurial activities in which both the upper strata of the immigrant Bengali Hindus and immigrant Bengali Muslims were involved contributed to economic and social rivalry between Hindu planters and Muslim planters over control of economic resources and, further, to the growth of narrow sectional identities among them. This tendency was reinforced by the Montford reforms which had widened the franchise but retained and extended a separate electorate. It is possible that important sections of the Noakhali Muslims, the most prominent among whom was Musharraff Hossain, viewed the post-1919 political set up as a means of improving and strengthening not only the economic but also the political position of their community. The withdrawal of the Khilafat-Non-Cooperation movements reduced the significance of nationalist Muslims like Sonaullah who had always been sought to be sidetracked by the Noakhali Muslims.

Musharaff Hossain had, by the end of the 1910s or even earlier, carved out an important place for himself in the public life of Jalpaiguri. In 1923 he was elected to the Bengal Legislative Council from Malda-cum-Jalpaiguri (Mohammedan) constituency and thus entered into a wider public arena. From the very beginning of his career as a member of the Council he took a communal as well as pro-government position as a means of promoting the cause of his community. His sectarian bias was quite pronounced in the stand taken by him in the Council debate in March 1924 over the issue of Das's Bengal Pact (December 1923) which promised to the Muslims, among other measures, 55 per cent of the government jobs after Swaraj. Musharraff Hossain moved a resolution demanding that 80 per cent of the jobs be given to the Muslims immediately. His speech in support of the resolution, in fact, his maiden speech in the Council, was marked by a pronounced communal tone[81]. Even a section of the Muslim members of the Council alleged that 'he has brought the resolution to make the [communal] situation difficult'[82]. In moving the resolution he had also reached some understanding with the government[83]. In fact, he took a pro-government position on a number of issues. For example, in August 1924 both Hindu and Muslim Swarajists moved a resolution rejecting the government's demand for grants on account of the salaries of the Ministers. Musharraff Hossain voted against the resolution and for the government demand[84]. In 1926 he was given the honorific title of Nawab. In 1927 he was appointed as Education Minister.

At the district-level he along with his associates like Waliur Rahman, a planter and big *jotedar*, was active in running the Anjuman-i-Islamia, an association to which reference has been made earlier. It was composed of selected Muslim members and its declared objectives were mainly the promotion and protection of the social, political, educational and other rights and interests of the Muslim community and the promotion of loyalty towards the British Government. In 1925 the number of members was 125 with the majority belonging to the land-holding group[85]. The 1924 enactment providing for the first time the system of a fixed percentage of government jobs for the Muslims and the introduction of the practice of advertisement of such posts through recognized Muslim associations, opened new scope for a body like the Anjuman-i-Islamia and also contributed to communalization of socio-political life in Jalpaiguri town, if not in the district.

The Hindus too had their contribution. Khagendra Nath was involved in the activities of the Hindu Sabha which had been formed in the mid-1920s. Many of the Hindu nationalists exhibited strong antipathy towards the Muslims and even denied the need for drawing in the Muslims in the freedom movement. Thus, *Trisrota*, one of the two regular nationalist weeklies published from Jalpaiguri town, in one of its issues of 1927 asserted that if 200 million Hindus could unite, then it was possible to attain Swaraj even without any Muslim support[86]. Such an attitude must have alienated Muslims and fed Muslim communal outlook.

Despite the growth of sectarian attitudes among both Muslims and Hindus, it is remarkable that the socio-political life in both the urban areas and rural areas of Jalpaiguri district remained totally free from communal disturbance and violence. Ample evidence is available to show that at the popular level the inter-community relations in the district and the countryside in particular were marked by amity. There was, in fact, no sharp Hindu-Muslim divide in the district. Perhaps the basic explanation for this lay in certain longterm tendencies in the socio-cultural life, agrarian society and urban structure which have been described and analysed earlier.

Political Currents and Cross-Currents,
    1930-1937

The process of political developments between 1930 and early
1937 when the elections were held under the Government of India
Act of 1935 came to be marked, as in earlier periods, by complicated and contradictory features. In fact, such was the basic
pattern of developments all over the country. But there were
pronounced and very significant regional and sub-regional variations. In this chapter our attempt will be to describe and analyse
the political trends which were in operation in Jalpaiguri district.

DEPRESSION AND ITS IMPACT

In considering the currents and cross-currents in the social and
political life of the district it is appropriate and important to keep
in view the economic changes during the period. The most out-
standing economic phenomenon was the world-wide Depression
that started in late 1929 and continued till the late 1930s. The ways
in which it affected India have been studied in several works [1] and
need not detain us here. In Jalpaiguri the impact of the Depression
was experienced very acutely in both the plantation industry and
peasant economy.

The fall in tea prices had begun in 1929 and in its annual report
for 1930 the Indian Tea Planters Association (ITPA) expressed
concern over the 'extent of depression in tea trade'[2]. In its report
for 1931 the Dooars Planters Association (DPA) reported that the
industry was 'passing through one of the worst crises in its
history'[3]. The fall in tea prices in 1932 was considered to be of
disastrous proportions and in all the tea producing areas of the
country including the Duars the industry was in 'a precarious

condition'[4]. By June 1933 a scheme for voluntary restriction of production and export was introduced. The Depression created a number of serious problems for the Indian planters in Jalpaiguri, but because of their dependence on government and European business interests in several ways their dissatisfaction remained subdued[5].

The economic situation faced by the Duars plantation workers seems to have been marked by two contradictory aspects. As a result of a fall in the prices of food crops perhaps there was some improvement in their real wages. At the same time, their miserable earnings were reduced and employment shrank[6].

As elsewhere in Bengal, in Jalpaiguri too, the Depression had disastrous consequences not only for the peasantry but also for the middle and petty land-holders. In the context of Jalpaiguri's agrarian economy the latter two categories referred to as middle and small *jotedars*, *chukanidars* and *dar-chukanidars* were caught between falling prices and inflexible rent/revenue demand. The price of jute, the most important single cash crop in Bengal and also in Jalpaiguri, marked an extraordinary fall. In Jalpaiguri, the jute price index (1926-9:100) went down to 35 in 1931-2, 30 in 1932-3, 28 in 1933-4; it rose slightly thereafter, but was still only 52 in 1937-8[7]. What is more, this fall was accompanied by a drastic fall in the price of rice. In earlier periods 'when jute prices fell abruptly the peasants partly made up for the loss by changing over to rice, particularly when its prices remained stable'[8]. But the simultaneity of fall in rice and jute prices made this short-term adjustment difficult.

Despite the fall in produce prices, the liabilities for revenue, rent and interest payments and other financial obligations, such as Union Board tax remained unchanged. Moreover, in the *khas mahal* areas in 1935-6 revenue demand was estimated to have been enhanced by as much as 45 per cent[9]. Such a development perhaps mostly affected the middle and small *jotedars* and *chukanidars*, that is, those who had some surplus to sell. Even the poor peasants and *adhiars* (who lived at bare subsistence level and somehow scraped a living from the soil, but resorted to distress sale for meeting their cash requirements) were hard hit by the slump[10].

In Jalpaiguri (as elsewhere in Bengal), such a situation led to widespread default on revenue payment. Under the influence of the Civil Disobedience movement there was considerable withholding or dodging of revenue payment (see below) and the authorities resorted to the certificate procedure for realization of arrear revenue[11].

One consequence of these developments was an increase in rural indebtedness. A large section of the rural population was in debt even before the onset of Depression. Fall in prices and fixed financial obligations led them to seek further credit. Newer sections too sought credit. But for a variety of reasons there was, as reported by *Deshabandhu*, 'drying up of credit' in the countryside[12].

Faced with the deepening crisis large sections of owner-peasants and tenants in both the permanently settled and *khas mahal* areas were forced to sell their land and faced foreclosure by the *jotedars*-cum-money/grain lenders. The former, however, were not totally dispossessed but kept on the land as *bargadars* or *adhiars*. This process led to accelerated growth of share-cropping and swelling of the rank of *bargadars* in Jalpaiguri and several other districts of north Bengal[13]. In 1939 an enquiry covering all the districts of Bengal was conducted to find out the extent of *raiyati* areas transferred and the manner in which the transferred area was cultivated. The enquiry revealed that in Jalpaiguri district the transferred area constituted 9.4 per cent of the total area enquired into in the district, and 42.1 per cent of the transferred area was cultivated by *bargadars* or *adhiars* and another 39.4 per cent by under-tenants. It is remarkable that each of the three figures were higher than the provincial average[14]. Thus, under the impact of the Depression the peasant economy was caught in a serious crisis. It has already been mentioned in an earlier chapter that between 1905 and 1910 there was an enormous growth of the *jotedar-adhiar* system in Jalpaiguri. In the 1920s the growth continued, but the process was slow. In the 1930s an accelerated growth and consolidation of the system took place. According to the Bengal Land Revenue Commission (or the Floud Commission), by 1939 in Jalpaiguri 26.6 per cent of all cultivating families lived mainly or entirely as *adhiars* and 25.9 per cent of the total cultivated area was cultivated by *adhiars*[15]. There are reasons to consider that the actual extent of share-cropping was much more extensive than these figures suggest[16].

The two-fold impact of the Depression on the economy of Jalpaiguri had an important bearing on politics in the district.

CIVIL DISOBEDIENCE MOVEMENT IN JALPAIGURI

On 26 January 1930, the national independence pledge was solemnly taken in gatherings all over the country. Gandhi's Dandi March from 12 March to 6 April 1930 provided the signal for the country-wide Civil Disobedience. The national week from 6 to 12 April was observed by war against the salt tax. The people were in a militant movement which provided a favourable context for the revolutionary groups functioning inside and outside the Congress.

The reverberation of the movement was felt throughout Bengal in diverse forms and varying degrees. It has sometimes been suggested that in Bengal the Civil Disobedience movement was an exclusively *bhadralok* affair[17]. But several studies have shown the popular dimensions of the movement in Bengal as well as the anti-colonial context of several popular movements that were not directly led by the Congress[18].

Jalpaiguri too was affected by the mass nationalist movement and popular political activities in the province, though to a much lesser extent than in a number of other districts. On 26 January 1930, the Independence Day was observed in Jalpaiguri town by hoisting the national flag in the morning at the Arya Natya Samaj ground. In the afternoon a large meeting was held and in the evening houses were illuminated and decorated by national flags[19]. On 28 March a Civil Disobedience Council was formed with Khagendra Nath Das Gupta as President and preparations were undertaken for Civil Disobedience in the district[20]. Like other districts away from the sea, in Jalpaiguri too it was decided to send a batch of volunteers to one of the centres that were set up on the sea coast of Midnapore and 24-Parganas districts for breaking the salt law. Dhiren Bose, Rabi Das, Pramatha Das and seven other *satyagrahis* commenced their journey on 6 April[21].

Within the district the Civil Disobedience took the forms of violation of orders, prohibiting meetings and demonstrations under Section 144 Cr.P.C. and picketing of shops selling foreign cloth and excisable drugs and liquor. For example, according to Congress Bulletin of May 1930, nine young men, one of whom was only 13 years old, were arrested at Gairkata for violation of Section 144[22]. With the opening of schools and colleges after the summer vacation in early July a call was issued for boycott of schools and colleges in Calcutta and different places of Bengal. In Jalpaiguri district all the students of Class IX and X in Fanindra Deb Institution and some students of Sonaullah School and Zilla School in Jalpaiguri town and educational institutions in Alipur Duar town gave up their studies[23]. From July onwards there was also extension and intensification of the different forms of civil disobedience, such as picketing of shops selling foreign cloth and opium, ganja and liquor, *hat hartal*[24] and violation of orders prohibiting assemblage of five persons or more at one place and raising of nationalist slogans.

The response of the district administration to all this was a resort to repression. The entire Duars area was brought under Section 144. Armed police pickets were posted at various places, particularly at the market centres. Scores of Congress volunteers were arrested and convicted for violating prohibitory orders and their attempts to organize *hat hartals* at different market places spread throughout the district[25]. Most of the *satyagrahi* volunteers were, however, students and youth coming from the urban middle class and rural gentry families of Rajbansi Hindu origin. Among those arrested and convicted were well-known Congress leaders like Khagendra Nath Das Gupta, Charu Chandra Sanyal and Sasadhar Kar, youth and student leaders like Birendra Dutta, Bijoy K. Hoare, Ajit Chakravarty and Chunilal Bose, and student volunteers like Swaprakash Datta, Sachindra Nath Das Gupta, Naresh Chandra Chakrabarty, Ajit Nath Bose, Aghore Sarkar and Sankar Sanyal, some of whom were mere school boys[26]. (Many of them in their later life developed into important political leaders and activists of the district). Kharga Narayan Das, Dhepai Das and several other Rajbansi Hindu students and youth too were arrested[27]. According to an incomplete report, the total number of convictions in Jalpaiguri between 12 April and 28 September 1930 was 56[28].

Following the Gandhi-Irwin Pact signed on 5 March 1931 the Civil Disobedience movement was suspended and there was a period of truce. The truce period that lasted from March to December 1931, was used for carrying the message of nationalist politics to the rural interiors. For example, *Trisrota* of 12 July 1931 carried a report of a meeting held at Jagdal village in Pachagar. In the meeting Anil Chandra Bagchi sang a song, the first words of which were 'Oh Peasant, firmly hold the plough', after which

Jogesh Chandra Datta and Rabindra Nath Sikdar spoke on 'Need for freedom' and 'Benefits of education' and Sasadhar Kar explained with the help of magic lantern slides the current situation in the country. Similar meetings attended by Rajbansi Hindu landholders and peasants were held at Tetulia, Rajganj, Bhajanpur, Berubari, Panda Para, Debiganj and Pachagar. Not only the well-known Congress leaders but also District Students Association leaders and activists like Bijoy Kumar Hoare and Bhabani Das Chakrabarty took active part in building up public opinion. The Students Association also held study circles and debating sessions around various national and international issues[29].

With the re-launching of the Civil Disobedience movement in early January 1932, Jalpaiguri once more became involved in it. On 5 January 1932 a students' strike in Fanindra Deb Institution and *hartal* were observed in Jalpaiguri town[30]. Throughout the month of January there were reports of *hat hartals* in many rural market centres and violation of prohibitory orders in Bhitargarh, Barnesh, Patgram, Boda, Debiganj, Changrabandha, Mainaguri, Dhupguri and many other places in the district[31]. Throughout the remaining part of the year the Civil Disobedience continued and it was during this movement that Keshab Datta of Changrabandha and Debananda Roy of Bhitargar emerged as two important rural-level Congress workers. (Debananda Roy, an illiterate Rajbansi, resigned from the post of Union Board *dafadar*[32]). The main forms the movement took were: hoisting of the National Flag on government and public buildings, violation of prohibitory orders including Special Power Ordinance, taking out of processions and holding of meetings, distribution of illegal leaflets, sale of illicitly manufactured salt, picketing of shops selling foreign goods and so forth[33]. On 3 April a serious disturbance took place at Banskata *mela* held a few miles away from Mainaguri. Three batches of Congress volunteers, mostly Rajbansi youth, resorted to picketing of shops that were selling foreign cloth and salt. They were detained by the *durwans* of the *mela ijaradar*. Later on when some volunteers gathered and took a procession in protest against this, they were beaten up by the *ijaradar's* men. At this an excited crowd assembled and attacked the *ijaradar's* office. In the ensuing confusion one *jotedar* present in the *mela* fired several rounds from the gun which he was carrying. However, no one was injured[34]. It deserves mention that it was in course of the Civil Disobedience movement that for the first time in Jalpaiguri, several women coming from *bhadralok* families took part in it and went to jail. Among them were Hiraprabha Sen, Nanibala Moulik, Sailabala Guha Thakur and Sailabamini Debi.

The government response to the Civil Disobedience movement in Jalpaiguri was, as elsewhere in Bengal and other parts of India, to resort to repression. Raids and searches of Congress offices and houses of persons suspected of having links with the Congress, seizure of leaflets and other materials considered objectionable by the administration[35], forcible breaking up of meetings and processions and largescale arrests became common occurences. The number of persons arrested in 1932 was 1273 and the number of convictions was 126[36]. Repression apart, the government resorted to propaganda and publicity to combat the Civil Disobedience movement through leaflets, coloured posters, inspired articles and news bulletins, magic lantern shows etc. For this purpose the government allotted a sum of Rs 5,000 for the Bengal districts taken together. Out of this Rs 200 was allotted for Jalpaiguri district[37].

Apart from the various forms of the movement mentioned above, the spirit of patriotism and social reforms were propagated in other ways too. On 16 June the death anniversary of C. R. Das was observed by taking out a silent procession[38]. A week-long celebration of Gandhi's birthday was made in the first week of October 1932. In the Gandhi week *khaddar* was hawked by Congress volunteers, and a large meeting held under the presidentship of Sreenath Hore, then District Congress Committee President, adopted resolutions on abolition of untouchability and acceptance of *Swadeshi*. In response to Gandhi's call for giving up untouchability the doors of Pateswari temple at Patgram were opened for the untouchables[39] and Kaviraj Satish Chandra Lahiri, himself a Brahman, organized the Durga Puja of 1932 with Jogesh Datta, a non-Brahman from one of the untouchable castes, as the priest. But these failed to take the shape of a movement for social reforms.

The years 1930 to 1933 in Bengal were also years of several strands of nationalistic political activity and popular movements other than the Congress-led Gandhian movement[40]. One of these was the recrudescence of revolutionary terrorism. Some of the militant students and youth of Jalpaiguri had become associated with revolutionary terrorist groups. Police raids and searches were often made on suspicion of terroristic activity and several young men were arrested for complicity in such politics[41].

Of much greater significance than revolutionary terrorism was a radical stirring within the Congress in the early 1930s. The growth of the young Communist movement in Bengal, the participation of Communists in some of the district youth and student conferences before their arrest in connexion with the Meerut Conspiracy Case, Jawaharlal Nehru's socialistic leaning, the role of Dr Bhupendra Nath Dutta in propagating socialism and other such aspects were influencing the minds of Bengal youth. Some of the Congressmen and youth of Jalpaiguri also came to be influenced by this new political trend. There was a vague leaning towards socialism and even Marxism among sections of students, young people and political workers[42]. Charu Chandra did a Bengali translation of the *Manifesto of the Communist Party* (*Samyabadir Adarsha*) and published it in 1933. 'Economic Interpretation of History' and 'Communism' were some of the topics discussed in the study circles organized by the District Students Association[43]. However, there was no perceptible radicalization of the Congress or broadening of its social base.

Unrest in those years had other dimensions too. One of these was the boycott of tea garden *hats*. For example, there was a dispute between shopkeepers and buyers at Mathurapur Tea Estate *hat* in Alipur Duars subdivision in December 1931. The buyers boycotted the *hat* and started two new *hats*, Khayerberi and Kamsingh, in nearby villages[44]. But from available reports it appears that these remained at the level of stray incidents and did not have the nature of rival *hat* movements as witnessed in early 1922.

Much more significant and widespread was the act of refusal to pay rent and revenue. Many government reports of those years speak of a widespread prevalence of 'no rent' mentality in a number of districts in Bengal. The Depression and the consequent extensive agrarian distress had hit large sections of peasantry and small land-holders and their response took the form of non-payment of rent and revenue[45]. Jalpaiguri, where, as shown above, middle and small *jotedars* and *chukanidars* and peasants were extensively affected by the slump in agricultural prices, was one of the districts most affected by this form of agrarian unrest[46]. A

Congress bulletin of March 1932 reported that the no-rent movement was going strong in Jalpaiguri[47]. Widespread revenue dodging took place and official reports reveal a drastic decline in the
collection of revenue in Jalpaiguri. The percentage of land revenue
demand actually collected fell from 90.28 per cent in 1929-30 to
78.38 per cent in 1930-1 and 62.26 per cent in 1931-2, 57.06 per cent
in 1932-3 and 55.69 per cent in 1933-4[48]. Part of the decline was also
just due to incapacity of the distressed peasants to pay revenue.

However, compared to the 1920-2 movement, the range of
participation in the Civil Disobedience movement in Jalpaiguri
district was much narrower both in terms of geographical spread
and sections of population involved. The small scale revival of
revolutionary terrorism and the incipient radical yearning were
two distinctive features of nationalist political activity in the early
1930s. But, on the whole, the forms and pattern of Congress-led
political activity were much less diverse than in the years of the
Non-Cooperation movement.

As for the Alipur Duars subdivision, that is, the entire eastern
part of the Duars which was very much involved in the earlier
movement, virtually remained outside the periphery of the movement in 1930-4. In July 1931 a local weekly commented that Alipur
Duars was backward in terms of participation in the movement[49]
and it remained so in the second phase of the movement.

With regard to participation of different sections of population
it needs to be mentioned that, though many Rajbansi rural youth
enrolled themselves as volunteers and courted arrest, there was no
mass participation in the rural areas. Muslim participation was
conspicuously absent. A very large proportion of the *satyagrahis*
came from Jalpaiguri town. In the rural areas volunteers were
enrolled, funds were collected, prohibitory orders were violated
in the rural market places (*hats*) and numerous *hat hartals* were
observed. But the sort of enthusiasm witnessed among the rural
masses in 1920-2 was totally absent. Non-payment of revenue was
surely a significant dimension. But this was largely the result of
popular initiative. The role of the Congress leaders and organization was hardly noticeable or at most marginal. Further, part of the
decline in revenue collection was because of the inability of the
distressed peasants and landholders to pay revenue.

It is, however, remarkable that despite the adverse impact of

Depression, the Duars plantation labour seems to have remained quiescent. It is reasonable to surmise that the labour force composed of numerous tribal groups resorted to individual and small group and informal forms of protest and dissent such as desertion, absenteeism, wilful damage to garden, and violence against individual manager or supervisor and also property[50]. There is some scattered evidence relating to a later year (1936) to show that tea garden workers sometimes took resort to poaching and killing of forest guards[51]. There are also stray reports of strikes in one garden or another. For example, in Totapara tea garden in Banarhat area in central Duars a strike took place on 7 and 8 September 1936. It was reported that the pluckers who were all women got excited and at one time the situation looked threatening[52]. It is quite likely that there were incidents of a similar nature. But these seem to have gone unrecorded. And there is no evidence to indicate any attempt on the part of the Congress workers to intervene in the labour situation.

AMBIGUITIES AND FRAGMENTATIONS

Nationalist politics: limitations

Several factors explain the limited impact and spread of the Civil Disobedience movement in Jalpaiguri. Some of these were of a general nature which go to explain the limited spread not only in Jalpaiguri but in most of the Bengal districts. The sweep of the Non-Cooperation movement is to a large extent accounted for by the novelty of the apocalyptic element as well as a faith in the impending end of the British rule and the coming of a Gandhi *raj*. These elements were, by and large, absent in 1930-4. The varying involvement of the Muslims in the 1920-2 and 1930-4 movements is at least partly explained by the presence and absence of the Khilafat factor.

But there were many factors which were particularly important in Jalpaiguri district. One of these was related to the specificities of the background of the Congress leaders in Jalpaiguri. Some of them like Khagendra Nath Das Gupta and Sasadhar Kar had a background of secret conspiratorial work (a characteristic of revo-

lutionary terrorism) and perhaps lacked the inclination for broad-based mass work. They as well as most of the leading Congressmen lacked any peasant and labour-oriented approach and failed to develop sustained mass-based activity and organization. The kind of rural Gandhian constructive workers found in some of the east Bengal districts[53] also failed to emerge in Jalpaiguri. Moreover, without any exception all the important Congress leaders belonged to families who had migrated to Jalpaiguri at the earliest only a generation ago and did not have any intimate and organic link with the autochthonous Hindu and Muslim population. Perhaps this along with their upper caste town middle class background explains to a large extent their failure to have any awareness, not to speak of any comprehension, of the continuing Kshatriya Samiti movement centring around Rajbansi socio-cultural, economic and political aspirations. The legal professional background and the planter connexions of many of the leaders also had an inhibiting influence on mass-oriented work.

The ambivalence in the attitude and position of the Congress leaders *vis-a-vis* peasant and labour problems and indeed any issue relating to the interest of the popular masses was also an important factor. Yet one more factor contributing to the generally hesitant approach was some features of the socio-economic background of the district Congress leadership. Town petty bourgeoisie composed of lawyers, doctors, teachers and businessmen had for all practical purposes the effective control in running the district Congress affairs. That some of the tea planters played an important role in the affairs of the Congress has been noted earlier. That the participation of rural and particularly Rajbansi Hindu and Muslim Congressmen was peripheral is indicated by the composition of the Jalpaiguri DCC[54], and also by the extremely limited representation of rural Congress workers in the delegation to the Provincial Political conferences. As late as 1938 the nationalist fortnightly *Deshabandhu*, edited by Pritinidhan Roy, himself a Congress leader, lamented the latter aspect[55]. In the rural areas sections of *jotedars*, in some cases fairly big ones, *chukanidars* and a substantial number of peasants provided the active support base of the Congress, and primary and local level Congress committee members came mostly from these sections. But even they, not to speak of the poorest rural masses and *adhiars*, had little representation in the Congress organization. Further, it relied on planters, businessmen and urban as well as rural propertied sections for a large part of the fund and various other forms of help.

Much of the ambivalence was also due to lack of clarity and understanding of the nature of Jalpaiguri's economy and society, the structure of the plantation system and its inhibiting impact and the agrarian changes and problems in the overall context of imperialist domination in India and, what is more, the links of all this with popular struggles. Congress interest in agrarian issues even in the days of Depression and crash in jute and paddy prices was marginal. Even when they showed some interest in agrarian problems, their concern mainly centred around the interests of *jotedars* and *chukanidars* and the issue of jute prices[56]. Its silence on the plight of the poor peasants and *adhiars* was glaring.

Apart from the lack of clarity about the issues involved, the ambivalence was also causally related to the ideological position derived primarily from Gandhi's position. The national movement was viewed as an anti-imperialist struggle on the broadest possible front. It is not that the Congress leaders were totally unaware of the misery of the *adhiars* or of the exploitation of the tea garden workers. But being afraid of disrupting the unity of the national movement and having no belief in class struggle, almost invariably they sought for a compromise and reconciliation between the exploiting *jotedars* and the exploited rural poor and *adhiars*[57]. The Congress leadership did not go beyond this. For it the national movement was primarily and fundamentally a struggle against the British rule and peasant issues were incidental to it[58]. All this, if not fully, at least to a considerable extent, account for not only the limited spread of the Civil Disobedience movement but also the somewhat limited influence of the Congress in the district even in later years.

The Congress leadership had another major anomaly. Many of them, consciously or unconsciously, identified nationalism with Hinduism. Sreenath Hore, the DCC President, was closely associated with the activities of the Hindu Sabha. Kaviraj Satish Lahiri, one of the DCC Vice-Presidents, was at the same time a Secretary of the Hindu Sabha[59]. At the time of the 1931 Census operations Sreenath Hoare, Satish Lahiri and Jogesh Ghosh, a leading tea planter of nationalist inclination, issued an appeal for recording the immigrant tribal groups like Oraons, Mundas and Santals as

Hindus[60]. Sometime later they along with others like Nalini Ranjan Ghose and Kumudini Kanta Chakrabarty became actively involved in the campaign to rally Hindu opinion against the Communal (MacDonald) Award (August 1932) and also the Poona Pact (September 1932)[61]. All this must have alienated broad sections of Muslims.

In May 1934, the Civil Disobedience movement was formally called off by the All India Congress Committee. Following this, a serious demoralization set in and the Congress organization in Jalpaiguri fell into a state of disarray.

Muslim politics

Muslims too of the district, as elsewhere in Bengal, were indifferent to the Civil Disobedience movement. Anjuman-i-Islamia led and controlled by Nawab Musharraff Hossain and his Noakhali compatriots took a hostile attitude, resorted to active propaganda to prevent the Civil Disobedience movement from spreading among the Muslims and supported government measures to suppress it[62]. Musharraff Hossain and his supporters had an unmistakable Muslim communal orientation. Prior to the 1937 Assembly election, he along with Khaja Habibullah of Dacca and Khaja Nazimuddin took an important part in the setting up of the United Muslim Party in May 1936. Musharraff became Vice-President of the party. But after some talks with Jinnah the party was voluntarily dissolved and Muslim League was launched in Bengal[63]. In the political position taken up by both the United Muslim Party and the Muslim League and also in the 1937 election campaign the stress was not on any socio-economic programme but on Muslim solidarity[64]. It is noteworthy that despite active support from Musharraff Hossain, in Jalpaiguri sectarian politics remained confined within the small but articulate and organized group of town-based Noakhali Muslims residing in Jalpaiguri town and failed to have any significant impact on the rural and local Muslims.

Even in Jalpaiguri town there were non-sectarian Muslim organizations like the Mohammedan Literary Society and the Distirct Mohammedan Association. The last-named one was established in 1935 at the initiative of, among others, Jaharatullah Ahmad, a nationalist-minded Muslim pleader of local origin. Both the organizations were mainly concerned with religious, social and cultural issues of a broad nature[65] and the Noakhali Muslim took little interest in the activities of these organizations.

It is remarkable that barring one or two incidents of fracas over the issue of musical processions before what was known as the Nawab's mosque or defilement of a Hindu temple[66], Hindu Muslim relations in Jalpaiguri remained remarkably free from tension and overt conflict. As late as October 1938 *Deshabandhu* observed, 'Till now there has been no acute communal conflict in this district... The lesson that religious sanctity has to be preserved by smashing each other's head has not yet been learnt'[67] Elderly people of Jalpaiguri town remember that till the late 1930s relations remained friendly and members of one community used to take part in the festivals and religious events of the other community[68].

Caste and politics

The complexities and fragmentation in the socio-political life were also revealed by the course of the Rajbansi Kshatriya movement Though many Rajbansi Hindus were associated with Congress, participated in the nationalist movement and went to jail, the Kshatriya Samiti kept away from it and persisted with loyalism to the Raj. In early 1931 an election of the Jalpaiguri Municipality was held. The Congress leaders were either in jail or did not take part in the election. Sections of the lower castes were, however, not averse to participation in the Municipality. On the urging from representatives of a few lower caste groups (Karmakar, Teli, Rajbansi and Beldar) of Jalpaiguri town, the government nominated Upendranath Barman, a rising Rajbansi Kshatriya leader, as a municipal commissioner. At the initiative of Nawab Musharraff Hossain and Rai Bahadur Bipulendra Nath Bannerjee, a *muktear* retained by the European tea planters and a known loyalist, Barman was also elected to the position of Vice-Chairman of the Municipality[69]. On 16 September 1931 several detenus were shot dead in Hijli jail and this incident revealed the dilemma which a person like Barman was put into. A resolution condemning the incident as a 'dastardly outrage' was moved. Barman, as he subsequently stated, was willing to vote in favour of the resolution provided the word 'dastardly' was deleted. But the movers reused to do so. Barman abstained from voting and the resolution was defeated[70].

An aspect deserving particular attention was that, against the background of the constitutional negotiation continuing since the appointment of the Simon Commission, the Kshatriya movement too became involved in the issue of political reforms and there was less stress on that of improvement of the ritual and social status of the Rajbansis. Bangiya Jana Sangha, an organization representing the Rajbansi Kshatriyas and several other backward but 'non-untouchable' caste groups, was formed[71]. It may be observed here that in a move to have a united lobby against the caste Hindus several low-caste *sabhas* formed the Bengal Depressed Classes Association which represented the Namasudras and other untouchable and depressed castes[72]. It is, however, interesting to note that the Kshatriya Samiti leaders because of their claimed higher ritual and social status were keen on demarcating themselves from the former and organized the Bangiya Jana Sangha[73].

In the Memorandum submitted to the Indian Franchise Commission (1932) on behalf of the Sangha, Panchanan Barman stated that the Rajbansis and other backward castes 'should be represented by reserved seats... through Joint Electorate'[74]. It is from this position that the Kshatriya movement supported both the government declaration of August 1932 with provisions for reserved seats and separate electorate for the 'depressed classes' and later on its modified version—reserved seats but joint electorate—under the Poona Pact[75]. To take advantage of job reservation, special educational facilities and electoral politics the Kshatriya Samiti asked for the status of Scheduled Castes and this was granted. There was some reservation within the community about this status, but the Samiti leaders argued that the term 'scheduled' was not related with ritual and social status of a caste and that the category 'scheduled castes' just referred to certain castes included in a schedule for electoral purposes; hence there was no ground for having any misgivings[76].

The policy of the colonial government was to encourage political aspirations of the lower castes including the Rajbansis in a bid 'to keep the nation divided and weak'[77]. Thus, addressing the fifteenth and sixteenth conferences of the Kshatriya Samiti held in Jalpaiguri on 18 July 1935 F.W. Robertson, the Rajshahi Divisional Commissioner, observed that the government had recognized the

Rajbansis as one of the Scheduled Castes and would surely especially consider their claim for government services and also other
matters of interest to them[78].

However, there were certain compulsions of the electoral politics. The Government of India Act of 1935 widened the franchise to
a certain extent and provided for joint electorate in the case of seats
reserved for Scheduled Castes. The first election under this Act
was held in early 1937. There is at least one piece of evidence to
show that in the election campaign of Upendranath Barman, the
Kshatriya Samiti candidate in the Jalpaiguri-Siliguri constituency
there was a new emphasis. There was less stress on the social rank
and separate identity of the Rajbansis. In the campaign the deplor-
able condition of the peasantry irrespective of their caste and
community affiliation was highlighted and in an election leaflet
written in verse the voters were asked to vote in favour of Barman,
a *krishaker pratnidhi* or peasant representative[79].

The 1937 election

On the occasion of the 1937 election attempts were made to revive
the Congress organization in the district. But in the election the
success of the Congress was limited. The Jalpaiguri-cum-Siliguri
general or 'non-Muhammedan' constituency had three seats of
which two were reserved for the Scheduled Castes. The Congress
contested in two seats. Khagendra Nath Das Gupta, its candidate
in the general constituency, won and secured 8,990 votes. But
Sarojendra Deb Raikat (son of Jagadindra Deb Raikat, the first
President of Jalpaiguri Congress), the other Congress candidate in
a reserved seat, was defeated. In one of the reserved seats Raja
Prasanna Deb Raikat was a formidable candidate with tremendous
social, political and economic influence. In many booths before
casting their votes the voters paid obeisance with money and
flowers to the ballot box which had the Raja's election symbol[80].
The network of zamindari organizations was turned into a powerful election organization for mobilizing votes and he won by
securing the highest vote of 16,244. The other reserved seat was
won by Upendranath Barman who, though drawing upon the
support of the Kshatriya Samiti, made the distress of the landholders and substantial peasants an important issue and could
even get the support of some caste Hindus[81]. In the

Jalpaiguri-Darjeeling Muhammedan rural constituency Musharraff Hossain won uncontested[82].

The election outcome once more revealed the complex and
fragmented features of society and politics in Jalpaiguri and the
failure of the Congress leadership to overcome the disjunction
between the nationalist forces and other social and political forces
which were active in the district.

8   New Political Trends and Emergence of the Left, 1937-38

PROVINCIAL BACKGROUND

The course of political movements in Bengal during the years 1937 to 1941 had several significant features. At the governmental level a Krishak Praja Party-Muslim League coalition ministry headed by Fazlul Huq and backed by the majority of the Scheduled Caste Assembly members came to be installed. An important feature of the political trends was considerable radicalization of politics at different levels. The Congress, which after the petering out of the Civil Disobdience movement, had become very much preoccupied with constitutional reforms and electoral politics came to be affected by this process. A 'mass contact' programme was launched by the Congress at Jawaharlal Nehru's initiative at its Lucknow session (1936) and a fairly radical agrarian programme was adopted at Faizpur (December 1936)[1]. The radicalization impact which all this had within the Bengal Congress was marked by the growth of left wing trends and elements. Important sections began to accept Marxism as the ideology of organization and movement[2]. The Communist Party of India (CPI) which was formally banned in 1934 eschewed the politics of 'left sectarianism' pursued by it earlier and adopted the programme of a broad united national front of all anti-imperialist forces. There was also a shift of many terrorists to CPI, providing the cadre-base for a major extension into districts. All this was accompanied by the revival and growth of the militant working class movement as well as the beginning of a new phase of the peasant movement. At the same time, there were several negative features. The Fazlul Huq ministry came to be dominated by the Muslim League and had to accommodate

Muslim communalism. Its tenure (1937-41) became a period of decline of the Praja   movement which had earlier reflected the anti-zamindar feeling of broad sections of peasant masses of east and north Bengal, mostly Muslims[3], and of the spread and crystal-ization of separatist Muslim politics led by the Muslim League[4].

This was in broad terms the provincial context in which impor-ant developments took place in the political life of Jalpaiguri district. One of these was some initiative on the part of the district Congress leadership to reach the masses. There was also a radicali-zation process reflected in the establishment of a district unit of the Congress Socialist Party and the formation of peasant and worker organizations and also of a nucleus of the CPI. All this culminated in what may be considered the first peasant movement of the district. These years also saw the beginning of a separatist and communal Muslim politics. This was paralleled by the activities of he Hindu Sabha. The Kshatriya Samiti too continued with its efforts to make its impact felt in political life.

STATE OF THE CONGRESS

In the years immediately following the withdrawal of the Civil Disobedience movement, the Congress in Jalpaiguri was in a very disorganized state. Congress organizational affairs came to be marked by intense factional squabbles—squabbles not around any policy issue but around personality clashes between leaders like Khagendra Nath Das Gupta and Charu Chandra Sanyal. Congress organization at different levels became virtually non-existent or non-functioning, even where they existed. False members were enrolled with an eye to the Bengal Provincial Congress Committee election. Further, the Congress did not have any mass-oriented programme and activity[5]. But soon several new political factors came into play bringing about significant changes. It deserves particular mention that before the decade came to a close the district, or at least part of it, witnessed the first mass movement specifically around peasant grievances.

New political dimensions

Fazlul Huq had been elected to the Assembly as the leader of the

Krishak Praja Party, a party that was committed to 'the abolition of zamindari without compensation'. Though the record of Huq was one of compromises, the fact that he headed the ministry had aroused high expectations among the peasant masses[6]. At the same time, following the 1937 election there was a noticeable change in the scale and nature of activity of the Congress in Bengal. In contrast to its earlier pro-zamindar and anti-tenant position which was most strikingly illustrated by the debate over the 1928 move to amend the Bengal Tenancy Act, the Congress in late 1930s took a less conservative view of the agrarian situation and issues[7]. It launched a mass contact programme and extended its propaganda and activity among the students and youth, peasants and labour.

A very significant political development was the introduction of a broad perspective of social transformation, brought in by intellectuals and large sections of revolutionary terrorists, and crystallized in the demand for abolition of zamindari within an anti-imperialist framework. In Bengal the Congress Socialist Party (CSP) and the Bangiya Pradeshik Krishak Sabha (BPKS), the provincial unit of the All India Krishak Sabha, were formed in 1934 and 1936, respectively. From the very beginning Communists were the most active within the BPKS. In the political life of Bengal, apart from the CPI, various other Marxist groups, such as M. N. Roy's League of Radical Congressmen, later renamed Radical Humanist Party, the Labour Party led by N. Dutta Majumdar, and the Communist League led by Soumyendra Nath Tagore were very active. Of these, the CPI, though a small illegal party at that time, began to emerge as a significant political force. From 1933 onwards it was functioning in a relatively organized and systematic manner. The formation of the Huq ministry gave the party new scope and the period 1939-41 was, according to CPI's own assessment made in 1943, one of expansion and consolidation[8].

It was against such a political background that new political developments began to take place in Jalpaiguri, particularly in some parts of the district. One of these was related directly to the Congress activity. Some of the district Congress leaders were seriously concerned at the prevailing state of organizational affairs and its distance from and indifference to the peasants and tea garden labour. This concern was unambiguously indicated in the pages of the nationalist fortnightly *Deshabandhu*.

Fresh initiatives were taken to revitalize the Congress organization, extend its activity to the peasant masses in the rural areas and
to students and youth in the two towns of the district, enrol new
and genuine members and form functioning primary Congress
committees[9]. *Deshabandhu* carried regular and detailed reports of
such activities. As part of a mass contact programme, some
Congress workers were placed at the *thana* and union levels with
the aim of organizing the rural people. Thus, Prafulla Kumar
Tripathi, who because of his connexion with the Bengal Volunteers
and alleged involvement in the Barge murder had been kept under
detention at the Buxa camp situated near the Jalpaiguri—Bhutan
border, was on his release in 1938 entrusted with the responsibility
of carrying on Congress work among the rural people in Changrabandha and Patgram areas in the Duars[10]. Madhab Datta (1910-85)
was posted at Boda. Born and brought up in Barisal district, he
came to be associated with the Anushilan Samiti in his boyhood.
He was kept in detention from 1932 to 1937. In Berhampore camp,
(Murshidabad district) he came into contact with some political
workers of Jalpaiguri and on his release came to Jalpaiguri[11]. On
being placed at Boda, Datta started work among the rural masses
with dedication and enthusiasm, began voicing their grievances
and soon endeared himself to large sections of the people. Congress workers were posted in some other areas also.

Meetings were held in different rural areas including faraway
places in the Alipur Duars subdivision and these were attended by
large numbers of people composed of the two major autochthonous communities. Many came from distant villages, and in
some meetings Muslims outnumbered Hindus. These meetings
were addressed by district and local Congress leaders and workers who exhorted the peasants to join the Congress and strengthen
it as a means of effectively solving their problems[12]. In these
meetings, among other things, the Huq ministry was strongly
criticized for imposition of education cess and its failure to fulfil
the promise of zamindari abolition. The reintroduction of the
certificate procedure for the realization of land revenue in the *khas
mahal* areas and the sharp increase in rent even before the recovery
from the disastrous consequences of the slump also came in for
attacks.

The ministry had two ministers from the district—Raja Prasanna
Deb Raikat and Nawab Musharraff Hossain. The district Congress

castigated them for their inability to look after the interest of the Jalpaiguri people. In the early years of the Huq ministry, the Kshatriya Samiti members in the Legislative Assembly including Upendranath Barman[13] extended support to the ministry with the expectation that it would take specific measures to ameliorate the condition of Scheduled Castes in general and Rajbansis of north Bengal in particular. Barman as well as the Samiti faced sharp criticisms from the Congress for their failure to wrest any significant concession to speak of and the Congress was projected as the only political organization that could effectively fight not only for national freedom but also for removal of specific grievances of various groups and communities[14]. The Congress campaign, however, did not go unopposed. In some places elements hostile to it tried to disrupt the Congress meetings. Thus, some persons made an attempt to break a Congress meeting that was being held at Bolar *hat* on the grounds that no meeting would be allowed in any place under Prasanna Deb Raikat's control[15]. It would not be inappropriate to mention here that the Raikat's Baikunthapur Estate authority later on refused to give permission for holding the Bengal Provincial Political Conference in a huge open space near the Rajbari or the palace[16]. Such attempts, however, failed to demoralize the Congress.

In fact, a certain rejuvenation of the Congress was achieved within a short time. The District Congress Committee felt confident enough to extend an invitation for the holding of the Provincial Political Conference in Jalpaiguri in early February 1939. At the same time, it made efforts to capture the local bodies and took organizational measures to contest the union board and Jalpaiguri municipality elections which were to be held in early 1939[17]. It was this revival and strengthening of the Congress which led *Deshabandhu*, which was often critical of various lapses in Congress activity, to make the observation: 'The victory of Khagendra Babu in the last election, the return of workers like Prafulla Kumar Tripathi and Sasadhar Kar and their involvement in Congress activity, the invitation for holding the Bengal Provincial Political Conference next year—all this sequence of developments has imbued in the minds of the Congress workers a new enthusiasm. They are turning to the villagers, advising the peasants to organize themselves, and are forming the primary Congress committees. All this is commendable'[18].

Issues in Congress campaign

The basic issue in the Congress campaign was that of political freedom. The keynote, according to Birendra K. Neogy, was the following: 'We must have freedom. Without freedom nothing purposeful can be done'[19]. The main demands voiced at the meetings included those for reduction of revenue in the *khas mahal* area, granting of occupancy rights under the Bengal Tenancy Act to the *khas mahal* tenants, stoppage of the practice of government nomination to the District Board and Union Boards, and repair of *jampois* (irrigation channels) in the Duars[20]. The Congress also campaigned around the issue of jute price. In a four-page Bengali leaflet entitled 'Jute Price and Mass Contact' issued in June 1937 under the signature of the then DCC President Charu Chandra Sanyal, a call was given for organizing the jute cultivators, formation of jute growers' associations at different levels, such as union, district and province, fixation of a minimum price for jute, and working out of a system of hypothecation and advances through the associations. Demands along these lines were also made at the meetings organized by the Congress[21].

The Congress leaders discussed and analysed agrarian problems also in the pages of *Deshabandhu*. Charu Chandra used to write a regular feature entitled *'Deshar Katha'* in a popular and easily intelligible style. Issues and problems close to the hearts of the rural people were raised and solutions suggested in the form of a dialogue between two or three villagers. Implications of the Debt Conciliation Board, jute price, education cess, plight of the *khas mahal* tenants, a comparison of the performance of the Huq ministry in Bengal with that of the Congress ministries in other provinces, defects of the amended Tenancy Act and such other issues were discussed under this feature[22]. Khagendra Nath also wrote several notes and articles dealing mainly with the problems of *jotedars* and *chukanidars* in the *khas mahal* area where the former did not have the right of occupancy tenants[23]. In some of the notes he also discussed the administrative policy with regard to the setting up of *hats*—a policy devised in the narrow interests of the tea planters, particularly European tea planters[24] or Jalpaiguri District Board's road construction programme which too was worked out to serve the interests of the planters [25] or government policy with regard to forest[26]. It is, however, significant that issues like abolition of zamindari or the plight of the *adhiars* or the condition of tea garden labour were still being excluded.

While the Congress activity in large parts of the district centred around the issues and problems mentioned above, in mid-1938 a situation of severe food scarcity and near-famine condition developed in several unions of Boda, Debiganj and Pachagar *thana* areas. In early July a Congress team composed of Prafulla Tripathi, Madhab Datta and Debananda Roy, a Rajbansi Congress worker mentioned earlier, was sent to make an on the spot enquiry, and after receiving a report from them the district leadership took measures for organizing relief[27].

The Congress, however, did not remain preoccupied with local or district issues only. Release of the political prisoners was a major issue of political campaign in Bengal in 1937 and 1938. A call was given by the BPCC, CSP, Bengal Labour Party and Bengal Provincial Students Federation to observe 14 March 1938 as the All Bengal Prisoners Release Day[28]. In response to this call processions and public meetings were held at different places in Jalpaiguri district[29]. The All Bengal Peasant Day was held on 29 July 1938. In meetings held at Boda, Burimari, Jalpaiguri town, Alipur Duar town and several other places Congress leaders and workers sharply criticized the failure of the Huq ministry to ameliorate the misery of the peasant masses and get the Governor's assent to the pro-tenant amendments to the Tenancy Act passed by the Assembly[30].

Organizational expansion

The intensified and multifarious activities on the part of the Congress got reflected in its organizational expansion. In many places where previously there was no Congress organization, primary Congress committees came to be formed. By 31 October 1938, the last date fixed by the BPCC for enrolment of Congress, the total number of Congress members was 4,980 which was about three times the membership strength attained in previous years[31]. The decision with regard to the composition of the district delegation to the Tripuri Congress session deserves notice. The Jalpaiguri DCC was entitled to send a five member delegation. It was decided that of them only one was to be from the town and the remaining four from rural areas[32]. In earlier years there was hardly any rural representation in such delegations. The decision reflected a change in the attitude of the Congress leadership.

Limitations of the Congress activity

Despite these advances, the political and organizational activities of the Jalpaiguri Congress had serious shortcomings. One of these was that the intensified political activity had no counterpart in the form of a mass, particularly peasant and labour movement-oriented programme. It is not that there was no rural protest action. Refusal to pay revenue or revenue dodging continued till as late as 1939. In the Assembly session held in December 1939 the Revenue Minister B. P. Singh Roy spoke of the 'no payment mentality of the tenantry' in the Duars and justified the re-introduction of Certificate Procedure for realization of arrear rents on that ground[33]. While the Congress held protest meetings against the re-introduction of Certificate Procedure as well as rent enhancement following the 1935 Settlement operations in the Duars, there is no evidence to indicate that the district Congress leadership had any direct role in the growth of the 'no-payment mentality'. To the extent that there was active refusal to pay, the initiative and leadership were most probably provided at the local level.

Another lacuna, in a sense a more serious one, was that the Congress campaign and activity were for all practical purposes oriented to the *jotedars* and *chukanidars*. The issues mentioned earlier covered the interests of the middle as well as petty landholders. But it had no programme for the poor peasants and *adhiars*. It is significant that in the fairly large number of reports published in *Deshabandhu* on the Congress meetings held in the rural areas there is not even the slightest reference to the miserable plight of the *adhiars*. Even the fairly radical-minded fortnightly which discussed a wide range of problems did not mention the *adhiar* issue except in one signed writing. And in that writing too the *adhiars* were viewed as just agricultural labourers and not as peasants without any tenancy rights. The writer stated, 'Though the *adhiar (bargadar)* is an agriculturist, he belongs to the class of labourers. The number of this type of labourer class is large in this area [Duars and Patgram]'[34]. In his address as Chairman, Reception Committee, Bengal Provincial Political Conference, Charu Chandra Sanyal focused on the problems of the *jotedars* in the district and particularly in the *khas mahal* area and ignored specific *adhiar* problems and demands[35]. All this revealed not only a lack of understanding of the agrarian structure and changes taking place in the district but, much more importantly, a class limitation of the nationalist leadership.

The class limitation was particularly manifest in the silence of the Jalpaiguri Congress over a specific and a most important problem of the district—the existence of a vast tea garden labour force and the terrible exploitation and oppression to which they were subjected. This lapse was critically commented upon in an editorial note of the *Deshabandhu* and a hope was expressed that this aspect would receive the attention of the socialist-minded Congressmen[36]. But this hope was not to be fulfilled till mid-1946. Though in his Welcome Address to the Provincial Conference held only a few months after the *Deshabandhu* observation, Charu Chandra referred to the Duars plantation entrepreneur as 'the pride of Jalpaiguri' and also to 'employment of nearly one lakh labourers'[37], there was no mention, even indirectly, of labour problems. It is noteworthy that the Address also failed to put forward any perspective for socio-economic changes in the district. The Address also did not show any awareness of the difficulties and complexities in the way of the spread of nationalist politics in a society composed of diverse social groups and communities. The Reception Committee Chairman made a reference to the Kshatriya Samiti which was not negative. But no perspective and policy with regard to the Rajbansi Kshatriya *andolan* was put forward. There was also no mention of autochthonous social groups like Meches or Rabhas or Garos or the immigrant tribal groups of Oraons, Mundas, Santals etc. or the Nepalis and their aspirations.

The nationalist leadership in the district failed to make any significant dent among the Muslim population. It is striking that of the total Congress membership of 4,890 in the district, Muslims numbered only 367[38] in a district in which the latter constituted nearly one-third of its population. But in the address no concern was expressed for such a state of affairs. It is also striking that among the six members of the executive committee and twelve secretaries of the different sub-committees of the Reception Committee there was no Muslim[39].

The failure of the Congress to create any noticeable impact

among the Muslims stands out particularly sharply against the background of the absence of any popular support behind the town-based elitist Muslim communal politics in the district. But there was the persistence of a quite pronounced sympathy for the Hindu Mahasabha among important sections of Congressmen in Jalpaiguri and the failure mentioned above was at least partly related to this. Differences between Hindu nationalists like Sreenath Hoare or Bhabaranjan Ganguly and non-communal elements came out in the open in early 1939 over the issue of nominations for the coming municipal election[40]. The communalism of Muslims, though of a small section, tended in its turn to feed the spread of Hindu communalism.

One may also note the neglect of Congress work among women. The membership breakdown for the year 1938-39 shows that women membership numbered only 137. The geographical spread too remained limited. *Deshabandhu* of 16 Asar 1345 observed in its editorial that large parts and even entire police station areas remained virtually uncovered by the Congress.

RAJBANSI KSHATRIYA POLITICS

One major problem complicating the political life in Jalpaiguri and the neighbouring districts of Rangpur and Dinajpur was the Kshatriya movement the influence of which among the Rajbansi Hindus, as shown by the election result, was considerable. Though many of the latter had turned into supporters of and some even actively participated in nationalist politics, large sections remained outside its sphere of influence. Some of the Congress leaders were, however, keen on having a dialogue with the Kshatriya Samiti and in finding out areas of common understanding. Upendranath Barman was invited to speak on the 'Ideal and Thinking of the Kshatriya Samiti' at the first special session of the Congress Study Circle held on 12 December 1937[41]. *Deshabandhu* also published the full text of the Presidential Address delivered by Gobinda Chandra Roy at the annual conference of the Samiti held at Dalgram (Rangpur district) in mid-February 1938[42]. The Address given by Charu Sanyal to the Jalpaiguri session indicated an appreciation of the social aspirations of the Rajbansi Kshatriyas[43]. At the same, the Kshatriya Samiti movement was criticized by the Congress leaders for its opposition to the Congress and support of the Huq coalition[44]. Nationalist-minded Rajbansis like Amar Chandra Deb Singha (a lawyer) came out with sharp criticisms of the Kshatriya movement[45].

In a situation of changing politics the Kshatriya movement was in a state of uncertainty about its socio-political perspective and particularly its relation with the nationalist politics and other political trends and groupings and also seemed to have its internal tension and differences. Thus, though stressing the sectional identity and aspirations of the Kshatriyas, Upen Barman in his speech at the Congress Study Circle also spoke of the links that the Kshatriya movement had with the rest of the polity. In the speeches and writings of Barman and other leaders and activists of the movement during this phase, the loyalism demonstrated earlier was watered down, if not abandoned altogether. The movement, in fact, continued to exhibit considerable ambiguity which was partly a result of a change introduced by the 1935 Act. It provided for seat reservation for the Scheduled Castes and thus conceded a major demand of the Rajbansi Kshatriya and other 'backward' and 'depressed' caste movements. (This demand was indeed accepted by the Macdonald Award and the Poona Pact.) Following this, the leadership of the Rajbansi Kshatriya movement was in confusion over the future course. Though initially the bulk of the Scheduled Caste leadership lent support to the Huq ministry, they were not happy with the performance of the Muslim League-dominated ministry. (For example, the Rajbansis had their resentment over the non-inclusion of a Rajbansi Kshatriya leader in the ministry.) But they had their misgivings about the Congress which was viewed by them as an organization dominated and controlled by the caste Hindus.

Their dilemma and confusion are clearly revealed from the account of a meeting of the Kshatriya and other non-Congress Scheduled Caste MLAs with Gandhi, Subhas Bose (the Congress President at that time), Sarat Bose and J.C. Gupta. The meeting held in early March 1938 tried to explore the prospect of reaching an understanding between the non-Congress Scheduled Caste movements and the Congress in Bengal[46]. Though nothing tangible in relation to the Congress emerged from the meeting, subsequent developments suggest that in the months following the meeting Upen Barman and other Kshatriya (and Scheduled

Caste) MLAs began to take a critical position in relation to the Muslim League-dominated coalition Government. Out of the 36 Scheduled Caste MLAs, 31 including 6 Kshatriya members formed a legislature group—the Independent Scheduled Caste Party (ISCP)—with Upen Barman as leader and Jogendranath Mandal, a Namasudra spokesman elected from a Bakarganj (Barisal) constituency, as secretary[47]. By June 1938 Barman was sharply criticizing the coalition ministry on the floor of the Assembly and on certain issues voting with the Congress. In early August he along with other Scheduled Caste MLAs voted in favour of no-confidence motions against the ministers[48]. Thus, under the impact of other political changes in Bengal there were shifts in the position of the Kshatriya Samiti. At the same time, there were reports of sections of the Rajbansi followers of the Samiti switching their allegiance to the Congress[49]. The shift, however, did not involve any radicalization of the socio-economic content of the programme of the movement. It is significant that it remained silent on issues like the problems of the *adhiars*, a very large proportion of whom in the north Bengal districts including Jalpaiguri were Rajbansis. Further, there were sections within the movement, as shown by a letter from the Jalpaiguri District Secretary Girija Singha Roy, published in *Deshabandhu* of 21 Magh 1345, who tended to stress the separate identity of the movement and highlight its demarcation from nationalist politics.

MUSLIM POLITICS IN JALPAIGURI[50]

The closing years of the decade also saw the beginning of organized manifestations of separatist Muslim politics in Jalpaiguri led by Musharraff Hossain. But, as mentioned earlier, till about the 1937 election there was no district-level organizational agency to give any popular dimension to the Muslim communal politics. The District Mohammedan Association was essentially concerned with religious, social and welfare activities mainly for Muslims of local origin and available evidence does not indicate its involvement in any separatist communal politics and rivalry with the Hindus over economic and political power. There was a district unit of the Krishak Praja Party with some support among sections of local Bengali and also non-Bengali Muslims. But it failed to grow as an active body. Anjuman-i-Islamia certainly had a separatist communal outlook, but its activities remained confined within very small groups.

In connexion with Muslim politics in Jalpaiguri an important feature deserving emphasis is that the Muslim society was not a homogenous one. A wide social, cultural and political gap existed between the Noakhali Muslims and the local Muslim masses. The majority of the Noakhali Muslims lived in the district town and were engaged in the legal profession and the tea business controlled by Musharraff Hossian and the coterie close to him. They were also employed in the subordinate government services and enjoyed the patronage and benevolence of the Musharraff group. In contrast, the local Muslim masses lived in the rural areas and earned their livelihood from agriculture and agriculture-related activities. A small section, however, came to reside in the town and were engaged in legal practice, teaching and petty jobs. Jaharatullah Ahmed[51], Sakhikul Islam and Ejarat Ali Ahmed, all legal practitioners, belonged to the local Muslim group and had considerable tension and contradictions in their relations with the group led by Musharraff Hossian. Sakhikul was one of the few known Congress-minded Muslims and in the Municipal election held in early 1939 he won on a Congress ticket[52]. Also, some of the non-Bengali Muslims active in the social and political life of the town were opposed to the Noakhali Muslims. Of them, Mohammed Shukurullah (1910-70), grandson of Ibrahim Sowdagar of Bhar, deserves particular mention. He had a large *jotedari* and considerable tea interests and also land and house property in Jalpaiguri town. He was Vice-Chairman of the District Board and Jalpaiguri Municipality for several years. He was also the Secretary of the Krishak Praja Party in Jalpaiguri[53]. Ejarat Ali openly voiced the grievances of local Muslims against the Noakhali Muslims and accused the latter for dreaming of enhancing the prosperity of Noakhali and Comilla at the cost of the people of the district in which they had come to settle recently[54]. The local Muslims found that so far as the distribution of service, jobs, professional opportunities etc. among the Muslims was concerned, the Noakhali group monopolized these.

Thus, the Muslim community was divided in terms of cultural practices, social mores, place in the economy, and social and political behaviour. In this context it would not be inappropriate to once more refer to a long-run tendency noticed earlier: at the popular level in the rural areas, even in late 1930s, the Rajbansi Hindus and Rajbansi or local Muslims had many important similarities and the syncretizing process that had been working earlier had not yet been disrupted. It is interesting to note several moves made by the organizations of local Hindus and local Muslims to move together on common issues. For example, in late 1937 the District Kshatriya Samiti and the District Mohammedan Association had a joint meeting which adopted a resolution on a government proposal for rural development and demanded active involvement of the local population in any programme for such development[55]. In another move an attempt was made to have joint activities of the Kshatriya Samiti and Jalpaiguri unit of the Krishak Praja Party headed by Shukurullah. A joint meeting of the two organizations held on 4 August 1939 and presided over by Upen Barman demanded the protection of the interest of the local Hindus and local Muslims in the activities of the District Board[56]. These were significant moves but failed to make any headway

Role of mullahs

As a matter of fact, by the late 1930s some unhealthy and even negative tendencies had also become noticeable. The presence and activities of itinerant *mullahs*–rural priests–hailing from Comilla, Noakhali and Chittagong became increasingly observable. They started village *maktabs* teaching children the elements of reading, writing and rudiments of Islamic law and theology. They also acted as the *imams* (prayer-leaders) of the village *masjids*, presided over *jumma* (the Muslim congregational prayers on Fridays) and *Id* prayers and officiated at other religious functions observed by the rural Muslims[57].

Most of the *mullahs* were semi-literate with bare rudiments of Islam and were often referred to as *kath-mullahs*, in the sense of ignorant and bigoted *mullahs*, even by some Muslims. But they began to exercise increasing influence over the illiterate Muslim rural masses. The rural population, virtually ignorant of the Islamic social code and doctrines, completely depended on these people for all religious ceremonies and functions. A major concern of these *mullahs* and *maulvis* was to Islamize the life-style of the ordinary Muslims, purify religious and social life of all non-Islamic influences and ensure that people conformed to Islamic principles and injunctions as interpreted by them. The deliberate move to Islamize the life style of the common people is exemplified by certain minor but significant innovations. For example, there was a tendency to substitute honorifics considered non-Islamic such as 'Sri', 'Srijukta' etc. by Arabic and Persian honorifics like 'Janab', 'Munshi' etc., and 'Nasya', the local Muslim title, came to be replaced by Ahmad, Mohammad etc.[58].

These *mullahs* coming from some of the east Bengal districts introduced elements of bigotry which led to a growth of intolerance of everything that was Hindu and supposedly un-Islamic. It was these *mullahs* and *maulvis*, known as *kath-mullahs*,[59] who became carriers of communal ideas. It was through them that communalism began to emerge and grow among sections of Muslims in the countryside of Jalpaiguri as a political factor. Their activity had another significant aspect. They played an important role in bridging the gap that existed between the town-based educated Noakhali Muslims, particularly those among them who were directly and indirectly involved in separatist Muslim politics, and the non-immigrant local rural Muslim masses who had earlier been by and large unaffected by such politics. It was primarily through the *maulvis* that the League politicians of Jalpaiguri like Musharraff Hossain who, besides making use of his economic and social position as a powerful tea planter and *jotedar* and also his influence as a minister in the first Fazlul Huq ministry (1937-41), began to mobilize the rural Muslims, particularly the *jotedars* among them.

Formation of the Muslim League

Mobilization of the Muslim masses was facilitated by another factor. Spread of literacy and education among them was relatively greater than that among the Rajbansi Hindu rural masses. Because of this, the magazines propagating separatist Muslim politics had a readership, though not large, in the countryside. Among these, *Nishan*, a weekly brought out from Jalpaiguri town under the editorship of a lawyer Abdul Khalek, had a role to play:

it became a purveyor of communal ideas to the literate sections of the rural Muslim masses of Jalpaiguri district.

It was in such a context that moves were made to set up a district unit of the Muslim League. An All Bengal Muslim Conference organized by the Muslim League and presided over by Jinnah himself was held in Berhampore, Murshidabad in late October 1937. Following that conference the League and its MLAs took initiative in setting up branches of the League at district and *thana* levels[60]. It was as part of these developments that in early December 1938, at the initiative of A.M.L. Rahman[61], the district unit of the Muslim League was set up in Jalpaiguri[62].

The formation of the League, however, did not have an immediate impact on mass politics. In early 1939 elections were held to the Jalpaiguri Municipality. Though a number of League-minded Muslims contested in the election, the Joint Secretary of the District Muslim League issued a public statement stating that it had no candidate in the election[63].

That separatist and aggressive Muslim communal politics was finding difficulty in spreading its message was also evident from the proceedings of the conference of the District Muslim Students League held on 23 and 24 June 1939. The Conference was presided over by Jaharatullah and inaugurated by P.D. Raikat. Among the speakers was Syed Badruddoja from Calcutta. Available reports, though scrappy, show that the proceedings were free from any communal overtone. The Conference President stressed the problems of the district. It is interesting that one Tachkin-uddin-Nuri drew attention to the *adhiar* problem. He raised the question that if the defaulting landholders could get debt relief from the government and also get loans on easy terms, why could the poor *adhiars* not get relief with regard to consumption loan on which they had to pay 50 per cent interest. This was one of the earliest references to the *adhiar* problem in Jalpaiguri. Tachkin-uddin-Nuri also spoke about the urgency of raising the salary of the teachers of traditional village primary schools (*pathsalas*)[64]. All this including the joint moves by the District Mohammedan Association and District Kshatriya Samiti or the latter and the District KPP show that at the ground level there were interesting possibilities. But these were thwarted by developments taking place at other levels.

LEFT STIRRINGS TRENDS

It was against such a political background that there emerged new stirrings and trends within the Congress in Jalpaiguri. A new generation of young men had entered the political arena in the late 1920s and early 1930s. Already in 1931 and 1932, there was new searching and questioning among sections of Jalpaiguri Congress workers. By 1937 and 1938 these trends gathered strength.

Some of the political workers, particularly the younger ones among them, became dissatisfied with the Gandhian leadership and programme. The earlier rejection of the Government of India Act of 1935 in its entirety by the Congress and the later decision to contest the election and even accept office under the same Act was viewed by them as glaringly inconsistent. The failure or, in fact, the virtual refusal on the part of the all India Congress leadership to take any concrete move for launching a mass struggle against the Raj added to their growing dissatisfaction. Their dismay increased because of the state of affairs within the BPCC—the constant squabble between a large section of Bengal revolutionaries led by Sarat Bose (who was later on joined by his far more indomitable brother Subhas Bose) on the one side and the staunch followers of Gandhi and other Congress leaders on the opposite side[65].

The dissatisfaction with the existing state of political activity along with a deep yearning for a new ideological and political opening among a large number of young political workers was an all Bengal phenomenon. The activists of Jalpaiguri district too did not remain unaffected by the new trend. Some of them had the first glimmerings of a new political philosophy that was radically different from and, in fact, opposed to the Gandhian ideas as well as revolutionary terrorism, the latter losing its romantic appeal by the mid-1930s. Ideas of socialism and of Marx and Lenin in particular began to exercise powerful influence[66]. The international setting, the Depression affecting the entire capitalist world, the rise of fascism in Italy and Germany, Japan's aggression against China, the Spanish Civil War and such other developments deeply stirred the minds of these political workers. The achievement of the Soviet Union set before them a new alternative. Jawaharlal Nehru's presidential address at the Lucknow session of the Congress and his writings, particularly *Whither India*, helped to pose questions regarding the political and economic content of independence. M. N. Roy who after his expulsion from the Comintern had returned to India and had been functioning within the Congress since the early 1930s, had a sort of charismatic appeal for sections of radical political workers. Thus, under the impact of all these trends, as elsewhere in Bengal, youth activists who had previous links with revolutionary groups, young Congress workers and politically advanced student cadres of Jalpaiguri, began to lean towards socialism and Marxism and some accepted these.

Some of the pioneers

Sachindra Nath Das Gupta was one of them. He was born in 1913 in a middle class family which was closely related to the 1911 martyr Birendra Nath Datta Gupta and the story of the latter's martyrdom told to Sachindra Nath in his childhood years left a strong impression on his mind. In 1930 he enrolled himself as a student in the newly established Jackson Medical School. That was also the first year of the Civil Disobedience movement and he enthusiastically joined the movement. For that he was sentenced to a short prison term. In 1934 he came out of the Medical School with a distinguished academic record and became actively involved in Congress activity. It was during his student days that he first came into contact with socialism and Marxism, particularly through Roy's writings. Chunilal Bose who had been active in the youth movement of the late 1920s persuaded Sachindra Nath to subscribe to Roy's *Independent India*[67].

Birendra Nath Datta, the acclaimed leader of Jalpaiguri youth in 1929, had to undergo prison and detention terms for a number of years in the early 1930s. While in the Hijli Jail, he read Marxist literature and soon accepted a Marxist position. Bijoy K. Hoare who had been active in the youth movement in the late 1920s came into contact with Bhupendra Nath Datta around 1931 and got initiated to Marxist ideas. While serving prison terms in 1932-4 he got in touch with some of his co-prisoners who were already inclined towards socialism and Marxism[68].

Birendra Kumar Neogy(1909-), the assistant secretary of the Jalpaiguri DCC in 1938, got his ideas of socialism and Marxism also through Roy's *Independent India* and was particularly impressed by the latter's stress on the role of the toiling masses in Congress activity[69]. Naresh Chandra Chakraborty (1916-70) had

participated in the Civil Disobedience movement as a schoo
student, graduated from Rangpur Carmichael College and joined
the Calcutta University Law College in 1937. He used to attend
Roy's meetings, soon became involved in the activity of the BPSI
which was, among other things, a most active force in the prison
ers release campaign in 1937 and 1938 and came into close contac
with Biswanath Mukherjee, one of the most prominent and dy
namic student leaders of those days. Soon Naresh Chandra made
his mark as a student cadre of considerable organizing ability and
in 1938 got himself elected as the Under Secretary of the Calcutta
University Institute which was, at the time a major area of studen
activity. Through Biswanath Mukherjee, Naresh Chandra also go
in touch with the illegal Communist Party[70]. In his activity Naresh
Chandra was joined by two other Jalpaiguri students, Birendra
Nath Bose who was a close friend of his and Bimal Kumar Hore
the younger brother of Bijoy Hoare. When they came back to
Jalpaiguri during the Summer and Puja vacations, they used to
bring in new political and organizational ideas and propagated
these among the Jalpaiguri students. Jalpaiguri District Students
and Ex-Students Association was changed into, Jalpaiguri District
Students Association (DSA). Later on the DSA became the district
unit of the BPSF[71].

In this context one should also mention Madhab Datta, a
Congress organizer placed at Boda. On his way to Jalpaiguri after
his release from Berhampore(Bengal) Jail he had come across
copies of the CPI publications *Ganashakti* (Bengali) and *National*
Front and got his initial ideas of communist politics from these. He
had a sensitive mind and at Boda came into close contact with the
peasant life. At that time Abdul Halim, one of the founders of the
communist movement in Bengal, was kept interned at Pachagar, a
few miles away from Boda, and was a source of new ideas.
Madhab Datta also had met Halim and discussed the political
situation and trends with him. All this helped him to move
forward to socialism[72].

Ideological and political differentiation

All this indicates that there was an urge among sections of Congress cadres and even some leaders for a clarification of the
meaning and social content of nationalist politics. The urge was

clearly reflected in the pages of *Deshabandhu*—not only in the reports it published but also in its editorials and editorial notes. While hailing the mass contact programme launched by the Jalpaiguri Congress, *Deshabandu* of 1 Jyaistha 1345 (mid-May 1938) observed in its editorial that in the earlier years under the leadership of Mahatma Gandhi the basis of mass contact was the temperance programme, introduction of *charkha* and abolition of untouchability. 'But at present', it wrote, 'we want to go forward by one more step. Being influenced mainly by the socialist-minded people, we are trying to organize the peasants on the basis of some economic demands'[73]. Given the state of political activity in Jalpaiguri in mid-1938, the latter claim was exaggerated. For at that time there was no organizational manifestation of the socialist trend. But it clearly indicated that socialism was having its impact upon some Congress leaders and cadres.

There was a certain degree of ideological and political differentiation which also got reflected in a debate in the pages of *Deshabandhu*. Some Congress leaders frowned upon moves that were being made for the formation of separate class organization of the peasantry. They argued that such an organization would divide and weaken the national movement. Representing this viewpoint Prafulla Tripathi wrote, 'We are noticing that some distinguished Congress workers are thinking of a separate peasant organization outside the Congress... But everybody should consider how disastrous will be the consequence of this attitude for the interest of the country... As a result of this the strength of this great organization [Congress] will certainly be reduced...'[74]. In a subsequent issue[75] Birendra Nath Datta wrote a rejoinder criticizing Tripathi's position. Pointing out the need for having a separate peasant organization, he contended that such an organization representing the peasant interests would strengthen the national movement against British imperialism. In support of his argument he made repeated references to the writings of Marx and Lenin.

District Students Association

The emerging new political trends with a distinct leftist and socialist orientation soon found organizational shape. Some time in early May 1938 at the initiative of Naresh Chandra, the BPSF leader Biswanath Mukherjee came to Jalpaiguri[76]. The Jalpaiguri

Students and Ex-students Association which was primarily concerned with student welfare and organizing of cultural functions was transformed into Jalpaiguri Students Association with the avowed purpose of not only having political discussion but also some political programme and activity. In response to an editorial comment in *Deshabandhu* expressing apprehension about harmful consequences of involvement of students in political activity[77], Bimal Hoare, in a letter to the editor defended the new orientation. He wrote, 'The ideals of freedom, peace and progress are now endangered in the country. At the altar of various (reactionary) interests such as imperialism and fascism, world humanity is now being sacrificed. So the oppressed mass spirit of the world has awakened to make itself free of all chains... The student community of the country is going to join this struggle...'[78].

Congress Socialist Party

Particularly significant was the formation of the district unit of the CSP. In a meeting held at the District Congress office on 22 December 1938 and attended by more than one hundred people the unit was constituted with Kaviraj Satish Lahiri, a veteran Congress leader, as President and Sachindra Nath Das Gupta as Secretary. Among other members of the District Executive Committee were Jogesh Chandra Datta, one of the DCC Vice-Presidents for the year 1938-9, Chunilal Bose, an associate of the youth leader Birendra Nath Datta in 1929 and an Assistant Secretary of the DCC at that time, Bijoy Hore and Sudhin Moitra, a medical student[79]. *Deshabandhu* of 15 Poush B.S. 1345 (end-December 1938) commented, 'We wholeheartedly approve it [i.e. its formation]'[80]. It suggested several areas of activity particularly noteworthy among which was investigation into the condition of tea garden labourers and publication of the findings of such an investigation. Its other suggestions were organization of a library containing books dealing with political and economic topics, holding of study circles and undertaking of a literacy campaign in nearby *bustees*[81].

The CSP in its public pronouncements put forward the ideal of political emancipation through social change. It was viewed as an instrument of struggle and mobilization of peasants and workers. Voicing the political outlook and policy Sachindra Nath wrote, 'It is necessary to base all political movements on an economic foundation... We will have to make people understand that it is necessary to totally change the social system which is at the root of poverty and to achieve that change the people must have political power'. Indicating the attitude towards the Congress, he stated that the socialists considered that the Congress with its existing character would not be able to launch movement in the interest of the people—the peasants and workers. That would have to be done by the Socialists. But he declared, '... they [i.e. the socialists] do not want to oppose the Congress. They want to transform Congress into an organization of the people'[82].

Krishak Samiti

Another highly significant development was the formation of the District Organizing Committee of the Krishak Samiti on 23 December 1938 with Gurudas Roy as Secretary and Sachin Das Gupta as Assistant Secretary[83]. Gurudas Roy (1913-61) hailing from Manikganj in Dacca district had earlier been associated with Shree Sangha and Bengal Volunteers, the latter organization being responsible for much of the daring revolutionary terroristic activities in the early 1930s. While in detention, he was attracted to socialism and Marxism. After his release in 1937, he came to Jalpaiguri and got in touch with leftist and socialist-minded Congress workers including Das Gupta[84]. Krishak Samiti was the first peasant organization in the district and its impact on the political life of the district soon came to be felt.

Workers Union

In December 1938, the first workers organization of the district came into existence. Through the Duars part of the district ran the lines of Bengal Dooars Railway(BDR). The BDR had also a small railway workshop at Domohani. A few hundred workers composed mainly of Bengalis and Biharis with a sprinkling of tribals (Oraons, Mundas etc.) and Punjabis were employed at the workshop. Most of the running staff and station staff were Bengalis. Those working as gangmen, linesmen etc. were mainly immigrant tribals. A unit of the Bengal Assam Rail Road Workers Union was formed with J.N. Gupta, a member of the Legislative Council representing Railway Labour constituency, as President and Birendra Nath Das Gupta, who was the founder Secretary of the All Bengal Students Association (1928) and by 1938 was close to the

Communist Party, as General Secretary. Amrita Lal Mukherjee (1912-), a political worker having links with revolutionary groups of Rangpur since his school days and an ex-detenue who had become a member of the Rangpur unit of the CPI some time in 1938, became the Organizing Secretary[85]. The formation of the union was not directly related to the political development within the district and was, in fact, a product of the revival of the working class movement in the province since the mid-1930s. In later years, however, it came to play a very important role in the unfolding of peasant and worker struggles in the district.

Early activities of the Left

With the formation of the CSP and Krishak Samiti units there was the beginning of changes in the orientation, goals and forms of political activity in certain parts of the district, specifically speaking in some areas under Boda, Debiganj, Pachagar, Sadar and Rajganj *thana* areas. Available accounts suggest that for the first time in the political life of the district serious attempt was made to organize and activize the peasants not only around broad national political questions but also around explicitly stated peasant issues. For Gurudas Roy and Sachin Das Gupta, both of them having already accepted Marxism, peasant agitation in 1938 or early 1939 was something totally new. They did not have much understanding of peasant life and problems and class relations in those areas. As Congress workers, their links in the rural areas were mainly with the *jotedars* and the well-off sections[86]. But inexperience and limited understanding were compensated by ideological and political fervour, a broad orientation towards work among the peasants, particularly the poorer sections of them, which in Jalpaiguri district by and large meant the *adhiars*, a strong urge a deeper understanding of what they saw and heard and a capacity for patient, hard work. Gurudas Roy had the additional quality of delving into the minds of the oppressed Rajbansi and Muslim peasants, talking in terms and language and also using symbols and idioms which were intelligible to the simple peasant families and keeping in mind their specific cultural propensities and traditions[87].

Gradually Sachin Das Gupta and Gurudas Roy began to gain an understanding of the problems of the peasants, various forms of exploitation and oppression to which the poor peasants and *adhiars* were subjected, and the exploitative practices of the Cooch-behar Raj and of the Raikats of Baikunthapur and also of the big *jotedars* and *mahajans*. They heard the unending tales of the woes of the peasants and urged them to stand on their own feet. Madhab Datta, assistant secretary of Boda Congress Committee, though initially not associated with the Krishak Samiti was on his own carrying on activities among the poor peasants and speaking against the oppression of the zamindars and *jotedars* and soon a link was established with the Krishak Samiti[88]. He, like Gurudas Ray, had the rare quality of easily identifying himself with the oppressed and exploited peasants[89].

Within the framework of basic political campaign for attainment of complete political independence and achievement of a broad national front Sachin Das Gupta, Gurudas Roy and Madhab Datta also raised peasant issues. The chief slogans were abolition of the zamindari system and land to the tillers. Along with these, demands were raised for stopping collection of *hat tola* or levy by *hat* owners and *ijaradars* from the middle and poor peasants who came to the *hats* (for details see next chapter), lowering of interest rates on *karja dhan* or paddy loan taken by *adhiars* from their *giris* and free primary education without imposition of cess. They exhorted the peasants to build up peasant unity and peasant organization. Initial response of the peasants was lukewarm. They looked upon these *babus* coming from Jalpaiguri town with distrust and suspicion. But within a short period they won the admiration of the peasants through their tireless work and propagation of concrete issues and demands vitally affecting the peasants. They began to attend meetings organized by these *babus* and enrol themselves as Krishak Samiti members. Soon the *babus* came to be known and affectionately addressed as 'comrades' indicating a process of fraternization.

First peasant rally

All this activity coincided with the preparation for the holding of the Bengal Provincial Political Conference. In view of the controversy then raging within the Congress at both the national and provincial levels over the attitude towards the Federal section of the 1935 Act and the pressure on the part of the Left for launching a nation-wide struggle, the Provincial Political Conference was viewed as an event of great political importance. Sarat Bose was to preside over the Conference and Subhas Bose to attend it as the Chief Guest. A Reception Committee was formed with Charu Chandra as Chairman, Khagendra Nath as Secretary and Sasadhar Kar as Chief of the Congress Volunteer Force. A detailed programme was chalked out to make the conference a success.

The newly formed Krishak Samiti as well as the CSP were anxious to link up their activities and emerging peasant movement with the Congress and nationalist politics. They were also keen to strengthen the Congress Left. They also wanted to give expression to peasant discontent and demands before the Conference. With such aims in view, the Krishak Samiti in co-operation with the CSP decided to organize a march of the peasants under its influence to Jalpaiguri town, and made preparations for these. The CSP also decided to hold a separate volunteer rally. According to one account, some of the local Congress leaders of Pachagar did not like the idea of a separate mobilization under the banner of Krishak Samiti and tried to create panic among the local peasants by spreading various rumours. But this move failed[90].

On the morning of 5 February 1939 Subhas Bose accompanied by the Conference President Sarat Bose and other leaders arrived in Jalpaiguri town and a most enthusiastic reception was given to them. On that day the people of Jalpaiguri saw for the first time a totally new kind of rally. According to the reports published in the *National Front*[91], thousands of peasants, many of whom had walked 30 to 40 miles to hear the leaders at Jalpaiguri, marched through Jalpaiguri town with Red and Tri-colour Flags and banners inscribed with peasant demands[92]. There was a fee of as. -/2/- for entry into the Conference pandal. But the peasants asked for entry without the payment of any fee. Initially this request was turned down by the local Congress leaders. But this led to an embarassing situation and eventually, at the intervention of Subhas Bose, they were allowed free entry into the Conference Pandal[93].

Subhas Bose and Bankim Mukherjee addressed the gathering. Bankim Mukherjee, a well-known peasant and labour leader as well as Congress leader, explained the necessity of organizing peasant movements and also dwelt on the evils of the zamindari system and problems of debt. He exhorted them to set up kisan committees in every village to protect their rights and carry on their movement[94]. *Trisrota* of 12 February 1939 commented, 'Though, because of the elegance of language, many of the thousands of illiterate and half-literate peasants could not fully follow his [Bankim Mukherjee's] speech, tears in the eyes of hundreds of aged people have clearly indicated what the peasantry of Bengal wants today'. *National Front* (9 March 1939) also reported that at the meeting order was maintained by a well-disciplined Kisan Volunteer Corp and great enthusiasm prevailed among the peasants who attended the peasant rally and Congress Conference. It was the first peasant rally of this kind in Jalpaiguri and thus occupies a distinct place in the annals of peasant agitations in the district.

It also deserves notice that it was from the Jalpaiguri Conference that the Congress in Bengal demanded for the first time not only the abolition of the Permanent Settlement but also of 'all the zamindari systems'. The Conference also called upon all the 'progressive organizations' in Bengal to present peasant grievances and demands before the Bengal Land Revenue Commission (the Floud Commission).

All this reflected the increasing radicalization of the masses including the middle class following of the Congress in Bengal. A major factor behind this radicalization was the slump of the early 1930s and the acceleration of the process of disintegration of the agrarian economy under its impact[95]. The beginning of a systematic work on the part of the Communist Party of India and other left political groups was also having its influence on the Congress. A related factor was the spread of the activity of the Kisan Sabha. The radicalization was also reflected in a resolution passed at the Conference demanding the lifting of the ban on the Communist Party.

Formation of the district unit of the CPI

Along with the holding of the Provincial Political Conference, a new development took place in the political life of the district. A cell of the Communist Party of India was formed on 6 February 1939 with three members—Biren Datta, Gurudas Roy and Sachin Das Gupta. The cell was formed in the presence of Somenath Lahiri who had come to attend the Provincial Conference. For a short period Biren Datta acted as Secretary. But soon he had to leave the district because of personal reasons and thereafter Sachin Das Gupta became Secretary and remained so till early 1948. The newly formed district unit of the CPI resolved to work within the CSP and strengthen the Krishak Samiti[96].

9 The First Left-Led Mass Movements, 1939-40

PREPARATORY PHASE

In the months following the Provincial Political Conference sustained propaganda and patient explanatory campaign around issues of peasant grievances and against exploitation and oppression on the peasantry and *adhiars* in particular became a regular feature of the Krishak Samiti activity. This activity was carried on mainly in three police station areas—Boda, Debiganj and Pachagar, the areas in which the Congress had a tradition of work since 1921. In view of this background these areas already had a body of rural political activists of nationalist movement.

Techniques and modes of campaign

Gurudas Roy, Sachin Das Gupta and Madhab Datta were the three most important political figures in this activity. Sometimes they were joined by a few other workers associated with the CSP. They used to lead a simple and austere life. They lived among the rural masses, particularly the poorer sections of them. They did not hesitate to stay in the peasant hovels and shared their meagre food and many of the hardships of their life. All this helped to create a new sense of credibility about them in the minds of the rural people.

The Krishak Samiti leaders used a variety of techniques to reach the people. *Baithaks* or small group meetings, gatherings at *hats*, previously announced meetings at some public places and public demonstrations were held to approach the rural population. Leafllets containing pointed slogans were distributed. These were usually

written in such a language that anybody having lower class
education could read them out and illiterate villagers could
understand them easily. Leaflets were often printed on coloured
paper resembling cinema handbills used in *mofussil* towns and
places in those days. Initial methods of propaganda sometimes
resembled modes of *hat* entertainer and canvasser[1]. *Dhols*, a local
variant of drums, were used to announce meeting places or
publicize information. In carrying campaign and propaganda
among the masses even in those early days CSP and Samiti leaders
tried to initiate the peasants to Left and radical politics. They spoke
about the implications of the end of the British rule for the peasant
masses. They taught them how the zamindars and certain other
sections of rural vested interests served the British Raj. The leaders
also told the masses what the Samiti was and what its relation with
the Congress was. They explained what the Red Flag, the flag of
the Samiti, signified.

But the Samiti leaders did not use and rely upon 'modern' or
more appropriately secular political ideas and arguments only.
Not only in those early days but much later too they made
considerable use of traditional idioms and religious symbols.
Stories from *Ramayana*, *Mahabharata* and *Puranas* were imaginatively
and skillfully used. For example, the behaviour of Dronacharya,
the Brahman arms instructor of the Kauravas and Pandavas, with
Ekalavya, a low caste young man who had attained an exceptional
proficiency in the use of arms or the *Ramayana* story according to
which Rama beheaded Shambuka, who being a Sudra had resorted
to austere religious practice (*tapasya*), considered to be a most
reprehensible offence on the part of a Sudra, were used to illustrate
class struggle in ancient India. Boda and Pachagar had a
preponderance of Muslim population. The Islamic injunction against
usury and any discrimination on the basis of wealth and the spirit
of *jihad* against oppression and injustices and also ideas of
brotherhood were used. In mobilizing women stories were used
relating to insults to and persecution of women, such as the
treatment meted out to Draupadi[2].

Along with the effort to organize the peasants and the
rural population, the Krishak Samiti tried to reach wider sections
of popular masses, particularly the town middle classes, and get
from them political as well as material support. With that aim in
mind it regularly published notices of meetings, circulars, resolutions,

reports on conditions in rural areas and Krishak Samiti activity in local weeklies like *Trisrota* and *Janamat* and provincial dailies like *Ananda Bazar Patrika*. For example, *Trisrota* of 2 April 1939 published the following news item sent by Sasanka Sekhar Bose, an office bearer of the Krishak Sangathani Samiti: 'At the initiative of local Krishak Sangathani Samiti many meetings have been held in various unions of the Sadar Subdivision and already nine Union Krishak Samitis have been formed. At present illegal exactions *abwab, tohuri*, etc., are extensively collected from the peasants of this district and if anybody protests against this practice the threat of realization of interest on arrear rent and compensation is being used as the main instrument for making these illegal exactions. This year the conditions of the peasants are very bad... For they have not obtained any relief from jute and are also getting very low prices for the paddy'.

Village-level links

In organizing the Krishak Samiti and in initiating subsequent peasant movement village and Union-level activists played an important role. These men such as Anath Saran Gautam, an Arya Samajist small *jotedar* hailing from Balia in the United Provinces and also a quack doctor, Pramada Chakrabarty, a poor village priest and Congress worker, Mahinath Jha, a Brahman middle *jotedar*[3] hailing perhaps from a UP district, Ashu Majumdar, Haripada Roy, a Rajbansi *jotedar*, and Upen Chanda, a cycle mechanic, provided the first link between the political leaders having urban middle class origin and the peasantry and acted as percolators of radical ideas. It is noteworthy that many of them were active in Congress work for quite some time. Further, most of these early Krishak Samiti activists of rural origin were non-local people, that is, persons who had come from outside the district, did not belong to peasant families and exercised considerable influence over the local society. Soon, however, they were joined by local Hindu and Muslim activists coming from peasant families.

Slowly but steadily the Krishak Samiti began to spread its influence and build up its organization. The *babus* from Jalpaiguri town who had, as seen earlier, been looked upon with some suspicion won the admiration of the peasants through their tireless work and propagation of concrete issues and demands vitally affecting different sections of the rural population, particularly the poorer sections. Soon these *naya* (new) *swadeshi babus*, as they were known[4], came to be addressed as 'comrades' indicating a process of fraternization. Formation of Union-level Krishak Samitis and enrolment of members began in earnest.

District Krishak Samiti conference

An office of the local Krishak Samiti was set up at Maidan Dighi in Boda. Four bighas (1.33 acre) of land were donated by Nandeswar Barman, a small peasant, for the purpose. By end–May 1939, that is, within six months of the formation of the District Organizing Krishak Samity 12 Union Krishak Samitis were formed and the number of members enrolled exceeded 1,000[5]. It was decided to hold the first regular conference of the District Krishak Samiti at Maidan Dighi in the last week of June and a Reception Committee was formed with Anath Saran Gautam as Chairman and Mahinath Jha as Secretary[6]. Hectic preparations were made to make the conference a success, membership drive was stepped up and a drive for collection of money, rice/paddy, vegetables etc. was also launched. Sachin Das Gupta, Satish Lahiri and Gurudas Roy published an appeal to the town people to make the conference a success and Gurudas wrote a three column write-up entitled 'Krishak Sabha O Congress'[7]. Explaining the specific role of Krishak Sabha and its relation with the Congress he stated: 'Congress is our national organization [platform]. As a constituent of the nation each of the anti-imperialist classes are with.n it. [But] Krishak Sabha is the class organization of the peasants. It is composed of only those peasant activists who support the peasants and their separate class organization... It is not an organization for opposing Congress. Opposition to Congress is against the ideal and principles of Krishak Sabha'.

Issues and demands

The conference was held on 27 June 1939. Large numbers of peasants including poor peasants and *adhiars* and other sections of rural population attended the conference. Many progressive-minded people of the Jalpaiguri town came to the conference[8]. Dinesh Lahiri, a peasant and Communist leader of Rangpur, hoisted the Red Flag and Abdullah Rasul, the then Secretary of the

Bengal Provincial Kisan Sabha(BPKS), presided over the conference. His presidential address, published in full in *Ananda Bazar Patrika* of 29 June 1939, was significant. It was one of the earliest Krishak Sabha documents in Bengal, perhaps the earliest one, in which the *jotedars* were considered as a distinct component of the agrarian structure and the question of exploitation of *adhiars* by the *jotedars* was addressed[9]. With reference to the consequences of the Permanent Settlement Rasul said:

> At present they [the peasants] are either doing labour as *adhiars* on land or trying to meet their hunger by working as agricultural labourers on daily-wage basis.
>
> In north Bengal in particular this preponderance of *adhiars* is a very big problem within the peasant movement. Being placed in a helpless situation, the peasants get *adhi* land for cultivation on condition of giving a higher rate [share] of produced crops. They do not have any permanent right [*swatwa*] over the land, they are bound to surrender the land at the sweet will of *jotedars*. Again, when at the time of cultivation because of their want they take paddy loan [*dhan karja*] they take it on condition that at the time of repayment after four or five months they will have to pay an interest of at least a half maund [paddy] on a principal of one maund [paddy]... The root of this exploitation is the Permanent Settlement. Krishak Samiti wants its abolition. The peasant wants land. He will not get it without its [Permanent Settlement] abolition[10].

Adhiar problem

Though Rasul was not clear in his perception of the *jotedar-adhiar* problem and did not raise any demand with regard to this problem other than the abolition of the Permanent Settlement, his speech unmistakably shows that the contention made by some scholars to the effect that the Krishak Sabha was not aware of the importance of the problem till the Tebhaga movement of 1946–7 is not correct[9]. Rasul also made a particular reference to the necessity of building unity of peasants and workers. He said:

> There are many tea gardens in your district. In those gardens thousands of labourers work... There too exists exploitation and oppression on the part of vested interests. So they are also an exploited class like you. They are your brothers and sisters and their joy and sorrow are tied with your joy and sorrow in one thread. There is no conflict between their struggle and your struggle.

With reference to anti-imperialist and anti-capitalist revolution he said:

> The united revolution [struggle] will make that [abolition of imperialism and capitalism] possible. So at the time of struggle of the tea garden workers you are not to hesitate in extending all possible help to them. If you can strengthen your movement and the workers can strengthen their movement and these two movements can make advances in co-operation with each other, then you will be able to achieve revolution—the revolution that would bring freedom for the country and emancipation of humanity.

The conference adopted eleven resolutions relating to peasant demands[11]. Among these, two deserve particular mention. For it is around the demands made in these two resolutions and also some other demands that the first major agrarian agitation involving peasants and *adhiars* in particular in parts of Jalpaiguri district and those of neighbouring Dinajpur and Rangpur districts broke out in the last quarter of the year and the early months of 1940. One of the resolutions stated, 'This Conference makes sharp protest against the collection of *gandi* or *tola* (tolls) in *hats* and markets from the peasants and demands immediate abolition of this practice'. The other resolution contained a demand specifically relating to the *adhiars*. It said:

> The conference makes sharp protest against the collection of interest on the paddy that is lent out to the *adhiars* as seed and for the purpose of consumption at the time of cultivation and demands the immediate abolition of this practice and institution of interest-free similar advance of paddy.

The resolution did not say anything about the various exactions realized from the *adhiars* on share of produce. Yet the resolution was significant, for here, according to available records, for the first time a clearly formulated demand relating to the problems of *adhiars* in terms of movement was raised at any district or provincial level of Bengal Provincial Krishak Sabha.

The remaining nine resolutions passed at the conference demanded (1) abolition of the zamindari system without payment of any compensation, (2) modification and amendment of the *mahajani* Bill in the interest of the peasants, (3) provision of rent-free grazing land, (4) free compulsory primary education without any tax, (5) payment of salary to the Union Board out of government funds and spending of money collected as *chaukidari* tax on rural development, (6) introduction of Tenancy Act in the *khas mahal* area, (7) right to collection of firewood etc. and grazing of domestic cattle in the forest areas and (8) release of all political prisoners. In one resolution it protested against the Federation Plan and efforts to intensify imperialist exploitation and called upon all the anti-imperialist forces to prepare for launching a struggle.

From the conference an executive Committee was elected with Kaviraj Satish Lahiri, a veteran Congress leader, Jogesh Dutta, a political worker who in 1929–30 had connexions with a revolutionary group and Dr Abanidhar Guha Neogy, a progressive-minded Congress worker as members of the Presidium, Gurudas Roy as Secretary, Sachin Das Gupta and Sachin Dutta as two Assistant Secretaries and Chunilal Bose as Office Secretary. Madhab Datta was elected as one of the members of the Executive Committee[12].

Post-conference activity

In July and August, the activities of the Krishak Samiti were stepped up. Enrolment of Krishak Samiti members and volunteers was continued and meetings and demonstrations were frequently held around peasant as well as broader political issues. Release of political prisoners was at that time a major issue throughout Bengal. In Jalpaiguri town a Political Prisoners Release Committee was formed with Sachindranath as Secretary. Krishak Samiti too took up the issue. On 15 July a peasant meeting was held at Maidan Dighi to demand release of political prisoners and also to protest against education cess[13]. On 30 July a day-long *hartal* was observed in Boda in support of the release demand and in the afternoon of that day meetings were held and processions were brought out in different places under Boda and Debiganj P.S.[14] On 31 August at the initiative of Left Coordination Committee a well-attended meeting with Birendra Nath Datta in the chair was held in Jalpaiguri town. On 1 September the All India Peasants Day was observed. A large number of peasants came from the rural areas and a big meeting was held on the Arya Natya Samaj ground in Jalpaiguri town. Satish Lahiri presided over the meeting and, among others, Sachin Das Gupta, Khagendra Nath Das Gupta, Charu Chandra Sanyal, Gurudas Roy and Debananda Roy spoke[15].

Women's organizations

It deserves particular mention that the Krishak Samiti leaders made a special effort to organize rural women. Stories from *Mahabharat* and *Ramayana*, such as the derobing of Draupadi and the acquiescence of Dhritarastra, Bhisma and others to such acts were used to arouse a sense self-respect among women and organize them. At the initiative of Sulekha Roy and Usha Roy a women's organization or *mahila* samiti, the first organization of the rural women in Jalpaiguri, was formed in Boda on 23 July. On that day a meeting and demonstration of about 200 women and girls was held[16]. On 30 July a women's procession led by Sulekha Roy, Sarojini Roy and Usha Roy[17] was brought out to demand release of political prisoners and later a women's meeting was held. Sulekha Roy and Pratima Debi, wife of Bhola Majumdar, a locally active Congress worker, explained the purpose behind the meeting[18].

HAT TOLA MOVEMENT

The Krishak Samiti activity, however, did not for long remain confined to general propaganda and campaign. Soon the campaign took the shape of concrete struggles and actions around specific issues. The first issue upon which the simmering agrarian discontent and anger of the oppressed and exploited peasants burst out was that of *hat tola* or tolls collected by those who owned or leased in and controlled the *hats*.

The practice of toll collection was found not only in Boda–Debiganj–Pachagar and adjacent areas. This was a practice that was widely prevalent in parts many of Bengal. From time to time broad sections of the rural population resorted to protest actions against this practice in different districts of Bengal. The incidents of *hat* boycott and setting up of rival *hats* in the *khas mahal* areas of Jalpaiguri in 1921–22 were in part connected with this practice on the part of *khas mahal* as well as tea gardens. Yet it remained a widespread practice in Jalpaiguri—both in the *khas mahal* area and the Permanently Settled tract—and other districts.

In view of extensive rural resentment against this practice the Government of Bengal made an enquiry in 1940. It was estimated that in that year there were about 6,000 *hats* in the province owned mostly by local zamindars who either managed them with their own staff or leased them out to *ijaradars* on a yearly rent. In almost all of these *hats* tolls were collected at exorbitant rates. The *tola* was collected from not only the sellers but in some cases also from the buyers[19].

The following table gives an approximate idea of the tolls levied at a *hat* in the year 1939.

Sl.No	Commodity	Load	Value	Toll Levies
1.	Vegetables	Head	Upto Rs 2	3 to 6 pices
2.	Vegetable	*Bhar*/Cart	Rs 2 to Rs 5	as.1
3.	Parched rice	*Bhar*	Rs 2 to Rs 5	as.1
4.	Pulses, salt, etc.	Head/*Bhar*	Rs 5 to Rs 10	as.to as.2
5.	Fish	—	Rs 3 to Rs 5	as.1
6.	Fowls	—	Rs 2 to Rs 4	as.1
7.	Goats	—	Rs 5 to Rs 10	as.2
8.	Paddy/rice	Cart	Rs 20 to Rs 30	as.2 to as.4

NOTE: *Bhar* refers to two baskets hung by a sling from the shoulders. Four pices made one anna and sixteen annas one rupee.
SOURCE: GOB, Agriculture and Irrigation Department Agriculture Branch 74/5. I owe this reference and information to Maitreya Ghatak.

In some *hats* the men of zamindars and *ijaradars* used to collect Rs 2 per cow and Rs 4 per buffalo as expenses for issuing receipts certifying such sales. The Senior Marketing Officer, Government of Bengal, conducting this investigation estimated that the income of a zamindar or an *ijaradar* from a *hat* was usually between Rs 1,500 to Rs 3,000 per annum.

Agitation against tola

Naturally enough, such toll collection had been a major issue of peasant discontent in different districts of Bengal in the past and from time to time disturbances took place around this issue. That Jalpaiguri district too witnessed such troubles has been noticed in an earlier chapter. Those disturbances were, however, essentially of a sporadic nature. But in the latter part of 1939 this discontent found coordinated manifestation in parts of Jalpaiguri as well as the neighbouring Dinajpur district.

In the Boda, Debiganj and Pachagar *thana* areas the hats were either directly owned and controlled by the Koch Bihar Raj Estate and Baikunthapur Estate or leased out by these two estates to influential big *jotedars* of the area. As elsewhere in Bengal, in these areas too the *hat* owners and *ijaradars* exacted levy from the stall holders as well as the peasants who came to the *hats* to sell or purchase something at exorbitant rates. The levy was exacted in some cases in cash and in some other cases in kind. In the case of cash collection, there was a fixed, though quite high, rate. In the case of collection in kind, the amount was determined totally arbitrarily. Even the poor peasants and *adhiars* who sold only a few seers of paddy or a meagre quantity of vegetables or some poultry products, usually a few eggs or some milk, were not spared. Not infrequently, such a toll was collected from the purchasers too. This was a form of exploitation that affected all sections of the peasantry and even small and middle *jotedars*. Various other sections of rural population, such as teachers, village doctors, small shopkeepers etc. too were subjected to this exaction.

In pursuance of the District Krishak Samity Conference resolution the peasants were called upon to refuse payment of *tola*. A movement around this issue took place in the closing months of the year 1939. The first action took place at Maidan Dighi *hat* under Boda P.S. With red flags and *lathis* (bamboo sticks) *kisan* volunteers marched into the *hat* and raised slogans: 'No tola payment by the Kisans'; 'Destroy the zamindari system', 'Down with the oppression of the zamindars and *ijaradars*' etc. The hat *ijaradar* did not remain a silent spectator to this. He and his hired men threatened the peasants. But that was of no avail. The police *daroga* came and took the side of the *ijaradar*. But his intervention too failed to cow down the peasants. Later on the Sadar S.D.O. came and in his presence a meeting was held. The Kisan Sabha leaders were asked to send their representatives. Gurudas Roy or Madhab Datta did not go to the meeting. Instead they sent a peasant delegation under the leadership of Radhamohan Barman, a local Rajbansi peasant cadre. Eventually a compromise settlement was arrived at. The assertion of the peasant right, the fact that they themselves could argue their case before the *jotedars* and *ijaradars* and even a powerful government official as equals, and the achievement of a settlement in their favour gave new confidence to the peasants[20].

The victory of 'no tola' campaign in Maidan Dighi *hat* enthused the peasants in Boda, Debiganj and Pachagar *thana* areas and the movement against arbitrary fixation and collection of toll spread to other *hats*. In many of the small *hats* in those areas the toll rate was reduced and in a number of small *hats* the toll collection came to a stop.

The toll collection, however, remained in force in some of the big *hats* and this became an issue of confrontation. One of these, the Boda *hat* was owned and directly controlled by the powerful Koch Bihar Raj Estate. Armed retainers and Koch Bihar Raj officials were posted there. The *thana* too was located there. So it was not easy for the Krishak Samiti and the peasants to agitate for the abolition of *tola* in Boda . There the movement took a novel form. At the call of the Krishak Samiti, the peasants boycotted the Boda *hat* and set up a *'dasher hat'* or people's *hat* outside the area of the Raj Estate. Thus, *tola* collection came to a stop in the Boda *hat* too[21]. The *ijaradar* of Lakshmir *hat* under Debiganj P.S. was a Muslim and he tried to arouse communal passion and in that way to divide the peasants. But that attempt was foiled by the unity of Hindu and Muslim peasants. *Tola* collection in Lakshmir *hat* too came to a stop. This was followed by stoppage of *tola* collection in Pachagar *hat*, one of the biggest *hats* in the area[22]. In response to these peasant agitations the District Board had to come forward. It fixed toll rates and directed the *hat ijaradars* to collect toll according to the rates fixed by the Board[23].

Spread of the campaign

This movement against *tola* collection did not remain confined to the areas within the Jalpaiguri district and soon spread to adjacent areas in the Dinajpur district. *Kalir Mela* or 'Kali's Fair' held every year during the days of Kali Puja (October–November) at Dumduma, stuated within the Thakurgaon Subdivision of Dinajpur district and separated from the Jalpaiguri district by a river called Bhulli, was famous as a centre for cattle purchase and sale. Thousands of people from Jalpaiguri, Dinajpur and Rangpur and even from nearby Bihar districts came to the *Mela*. The zamindar to whose estate the *Mela* ground belonged, employed his men for recording the sale and purchase of cattle and issuing necessary receipts. But for doing this work the *hat* authority charged Rs 2 per cow/bullock and Rs.4 per buffalo as *lekhai kharach* or recording expenses[24].

There was widespread resentment among the peasants and also the traders against this excessive recording expenses. The success of 'no *tola*' movement in adjacent areas of Jalpaiguri district made the peasants and broad sections of rural population attending the fair restive and they raised the demand for reduction of charges for issuing receipts and recording sales and purchases in *Kalir Mela*. The Union Krishak Samiti committees in Boda and Debiganj pressed the leadership for action to put a stop to the oppressive practices at the *Kalir Mela*[25].

In response to this, the Krishak Samiti leaders of Jalpaiguri decided to launch an agitation. Volunteers were enrolled and a camp was organized on the bank of the Bhulli river. Pramada Chakrabarty, the village priest turned into Krishak Samiti activist, was selected as the captain of the volunteer force. At some point of time, contact was made with the Dinajpur Krishak Samiti leaders. On the day fixed for action hundreds of trained and well organized peasant volunteers led by Gurudas Roy, Madhab Datta and Pramada Chakrabarty crossed the river and marched to the *Kalir Mela*. They carried with them red flags and *lathis*, spades and *bankua* or bamboo poles used to carry goods on shoulder. Several hundred volunteers came to the Mela place under the leadership of Dinajpur District Krishak Samiti too.

On entering the fair the volunteers raised the slogans: 'The charge for recording has to be reduced', 'Down with the oppression of the *mela* authority' etc. Peasants of all categories and dealers in cattle, many of whom were also peasants, supported the demand. But the *mela* authority was not in a mood to concede the demand. Armed police force came from Thakurgaon in Dinajpur. Section 144 prohibiting assembly of five or more than five persons was promulgated. Wearing of Samiti uniforms, such as red shirts and red caps and blowing of whistles were banned[26]. But the Krishak Samiti leaders belonging to both the districts resorted to a form that had earlier been adopted in the case of Boda *hat*. In a bid to avoid direct and physical confrontation with the *hat* authority and police, they called upon the peasants and traders to boycott the *Kalir Mela*. At the call of the Krishak Samiti, a *Dasher Mela* or 'People's Fair' was set up at a place on the other side of the Bhulli river and within Jalpaiguri district. Krishak Samiti activists began to write and issue receipts without any payment. As a result of this, the *Kalir Mela* was in the danger of being abandoned and the *mela* authority considered that this would entail a huge financial loss. Under the circumstances, the zamindar's men climbed down and agreed to charge only as. 2 per cow/bullock and as. 4 per buffalo[27].

After the success achieved in *Kalir Mela* movement in November, the *hat* agitation spread to those *hats* in which the toll collection was still being made. In an official report for the second half of December 1939 it was stated that the agitation 'has affected *hats* which are leased from an estate belonging to the Maharaja of Cooch Behar, and has succeeded in bringing about the closure of three *hats* and their re-opening on new sites without tolls'[28].

Significance of the movement

A brief account of these movements against toll collection in *hats* and fairs in Jalpaiguri district and also neighbouring Dinajpur and Rangpur districts was given in the Report placed before the Bengal Provincial Kisan Conference held at Panjia (Jessore district) on 8 and 9 June 1940. The Report stated that with the outbreak of the Second World War in September 1939 ordinances virtually prohibiting all meetings and processions throughout the province were promulgated. Many Krishak Samiti workers were arrested and jailed and numerous workers were warned against their movements and activities. The Report observed that for some reason or other this attack was less in Jalpaiguri district. 'Taking advantage of this opportunity the comrades working in that district created a situation of struggle among the peasants'[29]. Considerable success was achieved in a number of struggles. A major issue was that of collection of tolls at exorbitant rates. 'The movement [against this] first began in Jalpaiguri and later on spread to Dinajpur and Rangpur'[30]. It was also reported that 'the success with which about one thousand peasant volunteers and workers of Jalpaiguri and Dinajpur put to a stop in November [1939] the unjust exactions made by the zamindar in the Kalir Mela' led to the launching of extensive peasant movement in these two districts[31]. The All India Kisan Sabha (AIKS) reported, 'This year our committees and volunteers [of Jalpaiguri and Dinajpur district] launched with 900 volunteers a very successful fight against the tax [hat toll] and saved many thousand rupees of the poor peasants'[32].

The success of the *Kalir Mela* and other *hat* movements, to quote from the AIKS Report, 'proved a particularly sensational event in these areas and established the position of Kisan Sabha among the peasants'. In Jalpaiguri district, in terms of organization the impact of the 'no tola' movement was such that many of the primary Congress Committees in the Debiganj *thana* area were transformed into Krishak Samiti units[33]. In the Boda, Debiganj, Pachagar and Sadar *thana* areas peasants, particularly the poor peasants and *adhiars*, began to enthusiastically enrol themselves as Krishak Samiti members. Krishak Samiti units were set up at 15 unions and more than 2000 members were enrolled[34]. The *hat* movements and the *Kalir Mela* campaign in particular also exhibited tactical wisdom, innovative capacity and organizational ability of the Krishak Samiti leadership and peasant activists. Yet another aspect was that the movements based on a broad peasant unity badly hit the authority and economic power of the feudal/semi-feudal interests and their agents and also helped to reduce the fears in the minds of peasants about the police and local bureaucracy.

A NEW DIMENSION

The successful agitation against the arbitrary toll collection provided great impetus to the peasant movement. During the harvesting season in late 1939 and early 1940 the movement assumed a new dimension and a more militant outlook. The *hat* movement was based on broad peasant unity and drew the support of even sections of *jotedars*, particularly the lower ones, and the middle strata of rural population. The movement centred upon popular perception of what was just / unjust obligation.

This movement was immediately followed by and partly overlapped with one that was based on poor peasants, particularly the *adhiars*. The movement came to be known as the *adhiar* movement. It centred upon several aspects of relationship between the *jotedars* and *adhiars*.

Aspects of the adhiar problem

Along with the *adhi bhag* or half share, the *jotedars* collected several *abwabs* or additional levies which combined to intensify the oppression and exploitation of the *adhiars*. The latter were compelled by the *jotedars* to part with large portions of their produce at various points of time throughout the year. It may be recalled that Milligan in his *Settlement Report* had hinted at imposition of some fresh exactions on the *adhiars*. It seems that over the years, particularly in the inter-war years, still more new levies were imposed. By 1939 this became most perverse.

One of these collections was known as *gola mochani* or expenses for cleaning the store house at the rate of half a maund of paddy for every *adhiar*. Another levy was *angina chancha* or expenses on account of cleaning the threshing yard at the rate of half a maund per *adhiar*. Yet one more levy was *khamaru* or expense incurred for the maintenance of the person who helped to divide the crop at the rate of half a maund per each seven maund of paddy. *Dhula khaoa* or expense for spreading straw inside the bullock cart of the *jotedar* (half a maund per *adhiar*) was still another form of levy[35]. *Barkandaji* or expenses for maintenance of guards, *hari sabha* or expenses on account of religious of gathering, *hati bandha* and *ghora bandha* (maintenance of elephants and horses) were some more forms of levy. It is possible to mention some other forms of similar levies. The picture that emerges from a review of the various exactions made by the *jotedars* suggests that the extortions were entirely arbitrary, unjust and highly exploitative.

But the *adhiar's* obligation to the *jotedar* did not end with the payment of half share and all these exactions. The impoverished *adhiar* almost universally had to take consumption loan of paddy and seed loan usually from his *giri* or *jotedar*. Such borrowings were made mainly under three systems: (a) *dera bari*, (b) *duno bari* and (c) *dar kata*. Under *dera bari* and *duno bari* the *bargadars* had to repay the paddy borrowed at the rate of 50 per cent (*dera*) or 100 per cent (*duno*) interest for a loan incurred for a period of five or six months. Under the *dar kata* system a certain quantity of paddy was lent during the lean season in terms of prevailing market price which was very high and the loan was calculated in terms of money value of the paddy borrowed. Repayment had to be made after harvesting of the crop in the form of whatever amount of paddy was available at that amount of money. The price during repayment being low, the *bargadar* had to repay much more in terms of paddy than he had borrowed. Whatever might have been the particular system under which a *bargadar* borrowed, the consequence was further immiserization. Giving an account of the economic condition of the *adhiars*, *Ananda Bazar Patrika* (7 February 1940) observed that many *adhiars* remained indebted after paying to the *jotedar* his due half share.

The customary practice, as noted in an earlier chapter, was to stack all paddy after the harvesting was over in the *jotedar's kholan* or threshing place. This practice meant that the *adhiars* lacked any leverage and were under the total grip of their *giris*. Under the circumstances, the place where the crop was divided was a critical issue.

All this had created an acute resentment in the minds of the *adhiars* who constituted a very large proportion, according to a contemporary newspaper account, no less than 75 per cent[36] of the total population of Boda, Debiganj and Pachagar areas. The success of the 'no tola' campaign stirred them and provided a new confidence to them. The Krishak Samiti did not fail to gauge the minds of the exploited and oppressed *adhiars* and during the harvesting season in the winter months of 1939–40 it put forward several demands: 'Reduce interest rates on *karja dhan*' or consumption loan of paddy; 'No interest on seed loan'; 'Put an end to all *abwabs*' or unjust and additional exaction; and '*Nij kholane dhan tolo*' or stack paddy in your own *kholan*. The latter slogan '*nij kholane dhan tolo*' was put forward to assert the *adhiars'* right in the choice of the threshing place and protect their interests from the various illegal exactions made by the *jotedars* and their hirelings. The position was such that once the crop was stacked in the jotedar's *kholan*, the *jotedar* got unhampered control over the crop.

The adhiar movement

The *adhiars* in Boda, Debiganj and Pachagar *thanas* and parts of Sadar *thana* enthusiastically responded to the Krishak Samiti's call. It was as if a dam was burst asunder and the peasant movement gathering a new momentum entered into a new phase. In contrast to the earlier 'no *tola*' campaign, the new movement which came to be known as the *adhiar* movement gave expression to the discontent and demands of the poor and landless peasants.

The Krishak Samiti had raised a volunteer crops during the months of 'no *tola*' agitation. These Samiti volunteers and workers marched from *hat* to *hat* and village to village and called upon the *adhiars* to resist the oppression of the *jotedars*. It was officially reported from Jalpaiguri district that in early December 'a crowd of Red Shirts armed with lathis appeared at some *hats*'[37]. For the latter half of December officials reported tension and disputes between *jotedars* and *adhiars*[38]. With the help of the Samiti's volunteers and workers the *adhiars* collectively harvested the paddy and stacked it in their own places or *khamars*[39]. The movement spread to the Thakurgaon subdivision of the Dinajpur district and Domar thana area of the Rangpur district too[40].

The *jotedars* and their men used all kinds of threat against the *adhiars* and armed police pickets were posted at places. The *jotedars* also tried to sow all kinds of confusion in the mind of the peasants and raised various divisive issues. The Rajbansi Hindu *jotedars*, many of whom were supporters of the Kshatriya Samiti, called upon the Rajbansi Hindu peasants and *adhiars* not to believe the upper caste *bhatia* leaders. Muslim *jotedars* too resorted to communal propaganda[41]. But neither the repression nor the disruptive tactics succeeded. Faced with such a situation in January 1940 the officials of Jalpaiguri and also Dinajpur district called joint meetings of *jotedars* and *adhiars* and tried to settle the disputes[42]. These meetings were attended by local CPI leaders too. In both the districts the local officials conceded some of the demands of the movement. They agreed that all illegal exactions were to be stopped and laid down the maximum rate of interest on paddy loan. But they also ordered that the paddy had to be stacked in the *jotedars' kholans*. In Jalpaiguri the *adhiars* refused to agree to such a settlement and the movement continued.

Offensive of the jotedars and administration

Initial response of the local and district administration to the demands of the *adhiars* and Krishak Samiti, as stated above, was not unfavourable. But soon there was a sharp change in its attitude. Musharraff Hossain who was a Minister in the Huq ministry and who himself had large *jotedari* interests came to

Jalpaiguri, held meetings with the *jotedars* and called for total suppression of the movement. Police repression was let loose, Section 144 banning meetings, demonstrations, etc. was promulgated in Boda, Debiganj, Pachagar and Jalpaiguri *thana* areas and arrest warrants were issued against Gurudas Roy, Madhab Datta and other leaders. At places clashes between the police and peasants took place[43].

While continuing the *adhiar* agitation, the Krishak Samiti and CPI leaders did not lose sight of the fact that the agitation was also a part of the freedom struggle. It was decided to observe the Independence Day—26 January 1940—in a befitting manner, hoist the National Flag and hold a public meeting at Panchpeer under Boda P.S. Under the leadership of Laltu Barman, a militant poor peasant activist of the Samiti, the peasants brought out a procession and assembled in large numbers. The Sadar S.D.O. was present with a large police contingent and tried to break the rally. But the peasants were in a militant mood. A scuffle took place in which the peasants led by Ujani Barmani, wife of Laltu Barman, overturned the S.D.O's car and snatched the daroga's cap. It was an explosive situation. But because of the tactful handling of the situation by the S.D.O. any large-scale clash was avoided[44].

A setback

However, from the next day large scale arrests began to take place not only in Panchpeer but throughout the area of *adhiar* agitation. The Kisan Sabha office at Maidandighi was smashed to the ground by the police. Repression and police action were intensified. Marches of armed forces were undertaken. More than 200 peasants were arrested and many of them were not given bail. The repression was such that many peasants had to leave their villages and live in open fields and jungles for many days[45]. The police forcibly took away the paddy stacked at the *adhiars'* places to the *jotedars' kholans*. Even after this, the movement continued. In the second half of February it was officially reported that 'the Krishak Samiti created trouble in the areas under Boda and Debiganj police stations of Sadar Subdivision and held unauthorised meetings'[46]. Further repressive action was taken and more arrests were made. Some time in the mid-1940s Gurudas Roy, Madhab Datta and Monoranjan Das Gupta, a Krishak Samiti organizer, were arrested and after their trial were sentenced to prison for varying terms. In its Panjia Conference Report the BPKS observed that the police repression in Jalpaiguri was so severe that the movement suffered a serious setback[47].

CPI's anti-war campaign

At this point it should be mentioned that while the *adhiar* movement was the major factor behind this police repression, it was not the only factor. Following the outbreak of the War, the CPI Politbureau in a resolution adopted in October 1939 characterized the War as an 'imperialist war' and explicitly called for utilizing it for achievement of national freedom. In conformity with this political perspective, the local CPI leaders carried on anti-war propaganda through squads, meetings and posters[48]. This also brought the wrath of local officials and police and in December 1939 Madhab Datta was externed from the area. In January 1940 Sachindra Nath was warned under Rule 26 of the Defence of India Rules[49]. It should be added, however, that despite repression and temporary setback suffered by the Communists in the peasant movement, they and the various mass organizations led by them, the Students Federation in particular, continued to make their presence felt in the political life of the town and areas of their activity. Their policy of uncompromising anti-imperialism and building up of broadest possible unity of all nationalist elements enabled the CPI to make progress. All attempts to isolate the Communists from the main body of nationalism failed and even conservative Congressmen were forced to co-operate with them.

Sachindra Nath, the district CPI Secretary, was able to evade arrest and went underground. Some time between mid-1940 and late 1941 he was joined by Naresh Chakrabarty, Charu Majumdar, the future leader of the Naxalbari movement and then a young man of indomitable energy, Parimal Mitra, a medical student who had earlier been active in the student front and later on gave up his studies to do fulltime political work, Govinda Kundu, Abani Talapatra, Sudhin Moitra and Satyendra Narayan Majumdar, all of them being students or former students of Jackson Medical School, Paresh Mitra, a student, Saroj Gupta, Anil Mukherjee and a few others. Of them, the first three engaged themselves in work among the peasants, while the rest were active in other fronts.

SIGNIFICANCE OF ADHIAR MOVEMENT

Despite the setback suffered by the movement, it had several economic as well as political achievements. In terms of the immediate demands of the movement it succeeded in forcing the *jotedars* to agree to a reduction in the interest rate on consumption loan. It was also under the impact of the continuing movement around this issue that in mid-1942 the district administration officially announced limits on interest rate on such loans[50].

The significance of the *adhiar* movement and also the immediately preceding *hat tola* agitation for agrarian movement and organization in Jalpaiguri district and the adjacent districts of Dinajpur and Rangpur and, as a matter of fact, in Bengal as a whole can hardly be exaggerated. One thing is that the *hat* and *adhiar* movements enabled the Communist Left and Krishak Samiti of these districts to create and establish an extensive support base among the peasants—both Rajbansi Hindu and Rajbansi Muslim—in wide areas of these districts. These movements also drew the sympathy and support of sections of the middle class in Jalpaiguri town. The fact that Pritinidhan Roy, a lawyer and also the DCC President at that time, and Nagendra Nath Mahalanabish, an eminent lawyer with no known radical inclination, defended the arrested peasants and leaders without charging any fee indicates this[51].

A new phenomenon

The *adhiar* movement had still greater significance and wider implications for the agrarian movement in Bengal. The movement around *hat* tolls was the first movement in Jalpaiguri district organized specifically around peasant grievances and in that way was important for the district. But it had a very broad class basis and gave expression to the discontent and protest of wide sections of the rural population. Thus, it did not basically differ with the sort of peasant movement being organized till then in Bengal. Virtually all peasant movements were based on the demands and grievances of occupancy tenants and substantial peasants around the issues of rent enhancement, collection of *abwabs*, oppressive practices by the zamindars and other such issues. Even the peasant agitations organized by the BPKS or its units till 1939, by and large, represented global movements of tenants and under-tenants against the zamindars.

The *adhiar* movement in large parts of the three north Bengal districts was a distinctly new phenomenon. It was the first peasant movement in Bengal that organized and involved the *adhiars* or *bargadars*, one of the poorest and most oppressed and exploited sections of the peasantry, and unambiguously and firmly put forward their demands. The *adhiar* movement (and also the movement against the *nankar* and *bhaoali* systems in the Sherpur *pargana* of Mymensingh district in 1938 and 1939)[52] for the first time in Bengal gave expression to a more or less overt conflict between a most exploited section of the peasantry on the one hand and *jotedars* on the other. And it needs to be stressed that the Krishak Samiti and Communists of Jalpaiguri played a pioneering role in bringing to the forefront issues relating to the exploitation of the *adhiars* and also in the unfolding of the *adhiar* movement.

The movement also had elements of violence. The refusal of the *adhiars* to stack the harvested paddy at the *jotedars'* place and the stacking of it at places selected by the *adhiars* was an open defiance. It led at places to clashes with the *jotedars*, their men as well as the police. This was also a new aspect.

It is not that prior to 1939 *bargadar* agitation did not take place anywhere in Bengal. In the mid and late 1920s a few movements took place in parts of Mymensingh, Dacca and Jessore districts that voiced the grievances of the *bargadars*. In the movement in Jessore district the *bargadars* even raised the demand for two-third of the crops as their share thus anticipating the historic *tebhaga* movement of 1946–7[53]. But these movements reflecting a sort of autonomous pressure and demand on the part of the *bargadars* were sporadic in nature and were organized by peasant associations that were essentially local groups lacking any co-ordination and unified leadership[54]. In 1938 and 1939 too some 'troubles' between the *bhagchasis* or share-croppers and their landlords were reported from parts of Bogra, Faridpur, Birbhum, 24-Parganas and Midnapore districts[55]. But most of these too were of a sporadic and localized nature.

One major significance of the 1939-40 *adhiar* movement in Jalpaiguri, Dinajpur and Rangpur districts lay in the fact that this was led and coordinated by the district units of a province-wide peasant organization. In terms of political outlook the middle-class leaders of the movement were Leftwing Congressmen and Communists.

The movement was highly significant on another account too. For the first time in the history of peasant movement in Bengal concrete demands relating to the *adhiars* or *bargadars* came into prominence. In early 1939 the BPKS in its celebrated Memorandum to the Bengal Land Revenue Commission or Floud Commission demanded granting of legal status of 'peasant owner' to the *bargadars*[56]. In the Memorandum the emphasis, however, was on the abolition of the zamindari system and the protection of interests of tenants and under-tenants. In fact, there was considerable ambiguity in the BPKS position. Further, nothing was planned by the BPKS in terms of organization and movement involving the *bargadars* before the 1939-40 agitation. This agitation, though built primarily through the initiative of district-level Krishak Samitis and partly under autonomous pressure from below and not conceived and organized by the BPKS, helped to draw in the *bargadars* within the fold of an organization and made them more aware of their rights than ever before. All this including the nature of organization and political attitude of the Samiti leaders created a potential for building up of a sustained movement of the *bargadars*. This significance of the *adhiar* agitation was recognized in the Panjia Conference Report of the BPKS[57]. It was partly under the impact of this agitation and partly in response to the Floud Commission's recommendation for two-thirds share for the *bargadars* that the Panjia Conference gave the call for *tebhaga*. The potential that was created was at least partly realized a few years later in the winter months of 1946–7.

Political dimension

The activities of the Samiti and its core leadership constituted of Communists brought about a new kind of politicization of the rural masses. As seen earlier, Boda and its adjacent areas had some tradition of nationalist political activity since the days of Non-Cooperation movement. But while remaining within the broad framework of militant nationalism and anti-imperialist struggle the Communist Left introduced elements of radical politics. Conscious attempts were made to make the peasants aware of the links between the struggle against the British Raj and the struggle against zamindars, *hat ijardars* and *jotedars-cum-mahajans*. Experience gained in running the Union-level Krishak Samitis and, more importantly, through the mass struggles heightened the political consciousness of the peasant masses. They also became aware, though in an embryonic form, of class politics. Communists with their internationalist outlook also brought to them radical and socialist ideas and also information about Soviet Russia and international political development.

Social dimensions

Several social aspects of both the agitation against *hat tola* and the *adhiar* movement deserve special mention. Peasant women, particularly those coming from poorer families, participated in these movements in large numbers. They took part in meetings and demonstrations and exhibited considerable militancy as exemplified by Ujani Barmani's deed mentioned earlier.

Another important aspect was the sort of solidarity and fraternization that was built up. Rajbansi Hindu and Rajbansi or local Muslim peasants developed a militant unity and foiled various divisive moves on the part of vested interests. The movement drew support from sections of rural petty bourgeoisie or intermediate strata, and individuals belonging to these strata emerged as prominent village or *thana*-level Samiti activists. The movement also helped to break down certain deep-rooted taboos and barriers. Thus, Mahinath Jha, a devout upcountry Brahman, and Pramada Chakrabarty, a village priest, took food in the company of not only Rajbansi Hindus but even Muslims[58].

Social composition of the leadership

As shown above, the initial moves for activizing the peasant masses came from Communist and Left leaders having an urban middle class origin. It is they who brought forth the idea of launching exclusive peasant organizations and mobilizing the peasantry along explicitly formulated peasant demands.

Their early contacts with the rural masses were through individuals who did not belong to peasant stock. Initially men of some influence with a modicum of education—village priests, village doctors, mechanics, landholders, traders, shop-keepers, etc.,—provided the leadership at the local level. This early leadership pattern helped to give wider dimensions and scope to the Krishak Samiti.

But with the spread of the Samiti activities and unfolding of the two peasant movements in quick succession in the closing months of 1939 brought about a radical change in the local and village-level leadership composition. There took place the emergence of several local-level leaders and workers coming from middle and poor peasant families: Radhamohan Barman, Nandakishore Barman, Umesh Barman, Laltu Barman, Kalikanta Barman, Indramohan Barman, Jarif Mohammed, Machhiruddin Sarkar etc. Many of them remained active and in the forefront of all activities till the partition in 1947 when areas of their activities went to East Pakistan (now Bangladesh) and some even thereafter. Of them, Radhamohan of Langalgaon under Boda P.S. was a poor peasant who owned a few *bighas* of land and also took some land under the *adhi* system. He was active in village social life even before he joined the Krishak Samiti. He emerged as a leader of considerable organizational ability and political skill through the *hat tola* and *adhiar* movement. Nandakishore was a small peasant and donated 2/3 bighas of land on which the Samiti office was constructed at Maidan Dighi. Umesh was an *adhiar*. Laltu too was an *adhiar* of remarkable courage and militancy. Jarif Mohammed was a small *jotedar* and shopkeeper at Pachagar and had college-level education. He was initiated into CPI politics when Abdul Halim was interned at Pachagar. With the growth of militancy and emphasis on issues touching poor peasants including *adhiars* in late 1939, the initial rural links like Anath Saran, Haripada Roy and Pramada Chakrabarty became reluctant to involve themselves directly in the Samiti's activity and movement[59]. But dynamism, organizational thrust and radicalism in terms of the demand as well as forms of action were provided by a new category of rural leaders. Those coming from the middle and poor peasant families constituted the active nucleus of the movement. Social composition of the participants, however, varied from time to time and from issue to issue. While in the case of the global movement against toll collection at *hats* participants were recruited from wide sections of rural population, the poor and *adhiar* peasants predominated the *adhiar* movement.

Related to the above was another social dimension of considerable significance. As noted earlier, the entire leadership of the Jalpaiguri

DCC was dominated by non-local immigrant upper-caste Hindus and the Rajbansi Hindus and Muslims had little effective participation at different levels of the Congress organization. The district leadership of the CPI and also Krishak Samiti was, again, predominantly from the same social group. However, the latter leadership not only belonged to a new generation, projected radical politics and had a view of the organization that was significantly different from that of the official Congress leadership, but also sought to forge a new kind of link with the masses on the basis of a radical programme. In doing so it activized both the Rajbansi Hindu and Rajbansi Muslim peasant masses to a noticeable extent and ensured active participation and involvement of the Rajbansi Hindu and Muslim cadres at different levels of the leadership structure of the Krishak Samiti on the basis of class issues. It is also important to note that at no point of time did the Kshatriya Samiti, the Rajbansi caste organization, succeed in mobilizing the Rajbansi peasant masses to the extent that the Krishak Samiti managed even at that early stage. Further, as indicated in the preceding chapter, the Muslim League of Jalpaiguri did not have any broad and significant support base among the local Muslims in those years.

Worker movement

The year 1939 also witnessed the beginning of the worker movement in Jalpaiguri. The Bengal Dooars Railway Workers Union, which had been established in late 1938 as a branch of the Bengal and Assam Railroad Workers Union, was busy organizing the railway workers and giving expression to their grievances and demands. From time to time meetings were held and demands placed before the railway authority. In a meeting held at Domohani on 19 June the Birendra Nath Das Gupta, General Secretary of the Union and Amrita Lal Mukherjee, the Organizing Secretary, called upon the workers and employees to organize themselves for realizing their demands[60]. In another meeting held at Domohani on 13 August 1939, the Branch Council of the Union discussed the demands for monthly salary and sick leave for the locoshop workers, good quarters for all the workers and employees, full time allowance for work on deputation etc. and resolved to observe 21 September as the All India Railway Workers Day[61].

With the outbreak of the War curbs were put on the activity of the Union. In January 1940 Amrita Lal who was also associated with the Rangpur unit of the CPI was accused of attempts to stir up discontent among the workers of the Eastern Bengal and Bengal Dooars Railway and a warning under Rule 26 of the Defence of India Rules was served on him[62]. Later on a scheme was drawn up to deal with any strikes in the BD Railway[63].

Some limitations

Worker movement and Left-led political activity in the district, however, continued to suffer from a basic weakness. The two and half lakh tea garden workers remained outside the sphere of any activity led by the nationalists and leftists. There is, however no reason to consider that there was no labour unrest in the gardens. But the nature and manifestation of such unrest need to be investigated.

One main reason for this state of affairs was the way in which the planters exercised their control over the labouring population and kept them in isolation. But so far as the Left is concerned, the lack of adequate numbers of able organizers and cadres was an additional and quite important factor behind this limitation. The latter factor also explains another major limitation—the limited geographical spread of the CPI-led political activity. For several years to come the CPI activities remained confined to the Boda–Debiganj–Pachagar areas and Jalpaiguri town.

State of Congress affairs

So far as the district Congress organization is concerned, in late 1939 and 1940 it became primarily involved in what may be considered as the Gandhi versus Subhas Bose controversy. In the developments following the Tripuri Congress, the overwhelming majority of the district Congress leadership including its top leaders like Khagendra Nath and Charu Chandra supported Subhas Chandra Bose. When the Forward Bloc was organized, most of the district leaders joined it[64] and for some time Khagendra Nath functioned as the Secretary of the Provincial Forward Bloc. While the controversy created considerable excitement among the political workers and politically aware elements, there was little political activity at the mass level. In the autumn of 1940 Gandhi launched the individual satyagraha programme. But it too failed to have any noticeable impact either in Jalpaiguri district or in the rest of Bengal.

10 Popular Upsurge, Nationalist Leadership and Left Alternative, 1940-47

THE WAR YEARS

In the early forties there was not much Congress-led mass activity. The Quit India movement caused comparatively little trouble to the district administration, except *hartals*, processions and student strikes in Jalpaiguri and Alipur Duar towns, damage to a few post offices, cutting of wires and seizure of Kumargram *thana* for a few hours[1]. Congress leaders considered dangerous (Khagendra Nath Das Gupta, Sasadhar Kar, Rabindra Nath Ṣikdar, Satish Lahiri and a few others, all of whom were in Forward Bloc at that time) were arrested in early August 1942. In protest against government repression seven municipal commissioners elected on Congress ticket resigned from the Municipality. However, students and younger elements (Badal Sarkar, Deben Sarkar, Ghanashyam Misra, Prabhat Bose, Anil alias Buddha Roy, Bidhan Sinha, Debabrata Majumdar, Sachin Lahiri, Rathin Roy and others—most of whom soon joined various non-Communist Left groups within the Congress[2]), helped to maintain a skeletal Congress organization and carried on nationalist activities in the form of observance of various 'Days'—Independence Day, Students Day, anti-Repression Day, Asti-Chimur Day etc. under the cover of a students organization. Some 'Days' (for example, the Asti-Chimur Day) were observed jointly not only with the CPI-led Students Federation but also with the District Muslim Students League[3].

In terms of future potential for anti-feudal, anti-imperalist popular movement, perhaps the single most significant development in the years between 1942 and 1945 was the spread of Communist activities in Jalpaiguri town and particularly in the rural areas of Debiganj, Pachagar and Boda *thanas*. Despite the repression following the *adhiar* agitation of 1939-40, the Communists of the district[4], with the help of Rajbansi Hindu and Muslim peasant activists like Radhamohan Barman, Kishori Roy, Bachchah Munsi, and Uday Roy and peasant women workers most notable of whom was Punyeswari Debi, affectionately called *Buri Ma* (old mother), were able to maintain an effective underground network. After the withdrawal of the ban on the CPI in July 1942, they fanned out to the villages, and open activities of the Krishak Samiti were revived. An order issued by Deputy Commissioner W.J. Palmer in early July in response to the *adhiar* agitation continuing since late 1939 (a) putting a ceiling of 25 per cent on interest on subsistence loan given by *jotedars* and *mahajans*, (b) prohibiting all sorts of *baje adayas* (arbitrary exactions in addition to 50 per cent share of produce), and (c) asking the *jotedars* for providing customary paddy loan[5] gave a new stimulus to the Krishak Samiti activities.

Though Jalpaiguri district was spared the severity of the 1943 famine and mortality rate was relatively low[6], mass suffering was nonetheless extensive and acute. Large sections of rural and town population suffered from acute scarcity of food and widespread starvation, large-scale land alienation, ruin of artisans, and malnutrition and diseases. The exploitative grip of the *jotedars* and *mahajans* over the rural masses, particularly small peasants, *adhiars* and day labourers was intensified through famine and wartime inflation[7].

The response of the Communists to this situation, as elsewhere, was mass-oriented activities. But in conformity with the overall policy of the Party during the People's War phase they not only tried to avoid frontal confrontation with the British Government and, for a short while, to play down struggle against *zamindars* and *jotedars* but even sought to restrain militant action against hoarders and black-marketeers. For example, *Janyuddha* (CPI's Bengali weekly) of 9 June 1943 reported with appreciation the successful resistance given by two peasant activists Vidya Barman and Suren Barman in Kaliaganj under Debiganj *thana* to an attempt made by a band of 'fifth columnist' young men to incite people to indulge in looting of paddy. However, within a few months there was a modification in their emphasis and their actual programme came to consist of campaigns against hoarders and blackmarketeers, formation of broad-based food committees, de-hoarding and vigil against smuggling, organization of famine relief and other related activities, and interventions against bureaucratic bungling and corruption[8]. In these activities, they were successful to a noticeable extent in drawing in diverse social and political elements, such as top Indian planters, Muslim League-minded leaders and workers, Hindu Mahasabhites, Kshatriya Samiti leaders, and even some Congressmen[9]. At the same time, they carried on anti-fascist campaigns, voiced the demand for the release of national leaders, and organized various other political, social and cultural activities with the help of several front organizations like Soviet Suhrid Samiti, Pragati Lekhak O Shilpi Sangha, Mahila Atma Raksha Samiti, etc. Noresh Chakraborty, Bimal Hoare, Biren Bose, Kalyani Das Gupta and Kalpana Neogy were some of those who took leading roles in these activities. Through such activities, particularly the relief and de-hoarding campaign, the Communists and the Krishak Samiti were able to expand and strengthen their influence and support base among both the Rajbansi Hindu and Rajbansi Muslim peasants in the Debiganj–Pachagar–Boda area to a marked extent and the sort of resentment and opposition the Communists at times faced in the town was not a problem in the rural areas[10]. The District Krishak Samiti conference held in Pachagar in late February 1944 raised, among other demands, the ones for introduction of rationing in both town and rural areas, import of foodgrains in deficit areas, suspension of rent collection in the distressed areas and reduction of interest on paddy loan[11]. The Krishak Samiti activities of those days, however, lacked any militant thrust against the government and also the rural vested interests.

These years also witnessed the growth and consolidation of the BDR Workers' Union. Parimal Mitra, a full-time Communist functionary, Bimal Das Gupta (1919 –), Assistant Station Master at Domohani where the Union office was located, Jadunath Singh and Lal Bahadur Chhetri (both traffic *jamadars*), points-man Man Singh and gangman Budhan were some of those who took prominent part in Union activities. Its activities included not only negotiations with the authority relating to workers' grievances, but also famine relief work including running of gruel kitchen and political propaganda. Several copies of *Janayuddha* and *Naya Rashmi* (Hindi) were subscribed and read out to those who could not read themselves[12].

Some of the activities of the Communists, particularly the campaign for seizure of food hoards and criticisms of the bureaucracy for its handling of the food and cloth situation, increasingly brought them into conflict with the administration. In fact, throughout the later years of the War the activities of the CPI in Jalpaiguri and other Bengal districts repeatedly drew adverse comments in secret official reports[13]. By March 1945 there were complaints that the Communists 'were causing disquiet to the District Officers of Jalpaiguri and Rangpur' and in Jalpaiguri they were 'inciting *adhiars* against *jotedars*'[14].

While the above were some of the political trends at the popular level in the district, there were certain other noteworthy happenings. One of these was that as a part of the changing political alignments at the provincial level in the early 1940s the Independent Scheduled Caste party leader Upendra Nath Barman became a minister in charge of Forest and Excise Departments in the Progressive Coalition Party ministry headed by Fazlul Huq or the second Fazlul Huq ministry (December 1941 to March 1943)[15]. This was for the first time that a Rajbansi, and, someone not from a landowning background, was made a minister. Though at times privately derided by sections of town *bhadraloks* as a *bahe*, the event of Barman's becoming a minister aroused considerable expectations among broad sections of people of the district. *Trisrota*, in its editorial, welcomed his appointment as a minister[16]. The District Mohammedan Association led by Jaharatullah Ahmad and the district unit of the Kshatriya Samiti gave him a joint reception[17] which once more indicated possibilities of political development along positive, non-communal lines and of joint activities. But neither of the two organizations could put forward any meaningful socio-political perspective either at the district or wider regional level of north Bengal. The district Congress leadership too failed to work out any programme of action in this regard.

In the meantime a disturbing development in the form of crystallization of both Hindu and Muslim communal politics in the district was taking place. League leaders had realized that for spreading Muslim League politics and organization in the rural areas and among the local Muslims, it was necessary to involve big Muslim *jotedars* like Mechhua Mohammed of Falakata and Dhupguri, Aftaruddin Dewania of Batabari, Nepucha Mohammed of Nepuchapur and Tajammal Hossain Pradhan of Bakali (all in the

Duars) and big Muslim *jotedars* in the Permanently Settled area.
Aided actively by the *kath mullahs*, some of whom had married into
families of Muslim *jotedars*, the League began to forge links with
large Muslim landed interests and consolidate its position. At the
district and town levels Musharraff Hossain, Kazi Abdul Khalek
and Enamal Hossain (both nephews of Musharraff), Khan Bahadur
Mokaleswar Rahman (also a close relation of Musharraff), Abdus
Sattar, a lawyer, and Maqbul Hossain, son of Mokaleswar Rahman
were among the prominent leaders and chief organizers of the
League. Gamiruddin Pradhan, Golam Hafez, Nurul Huq and
Abdur Rahman—all sons of middle and small *jotedars* mostly of
local origin—emerged as younger League activists and helped to
link up Noakhali Muslims and local Muslims[18].

Diverse activities and issues were used to spread the League
politics. A Pakistan Club and Library were organized in the town
and observance of Pakistan Day became an annual feature. As in
other districts, music before mosques, holding of Saraswati *puja* in
the school premises, spraying of *abir* and coloured water during
Holi and sale of beef in public view became recurrent issues of
friction which was used to raise the slogan of 'Muslim identity in
danger'.

The District Mohammedan Association tried to maintain a non-
communal and non-separatist position. Its politics continued to
reflect a conflict between local Muslims and Noakhali Muslims
and partly between the interests of small landholders and those of
planters in alliance with big landholders. But within a short period
of four or five years the League emerged as the dominant force
within the Muslim community. However, among the League
activists there were elements like Dr. Mohammad Solaiman of
Pachagar and student leader Golam Rahman who on certain issue
acted jointly with the Communists and even non-Communist
nationalists[19].

Hindu communalism too gained ground considerably. Led by
Hindu Mahasabha leaders and organizers like Kumudini Kanta
Chakrabarty, Nalini Ranjan Ghose, a leading lawyer and also a
planter, Biren Ghose, a leading planter, Jagadish Ghose, also a
lawyer, Satish Lahiri, Jogesh Dutta and Bijoy Hore, all three being
active in the Congress politics since late 1920s, the Hindu Mahas
abha stepped up its activities. It is interesting that the last three had

been closely associated with the CSP in 1938–40 and their later turn towards the Mahasabha showed the strength of Hindu nationalism which was not fought seriously. By late 1944 Upen Barman too became involved in the Mahasabha activities. The Mahasabha started to spread its politics and organization among the Rajbansi Hindus, Santals, Meches and Christians through a variety of activities, such as relief work among distressed peasants in Dhupguri and Falakata, *shuddhi yagna* for a Rajbansi woman alleged to have been kidnapped by Muslim miscreants, *shuddhi* ceremony for Santals, conversion of Christians into Rajbansi Kshatriyas and organization of anti-Pakistan public meeting[20]. By late 1944 the district leaders felt confident enough to convene the All Bengal Hindu Sabha Conference in Jalpaiguri. The Conference, held on 24 and 25 February 1945, was attended by all India and provincial leaders like B.S. Munje, Babaji Khaparde, Shyamaprasad Mukherjee and Ashutosh Lahiri. Nalini Ghosh, the Reception Committee Chairman, delivered the welcome address. Barman seconded the resolution on Pakistan moved by Khaparde calling upon the people to resist the Pakistan proposal by all means[21]. Thus, the first half of the decade saw the spread and consolidation of the two forms of communalism which fed each other. However, because of certain long-run socio-economic features and trends noted in an earlier chapter, spread of communalism did not lead to any serious and violent confrontation.

SMALL TOWN AGITATION, RURAL UNREST AND ELECTIONS: MID 1945–1946

The end of the War in August 1945 did not bring much of relief to the people. Acute food shortage, scarcity of essential commodities, continuing inflation, blackmarketing and bureaucratic corruption and inefficiency plagued the life of common people.

But socio-economic dislocation, though very important, was only one element in the post-War situation. The defeat of fascism, the demonstration of the might of the Soviet Union, a perception of the coming collapse of British rule in India—all combined to provide the background in which a new stage began in the history of political currents and cross-currents in the district.

The first spark in post-War popular agitation not only in Jalpaiguri but also in Bengal was supplied by what came to be known as the Koch Bihar incident. On 21 August 1945 students and teachers of Koch Bihar Victoria College were brutally assaulted by the State Military Force. In protest against this, students all over Bengal were in ferment and at the call of both the Communist-led Students Federation(SF) and the non-Communist SF, 29 and 31 August were observed as Koch Bihar Days. Students of Jalpaiguri, Alipur Duar and other places in the district took active part in protest actions and strikes on a large scale. Though apparently a protest against assault on students, the agitation was directed against a feudal autocracy propped up by the British and anticipated the upsurge that was soon to follow[22].

In Jalpaiguri town the discontent of the town poor hard hit by economic difficulties at times took the form of direct action, such as the CPI-led strike of the rickshaw pullers in protest against increased municipal taxes in the third week of September 1945[23]. However, much more significant was the undercurrent of labour unrest in the Duars gardens that found occasional manifestations. For example, on 22 September, 'incensed' at the wages they received, the women workers of Dalgaon T.E. damaged the European manager's bungalow, the office and staff quarters by pelting stones. There was also a trouble in Rangamati T.E. under Mal P.S. on 12 November. The European Assistant Manager was assaulted, some arrests were made and a police force was posted in the garden[24]. All this foreshadowed the upsurge in worker action in late 1946.

The Koch Bihar agitation was, however, followed by a political lull. In late 1945 Khagendra Nath Das Gupta and other Congress leaders arrested in 1942 were released. With their prestige enhanced through the spell of prison life, they set about refashioning the district Congress organization[25]. But the activities of the district Congress leaders, as at the national and provincial levels, were not geared to the launching of any mass agitation but primarily to the preparation for the coming Assembly elections[26]. At the same time, a campaign was started against the Communists for their 1942 stand. The different Left groups working within the Congress—the Congress Socialists[27], the Forward Bloc and the R.S.P.—however, propagated the belief that a violent and popular revolution would be necessary to overthrow the British rule.

Of all the parties and groups, according to secret official reports and also other sources, the C.P.I., however, was most active in giving shape to popular discontent, particularly in the rural areas[28]. And in addition to the adverse remarks made by the district officials, in September 1945 the Bengal Government itself complained of a change in Communist attitude 'from one of avoiding embarrassment to Government to that of active opposition to Government in accordance with its programme of anti-imperialist struggle'[29]. But, despite their constructive work and emphasis on certain national issues, with the launching of a tirade against them the Communists faced a swing of public opinion against them[30]. The difficulties and the consequent 'stagnation' in activities experienced by the Jalpaiguri Communists were also noted in a District Committee meeting of the Party held in October 1945[31]. Placed in such a situation the Communist leaders of the district— the leading figures being Sachin Das Gupta, Naresh Chakraborty, Biren Neogy, Madhab Datta, Parimal Mitra and Govinda Kundu— chalked out a programme of mass agitation for relief and de-hoarding and against interest on *karja* or consumption loan taken by the rural poor and *adhiars*[32].

However, by late 1945 the party along with other political parties began preparations for the election scheduled to be held in early 1946. For the Jalpaiguri-cum-Siliguri three member non-Mohammedan general constituency with two seats reserved for Scheduled Castes, Congress fielded Khagendra Nath Das Gupta and Mohini Mohan Barman as its candidates. It is noteworthy that Barman, a Rajbansi Hindu lawyer with considerable *jotedari* interests, did not have any record of involvement in nationalist politics. For the other reserved seat the Congress did not put up any candidate. Perhaps the consideration was avoidance of splitting up of Congress vote to ensure victory of Mohini Barman. However, it also meant an indirect support to Raja Prasanna Deb Raikat, an Independent candidate, who had earlier always taken a loyalist position and had been a minister in the League-dominated first Huq ministry. The Communist Party put up Radhamohan Barman, a Krishak Samiti leader coming from a poor peasant family, as a candidate for one of the reserved seats. The Kshatriya Samiti set up two candidates—Upendra Nath Barman and Girija Singha. In the non-reserved seat Nalini Ghose contested as a Hindu Mahasabha candidate. In the single member Jalpaiguri-cum-Darjeeling Mohammedan constitutency Musharraff Hossain was the League candidate. But he was opposed, among others, by Jaharatullah Ahmed who was backed by the District Mohammadan Association and various other elements opposed to the Nawab group.

The electioneering and the political lull were, however, interrupted by eruptions of massive popular outbursts over the issue of release of INA prisoners first in November 1945 and then again in February 1946 as well as the RIN Revolt, also, in February[33]. The impact of all this was felt in the district, particularly in the two towns of Jalpaiguri and Alipur Duar, in the form of popular agitations—frequent strikes in schools and colleges, *hartals*, processions, meetings, hoisting of National Flag etc. While the Congress leaders like Khagendra Nath Das Gupta or Dr Dhiraj Sen or Dr Abanidhar Guha Neogy were not actively involved in these agitations, all the Left groups and parties—FB, Congress Socialists, RSP and CPI—particularly their student organizations, took leading part in these agitations. (Forward Bloc's Nirmalendu Sanyal, Nirmal Bose, Aruna Sanyal and Dipti Roy, Socialist Badal Sarkar, Anil Guha Neogy, Prabhat Bose and Nikhil Ghatak, RSP's Anil Roy, Bidhan Sinha and Debabrata Majumder and CPI-led SF's Abdus Samad, Dilip Ghosh, Jiten Guha, Abul Huda and Narayan Bhattacharya were some of the student leaders of those days.) Muslim students and District Muslim Students League also joined these agitations. There was a marked upswing in anti-imperialism. The upheaval was by and large spontaneous with little guidance and coordination and the students and other youthful elements constituted the bulk of the militant mass[34]. These agitations, however, mostly remained confined to the urban and semi-urban centres and their rural repercussions were limited[35].

But the rural areas, particularly the Debiganj, Pachagar and Boda *thana* areas, were also in the midst of a peasant agitation against exploitation by *jotedars* and *mahajans*. In this agitation taking place in the winter months of 1945–6 the key demand put forward by the District Krishak Samiti was the demand for putting to a stop the practice of charging interest on *karja* or paddy loan for consumption—a demand around which widespread *adhiar* unrest had taken place earlier in 1939–40. With this demand, an agitation was started from November 1945[36]. In some places the *adhiars* resorted to strikes, that is, stoppage of threshing of paddy and forced some *jotedars* to concede the demand[37]. The issue was a vital one. It was not only a struggle against exploitation by the *jotedars* but also a struggle against a system—the *karja* system—that reduced the *adhiars* to permanent indebtedness and a semi-servile status.

This and other issues relating to grievances of the rural masses figured prominently in the election campaign of the CPI in favour of Radhamohan Barman. In their campaign the Krishak Samiti and the Communists tried to link up the *adhiar* agitation and also the issue of abolition of *zamindari* system with the struggle for freedom. They also projected that the fulfilment of socio-cultural aspirations of the Rajbansis and other Scheduled Caste groups depended on the progress of such struggles.

The *adhiar* agitation caused the ire of the *jotedars*. The Rajbansi Hindu big *jotedars* flocked to the Congress or to the Kshatriya Samiti and the Muslim *jotedars* to the League. The Congress leadership, not to speak of the Kshatriya Samiti and the League, took an indifferent and even hostile attitude to the *adhiar* agitation[38]. This indicated the sort of tension that existed at the local level between two major segments of anti-imperialist leadership—one imbued with Marxist ideology and working for radical social transformation and the other one, much older, more powerful and commanding far greater popular support and prestige but afraid of attacks on the existing social order. The reality of almost all the Hindu planters of Jalpaiguri fully backing the Congress with men, money and other resources such as cars and lorries also brought out some of the components of the divergent character of the two segments of leadership. The situation was being made more complicated by the rapid growth of the Muslim League.

In the election held in late March 1946 Jyoti Basu, then a young Communist labour leader, won from the Railway Labour Constituency in which the CPI-led BDR workers formed an important chunk. In the Jalpaiguri general constituency Khagen Das Gupta secured nearly thirty-one thousand votes and defeated his Hindu Mahasabha rival who got just above five thousand. In the two reserved seats, as against more than twenty-six thousand votes secured by the Congress candidate Mohini Barman and nearly fourteen thousand votes got by P.D. Raikat who seems to have enjoyed the tacit support of Congress[39], the Communist candidate obtained more than nine thousand votes. Upendra Barman and

Girija Singha, the two Kshatriya Samiti candidates, secured more than five thousand and three thousand votes, respectively[40]. In the Muhammedan constituency Musharraff Hossain obtained nearly fifteen thousand votes, while his nearest rival Jaharatulla Ahmed could get a meagre two thousand votes[41].

The election result gave an indication, though in a broad sense, of the complex and changing relationship between various political parties and groups and social forces in general and the strength and limitations of the CPI and Krishak Samiti in particular. The striking growth in the electoral support of the Congress compared to its 1937 electoral performance and also the undeclared understanding with the Baikunthapur zamindar were signs of the complexity in the role of the Congress. The Congress, which in 1945–7 included the various non-Communist Left elements, came to represent the major segment of the anti-colonial forces and also sought to incorporate elements or forces which were earlier outside and even opposed to the Congress nationalism. The later election of Raikat to the Constituent Assembly and, on his sudden death in December 1946, of Upendra Nath Barman as Congress nominee[4] once more revealed this trend.

The Communists and the Krishak Samiti represented the most active and most militant segment of the forces of anti-colonialism and anti-feudalism. The polling of about nine thousand votes in those days of limited franchise and in a situation where the rural poor and *adhiars* who constituted the major support base of CPI did not have franchise was no mean achievement. In the Communist strongholds of Debiganj–Paschagar–Boda area the Congress campaigners failed to make much headway. In those areas it was the Krishak Samiti activists, mostly illiterate or at most half-literate, who did the bulk of the election work ranging from scrutiny of the voters' list to the organization of resistance to intimidation and violence from the rival sides[43]. In some places meetings organized in favour of rival candidates were turned into platforms for CPI campaigners[44]. But the overwhelming majority of CPI votes came from the above area and certain pockets under Kotwali and Rajganj *thanas*. It did not have any support base to speak of in the remaining parts of the sprawling constituency particularly in the Duars part. Dearth of cadres was one major factor behind this localized influence. In the two towns also the party secured poor votes partly because of its 1942 stand and also because of its response to the Pakistan proposal. Those positions had created serious misgivings in popular minds and hindered its spread to newer areas.

The election, however, turned out to be a major political campaign involving projection of divergent approaches to the issues agitating the minds of the people. While the Congress asked for votes to strengthen the hands of the national leadership (which had already opted for a negotiated settlement) and the Muslim League pressed the demand for Pakistan, the Communists put forward the perspective of a final bid for power through mass struggles along non-communal lines. They also gave a radical social content to the campaign[45]. In the months following the election, mass political activities were at a low ebb in the towns. The attention of the district Congress leadership remained almost exclusively focused on the Cabinet Mission talks. The Left parties and groups both within and outside Congress, however, carried on the campaign for launching of mass struggles and were engaged in propagation of their respective political viewpoints, in particular through running of, among others, Azad Hind pathagar by the Forward Blocists, Cultural Institute by the Communists and Sanskriti Sadan by the RSP. They also tried to involve the town poor through multifarious activities. Middle class employees were also being organized. In response to the call for an all-India postal strike, the Jalpaiguri employees held a meeting as early as 20 January[46]. A co-ordination Committee composed of representatives of different political groups and various mass organization with Dr R. M. Lahiri, a College teacher, as the President (the first of its kind in Jalpaiguri), was formed to carry on a solidarity campaign. On 29 July 1946 at the call of the Bengal Provincial Trade Union Congress a historic general strike was observed throughout Bengal. Jalpaiguri too participated in it through complete *hartal*, processions and meeting[47].

The *hartal* on 29 July was, however, virtually the last but one major event in the history of anti-imperialist popular movement in Jalpaiguri town. The mood reminiscent of the months between November 1945 to February 1946 was at least partly revived in late January and early February of 1947 when following police firing on Calcutta students observing Vietnam Day on 21 January 1947, leading to killing of several students and two days later on Mymensingh students protesting against the Calcutta incident again resulting in one death, students all over Bengal were once more in ferment[48]. Jalpaiguri students and youth too did not fall behind. But in Jalpaiguri feelings ran particularly high, because the then Bengal Governor Frederic Burrows was scheduled to visit Jalpaiguri town as a part of his programme to tour Darjeeling and Duars (which were considered as seriously disturbed at that time)[49] within a few days of the Calcutta and Mymensingh killings. Students struck schools and colleges, merchants and traders closed down shops and huge crowds composed mainly of angry students and youth took to the streets with slogans 'Burrows pucca khuni hai' (Burrows is a perfect murderer) and 'Go Back Burrows'. Though the other part of his tour programme was retained, Burrows had to cancel his proposed visit to Jalpaiguri town[50].

Barring this anti-Burrows agitation and one or two other incidents, for the one year period 15 August 1946 to 15 August 1947 one can hardly speak of any anti-colonial mass movement in Jalpaiguri town. Anti-British activities remained confined at most to occasional mass meetings addressed by Left leaders.

This decline in the popular movement in Jalpaiguri town was coincidental with and to a considerable extent the result of the outbreaks of communal riots from mid-August onwards. The political atmosphere of the town, as elsewhere, became communally surcharged. Fortunately, despite some provocations from certain elements on both sides, the town or the district did not go through any communal violence. The rural areas in particular, by and large, remained free from aggressive communalism, though communal distrust and tension were not absent. For this, apart from other factors mentioned earlier and particularly the age-old socio-cultural relations between the Rajbansi Hindus and Rajbansi Muslims, the Krishak Samiti and the Communists had an important contribution.

From what has been said above it must not, however, be construed that there was a decline in mass struggles in the district as a whole. In fact, in the post-election months and even in the months immediately following the Calcutta riot, the Krishak Samiti remained actively involved in a series of peasant agitations around the issues of *karja*, worsening food situation, hoarding and smuggling of paddy out of the district, and official inefficiency and corruption[51]. Apart from the Communists, the Congress Socialists and the Revolutionary Socialists too were attempting to find rural contacts and spread their activities beyond the limits of Jalpaiguri town.

The earlier half of 1946 was also marked by intensified activities on the part of the BDR Union to make a success of the call for a nationwide rail strike for pressing their long-standing demands. The railway authority conceded some of the major demands and the strike call was withdrawn. This victory was celebrated with great fanfare. In Duars the impact of this went far beyond the railway workers[52].

In late 1946 and early 1947, Jalpaiguri witnessed an upsurge in popular movements of a nature and magnitude that had never before been experienced in the district.

LABOUR UPSURGE IN DUARS

One entirely new and highly significant dimension that was added to the story of popular movements in Jalpaiguri district was the beginning and rapid spread of trade union as well as nationalist and leftist political activities among the Duars plantation labourers.

Prior to mid-1946 these labourers had not been organized in a trade union and on the whole remained untouched by the national movement. But several developments during the War and immediate post-War years converged to bring about a critical change in the life-situation of the labourers. The sort of exploitation and bondage to which the labourers had been subjected under the plantation system has been indicated earlier. In the War years the extent of exploitation was greatly increased. There was a sharp rise in the cost of living which was not offset by the meagre concessions made. An official enquiry made in 1946 revealed that between 1939 and 1945 while the cost of living had gone up by at least 200 per cent in the Duars plantation area since 1939, the labourers' total earnings including concessions had only doubled. The planters, however, minted money[53].

The workers suffered from irregular and inadequate supply and very bad quality of rice, adulterated mustard oil, scarcity of kerosene oil and short supply of sugar[54]. Cloth shortage was so acute that in the Annual Report for 1945 the ITPA Secretary had to state that 'a large number of female labourers were compelled to use hessians to cover themselves up due to want of cloth'[55].

The end of the War did not bring any improvement. On the contrary, there was a worsening. Thus in his Report for the year 1946 the Chairman of the DPA representing the European planters' interests said, 'The past year should go down in the history of our Association as the year of shortage...'[56]. Wheat and wheat products partly substituted rice, while the labourers were used to taking rice. The annual cloth quota was reduced from 20 yds. per capita to 10 yds[57]. Evidently enough, the problems were more acute than these had been when the War came to an end a year earlier.

At the same time, the workers' perception of deprivation and exploitation must have been accentuated by other developments. As the Indian Tea Association (ITA) Chairman in his address before the DPA's 1946 Annual meeting observed, '... the war has stimulated new demands and new standard of living for labour...'[58].

Another factor was the emergence of a situation of relative labour shortage in the gardens. The Eastern Front projects led to increased demands for labour and C.P.W.D. and M.E.S. contractors enticed away large numbers of tea garden workers[59]. Such a situation perhaps helped to create bargaining power in favour of labour.

But economic factors alone do not provide explanation of the widespread upsurge that broke out in the Duars tea garden area. In the country as a whole there were critical shifts in popular perception and awareness. These shifts and tumultuous developments that had been taking place both within the country and abroad must have been affecting the Duars labourers. Through some channels information or just 'rumour' about all this must have percolated to them. That the British rule was coming to an end was, may be vaguely, being perceived.

Already Assam and Darjeeling labourers were in ferment. The Duars labourers too were in a restive mood that found expression in sporadic incidents of labour outbursts. Already in June 1946 it was being officially reported that the labour situation in tea gardens was 'far from normal'[60] and by the end of the year the Communist Party, Congress and Gurkha League, as noted by the Rajshahi Divisional Commissioner K.A.L. Hill, were active in the area[61]. But to the typical imperialist bureaucratic mind and also to the planters the workers were, in the words of ITA Chairman G.A. Rainey, 'thoroughly health in themselves', but 'new forces, working amongst an illiterate labour force are bound ... to produce stresses and strains'[62]. ITPA Chairman T.P. Roy who was noted for his support to the Congress and public cause observed that labour unrest was 'caused by agitators who seem to take advantage of the present difficult conditions of the country to excite labourers for the purposes of party strength'[63]. The Divisional Commissioner commented, '... Political parties are seeking new sources of power and they often find it in labour agitation'[64]. But, as indicated above, deeper causes were in operation.

Among the different political forces active in the Duars gardens in 1946, the CPI was the most potent force and even a cursory reading of both DPA's and ITPA's annual reports for 1946 shows that the planters, irrespective of their racial origin, considered the Communists as the 'villain of the piece'. Now, available evidence suggests that the message of the Red Flag, and in large parts of the Duars, even that of nationalism and freedom were for the first time carried to the plantation workers at the time of the 1946 election campaign. That campaign aroused the political interest, though very vaguely, of at least some workers. This was heightened by the victory of Ratanlal Brahman, the Communist candidate from the Darjeeling Labour constituency.

Perhaps much more important were the activities of the Domohani Branch of the CPI-led B.A. Railroad Workers Union and particularly the impact of the victory won by the unionized railway workers as part of the all India agitation mentioned earlier. The Union leaders and activists carrying the news of the concessions granted by the authority to far-flung areas moved in a railway engine and bogey bedecked with Red Flags, victory banners and flowers. This highly visible demonstration of the strength of the Union and the news that even the powerful railway *sahibs* had to bow down to the Red Flag had a great impact on the tea garden workers. Further, these workers, living and working in a rural atmosphere and having little knowledge of mechanical appliances and modern technology viewed railway engine and train with great awe, and the sight of an engine moving at the bid of the Union greatly stirred their mind[65].

For quite some time the district leadership of the CPI had been trying to spread their work in the rural and plantation areas of the Duars. Around mid-1946 some of the Union leaders and railway

worker cadres took initiative for mobilizing first the tea garden
workers and later on the peasants, particularly the tribal *adhiars*.
Their work was partly facilitated by locational factors. The railway
lines went by the side of or even through the tea gardens and
railway stations like Mal, Banarhat or Madarihat had a cluster of
tea gardens around them. Moreover, the lowest ranking railway
workers—the unionized pointsmen and gangmen, themselves
mostly tribals, and with some relatives in the gardens—came into
frequent contact with the plantation labourers.

Deba Prasad Ghosh (popularly known as Patal Babu, 1916–
1972), who was for quite some time engaged as a whole time
organizer in the railway union, Parimal Mitra, Domohani Branch
Secretary Bimal Das Gupta, Jadunath Singh, Lalbahadur Chhetri,
Budhan, Man Singh, Guhi and Mahavir—all railway workers—were
some of those who took leading parts in mobilizing tea garden
workers. They had, however, to do their work in a clandestine
fashion and often at night. As the 'cooly' lines and most of the
roads and pathways through the tea gardens belonged to the
private property of the estate, contacting the labourers openly or
within the gardens was virtually out of question. Initial contacts
and group meetings had to be held on railway lines, in a dark
corner of a railway platform or in the gangmen's quarters[66].

Haihaipatha T.E. situated near Mal railway station and belonging
to a British managing agency concern was one of the first few
gardens whose workers were drawn into organized activity.
Among others, Faguram Oraon, Jagannath Oraon, Arjun Bhagat
and Lawrence Sukdeo, all working in Haihaipatha garden, responded
enthusiastically to their early contacts and took the lead in organizing
their fellow workers[67]. Contacts were made with workers of some
other gardens and from a meeting of representatives from about 30
gardens held in Mal sometime in June or early July 1946 the Zilla
Cha Bagan Mazdoor Union (Registration No. 246, dated July
1946)1—the first union of the Duars plantation workers—was
formed with Ratanlal Brahman as President and D.P. Ghosh as
General Secretary. On that occasion a meeting of more than 2,000
workers was held and a procession paraded the roads of Mal[68].
Soon thereafter a Memorandum containing demands for wage
increase, regular supply of ration, supply of good quality rice and
other commodities, better housing, improved medical facilities
and introduction of welfare measures was prepared and submitted

to the government, and the Memorandum was considered in several meetings of both the DPA and the ITPA.

In the meantime, the seething labour discontent burst forth in a series of protests and agitations—petitions and representations, *gheroas*, sudden work stoppages, strikes, riotous actions, assaults on *sahibs* and *babus* notorious for their *zulum* and corruption, and violence against *kayas* or Marwari shopkeepers considered to be responsible for high prices, adulteration, short weight etc. The secret political report for the first half of July mentioned 'signs of trouble developing in some of the Duars gardens ....'[69]. In the second half of July two strikes 'in one of which labour made an organised attempt to cut off the garden from the outside world and to sabotage the factory arrangement' was reported[70]. A DPA Committee meeting held on 30 July considered labour troubles at Dumchipara, Banarhat, Naya Sylee and Jiti tea gardens. The disparity in earnings between gardens was held to be a major factor behind disturbances in these gardens. In August it was reported that the situation was 'not normal in Jalpaiguri gardens' and that the Communists were 'active in organising unions'[71]. In September the Rajshahi Divisional Commissioner reported 'unrest, rioting and a strike in three different gardens'[72].

In October it was reported that the efforts of the Alipur Duars Congress to organize unions in that area and to have mass meetings have been prevented by the Alipur Duars SDO[73]. But it was only a temporary respite. In early November +troubles broke out in nine tea estates of the Alipur Duars subdivision. It was officially reported that 'the stoppage of work in each case was of short duration but considerable violence was used by the staff, particular targets being the houses and property of Bengali clerical staff and the shops of some Marwari garden shopkeepers'[74]. *Ananda Bazar Patrika* reported that there was a 'revolt' on the part of the labour of Salbari, Dima, Kalchini, Gangutia, Raimatang, Chinchula and some other tea estates. The immediate factor behind this unrest was, according to an official report, cut in the rice part of ration. But the basic reason was acute scarcity of food. Not only the workers but also the peasants of the area joined the 'revolt'[75]. In two other gardens there was a 'renewed agitation' following the *hata bahar* or expulsion of labourers alleged to have been implicated in earlier disturbances[76] along with all of their family members. At Dumchipara tea garden not only the worker leaders but families of arrested leaders including 19 women and 5 children of ages ranging from two to six years were expelled from the garden. This led to serious disturbances[77]. In February 1947 there was report of further trouble in several Duars tea estates. The workers were reported to be stirred to action by Communists and there were cases of assaults on guards and clerks. The main reasons were 'the alleged harsh treatment of the workers by the clerks and the insufficient supply of rations'[78].

It has been noted that the planters as well as the officials held instigation given by 'outside agitators', usually Communists, as primarily responsible for the labour unrest in Duars. But while the Communists certainly acted as the catalytic agent in the unfolding of the process of labour upsurge, and also were the first to carry even the message of nationalism and anti-imperialism to large sections of labour, in a situation of social and political turmoil perhaps in a very large number of cases the workers acted on their own, set up impromptu organizations and threw up leaders from their own ranks.

This is what seems to have happened in Dumchipara garden in June 1946. In this garden, under the management of Duncan Bros., workers were not allowed to go to their houses during the noontime meal recess. Some Nepali workers sought permission for going to the 'lines' from the Manager. Permission was refused, yet they went to the 'lines' for meal. The management considered it as a defiance and dismissed the workers involved. Following this a long-drawn labour agitation began. Biradhawaj Rai, whose mother and brothers worked in the garden and who himself was a supervisor in a coal quarry near Bagrakote, was one of those who took lead in organizing protest action and in course of time emerged as a major leader of the Socialist-led trade unions[79].

In some gardens political elements other than the Communists, for example, Piyush Mukherjee and Sunil Sarkar of Alipur Duars Congress took initiative in mobilizing the plantation workers. While the substantial links of the district Congress leaders based in Jalpaiguri town with the Jalpaiguri planters cramped their approach to labour, Alipur Duars Congress leaders had no such links[80]. Socialists working within the Congress, Ghanashyam Misra being the most prominent of them, started to organize the workers of some gardens around Bagrakote in late 1946 and early

1947[81]. Around that time the RSP also began work among the tea garden workers[82].

The Gurkha League was also active. But it acted mainly as a divisive force and received support from the European planters. In August 1946 a DPA Sub-Committee meeting noted with appreciation that the Gurkha League 'had done good work during recent disputes' and recommended that 'permission and sympathetic consideration should be given by Managers to request from this organization in the future'[83]. The Gurkha League along with several other elements was a major force behind a subsequent move backed by the European planters to form a separate regional political unit comprising Darjeeling, Duars, Koch Bihar and Assam[84].

But such disruptive tactics could not put a halt to the labour upsurge that continued to surge forward and engulfed gardens previously unaffected. Proceedings of the meetings of the DPA or its subcommittees held in the earlier half of 1947 abound with reports of such labour unrest. Reports of strikes and work stoppages continued to pour in. Violence and assaults provided a sort of perpetual background[85]. Though these took place around economic demands, the unrest was not a reflection of mere economism. In the complex political situation prevailing in the country marked by firm rejection by the Congress leadership of any confrontation with the British rulers and tortuous negotiation between the two sides, the rapid growth and consolidation of communal forces, and sporadic popular outbursts of near-revolutionary nature the Duars labour upsurge came to have an anti-imperialist political content. Communists played a key role in imparting such a content. In large parts of the Duars, as already mentioned, they were the first to convey the message of nationalism and also Left, radical politics[86]. But other political elements like the Congress Socialists or Alipur Duars Congressmen also helped to give an anti-British colour to the labour unrest. Slogans such as *hamara mang dene hoga* (our demands must be met), *Belati malik London bhago* (British owners go back to London), *Inquilab Zindabad* etc. rent the air. That a situation of labour 'revolt'—the term was used in the *Ananda Bazar Patrika* report mentioned earlier—joined in by peasants had developed in parts of Alipur Duars has already been noted. In early 1947 potentially a much more explosive situation developed in the Oodlabari–Dam Dim–Mal–Chalsa–Baradighi area.

All this caused most serious alarm to the planters, particularly the European planters, and the British rulers, and Communists came to be considered as the main enemy. The alarm was compounded by the knowledge that the upswing in labour unrest was not a phenomenon localized in the Duars. The whole of plantation area extending from Darjeeling to Assam was in the midst of an unprecedented upheaval[87]. In a sense it was an integral component of the labour situation in the entire country which, according to a secret note by the Director of Intelligence Bureau (dt. 9 August 1946), was 'becoming increasingly dangerous'[88]. Making a similar point the Jalpaiguri Superintendent of Police Cottam told an Emergency General Meeting of the DPA held on 19 February 1947:

> Trouble now being experienced on Duars gardens was by no means local; Communist activity was, in fact, widespread throughout India[89].

A 'Top Secret' Note prepared by the Bengal Governor Burrows on his return from a north Bengal tour in February 1947 (see Appendix II) specifically referred to the 'situation of widespread disorder and confusion' prevailing in the tea gardens of north Bengal[90]. Earlier in December 1946 in their communication to the British High Commissioner in India, the Calcutta-based European Association had spoken of 'the danger of a complete breakdown of law and order' in the planting areas of Bengal and Assam and also of the 'crude form of Communism' assuming in the planting areas 'an anti-British form' (see Appendix II).

The response of the planters and the British officials to the situation prevailing in the Duars plantation area and also elsewhere was essentially four-fold. One response, an adroit one, was to admit the genuineness of some of the grievances and redress these. Thus, in one official report it was noted that the Rajshahi Divisional Commissioner 'emphasises that the whole problem of the tea garden labour required the careful attention of the Labour Commissioner'[91]. In conformity with this approach of at least partly conciliating their conditions but to considerable chagrin of the planters, pending a long term review of the industry's wage structure, interim increases in wages and allowances were made in two instalments, one in October 1946 and another one in February

947[92]. This was a significant achievement on the part of labour.

In part related to this approach was the appointment of a Labour Officer to look after the labour problems. But J. L. Jenkins, the person so appointed, was a retired Deputy Inspector-General of Police. It is revealing that the first Labour Officer appointed by the Indian Jute Mills Association in late 1930s and the first ITA Labour Officer too were also ex-police officers. Such appointments were dictated by the view that labour problems were basically law and order problems. Thus, essentially the second response was to handle the labour agitation and the Communist agitators firmly, that is, to resort to repression. These included dismissals, *hatasahar* and arrests. And the Jalpaiguri SP advised the Emergency General Meeting of the DPA that 'complaints require to be made to the Police before action can be taken either by the police or the authorities'. He told the meeting that wide powers existed under the Special Powers Ordinance which was already in force. But to enable the police to use these powers 'clear cases' should be made out[93]. The third response was the panicky planning for evacuation of the Europeans from the plantation belt (see Appendix II). The fourth one was a political response in the form of a close co-ordination between the Indian Tea Planters Association, the Duars Planters Association and the District Congress Committee (see Appendix II). In the face of continuing labour agitation and 'disturbances' and increased activities on the part of the Communists, the planters, both Europeans and Indians, on the one hand and the district Congress leadership on the other were devising plans to help each other. This once more brought out some of the limitations and the contradictions within the national movement in Jalpaiguri. Despite such moves, the militant labour movement led mainly by the Communists continued to make progress[94].

THE TEBHAGA STRUGGLE

While the Duars plantation area was going through a wave of labour agitation, a major peasant outburst took place in large parts of the district (and also in adjoining areas of Dinajpur, Rangpur and Malda in north Bengal). In September 1946 the Bengal Provincial Kisan Sabha gave the call for *tebhaga*, that is, two-thirds share of the harvests in favour of the *adhiars* recommended by the Floud Commission in 1940. (It may parenthetically be observed that th BPKS call was preceded by a Resolution adopted by the CP Central Committee meeting held from 23 July to 5 August 1946 The resolution concluded that the freedom struggle had entere 'the revolutionary phase' and pointed out, among other thing: that 'the peasantry is lagging behind the working class in thi phase of mass upheavals'[95]. There are reasons to consider that thi understanding of the CPI leadership was an important facto behind the call issued by the BPKS.) This call coincided witl economic grievances, intensified by scarcity of food, continuin; peasant agitation against the exploitation made by *jotedars*-cum *mahajans*, sharpened perception of the increasing non-viability o *jotedar-adhiar* system already tellingly revealed by the 1943 famin and, perhaps more importantly, the growing awareness that th days of British rule in India were numbered. The *Fortnightly Repor* considered the call as 'clearly most dangerous for the peace of th countryside'[96].

(a) *Debiganj–Pachagar–Boda Area*

In Jalpaiguri the Debiganj–Pachagar–Boda area provided à favourable setting for response to the BPKS call. By the time th call was issued or even earlier the area and, one may add, also th adjacent areas in Dinajpur and Rangpur districts came to have three major elements in their socio-political complexion. First, the area had a long tradition of political activity and peasant move ment. From the experience of the Congress-led nationalist activity (1921–39), and from 1939 onwards the Communist-led *adhia* agitation (1939–40), relief and dehoarding campaign (1943–5), agitation around interest on *karja* (1945–6) and 1946 electior campaign broad sections of the Hindu and Muslim peasants, particularly the rural poor and *adhiars*, of the area came to have ar orientation for peasant struggles and also for viewing such struggle: as part of struggles for national freedom. The experience of their life situation as well as movements since 1939 also fostered a certain degree of class awareness among large sections. Second, there was a band of dedicated Communist organizers who, though coming from petty bourgeois intelligentsia background, sank themselves deep into the masses. Third, there were scores of

Rajbansi Hindu and Rajbansi Muslim peasant activists and cadres (the latter, however, in much lesser number), many belonging to poor peasant and *adhiar* families, who were steeled through their experience and, given their initial background, had a fair degree of political knowledge and organizational skill. These peasant cadres made possible a regular and lively functioning of the Krishak Samiti committees at the Union level. Thus, the area also had an organizational structure for mass struggles[97].

With the call for *tebhaga*, the district leadership of the CPI and Krishak Samiti began active preparations for launching the movement. Krishna Binode Roy, the BPKS President, came to the area in late November, had meetings with the DKS and Union committees and addressed mass meetings in which the significance of the *tebhaga* call and its links with the solution of the food problem and also the broader struggle for freedom were explained[98]. Area-wise allocation of work was made among the leaders and activists like Charu Mazumdar, Biren Pal, Madhab Datta, Biren Neogy, Dipen Roy, Dulal Basu, Nripen Roy, Monoranjan Das Gupta, Hara Ghose, Gurudas Roy and Samar Ganguly(-1989). Group meetings, mass meetings, demonstrations, *hat* squads, peasant marches through the countryside and other such forms of both propaganda and mobilization became regular features; volunteers were recruited, trained and assigned with specific responsibilities; and slogans like *adhi nai, tebhaga chai, nij kholane dhan tolo, jan debo to dhan debo na, patit jami dakhal karo, Inquilab Zindabad,* etc. broke the silence of the winter night. *Ek bhai, ek taka, ek lathi,* became a major rallying slogan. It signified a militant peasant solidarity[99].

The first report on enforcement of *tebhaga* in Jalpaiguri district came in late November from a village under Pachagar *thana*[100]. Thereafter it began to spread to newer and newer areas. On 20 December an attempt was made to enforce *tebhaga* on the land of Digen Roy, a big *jotedar* in Sundardighi Union under Debiganj P.S. But the *jotedar* was forewarned. Madhab Datta, Vidya Barman, Chaitu and few other peasant cadres were assaulted by the *jotedar's* men and arrested by the police. Local peasants were somewhat taken aback by the incident. Next day a cadre meeting attended by Sachin Das Gupta and Biren Neogy, the DKS Secretary, was held. A peasant woman activist stood up and declared that there was no going back, '*Tebhaga* has to be enforced on the land of this particular *jotedar*', she asserted. This roused the morale of the peasants, particularly of the poor peasants and *adhiars* Renewed preparations were made and on 22 December more thar 200 volunteers, both men and women, carrying *lathis* and Rec Flags with them assembled, collectively harvested the paddy grown on that *jotedar's* land and carried it from the field not to the latter's *kholan* but to a place chosen by the peasants for the purpose of threshing. This time there was no resistance from the *jotedar':* side[101].

This was viewed as a great victory by the peasant agitators and the movement spread rapidly from village to village under Debiganj Pachagar, Boda and parts of Kotwali and Rajganj *thanas*. (Charu Majumdar was one of the most important and beloved leaders of this movement). Paddy was harvested collectively. After stacking it in the *adhiar's* place or a common place, the *jotedar* was asked to come there and receive his one-third share of the crop. The police was also informed. But neither the *jotedars* nor the police turned up[102].

According to a report submitted by the Sadar Sub-Divisional Officer (SDO) A.M.S. Mahmood in March 1947 :

> ... the movement was organised ... by educated Communist workers of town and outside agitators. Without [them] there would be no movement ... in the sub-division[103].

But as *The Statesman* correspondent covering the movement reported, the peasants were 'moving with a momentum that does not need any aid from outside'[104]. In fact, the SDO himself indicated the mass character of the agitation.

He stated :

> ...during the harvest season Communist volunteers in batches visited different localities, established camps in the interior, en-listed local support and they helped the selected *adhiars* to cut and take away the entire produce from their lands and stack these in places suitable for the purpose of the Communists. The *jotedars* could not oppose ... Large number of volunteers armed with lathis, scythes etc. would gather together and cut paddy of some land on each occasion ...[105].

Thus despite his overt anti-Communist biases and typical bureaucratic frame of mind, the SDO could not but mention certain features which showed that in extensive parts of the Debiganj–Pachagar–Boda area the *tebhaga* agitation assumed the shape of a mass upheaval.

One major indicator of the broad peasant awakening was the participation of Rajbansi peasant and *adhiar* women activists like Sagari Barmani, Buri Ma (Punyeswari), wives of peasant cadres of Debiganj area and Tilak Tarini Nandi, Sikha Nandi and a host of militant peasant women activists of Pachagar area. Rajbansi peasant women took part in meetings, processions, paddy harvesting and threshing and even resistance to the police. Once when police came to arrest Biren Pal, the DKS Assistant Secretary and some other leaders staying at one place, Tilak Tarini stood on guard with a *banti* (large fish-cutting curved knife) while the leaders slipped away. In Kharija Berubari under Kotwali *thana* and several other places militant peasant women chased away armed police with broomsticks, scythes and *bantis* in their hands[106]. (An aspect that needs to be explored is whether the militant role played by Rajbansi peasant women had any relation with their position in Rajbansi society mentioned in chapter 2).

As *The Statesman* correspondent observed :

> Dumb through past centuries, he [the peasant] is today transformed by the shout of a slogan. It is inspiring to see him marching across the field with his fellows, each man shouldering a lathi like a rifle, with a red flag at the head of the procession. It is sinister to hear them greet each other in the silence of bamboo groves with clenched left fists raised to foreheads and whisper 'Inquilab, comrade'[107].

For several weeks, that is, from late November to early February the peasants and *adhiars* in particular remained on the offensive. (The height of the *tebhaga* movement in the area and also in Dinajpur and Rangpur in January–February 1947, it may be noted, coincided with a new wave of anti-imperialist student and youth agitation in Bengal marked by the 'Hands off, Vietnam' campaign, renewed surge of strike action involving the historic 85-day Communist-led tram strike and strikes of port employees and Howrah engineering workers and Hajong revolt in northern Mymensingh). In the face of unity, sweep and organizational strength of the *tebhaga* movement many *jotedars* made a retreat and arrived at compromises. Some *jotedars* fled to the town. According to the SDO's report, '... the *jotedars* were on many occasions kept confined in their houses under threat of assault and violence'[108]. For two months or so administrative control over these areas was virtually non-existent and the provincial government expressed its serious worry over the 'parallel government' run by the Communists in Jalpaiguri, Dinajpur, Rangpur and some other parts of the province. The spread of the movement was such that in some localities even elements known as dacoits gave up dacoity and joined the movement. The *jotedars* sought police help. But for several weeks the police did not dare to enter the strongholds of the *tebhaga* movement. With the help of children, young boys and girls and women an elaborate forewarning arrangement was organized[109].

The *jotedars*, however, were only biding their time and carried on the conspiracy to smash the movement. Many of the big *jotedars* in Pachagarh were Muslims and they tried to divide the peasantry along communal lines and rouse communal passions. Though they failed to create any communal clash, they succeeded to a certain extent in keeping the Muslim peasants away from the movement. They held confabulations among themselves, raised funds and put increasing pressure on the district administrative officials and the Muslim League government in Bengal for police intervention.

Soon an opportunity was provided by a new turn of the movement which, once begun, tended to generate its own momentum that was not anticipated by the leadership. In villages and areas where the Krishak Samiti had no previous base or strong organization, the *adhiars* had stored the paddy in the *jotedar's kholan* (threshing place). But the success of the movement in the organized areas and also the publication of the Bargadar Bill in January 1947 gave a new impetus to the *tebhaga* struggle. The *adhiars* in the unorganized areas such as parts of Kharija Berubari Union under Sadar P.S. and certain areas under Debiganj, Pachagar and Boda P.S. too, previously untouched by the movement, now on their own and without any directive from the Kisan Sabha leadership, started what came to be known as the *kholan bhanga andolan*. (Biren Neogy, however, asserts that a call for such a movement was given by Bhowani Sen at a meeting of the district leadership held at Pachagar in February 1947 and also at a peasant meeting held immediately thereafter. According to one Intelligence Branch Report Sen called for forcible possession of arable land[110].).

This was the second phase of the movement both in Jalpaiguri and other districts of movement, particularly Dinajpur and Rangpur. The peasants and *adhiars* began to seize paddy in the *jotedars'* stacks and removed it to their own places for their shareout. The Sadar SDO reported:

> The second phase of the movement was forcible taking away of paddy stocks and plough cattle from the Khamars and houses of the *jotedars*. Some cases of removal of paddy from *golas* [granaries] were also received. Allegations were also made by many *jotedars* that the volunteers were armed with *lathis, daos* [chopper], bows and other weapons and the *jotedars* were threatened with violence and assaults...

With reference to this phase *The Statesman* correspondent commented

> It was an attempt to alter custom by force, but it is doubtful if it amounted to criminal breach of the law...[111].

But these actions provided the opportunity sought for by the *jotedars*. They lodged charge of dacoity and looting and immediately thereafter a well-prepared police offensive followed. Section 144 was declared in Pachagar, Debiganj, Boda, Kotwali and other adjacent police station areas, large scale arrests were made and severe repression was launched [112]. In the face of such offensive and repression the gains previously made in the organized areas could not always be successfully defended.

(b) Worker—Peasant—Tribal upheaval

But while by late January or latest by early February the *tebhaga* movement was put on the defensive in its old bases and severe repression was let loose also in Dinajpur and Rangpur, the other two North Bengal districts in the forefront of the *tebhaga* struggle, peasant unrest again took a new turn, which was neither planned nor even foreseen by the district leadership of the CPI and Kisan Sabha. This was a virtual tribal peasant uprising in wide areas under Mal and Matiali P.S. in the Duars.

In the countryside of the Duars, basic production relations existed between *jotedars* and *adhiars*. Exploitation and oppression of the *adhiars*, overwhelmingly tribals—Oraons, Mundas, Santals, etc.,—in large parts of the Duars, particularly the parts under Mal and Matiali P.S., by the *jotedars*, mostly Muslims and Rajbansi Hindus but also some Marwaris and immigrant Bengalis knew no limits, and elements of peasant discontent had been accumulating in such areas for over a long time. But there was no tradition and experience of peasant movement and organization in most parts of the Duars.

However, between late January—early February and April 1947 a peasant upsurge around the issue of *tebhaga* flared up in the Oodlabari—Dam Dim—Mal—Chalsa—Baradighi area. It is not quite clear how the tribal peasants and *adhiars* of this area came to know of the *tebhaga* agitation. That this peasant outburst have some elements of autonomy is certain. Moreover, some factors operating within the world of tribal peasant community might have helped in triggering off the peasant unrest[113]. (All this constitutes an important area that needs to be explored further.).

However, a close examination of the unfolding of the movement shows that it did not begin so 'spontaneously' as has been suggested by some scholars[114]. In the first place, in this area too, according to available accounts, the organized railway workers and their Union having a nearly decade-long experience of mass activities and movement played a crucial role. Some of the railway workers, particularly the leading cadres[115], must have come to know about the *tebhaga* struggle and its advance from *Swadhinata*, Krishak Samiti leaflets and various other sources.

Further, in early December 1946 the Fourth Annual Conference of the Bengal and Assam Railroad Workers' Union (the Union to which the Domohani Branch was affiliated) was held at Lamding in Assam. This Conference, attended by a number of Domohani Branch organizers and cadres and also two tea garden worker activists, Jagannath Oraon and Arjun Bhagat, adopted a Resolution in support of the *tebhaga* demand. The Resolution read:

> The peasants of Bengal and Assam have started *tebhaga* movement for getting legitimate share of produce. This Conference considers that those landowners who do not take due part in the process of production are not entitled to get more than one-third of the produce. The Conference appeals to the Bengal Government to pass legislation in favour of this demand[116].

This Resolution and the experience of participation in the Conference perhaps opened the floodgates of the *tebhaga* movement in the Duars[117]. After coming back from the conference the railway union cadres, some of whom themselves were tribals, carried the message of the *tebhaga* movement to the tribal peasants. In the meantime, the story of successes achieved by the *tebhaga* struggle in the organized bases in the district had spread to the peasants of the Mal–Matiali area through the railway workers and union activists and also through various other channels. Thus, Jagannath and a few other tea garden workers were arrested in connexion with the labour unrest and were lodged in Jalpaiguri Jail[118]. There they met some of the peasant activists from the Debiganj–Pachagar–Boda area and heard from them the story of the *tebhaga* struggle. The *tebhaga* message must have also circulated through 'rumour'. *Tebhaga* leaflets including one entitled 'Communist Party's Appeal to Duars Peasants' were widely circulated[119]. The wave of labour unrest continuing in the surrounding plantation areas for several months had also certainly stirred their minds.

All these elements—some determinate and others indeterminate—converged to give shape to the seething discontent and anger of the peasants. In early 1947 four distinct forces—the Communist leaders and cadres (some coming from middle class families and some others from a working class background), the railway workers who had been unionized and were being led by the Communists for several years, the plantation labourers who were just in the midst of a process of being organized and were in a state of turmoil, and the peasants (mostly tribals), unorganized in the conventional sense but in a militant moods—joined hands and the outcome was virtually a peasant–worker–tribal rebellion.

Samar Ganguly who had earlier been an organizer in Debiganj and had come to Mal to attend a conference of the tea garden workers was assigned with the responsibility of looking after the peasant struggle in the Duars. He along with Deba Prasad (Patal) Ghosh addressed several meetings of workers and peasants and urged them to enforce *tebhaga*[120]. Ganguly set up a sort of operational camp at a place near Mal—a *jote* owned by Balgovinda, a Marwari *jotedar*. The peasants took possession of it without any resistance from any quarter[121]. Apart from Samar Ganguly, Patal Ghosh and Parimal Mitra too were available for consultation and necessary guidance. At one stage, Charu Mazumdar, Hara Ghosh, Raghunath Routh, an Oriya Communist and Anil Gupta also were placed in the Mal–Matialy area for providing active assistance.

Along with them, a host of peasant leaders and organizers like Birsa Oraon and Sukra Oraon (popularly known as 'Lal' Sukra) of Matha Chulka near Baradighi, Sarbaru Mohammad, Buni Oraon and Deocharan Nayak of Oodlabari, Puria Manki Munda of Dhumsigara, Sabaruddin Mohammad and Hopna Majhi of Khagrabari or Basiruddin Mohammad of Manabari were thrown up from amongst the peasants. Jagannath Oraon, a victimized ex-tea garden worker, was also given the responsibility of looking after the peasant movement. Several militant peasant women activists too—Naihari Oraoni, wives of Buni and Chhotan and Poko Oraoni amongst others—emerged [122]. The peasants of the areas also showed a remarkable degree of organization and leadership pattern. They fairly rapidly set up an organizational network. Thus, in the Oodlabari area an organization was formed with Sarbaru as Captain, Sabaruddin as Vice-Captain and Deocharan, Buni and a few others as their lieutenants[123].

The pattern of unrest was fairly uniform. Hundreds of peasant men, women and even children—mostly tribals with a sprinkling of Nepalis, Rajbansis and Muslims—joined by large numbers of tea garden labourers who had struck work in support of the agitating peasants and bands of railway workers, carrying Red Flags and in many cases armed with *lathis*, spears, and bows and arrows marched from village to village. Tribal drums (*nagras*) and *madals* were used to spread the struggle message and mobilize the peasants. By the time this upheaval took place, in the Duars harvesting was over and paddy was already stored in the *jotedar's* stacks. Under the circumstances, the *tebhaga* struggle in Duars inevitably took the form of forcible seizure of paddy for securing a two-thirds share of the paddy. Here one witnessed not only something unprecedented in the history of popular movements in Jalpaiguri but also one of the rare instances of close physical interaction, in the sphere of action, between peasants, workers and tribals in the history of popular movements in India, reminiscent of the historic Punnapra–Vyalar revolt.

Describing the course of movement the following observation was made in the ITA's Annual Report for 1947 :

[Early in 1947] as a result of outside agitation bands of labourers had left their work and, headed by Communist leaders, were roaming the countryside, in many cases armed with *lathis* and spears, with the object of entering *bustees* and raiding paddy stocks in support of the general demand by the ryots of the district for a two-thirds share of the crop, instead of half the share which they had always received in the past from the Zamindars[124].

Nani Bhowmik, a well-known litterateur of the 1940s and a Communist, who was on the staff of *Swadhinata*, spent several days among the rebel peasants and workers. Here is an extract from his long first-hand account[125]:

The spectacle of how the down-trodden people got roused up into a new life of unbounded vitality that is what I witnessed. Nobody lent hand to the paddy accumulated in the *kholans* of *jotedars*, no threshing till *tebhaga* is realized. A mammoth contingent of Santal, Oraon and hill peasants are on the march night and day. Each and every village and hamlet in two to three *thanas* are being covered. Only a few words to the village folk and they instantly realize what is afoot. With head covered in dirty *chaddars* they leave their homes and join this thrilling procession. The coolies at work in the fields look afar in eager expectation as the noise reaches their ears. They too go on strike and join in. They lend their support to their *kisan* brothers. In the gang quarters inside the jungles the gangmen troop out. They hoist high the iron gang plates like banners and head the demonstration.

Continuing, Bhowmik narrated :

In all the corners of the hills, forests and lands, amongst all the sections of the people a new wave of inspiration finds its way through.

One such demonstration was once moving deep inside a sal forest at dead of night. With eager steps I attached myself to the fag end of that procession. In the darkness of the forest it is difficult to realize how far that wondrous stream of humanity stretches out ... Those amongst them who are smart shout *'Inquilab'*. It seems all of them have not as yet learnt about *'Zindabad'* too. *'Lal Jhanda Ki'*—everybody says—*'Jai'*. *'Kisan Majdoor'*—*'Ek Ho'* that is what should follow. But this is not known to them. *'Jai'*—that is the only word they shout in an outburst of a still not well-defined emotion. Even the word 'Jai' is not uttered any too distinctly.

They can shout, they have to go on shouting, this is the new emotional experience of their life. The word '*Jai*' cannot be singled out in that shouting, a long stretched-out *Jai-i-i* in the shape of a primordial wild shout that is what penetrates the ears. A drawn-out hoarse age-old primitive shout whirls through the dark *sal* forest.... I found ringing in that shout an age-old pain as well as an age-old anger.

The *jotedars* were totally taken by surprise. Not only the big Rajbansi and Muslim *jotedars* but even some tribal *jotedars* were affected[126]. Particularly exposed were the Muslim and Rajbansi *jotedars* in villages and areas with a large tribal peasant population. In many cases they had no alternative but to concede the demand. Where necessary, coercion was used against the *jotedar*. Government officials too were not prepared for such a situation. Sometimes one *daroga* with a small police force appeared, but on seeing large crowds of armed villagers made hasty retreat. There were also a few instances of a *daroga* or a police party being surrounded and temporarily confined by rebellious peasants. Once on hearing that two Communist leaders had been arrested and kept confined in the Mal police station, hundreds of armed peasants and workers *gheraoed* the *thana* demanding the release of allegedly reportedly arrested leaders. It was a tense situation and the assembled crowd dispersed only after being fully satisfied that none of their leaders was under detention[127].

It was in the context of such a rebellious situation that the terrified *jotedars* begged for police help. Their plea was joined in by the planters. An emergency meeting of the Dam Dim Sub-District of the DPA held on 4 February 1947 'decided to instruct the Chairman to request the Superintendent of Police to provide an adequate armed police force in the Dam Dim Sub-District and to remain there until the wave of unrest, now being experienced, subsides, and conditions return to normal'[128]. In the Emergency General Meeting of the DPA held immediately after the above meeting the SP gave a resume of the Communist effort 'to stir up troubles amongst our labour and *adhiars*', assured the members present that 'wide powers now exist under the existing Special Powers Ordinance' and advised them to take advantage of these powers[129].

By late February the situation began to change and the police force was strengthened. On 1 March at Neoramajhiali near Baradighi under Mal P. S. a large number of peasants and tea garden workers carrying lathis, bows and arrows, spears etc. raided the paddy stocks stored in a *jotedar's* granary. An armed police force was already posted there. A scuffle took place and the peasants snatched away some guns from the police. Thereafter, the police opened fire and killed five peasants including one woman[130].

The leadership was taken aback by this incident and displayed utter confusion. Samar Ganguly himself was present at a place very close to the spot where the firing took place. He went to Mal which was a few miles away. On that day a huge meeting organized by the Rail Union was being held at Domohani where many district leaders and also Jyoti Basu, the main speaker at the meeting, were present. Ganguly sent couriers to Domohani seeking advice and instruction from the district leadership. While several leaders along with a large number of Rail Union activists and railway workers rushed to Mal and made arrangements for immediate relief and also for carrying the wounded and the dead to Jalpaiguri hospital and thus showed exemplary fraternity,[131] the advice sent by the leadership was two-fold :(a) Throw away the snatched guns in wells; and (b) Ganguly was to evade arrest[132]. The peasants did not expect this brutal attack. But they were not demoralized. In fact, they were incensed and shouted for retaliation. The movement continued to spread throughout the month of March.

Occasional skirmishes used to take place. But another major incident of indiscriminate firing by a police party led by the Sadar SDO himself on a group of peasants and tea garden workers took place on 4 April 1947 at village Mahabari situated near Mangalbari *hat* (Chalsa area) under Matiali P.S.. Nine persons including one thirteen year-old boy were killed instantaneously and a few others were seriously injured. One of them died the next day (Appendix I). Among those killed and injured, two—Jitia Oraon and Natai Nagesia—were workers of Oodlabari tea garden and thus a new kind of worker-peasant alliance was forged in blood. Available unofficial accounts show that there was no attack on the police or no scuffle and that the brutal firing was a pre-planned one with the aim of smashing the spread of peasant–worker rebellion[133].

Decline of popular upheaval

Following this incident the police repression which had earlier been unleashed was intensified. By late February Section 144 had been in force in as many as eleven police stations: Kotwali (Sadar), Pachagar, Boda, Debiganj, Rajganj, Tetulia, Mainaguri, Patgram, Mal, Matiali and Nagrakata[134]. By the end of April criminal cases were lodged against more than 1,000 persons, more than 200 leaders and peasants and workers including D.P. Ghosh, the Secretary of the Cha Bagan Mazdur Union were in jail, and arrest warrants were issued against 250 leaders and activists[135].

Here it deserves mention that though the town middle class people were by and large apathetic to the *tebhaga* struggle and some even overtly hostile to it, at least sections of them reacted against the brutality of police repression. Thus, following the Mahabari police firing three enquiry teams went there. One team included several non-Communist doctors and one college teacher[136]. The second team consisted of representatives of the Students' Congress (the students' organization of the Congress Socialists and RSP), District Muslim Students' League and Students' Federation[137]. The third one was composed of Khagendra Nath Das Gupta, the Congress MLA from Jalpaiguri, another district Congress leader Prafulla Tripathi and the well-known BPCC leader Arun Chandra Guha. All the teams condemned the police firing in most unequivocal terms[138].

It was also possible to organize a successful students' strike and hold a students' demonstration in Jalpaiguri town in protest against the police firing. Even Forward Blocist student leaders like Sm Aruna Sanyal paid homage to the peasant and worker martyrs[139]. A Civil Liberties Committee was formed with Subdoh Sen as a leading organizer.

Despite all this, the *tebhaga* movement in general and the peasant–worker upsurge amounting to a rebellion in the Oodlabari–Dam Dim–Chalsa area received a most serious set-back. Massive state repression was certainly a major factor. But explanation of the set-back in terms of repression and terror alone is not adequate. That the movement, even at its height, remained in a state of isolation from most of the rural areas in the district and from Rajbansi Hindu and Muslim peasants in the Duars as well as from the masses of urban population, was much more important[140]. But no less important was the transformation in the political climate of the province in general and Jalpaiguri district in particular. That Freedom with Partition was in the horizon, overshadowed all other events.

MAY–AUGUST 1947

By the third of week of April 1947 the main lines of partition of the country were accepted by both League and Congress leaderships. Following this, at the initiative of most of the Bengal Congress leaders and also Hindu Mahasabha regional and local conferences demanding partition of Bengal and formation of a province with non-Muslim majority areas, came to be organized throughout Bengal. As a part of this campaign North Bengal Jatiya Mahasabha, a conference of more than 500 delegates from the eight districts of Rajshahi Division was held in Jalpaiguri on 17 and 18 May. Among others, the Hindu planters and Marwari businessmen of Jalpaiguri played an important role in the organization of the conference. Welcoming the delegates on behalf of the organizers, Upendranath Barman who had fully identified himself with the Hindu nationalists said that 'Bengal was confronted with a terrible catastrophe' and that the plan put forward by Sarat Bose and H. S. Suhrawardy for a united, independent Bengal was 'a great political trap' for the Hindus. The conference presided over by Pandit Lakshmikanta Maitra lent support to the demand for partition of Bengal and rejected in unambiguous language the Bose–Suhrawardy plan. Khagendra Nath Das Gupta moved a resolution calling upon all nationalists of Bengal to immediately organize defence parties in every village, town and city. Another resolution moved by Nagendra Nath Mahalanabish, a leading lawyer of Jalpaiguri, resolved to form a Committee of Action to implement the Das Gupta resolution. By that time any distinction between Congress and Hindu Mahasabha had been virtually obliterated[141]. In a by-election held in Jalpaiguri—Siliguri constitutency in early June, according to the contemporary Communist source the Congress sought votes on a Hindu solidarity platform[142].

The League leadership of the district did not sit idle. Once it became clear that the province was going to be partitioned, Nawab Musharraff Hossian, having considerable stake in the form of large *jotedari* interests and a large number of tea gardens, and other League leaders mounted a campaign for inclusion of the whole of Jalpaiguri district in Pakistan.

The political situation was further complicated by the projection of the slogan of Rajasthan or creation of a separate Rajbansi Kshatriya land under Koch Bihar State. The Jalpaiguri Kshatriya Samiti which was in early 1947 being led by Girija Singha and Mukunda (Singha) Sarkar, both of them having links with Nagendra Narayan Roy of Rangpur, a Rajbansi Minister in the League ministry, tried to popularize the slogan among Hindus and Muslims of local origin. In early May Jogendra Mandal, a Scheduled Caste leader who had become a Minister in the Interim Government as a League nominee, toured north Bengal and in meetings held in Jalpaiguri and several other places lent support to the Rajasthan idea. In the June by-election in which Sarkar was the Kshatriya Samiti candidate the Samiti campaign centred around this slogan[143]. In the Alipur Duars area and elsewhere influential Hindus and Muslims of Rajbansi origin circulated leaflets in support of the Rajasthan slogan and emphasized that their ancestors had a glorious history of empire-building (see Appendix II). There are reasons to consider that the Rajasthan move had the support from Koch Bihar Hitasadhini Sabha, an outfit of Hindu and Muslim *jotedars* of Koch Bihar and also from the *dewan* and ministers of Koch Behar State perhaps with a wink from Maharaja Jagaddipendra Narayan Bhup Bahadur. There were several other separatist moves and schemes by the European planters[144].

All these moves and counter-moves generated considerable uncertainty, anxiety and tensions in the minds of the people. In view of the League effort to get Jalpaiguri district or at least a large chunk of it included in Pakistan, communal tensions were rising and were having repercussions even in the areas of the *tebhaga* struggle. Among the organized political forces, only the Communists took an unqualified unambiguous anti-communal position. RSP and Forward Bloc too strongly opposed the partition move. But on the whole the Left showed its utter helplessness before the unprecedented growth of communalism and failed to mobilize popular forces against the move for Partition.

When Freedom came, the Debiganj–Pachagar–Boda areas—the areas of peasant movement since 1939—went to East Pakistan (present-day Bangladesh). The Duars upheaval, however, created durable bases for future Communist-led popular movements. The years 1946–47 also saw initial moves on the part of the non-Communist Left groups and parties, particularly the Congress Socialists and the RSP, to spread out among the peasants and plantation labour. The Congress had, by the end of the period, transformed itself into a component of the ruling political force oriented basically towards preservation of the social, political and economic stability and containment of popular yearning for a break with the status quo. What all this meant for the peasant masses, *adhiars*, plantation labour, tribals and various other subordinate groups as well as for the economy and society of the truncated district, is a theme for another study.

11 Conclusion

The preceding survey of certain dimensions of the historical processes that had been in operation in the district of Jalpaiguri for nearly eight decades indicates the persistence of a curious dichotomy between potential for fundamental social, economic and political transformation and eventual non-realization of the potential.

The district had all the distinctive characteristics of a colonialized economy and society. Even the administrative arrangement in the form of demarcation of an extensive tract as non-Regulated area implying the prohibition of any anti-colonial political activity highlighted the colonialized feature. The peasant economy suffered from stagnation and disintegration resulting from the rapid spread of *jotedar-adhiar* relations and multi-form exploitation of the peasant masses. The process was closely linked to the penetration of capitalist exploitation in the form of tea plantation enterprise dominated by European capital. Alongside this, there was an early growth of a small Indian sector pioneered by Indian enterpreneurs—both Hindu and Muslim—all significantly immigrants with no deep roots in Jalpaiguri's economic and social life. Despite occasional tensions in the relationship of the Indian entrepreneurs with the British capital, they remained dependent on the latter and collaborative in nature.

It was in such a context that divergent and sometimes even conflicting political trends and forces worked. The nationalist politics that had emerged in the early twentieth century, by and large, remained limited and feeble. It is not that it did not have any possibility of vigorous development. The years of the Non-Cooperation movement revealed various significant possibilities in the form of making nationalists out of Rajbansi Hindus and also Rajbansi Muslims, peasant militancy, sparks of labour-tribal protest and even creation of parallel political authority. But such possibilities remained basically unrealized. The political trends discussed earlier revealed the inability of the nationalist leadership to unite the diverse subordinate social groups: peasants including *adhiars*, plantation labour, autochthon social groups and communities, and immigrant tribals at the base level.

Class outlook and ideology of the Congress nationalists and their links with the dominant groups, the planters and *jotedars*, largely lay at the root of their default. For Jalpaiguri it could particularly be said that the small town-based immigrant *bhadralok* leadership lacked adequate integration with the broad sections of Rajbansi Hindus, Rajbansi Muslims, tribals like Oraons, Mundas or Santals and other linguistic-cultural groups and communities. This lack of integration was in striking contrast to the composite culture that the local Hindus and local Muslims had at the grass roots. But for the immigrant Hindus and also Muslim élites even language constituted a barrier. The historical processes were such that the Congress leadership at the district level failed to evolve any programme oriented towards the subordinate groups and classes at the base. In their political programme and practices it could not incorporate and address even those issues which had been thrown up earlier by government reports (for example, Milligan's Settlement Report) or cases of self-mobilization of the subordinates or the Non-Cooperation movement. On the contrary, there were instances, as at the time of the 1929 district youth conference, on the part of the Congress leadership steadfastly avoiding any activity that might annoy the colonial officials and the dominant groups. In the period mid-1946 to August 1947 there were moves which even amounted to entering into conspiracy with the superordinates to contain and break popular upsurge, the most striking one being the understanding reached between the Congress leadership and the planters, both foreign and Indian. The ambivalence of the nationalist leadership was also manifested in the Hindu nationalist attitude that prevailed among its important segments, its failure to make any dent among the Muslims despite the fact that in Jalpaiguri Muslims of local origin remained outside the purview of separatist Muslim communal politics till at least the early 1940s, and its undisguised effort in early 1947 to develop Hindu nationalist consolidation.

The social and political life in the district had other dichotomies in addition to the one between the *bhadralok* nationalists and the popular masses. One of these found expression in the absence of integration between the immigrant Muslim leadership and the multitude of local Muslims resulting in considerable tension between these two segments of the Muslim community.

It is interesting that since early 1930s from time to time attempts were made on the part of the District Kshatriya Samiti and District Mohammedan Association to build a local political network involving Hindus and Muslims of local origin as a move against domination by immigrants. But both the organization being based on *jotedar* support did not have any peasant perspective and programme and remained on the periphery of élitist nationalist politics, communal activities and radical peasant movement.

The fragmented political experience in Jalpaiguri was also seen in the course of the Rajbansi caste movement which combined elements of social resentment against *bhatia* or immigrant domination, conservative socio-cultural attitude that did not even question the Brahmanical caste structure, loyalism depending on the British patronage and distancing itself from the nationalist politics, agrarian conservatism and Hindu communal overtone. But the movement was not free from tensions and internal contradictions which became particularly manifest after the introduction of the 1935 constitutional reforms. It tended to fluctuate between casteist sectarianism, Muslim communalism, Hindu Mahasabhaite programme and ideology and Congress politics. Eventually, in Jalpaiguri, one segment aligned with Hindu nationalism as projected by the Congress and another segment for a brief period before Independence hesitantly collaborated with the League and a section of the Namasudra movement and with encouragement from elements within the Koch Bihar State ruling circle even toyed with the idea of a separate Rajbansi land. Jalpaiguri, however, was one of the few districts in Bengal where despite the ambivalences of the leadership of the caste movement the Communist Left could create a powerful base among the Rajbansi peasants.

As against the fragmented experience and deep-seated anomalies of the different versions of élitist politics, Jalpaiguri during the long period under survey witnessed numerous popular protests which, however, for most part remained disjointed from each other and lacked any distinct direction. It was only during the closing decade or so of the period under study that popular forces—peasants and later on railway workers, plantation labour and tribals—began to combine against common enemies which took the shape of a popular insurgency in large tracts of the district. The upsurge went, in one form or another, against the two sub-systems of colonialism in the district—the plantation system and the *jotedar-adhiar* relations—which had kept broad sections of the people under multiple and often interpenetrating forms of exploitation and in a state of semi-bondage. This upsurge of the mass forces was made possible largely by the role of radical Left politics, particularly of the Communist Left.

But the radical potential created by the Left and the popular forces could not develop into reality. The Left failed to transcend the ambiguities of the processes of social change indicated in this study. Part of the reason was rooted in the continued dominance exercised by different strands of elitist political leadership. But did the Left itself have adequate perception of the complexities of the situation? Could the Left work out an appropriate strategy and policies to meet the challenge of the situation? The story of Jalpaiguri suggests that the Left too including its Communist segment had its confusion and weaknesses. The radical potential was thwarted also by the developments that had been taking place at the provincial and national level. This leads us back to the issue of the relationship between developments at different spatial levels. But this is another aspect that needs further study both in its historical and contemporaneous dimensions.

Appendix I

LIST OF TRIBALS CONVICTED IN JALPAIGURI DISTRICT FOR PARTICIPATION IN TRIBAL WORKER AGITATION 1916

Sl. No.	Date of conviction	Name	Parentage and address
1	29 June 1916	Sunia Uraon of Tondoo T.E.	Naru Uraon of Makunda, P.S. Marar, (Ranchi)
2	- do. -	Jambua Uraon of Tondoo T.E.	Dasha Uraon of Purana, Ranchi P.S. & Dist. Ranchi
3	24 August 1916	Lalmohan Teli of Hatipotha T.E.	Parmand Teli of Burmu, P.S. Manda (Ranchi)
4	- do. -	Sukha Uraon of Hatipotha	Sudhu Uraon of Hatipotha T.E. P.S. Kumargram (Jalpaiguri)
5	- do. -	Jahuru Uraon of Hatipotha T.E.	Latia Uraon of - do. -
6	- do. -	Jethu Bhakta of Hatipotha T.E.	Aklu Bhakta of Sarle, P.S. Marar (Ranchi)
7	- do. -	Dukhan Goala of Hatipotha T.E.	Harku Goala, Hatipotha T.E., Kumargram
8	- do. -	Mangra Uraon of Hatipotha T.E.	Dhouna Uraon of -do.-

9	- do. -	Jagarnath Mahali	Munnu Mahli of - do. -
10	- do. -	Gahnoo Uraon of Hatipotha T.E.	Makhawa Uraon of Sarle, P.S. Marar (Ranchi)
11	- do. -	Baijnath Mahali of Hatipotha T.E.	Sahdeo Mahali of Tatkundu, P.S. Marar (Ranchi)
12	- do. -	Charwa Uraon of Hatipotha T.E.	Sukhu Uraon of Hatipotha T.E., P.S. Kumargram, (Jalpaiguri)
13	- do. -	Bahura Uraon	Unknown of Hatipotha T.E.
14	- do. -	Jahuria Uraon	Krishna Uraon of Hatipotha T.E., P.S. Kumargram, (Jalpaiguri)
15	24 August 1916	Ghengtu Munda of Hatipotha T.E.	Mania Munda of Ramjari, P.S. Kalibira, (Ranchi)
16	- do. -	Debi Uraon of Hatipotha T.E.	Aghna Uraon of Katangdir,P.S. Manda, (Ranchi)
17	31 August 1916	Dosra Somra Uraon of Hatipotha T.E.	Lalu Uraon of Umedand, P.S. Marar, (Ranchi)
18	- do. -	Chengna Uraon of Hatipotha T.E.	Makhoa Uraon of Hatipotha T.E., P.S. Kumargram, (Jalpaiguri)
19	- do. -	Gendwa Uraon of Hatipotha T.E.	Makhoa Uraon of Hatipotha T.E., P.S. Kumargram, (Jalpaiguri)
20	- do. -	Porha Munda	Mathura Munda of Jalpaiguri

21	1 September 1916	Manghu Uraon of Gandrapara T.E.	Raina Uraon of Kita, P.S. Chandwa, (Ranchi)
22	- do. -	Sibu Uraon of Gandrapara T.E.	Bhikari Uraon of Gandrapara T.E. P.S. Dhupguri
23	- do. -	Jallah Uraon of Gandrapara T.E.	Kare Uraon of Kharcha, P.S. Lohhrdaga, (Ranchi)
24	- do. -	Budhu Uraon (Chotta) Gandrapara, T.E.	Somra Uraon of Nawaguda, P.S. Latehar, (Ranchi)
25	- do. -	Budhu Uraon (Bara) of Gandrapara T.E.	At present of Gandrapara T.E., P.S. Dhupguri
26	- do. -	Etwa Uraon of Gandrapara T.E.	Chamru Uraon of Dhupguri
27	- do. -	Chuttia Uraon of Gandrapara T.E.	Sukra Uraon of Bhushur, P.S. Latehar, (Ranchi)
28	- do. -	Gharwa Uraon of Gandrapara T.E.	Charwa Uraon of Sakoar, P.S. Latehar, (Ranchi)
29	- do. -	Somra Uraon of Gandrapara T.E.	Bhorwa Uraon of Ranchi

SOURCE : *DPA Report* for 1917, pp. 426-7.

NAMES OF PEASANTS AND WORKERS KILLED IN POLICE
FIRING

A. *Police firing at Mathachulka (Neora Majhiali near Baradighi)
under Mal P.S. on 1 March 1947.*

1	Maharani Oraoni	(Peasant woman)
2	Sukhu Oraon	
3	Bacchu Oraon	Two brothers
4	Budhu Oraon	
5	One Santal	Name not known

B. *Police firing at Mahabari (near Mangalbari Hat-Chalsa) under
Matialli P.S. on 4 April 1947.*

1	One local peasant woman	Name not known
2	Murla Oraon	
3	Jitia Oraon	Worker, Oodlabari T.E.
4	Lachu Oraon	
5	Natai Oraon	Worker, Oodlabari T.E.
6	Chama Oraon	Owner of 5 acres of land
7	Pola Qraon	
8	Era Patras(Turi)	
9	Bhulu Oraon	
10	Name not known	

Appendix II

NOTE BY SIR F. BURROWS, GOVERNOR OF BENGAL

EXTRACTS ONLY   14 February 1947

'I understand that the contingencies for which planning is required are :

    A. An announcement by H.M.G. that they intend to withdraw their power in India within a time limit irrespective of a constitutional agreement :

    B. A situation of widespread disorder and confusion.

'The Communists are actively fishing in all our troubled waters and would give the disorders both an agrarian and an anti-British colour—the latter would not be difficult in the tea gardens of North Bengal, in the industrial areas along the Hooghly in West Bengal and at Narayanganj (Dacca).

'The "Internal security" problem as it presented itself from time to time during the past ten months has been the subject of frequent discussion by me with successive Army and Area Commanders, and as a result of my recent tour in North Bengal I am proposing to discuss more especially the arrangements to be made in that area when I see the Army Commander on the 15th February. (In this matter I share the apprehensions of the Commanding Officer of the Northern Bengal Mounted Rifles regarding the suitability of the existing scheme in present conditions in the Jalpaiguri and Darjeeling districts. The scheme, I understand, even in its most recent form, still envisages the evacuation of the European population of the Jalpaiguri (plains) tea area by the very vulnerable "Cart road" to Darjeeling. That may have been a good—and the only safe plan–when there were no aerodromes in the Duars, when the loyalty of the hill people was not questioned, and when retreat to Darjeeling would have been only till restoration of order in the plains. In all these respects the situation has now changed. The existence of an airstrip at Baghdogra (near Siliguri) and of an airfield at Hasimara (in the east of Jalpaiguri district) render evacuation to Calcutta or even out of India feasible if aircraft can be made available and this would obviate retreat to Darjeeling where (if it could be reached at all) the friendliness of the hill population can no longer be counted on to anything like the former extent and where, with the plains in chaos and no airfield available, the European community may find themselves quite cut off amid a population which may soon be very short of food. Evacuation from East Bengal (Dacca and Chittagong) will have to be by air (for the former) and by sea or air (for the latter). There are possibilities of road, rail and air evacuation from West Bengal. I do not at present know how we could evacuate Darjeeling except by air from Baghdogra'.

SOURCE: N. Mansergh(ed.), *Transfer of Power*, Vol. IX, London, Document No. 395, pp. 705, 707 and 708.

FROM J.D. TYSON ON BEHALF OF THE CENTRAL
CONSTITUTIONAL COMMITTEE OF THE EUROPEAN
ASSOCIATION, CALCUTTA TO SIR T. SHONE,
BRITISH COMMISSIONER IN INDIA.

EXTRACTS ONLY   20 March 1946

'Recent events in many parts of India have demonstrated how easily disorder can become widespread and how helpless the authorities are to cope with it under present circumstances. This danger of a complete breakdown of law and order, and of a resulting orgy of plunder and murder is particularly great in the outlying districts where large number of Europeans live, as for example in the planting areas of Bengal and Assam, of Bihar and

South India, while there are numerous other pockets of Europeans in rural areas elsewhere.

'At the moment feeling towards the British is probably more friendly than it has been for some years and there is thus no immediate reason to expect the growth of any movement directed specifically against our community. There are signs, however, that both Hindus and Muslims are assuming that H.M.G. will have to make an award in June 1948 and each hopes that the award will be in its favour. Whatever then may be the decision of H.M.G. as to the Government or Governments to whom power is to be transferred it is likely to be regarded by one or other of the parties as a betrayal. The resulting anger may well provide the starting point for a violent anti-British movement throughout large parts of India.

'Another, not dissimilar, potential danger arises from the crude form of Communism which is rampant in many parts of India today. Already in some localities Communist agitators have sought to stir up labour to personal violence against managers and employers, and in areas such as the planting districts, where the employing classes are mainly European, Communism may assume an anti-British form and, in the event of any breakdown in law and order, lead to general attacks on British residents.

'To put it briefly the situation today is full of explosive elements. It is impossible to forecast when, where or in what form violence will break out, but in view of the special place occupied by the British in the life of the country they are by no means an unlikely target'.

SOURCE: N. Mansergh (ed.), *Transfer of Power*, Vol. IX, London, Document No. 552, p. 994

CONGRESS, DUARS PLANTERS ASSOCIATION AND
INDIAN TEA PLANTERS ASSOCIATION

A.*Extract from the Proceedings of the Special Meeting of the Executive Committee of the ITPA held on 13-4-47*

'Resolved that Trade Unions be encouraged to be formed on every garden under the Association on proper and non-political and healthy basis and the Association should help in forming such Unions with model rules'.

SOURCE: *ITPA Annual Report* for 1947, pp. 102-03

B.*Extract from the Proceedings of the Special Meeting of the Executive Committee of the ITPA held on 2-8-47*

'The meeting considered the letter dated the 25th July 1947 from the Jalpaiguri District Congress Committee wherein the Congress informed the Association of its desire to organise Trade Unions amongst tea garden labourers. The Congress in its letter made it clear that as designing parties were exploiting the labourers for purposes other than for real benefit of the labourers, it intended to establish Trade Unions which would be run on the proper Trade Union lines. The meeting also considered the report of an informal discussion held on the 25th July 1947 between the representatives of the D.P.A., the Congress and the Association on the subject ... the meeting decided to advise member bodies to give every possible help and assistance to the Congress, it being the policy of the Association all along to promote all-round welfare of the labourers ...'.

SOURCE: *Ibid.*, p.112.

C.*Extract from the Proceedings of a DPA Committee Meeting held on 11-8-47*

'The Labour Officer elaborated points brought up regarding Gurkha League and Congress Trade Unions. Agreed that Congress members with cards of identification will be given permission to hold meetings in gardens with a view to forming Trade Unions.'

SOURCE: *DPA Annual Report* for 1947.

D.*Extracts from the Proceedings of the Nagrakata Sub-District Committee Meeting held on 17-9-47*

'Letter from Deven Sarkar, Secretary of Jalpaiguri District Congress Committee to the Chairman, Duars Planters Association dated 8-9-47 was read and discussion ensued. It was hoped by all members that Mr. Jenkins (Labour Officer) would be able to arrange for a Senior Congress Official to be appointed to Trade Unions rather than a local minor official appointed by the Secretary, Jalpaiguri District Congress Committee'.

SOURCE: Ibid., p. 259.

TWO DOCUMENTS ON MOVE FOR INCLUSION OF DUARS INTO KOCH BIHAR STATE

A. An Appeal

Our Brothers living in Western Duars,

You might have heard from the elderly persons that in the days of our forefathers these Duars areas constituted a part of the Koch Bihar kingdom. Many of them were engaged as service-holders in the royal court, jagirdars, sardars [chiefs], village *patwaris* and supervisors. The frontier of the Koch Bihar kingdom lay extended up to the foothills. Due to various reasons in the last two or three generations we have become detached from the Koch Bihar kingdom. In fact, in language, feeling, social custom, ethnic features, work, myths, and culture, education and domestic life we were and still are one with the subjects of the present-day Koch Bihar State.

Now, the British will shortly leave the country after giving up the responsibility of ruling the country. Under the circumstances, the land of our forefathers — the happy and prosperous Koch Bihar is the source of our strength and security. In order that our peace and happiness get protection and in order that our previous beliefs and civilization are preserved we consider that our re-inclusion into the Koch Bihar kingdom is reasonable. Let us all submit our appeal by presenting ourselves at the Maharaja's palace. We hope that he will fulfil our wishes and will take measures for inclusion of the Duars area in the Koch Bihar kingdom.

Shri Bidhu Bhusan Karji, Vill. Parorpar
Shri Gopal Chandra Roy, Vill. Silbari
Shri Tarinikanta Roy, Vill. Raicheng
Shri Tarakeswar Basunia,Vill. Ksheti Fulbari
Mohammad Abduchhebahan, Vill. Falakata

B.   An Appeal

To the Rajbansis and Indigenous Muslim Inhabitants

Brothers,

For the Rajbansis and indigenous Muslim inhabitants present time is not the time for remaining asleep. You know that before the British period the Western Duars area of Jalpaiguri district was under our Rajbansi kingdom of Koch Bihar *rajya*. During the British period we have become separated from the [Rajbansi] national empire of Koch Bihar. The British rulers are leaving and the Maharaj (Koch Bihar ruler) has demanded the restoration of our ancestral land–the Duars area [to Koch Bihar]. To make this demand a success and the national movement victorious each and every Rajbansi and Muslim of the area will have to unite. So we make a sincere request to our indigenous brothers to devote themselves in the sacred task of strengthening a united Rajasthan and ... build up the national glory through the inclusion of the Duars area into the Koch Bihar kingdom.

Brothers,

We need Awakening. We need Solidarity. We need Patriotic Inspiration. We need Emancipation of the threatened Duars people. We need Patriotism.

N.B. Every country, every nation is engaged in life and death struggle for founding national empire. During these days of national awakening we also similarly have to awaken ourselves.

Shri Rajendranath Roy Sarkar (Chengpara)
Shri Nilkantha Das Muktear (Damanpur)
Shri Chabiballabh Roy (Bhothuri)
Shri Surendra Nath Barman (Alipurduar Court)
Shri Maheshchandra Gabur (Nimti)
Shri Upendranath Adhikari (Chaparer Par)
Maulvi Mainuddin Basunia (Alipurduar)
Shri Bidhubhusan Karji (Paror Par)
Shri Dudhkanthalal Roy (Alipur Duar Court)
Raj Mohammad Raichhuddin Basunia (Alipurduar)
Shri Kailaschandra Das Sarkar (Chaparer Par)
Shri Lankeswar Das (Bara Chowki)
Shri Kesharimohan Mech Mandal (Satali)
Shri Nagendranath Karji (Satali)
Maulvi Meheruddin Ahmed (Salsalabari)

I have obtained copies of these two appeals through the courtesy of Dr Anandagopal Ghosh.]

Notes and References

CHAPTER 2

1 Jalpaiguri district and Bengal in this work refer to pre-1947 administrative divisions.

2 'The name Duars, divided into western and eastern, the term western applying to that portion which falls in Jalpaiguri district, refers to that tract of the country which affords gateways or *duars* to Bhutan from India. There are supposed to be 11 recognised *duars* or passes into Bhutan from India, of which 5 happen to be in Jalpaiguri district. These are from the west eastwards, Chamurchi, Lakhimpur, Balla, Baksha (Buxa), and Kumargram'. *Jalpaiguri DH*, p. viii.

3 *Jalpaiguri DG*, ch.II; and *Jalpaiguri DH*, pp. iii-v.

4 See Manikrishna Sen, 'Tebhaga Andolane Rangpur' in Sumit Chakrabarty (ed.), *Tebhaga Sangram: Rajat-Jayanti Smarak Grantha*, Calcutta, 1973, p. 57.

5 See the extract from *Himalayan Journals* by Sir J. D. Hooker in *Jalpaiguri DH*, p. ccxl.

6 *Jalpaiguri DG*, p. 80.

7 For these accounts see, among others, 'Extracts from Dr. Francis Buchanan-Hamilton's Account of the District of Rangpur, 1810' (hereafter Buchanan-Hamilton's Account) in *Jalpaiguri DH*, pp. cxxxii; Khan Chowdhury Amanatullah Ahmed, *Koch Biharer Itihas*, Pt.1, Cooch Behar, 1342, ch.VII; and *West Bengal District Gazetters: Koch Bihar* by Durgadas Mazumdar, Govt. of West Bengal, Calcutta, 1977, ch.II, pp. 30-1.

8 See 'Buchanan-Hamilton's Account' in *Jalpaiguri DH*, pp. cxxxii-cxxxiii; Khan Chowdhury, *op.cit.*, ch. XIII; and *West Bengal District Gazetters: Jalpaiguri*, Calcutta 1981 (hereafter *Jalpaiguri DG 1981*), pp. 55-62. According to some accounts, Darpa Dev, the Raikat in 1770s and 1780s, had entered into an understanding with the Dev Raja of Bhutan and went against the Koch Bihar kingdom which was in alliance with the British and that was the reason for interfering with the status of the Raikats ('Buchanan-Hamiltons' Account' *Jalpaiguri DH*, pp. cxxxii). It is, however, widely believed that Darpa Dev Raikat had pro-

vided support to the Sannyasi rebels and that is why his status was adversely affected.

9 *Jalpaiguri DH*, pp. viii-ix; and D. K. Roy, 'Administrative and Jurisdictional Changes in the District of Jalpaiguri since its Formation' in *Centenary Souvenir*, p. 59.

10 In the district there were two subdivisions—Sadar and Alipur Duars.

11 For details of physical aspects and river system see *Jalpaiguri DH*, pp. viii-xxxi.

12 *Jalpaiguri DG*, p. 31.

13 *COI. Report*, para 103.

14 For the Meches see 'Buchanan-Hamilton Account' in *Jalpaiguri DH*, pp. cxxxix-cxl; *Duars SSR*, ch.VII, 'Social Life and Religion of Certain Tribes'; *Jalpaiguri SSR*, p. 135, para 115; and *Jalpaiguri DG*, pp. 36-8.

15 In most of the writings on the composition of population in Jalpaiguri and other north Bengal districts and also often in popular perception Rajbansis are only Hindus and by implication Muslims of local origin are non-Rajbansis. But the evidence that I have come across which has been referred to below clearly shows that, as stated in the text too, the bulk of the local Muslims were converted Rajbansis. Some of them, for example, the well-known big *jotedar* Mechhua Mohammed of Dhupguri area, was Meches. In view of this, throughout this work I have used the category Rajbansis in the sense of Hinduized Rajbansis and Islamized Rajbansis. For a similar use see Debesh Roy's significant novel relating to a part of the Duars *Tistaparer Brittanta*, Dey's Publishing, Calcutta, 1988.

16 G.A.Grierson, *Linguistic Survey of India*, Vol. I, Pt.1, Introduction, 1927, Reprint, Motilal Banarasidas, Delhi, 1967, p. 153.

17 See *Jalpaiguri DG 1981*, pp. 52-9.

18 'Buchanan-Hamilton Account' in *Jalpaiguri DH*, p. cxxxv.

19 Ibid.

20 Edward T. Dalton, *Descriptive Ethnology of Bengal*, Calcutta, 1872, Reprint, Indian Studies Past & Present, Calcutta, 1960, pp. 89-93.

21 H. H. Risley, *The Tribes and Castes of Bengal*, Vol. I, Calcutta, 1891, Reprint, Calcutta, 1981, p. 491.

22 Chatterjee, *Kirata-Jana-Kirti*, The Asiatic Society, Calcutta, 1951, Reprint, 1974, p. 112.

23 See in this connexion *Rangpur SSR*, p. 12, para 21; and also *Dinajpur SSR*, p. 11, para. 13.

24 Charu Chandra Sanyal, *The Rajbansis of North Bengal (A Study of a Hindu Social Group)*, The Asiatic Society, Calcutta, 1965, p. 13.

25 See Upendranath Barman, *Rajbansi Kshatriya Jatir Itihas*, 3rd edition, Jalpaiguri, 1981, pp. 26-55; and 'Buchanan-Hamilton Account' in *Jalpaiguri DH*, p. cxxxv.

26 Op.cit., p. cxxxv.

27 H.H. Hunter, *Statistical Accounts of Bengal* (hereafter *SAB*), Vol. X, Darjeeling, Jalpaiguri and State of Kuch Bihar, London, 1876, Reprint, 1974, p. 255.

28 *Census Report of the District of Jalpaiguri 1891*, p. 21, para 77.
29 Ibid; and *SAB*, Vol. VII, *Maldah, Rangpur and Dinajpur* p. 225.
30 *Duars SSR*.
31 For the north Bengal districts like Jalpaiguri or Rangpur or Dinajpur and the Koch Bihar State three categories of
   Muslims—Pathans, Sheikhs and Nasyas—were mentioned in the
   Census reports. Of these, the latter two were considered to be of
   local origin. The Nasyas or 'unspecified', as they were returned in
   the Census of 1872, were numerous and most probably they and
   also the Sheikhs were converts. See in this connexion *Jalpaiguri DG*,
   p. 35; *Rangpur SSR*, p. 11; *Dinajpur SSR*, p. 10; and J.A.Vas, *Eastern
   Bengal and Assam District Gazeteers : Rangpur*, 1911, p. 41.
32 *Jalpaiguri DG*, p. 102.
33 Referring to this aspect Hunter quoted the following from an
   account of a Deputy Commissioner : 'A witness in the courts, being
   asked in what village or where he lives, answers by giving the
   name of the *jot* in which he lives. These jots either bear the name of
   the original settler who first held them, or of the mass in whose
   name they may have been afterwards registered ...' (op.cit., Vol. X,
   p. 287).
34 The following account is based on Sanyal, op.cit., chs. VII and VIII,
   pp. 134-73.
35 The account that follows is based on Sanyal, op.cit, ch.IV, pp. 88-
   137. In discussing the marriage customs Sanyal observes, 'In
   matters of marriage the Rajbansis [were] in a state of transition' (p.
   88).
36 *Duars SSR*, ch.VII, 'Social Life and Religion of Certain Tribes'.
37 Ibid.
38 Cf. *Rangpur SSR*, p. 11.
39 *Jalpaiguri DG*, p. 35.
40 *Duars SSR*, Ch.VII, 'Social Life and Religion of Certain Tribes'; and
   Jalpaiguri DG, p. 35.
41 Hunter, *SAB*, p. 35; and *Dinajpur SSR*, p. 10.
42 Cf. Chatterjee, op.cit., pp. 127-8.
43 Interviews with Sabed Ali Ahmed and Dr Taiyab Chowdhuri. See
   also J.A.Vas, *Eastern Bengal and Assam District Gazetteers: Rangpur*,
   1911, p. 41.
44 *Rangpur SSR*, p. 11.
45 See *Imperial Gazetteer of India*, Vol. XIV, p. 35; Hunter, op.cit., p. 260;
   and *Jalpaiguri DG*, p. 36.
46 Ibid., pp. 35-6; and *Rangpur SSR*, p. 11. Here are some such names:
   Khaichalu, Tepua, Bhaichalu, Dhipiri, Parai, Bhola, Bacha Bau,
   Chhota Bau, Bara Bau, Baisakhu, Jaso, Bhasani and Chengroo.
   (Courtesy: Taiyab Chowdhuri and Sukhamoy Das Gupta.)
47 *Duars SSR*, Ch.VII, 'Social Life and Religion of Certain Tribes'.
48 Cf. Rangpur SSR, p. 11.
49 Charu Chandra Sanyal, 'Jalpaiguri Saharer Eksho Bachhar' in
   Centenary Souvenir, p. 99.

50 *Jalpaiguri DG*, p. 102.
51 Ibid., p. 36.
52 *Jalpaiguri DG 1981*, pp. 79-80.
53 *Jalpaiguri DG*, p. 36.
54 See Sharit Bhowmik, *Class Formation in the Plantation System*, PPH, New Delhi, 1981, Ch.4, pp. 105-35.
55 *Jalpaiguri DG*, p. 41.

CHAPTER 3

1 *Jalpaiguri SSR*, p. 74, para 76, and *Jalpaiguri DG*, pp. 80-3.
2 For 'Government Estates' and diversity of land tenures in these estates in different parts of Bengal see *BAR* 1921-22, pp. 105-07, para 205, and for details of the arrangement in the Duars see *Jalpaiguri DG*, p. 86 and *Jalpaiguri DH*, p. lxxv.
3 *Jalpaiguri DG*, p. 83. See in this connexion Partha Chatterjee, *Bengal 1920-1947*, Vol. 1, *The Land Question* (hereafter '*Bengal 1920-1947*'), K. P. Bagchi, Calcutta, 1984, pp. 25-6.
4 *Jalpaiguri DG*, p. 84.
5 Reprinted in *Census Report* 1951 Vol. VI, Pt. IC, p. 193. See in this connexion Ratnalekha Ray, *Change in Bengal Agrarian Society 1760-1850*, Manohar, Delhi, 1979, ch.3, pp. 53-72.
6 *Jalpaiguri DG*, pp. 80-1,
7 See Binay Bhusan Chaudhuri, 'The Process of Depeasantization in Bengal and Bihar, 1885-1947', *The Indian Historical Review*, Vol. II, No.1, July 1975 (hereafter Chaudhuri, *IHR, 1975*) p. 146, and Partha Chatterjee, 'Agrarian Structure in Pre-Partition Bengal', in Asok Sen, Partha Chatterjee and Saugata Mukherjee, *Perspectives in Social Sciences 2*, Oxford University Press, Calcutta, 1982, pp. 113-224.
8 See the account given by Deputy Commissioner of Jalpaiguri in early 1870s W.W. Hunter, *SAB*, Vol. X, pp. 280, 283-4, 288.
9 Ibid., pp. 279-80.
10 Ibid.
11 Tweedie's findings as referred to by P. Nolan, Rajshahi Divisional Commissioner in his 1894 'Note on the Settlement of the Western Duars', (hereafter *Nolan Note*) para 6 as reproduced in the GOB's Revenue Department Resolution on *Duars SSR*, p. 16. For further details see *Jalpaiguri SSR*, p. 78, para 85, pp. 82-3, paras 87-8.
12 Hunter, op. cit., pp. 279-80.
13 Special Report from the Jalpaiguri Deputy Commissioner, dt. 2 August 1872 extensively cited in ibid., pp. 286-92.

14 Hunter, op. cit., pp. 278, 279.
15 See the text above.
16 *Duars SSR*, pp. 138-9, para. 734, p. 141, para. 746, p. 148, para. 791; and *Jalpaiguri DG*, p. 110.
17 *Duars SSR*, pp. 46-7, para. 172.
18 *Census Report of the District of Jalpaiguri 1891* (hereafter Jalpaiguri District Census), p. 26, para. 89; *Duars SSR*, p. 130, para. 684; *Jalpaiguri DG*, p. 36; and Chaudhuri, *IHR*, 1975. p. 109.
19 *Jalpaiguri District Census 1891*, p. 26, para 89.
20 Ibid., p. 26, para. 87.
21 Ibid., p. 26, para. 89.
22 Ibid., p. 27, para. 96.
23 Referred to in *Jalpaiguri SSR*, p. 89, para. 89.
24 *Duars SSR*, p. 119, paras. 647-52, p. 120, para. 655. Cf. Asok Sen, 'Agrarian Structure and Tenancy Laws in Bengal 1850-1900' in Sen, Chatterjee and Mukherjee, op. cit., pp. 45-6.
25 WBSA. Revenue Dept. Land Revenue. Amendment of the Bengal Tenancy Act. File 3-A/14 1-3 Nos. 18-21 of November 1914.
26 Cf. Adrienne Cooper, 'Sharecroppers and Landlords in Bengal 1930-50: The Dependency Web and Its Implications', *Journal of Peasant Studies*, Vol. 10, Nos.2 and 3, January/March 1983 and also Cooper, *Sharecropping and Sharecroppers' Struggles in Bengal 1930-1950*, K.P. Bagchi & Co., Calcutta, 1988, pp. 85-7.
27 Cf. *ibid.*, pp. 99-102. I have personally come across many instances of the prevalence of such practices in different parts of Jalpaiguri as late as the 1950s and even thereafter.
28 *Nolan Note*, para 18.
29 Referred to by Milligan in *Jalpaiguri SSR*, p. 88, para. 89.
30 *Nolan Note*, paras. 6 and 17.
31 *Jalpaiguri SSR*, p. 135, para. 115.
32 Ibid.
33 *Jalpaiguri DG*, p. 98.
34 *Dinajpur SSR*, p. 22.
35 Ibid., and also Chaudhury, *IHR*, 1975, pp. 147-8.
36 See in this connexion Upendra Nath Barman, *Uttar-Banglar Sekal O Amar Jivan-Smriti*, Jalpaiguri, B.S. 1392(1985), pp. 10-12.
37 *Jalpaiguri DG*, p. 59.
38 *Duars SSR*, p. 117, para. 631.
39 *Jalpaiguri DG*, p. 97.
40 Ibid., pp. 110-11.
41 Ibid., pp. 110, 113-14; and *Jalpaiguri SSR*, p. 14.
42 For the place of jute cultivation in Bengal agriculture in the context of international economy and Britain's international economic network see Sen, op.cit., 83 ff.
43 See *Jalpaiguri DG*, p. 58.
44 Cf. Sen, op.cit., p. 91.
45 *Jalpaiguri SSR*, p. 14.

46 Ibid., p. 15.
47 Ibid., pp. 135-6.
48 *Jalpaiguri DG* ,p. 101.
49 Ibid., p. 98.
50 Ibid., p. 99.
51 Ibid., p. 101.
52 Ibid., pp. 93-5.
53 *Duars SSR*, Resolution, p. 2, para 5.
54 Ibid., Resolution, p. 3, para 6.
55 Ibid., Resolution, p. 5, paras 12,13; *Jalpaiguri DH*, p. xcvii.
56 *Duars SSR*, p. 118.
57 *Jalpaiguri SSR*, p. 14.
58 Ibid., p. 91.
59 Ibid.
60 *Jalpaiguri DG*, p. 76.
61 Ibid., p. 101.
62 *Jalpaiguri SSR*, pp. 87,90.
63 Omkar Goswami, 'A Reply', *IESHR*, Vol. 23, No.2, 1986, p. 352.
64 *Duars SSR*, p. 121, para 663; and *Jalpaiguri SSR*, p. 90.
65 Ibid.
66 WBSA. Land Revenue, File 3-A/14 1-3 Nos. 18-19 of November 1914. Such high percentage was, however, considered by McAlpin as 'abnormal'.
67 *Jalpaiguri SSR*, pp. 88-92. McAlpin reported 43 per cent of the *adhiars* in the permanently settled area of Jalpaiguri were 'classi fied as dependents, that is to say their landlords provide cattle and ploughs' (op.cit.).
68 *Jalpaiguri SSR*, p. 74.
69 Ibid., pp. 74-5.
70 See note 66 above.
71 *Jalpaiguri SSR*, p. 91.
72 Ibid.
73 Cf. Hamza Alavi, 'Peasant Classes and Primordial Loyalties' *Journal of Peasant Studies*, Vol. 1, No.1, October 1973.
74 *Cheka* was prepared from ashes obtained by burning the root and stumps of cotton plant, mustard plant, *kalai* (a pulse) and plantain tree. See *Duars SSR*, para 361.
75 *Jalpaiguri DG*, p. 83.
76 Chatterjee, *Bengal 1920-1947*, pp. 151-2.
77 *Dinajpur SSR*, p. 16; and *Rangpur SSR*, pp. 14-5, para 25.
78 Based on Chatterjee, *Bengal 1920-1947*, pp. 44-54.
79 Ibid., p. 163.
80 *Jalpaiguri SSR*, pp. 90-1; and Chatterjee, *Bengal 1920-1947*, pp. 45-9
81 *Jalpaiguri SSR*, p. 92.
82 Ibid.
83 Ibid.
84 Chatterjee, *Bengal 1920-1947*, pp. 1-3.

85 Cf. Ray, op.cit., p. 291; and also Rajat Ray and Ratnalekha Ray, 'The Dynamics of Continuity in Rural Bengai under the British Imperialism', *IESHR* 1973.

86 The Raikats went up to the Privy Council several times around the issue of succession to the Baikunthapur Estate, and Prasanna Dev Raikat (1946), the last of the Raikats, was fond of horse-racing and hunting. See Jagadindra Deb Raikat, *Raikat Bangsa O Tahader Rajyer Sankshipta Bibaran*, edited by Nirmal Chandra Choudhuri, Jalpaiguri, B.S. 1389.

87 Op.cit., p. 83.

88 *Duars SSR*, ch.VII, 'Social Life and Religion of Certain Tribes'.

89 *Jalpaiguri SSR*, p. 21.

90 *Jalpaiguri DG*, p. 58.

91 Partha Chatterjee, 'Agrarian Relations and Communalism in Bengal, 1926-1935' (hereafter briefly 'Agrarian Relations and Communalism in Bengal') in Ranajit Guha (ed.), *Subaltern Studies I : Writings on South Asian History and Society*, OUP, Delhi, 1982, particularly pp. 19-34.

92 The Koch Bihar Raj family, however, deliberately strove to improve their social status by entering into matrimonial alliances with Rajput princely houses of Baroda and Jaipur and upper caste Bengali families. Many of the Raj *amlas* or officials were high caste Hindus.

93 See, among others, Jatin De, 'The History of the Krishak Praja of Bengal, 1929-1947 : A Study of Changes in Class and Inter-Community Relations in the Agrarian Sector of Bengal', unpublished Ph.D. dissertation, Delhi University, 1977, 23 ff.

94 Cf. Chatterjee, 'Agrarian Relations and Communalism in Bengal ', in Guha (ed.), op.cit.

CHAPTER 4

1 Amiya Kumar Bagchi, *Private Investment in India 1900-1939*, Cambridge, 1972. p. 48.

2 Cf., among others, G.L. Beckford, *Persistent Poverty: Underdevelopment in Plantation Economies of the Third World*, OUP, 1972; and Sidney W. Mintz, *Caribbean Transformation*, John Hopkins University Press, Baltimore, 1974.

3 S. Mukherjee, 'Emergence of Bengalee Entrepreneurship in Tea Plantation in a Bengal District, 1879-1933', *IESHR*, October--December 1976, p.489.

4 *Jalpaiguri DG*, p. 103.
5 Ibid.
6 Percival Griffiths, *The History ot the Tea Industry in India*, Weidenfeld Nicholson, London, 1967, pp. 143, 170, 179-80.
7 Cf. Bhubanes Misra,'A Study of management structure of the Indian tea industry from colonial era to recent times' (mimeo), Indian Institute of Management, Calcutta, p. 30.
8 *Jalpaiguri DG*, p. 105; and B.C. Ghose, *The Development of Tea Industry in the District of Jalpaiguri 1869-1968*, Jalpaiguri, 1970, pp. 30-7.
9 *Duars SSR*, p. 103, paras 544-6; *Jalpaiguri DG*, pp. 84-6.
10 Bagchi, op.cit., pp. 161-2.
11 The Duncan Group, *Being a Short History of Duncan Brothers & Co. Ltd., Calcutta and Walter Duncan and Goodricke Ltd., London, 1859-1959*, London, 1959, pp. 34-8, 40-4, 47-8.
12 Ibid.
13 Andrew Yule and Co. *Andrew Yule and Co. Ltd.*, Great Britain, 1963.
14 Md. Habibar Rahman, 'A Short History of Introduction of Tea in India and a Century of Progress of Gurjangjhora Tea Estate' in Gurjangjhora Tea & Industries Ltd., *Souvenir : A Century of Progress*, Jalpaiguri, 1982. It is curious that in most of the accounts of the Indian entrepreneurship in the Duars tea the role of Rahim Baksh as the first Indian pioneer is ignored.
15 Ghose, op.cit., p. 14. It may be noted that Bose was the father of the renowned scientist Jagadish Chandra Bose.
16 Mukherjee, op.cit.; Ghose, op.cit., pp. 14, 30-7; and B. De, 'Local Entrepreneurship in Tea Industry in the Dooars' in *Dooars Branch of Indian Tea Association 1879-1978* (hereafter DBITA Souvenir), Binnaguri, 1978, pp. 48, 50. (It contains articles and speeches on the occasion of the DBITAS's centenary celebration.)
17 Mukherjee, op.cit., Annexure I, Table 4 and Annexure II.
18 Ibid., Annexure II.
19 Ibid., pp. 488-90.
20 Indian Tea Planters' Association, *Golden Jubilee Souvenir* (hereafter ITPA Souvenir), Jalpaiguri, pp. 13,17,19.
21 Ghose, op.cit., pp. 30-31.
22 Mukherjee, op.cit., Annexure III, p. 512.
24 Mukherjee, op.cit., Annexure III, pp. 510-2; and Ghose, op.cit., pp. 23,26.
25 Ibid., pp. 495-6.
26 Ibid., pp. 488-90.
27 Bagchi, op.cit., pp. 165,166.
28 For details see *DPA Report* for 1915, pp. 29-30, and also for 1917, pp. 164,165-9.
29 Interview with F.M. Kerr, a retired manager and supervisor in Macneil Berry gardens in the Duars.
30 Ghose, op.cit., pp. 30,35, and *ITPA Souvenir*, p. 33.

31 For specific instances see Ghose, op.cit., p. 37, and also *DPA Report* for 1927, pp. vii, 81-2.
32 Interview with Nirendranath Bagchi, a well-known planter; and also Ghose, op.cit., pp. 22,31,42.
33 *ITPA Souvenir*, pp. 25-31.
34 COI *1901 Report*.
35 COI *1911 Report*.
36 Griffiths, op.cit., p. 284. See also *Report of the Labour Enquiry Commission*. 1896 (hereafter *LEC Report*), Appendix Q. Mr. Thompson's and Babu Akshay Kumar Sirkar's evidence.
37 GOI. Labour Investigation Committee, *Report on an Enquiry into Conditions of Labour in Plantations in India* by D.V. Rege (hereafter Rege Committee Report), Delhi, 1946.
38 Ranajit Das Gupta, 'Structure of Labour Market in Colonial India', *EPW*, 1981 Special Number.
39 For details of recruitment methods see, among others, *Duars SSR*, pp. 106,107; *DPA Report* for 1920; *Rege Committee Report*, p. 76; and Sharit Bhowmik, *Class Formation in the Plantation System*, pp. 56-7.
40 J.C. Arbuthnot, *Report on the Conditions of Tea Garden Labour in the Dooars of Bengal, in Madras and in Ceylon* (hereafter Arbuthnot Report),Shillong, 1904, p. 2, para. 4.
41 S.K. Haldar, *Report on an Enquiry into the Living Condition of Plantation Workers in Jalpaiguri District (Dooars)* (hereafter Haldar Report), West Bengal, Labour Directorate, GOWB, Calcutta, 1951, pp. 9-10.
42 I have heard such accounts during my field work. Asit Sen, a leading Congress activist in the late 1940s and early 1950s and later on a Communist leader hailing from a planter family, also told me of such incidents.
43 See Hamdi Bey, 'A Centenary Survey' in *DBITA*, op.cit., p. 67.
44 For example, the DPA urged the administration to prevent Baradighi *hat* for being open on any day except Sunday. WBSA, File, p. 46, B. Nos.103-10 of August 1913.
45 For an example of this sort of use NBMR see *Jalpaiguri DG*, p. 110.
46 *Jalpaiguri SSR*, pp. 13, 16-7.
47 *Duars SSR*, p. 103, para 553. See also Royal Commission on Labour in India (RCLI), *Evidence*, Vol. VI, Assam and the Dooars, Pt. II Evidence by Bhirsa F 4216-4219.
48 For details see *Arbuthnot Report*, p. 5, para. 10.
49 *LEC Report*, para. 102. That there was little change in all this is indicated by later official reports. See *Rege Committee Report*, and *Haldar Report*, pp. 9-10.
50 *Arbuthnot Report*, p. 5, para. 10.
51 See R. Das Gupta, op.cit. For conditions of Assam plantation labour see Sanat Kumar Bose, *Capital and Labours in the Indian Tea Industry*, All India Trade Union Congress, Bombay, 1954; and Guha, op.cit.
52 RCLI. *Report of the Royal Commission on Labour in India*, 1931, p. 398.

53 *Duars SSR*, p. 103, para. 554.
54 *Arbuthnot Report*, p. 4, para. 7.
55 *Jalpaiguri DG*, p. 96.
56 *Arbuthnot Report*, p. 5, para 10 and p. 6, para. 11.
57 *Duars SSR*, p. 106.
58 *Rege Committee Report*, pp. 87-8; and *Haldar Report*, p. 14.
59 Ibid., p. 13.
60 *Arbuthnot Report*, p. 7, para 14.
61 Quoted from J.C.K. Peterson, 'Industrial Development in Bengal' *The Englishman*, 4 March 1918, p. 11, in A.Z.M. Iftikduar-ut Awwal, *The Industrial Development of Bengal 1900-1939*, Vikas, New Delhi, 1982, p. 19.
62 *Jalpaiguri DG*, pp. 113-4; and Griffiths, op.cit., pp. 647-8.
63 Santosh Ghosh, 'Shata Barser Darpane Zillar Swayatwasasan' i *Centenary Souvenir*, Jalpaiguri, 1970, pp. 241-2.
64 For evidence of this pertaining to as late as 1930s see Khagendr Nath Das Gupta , 'Jalpaiguri Zilla Board' in *Desha Bandhu*, Vol. No.11, pp. 133-5.
65 See in this connexion Asim Chaudhuri, 'Development, Urbaniza tion and Rural-Urban Relationship in a Plantation Dominate Economy—Myth and Reality: The Case of Jalpaiguri District i North Bengal' in Biplab Das Gupta (ed.), *Urbanization, migratio and rural change ; a study of West Bengal*, A. Mukherjee, Calcutta 1988.
   Our analysis shows that the spread effects as well as the links the two small towns with the wider rural economy in the distri were extremely limited and in view of this it is hardly appropria to speak of urbanization in the sense of a sustained and broader ing process.
66 *Jalpaiguri DG*, p. 111.
67 Charu Chandra Sanyal, 'Jalpaiguri Saharer Ekso Bachhar' i *Centenary Souvenir*, pp. 82, 85-6. The main reasons behind the us of straw and wood as roofing materials were easy availability an cheapness and proneness of the area to earthquake. From 1920 onwards corrugated iron roofing became a common practice. B till early 1950s only a few residential houses of Indians had *pucc* roofing. The Raikats who had zamindari right over most part of th town put severe restrictions on construction of *pucca* buildings an asked for heavy *salami* for granting such permission.
68 Ibid., pp. 83-4; and Jatindranath Sinha, 'Ekjan Shikshaker Chokh Saharer Adim Rup' in *Centenary Souvenir*, pp. 276-7.
69 The lawyers often charged fees according to the Section No. und which a case was instituted. Thus, if a case was under Section 10 the simple-minded peasants had to pay Rs.107 as the lawyer's fe
70 COI *1921 Report*, Chapter II, Subsidiary Table II, p. 128.
71 For the nature of eastern and northern Bengal towns see Parth Chatterjee, *Bengal 1920-1947*, p. 130.
72 See, for example, Ananda Gopal Ghose, 'Jalpaiguri Jelar Musalma

Samanj' in *Madhuparni*, Jalpaiguri Jela Sankhya, B.S. 1394, pp. 122-32.

73 Sanyal, op.cit., p. 92; and interview with Sabed Ali Ahmed, a septuagenarian Muslim resident of Jalpaiguri town.
74 Dr Taiyab Chowdhury, 'Bidhwasta Nilay' in *Ateet*, a Souvenir on Raikatpara, Senpara and Rajbaripara, Jalpaiguri 1980, p. 84; and interview with Nikhil Ghatak, scion of one of the earliest settler families.
75 See Santosh Ghosh, op.cit., pp. 233-42.
76 Sanyal, op.cit., pp. 88, 100.
77 For a short life sketch see *Akalanka Shashi*, Jalpaiguri, n.d.
78 For a brief life sketch of Md. Sonaullah see Md. Habibar Rahman, 'Danbir Vidyotsahi Mohammad Sonaullah' in *Sonaullah Uchcha Madhyamik Vidyalay Diamond Jubilee Souvenir*, 1984. He founded a high school, donated towards the opening of a ward in Jalpaiguri hospital, contributed liberally both in money and materials for the construction of Arya Natya Samaj building and promoted sports. In addition, he took an active interest in the Khilafat-Non-Cooperation movement. It is curious that Sonaullah's activities are neglected in most of the writings on Jalpaiguri.
79 Bhabaranjan Ganguly, 'Jalpaiguri Zelar Sambadpatrer Sankshipta Itihas' in *Centenary Souvenir*, pp. 195-6; and Sanyal, op.cit., p. 93.
80 Ibid., p. 93; and Arya Natya Samaj, *Platinum Jubilee Souvenir*, 1979.
81 It is interesting to note that a Brahmo Muslim couple Jalan Mian and his wife took initiative in the running of a Lower Primary School around 1902 which later on grew into the town's first high school for girls. (Suniti Bala Chanda, 'Jalpaiguri Jelar Eksa Bachhare Stree Shikshar Kramabikash' in *Centenary Souvenir*, p. 147.).
82 Interview with Anil Ganguly who belongs to one of the earliest settler families, and also with Piyus Kanti Mukherjee who too is from an old family. See also Suranjan Datta Ray, 'Sahar Alipurduarer Ateet Ebong Bartaman' in ibid., pp. 102-10.

CHAPTER 5

1 John Gallagher, Gordon Johnson and Anil Seal (eds.), *Locality, Province and Nations : Essays in Indian Politics 1870 to 1940*, Cambridge, 1973, pp. 1-28.

2 Sumit Sarkar, *The Swadeshi Movement in Bengal 1903-1908*, PPH, New Delhi, 1973, pp. 418-44.

3 Cf. Rafiuddin Ahmed, *The Bengal Muslims 1971-1906 : A Quest for Identity*, OUP, 1981, p. 180.

4 One stray report suggests that Jalpaiguri had a branch of the Indian National Congress with Umagati Roy, a legal practitioner, as Secretary as early as 1893. (*Madhuparni, Jalpaiguri Jela |Sankhya*, B.S.1394, Balurghat, Annexure facing p. 402). But nothing is known about its activities or subsequent course.

5 Mukulesh Sanyal, 'Swadhinata Andolane Jalpaiguri' in *Centenary Souvenir*, p. 322. The names of the arrested three, according to this account, were Durgadas Chakraborty, Adyanath Misra and Ananda Biswas.

6 Durga Charan Sanyal, *Banglar Samajik Itihas*, Calcutta, B.S. 1317.

7 Sumit Sarkar, op.cit., p. 161.

8 Khagendra Nath Das Gupta, 'Swadhinata Sangrame Jalpaiguri Zilla', *Jalpaiguri Zilla School Shatabarsikee Smarak Patrika*, Jalpaiguri, 1976, p. 2. The Rangpur national school set up on 8 November 1908 was incidentally the first national school. Sarkar, op.cit., p. 162.

9 Satyendra Nath Biswas, Taranath Ghatak, Jaichandra Chakraborty, Prantosh Sanyal, Kumudini Kanta Chakraborty and Santosh Neogy were some of them. For details with regard to the school see Khagendra Nath Das Gupta, op.cit,, p. 2.

10 Sarkar, op.cit., pp. 377-8.

11 Ibid., p. 127, and M. Sanyal, op.cit., p. 323.

12 Rajendra Neogy, a brother of Sasi K. Neogy, took the initiative in setting up the former and Makhan Chandra Bhowmik, a contractor, Kishori Mohan Moulik and some other gentlemen organized the latter. See K.N. Das Gupta, op.cit., p. 2.

13 Ibid., p. 2.

14 Jadu Gopal Mukhopadhyay, *Biplabi Jivaner Smriti*, Indian Associated Publishing Co., Calcutta, B.S. 1363, p. 634. Panchanan Neogy, Khagendra Nath Das Gupta (younger brother of Birendra Nath Das Gupta), Purna Chandra Bagchi and a number of .other students and young men joined the unit. K.N. Das Gupta, op.cit., p. 3.

15 WBSA. Eastern Bengal and Assam. Political Dept. Special Branch. No.44 of 1910; 514 of 1910; and 234 of 1911.

16 Kali Charan Ghosh, *Roll of Honour*, Vidya Bharati, Calcutta, 1965, pp. 213-5.

17 K. N. Das Gupta, op.cit., p. 4.

18 Rafiuddin Ahmed, *The Bengal Muslims 1871-1906 : A Quest for Identity*, OUP, Delhi, 1981, p. 166.

19 In 1910 Musharraff Hossain promoted three companies—Nuxalbari, Rahimia and Diana—based on community identity and with it began the phase of 'closed group' activity of the Muslim entrepreneurs. In the post-1910 period Hindus too launched tea companies which had overt sectional character. For details with regard to 'closed group' and 'open group' activity see S. Mukherjee, 'Emer-

gence of Bengalee Entrepreneurship in Tea Plantations in Jalpaiguri Duars (1879-1933)', North Bengal University Ph.D. thesis, 1978, pp. 80-9.

20 The first two decades of the twentieth century witnessed, in addition to the Rajbansi Kshatriya movement, two major caste movements—one among the Mahisyas of Midnapore, Howrah, Hooghly and 24-Parganas, and the other one among the Namasudras of Khulna, Faridpur and Jessore. See in this connexion Hitesranjan Sanyal, 'Dakshin-Paschim Banglay Jatiyatabadi Andolan', in *Chaturanga*, Vol. 38, No.3, 1976-7, pp. 183-207; also Vol. 38, No.1, pp. 1-26, Vol. 39, No.1, 1977-8, pp. 68-83; and Sekhar Bandyopadhyay, 'Social Protest or Politics of Backwardness? The Namasudra Movement in Bengal, 1872-1911' in Basudeb Chattopadhyay, H.S. Vasudevan and Rajat K. Ray(eds.), *Dissent and Consensus : Social Protest in Pre-Industrial Societies*, K.P. Bagchi, Calcutta, 1989, pp. 170-232.

21 See Upendranath Barman, *Rajbansi Kshatriya Jatir Itihas* (hereafter *Kshatriya Itihas*), Jalpaiguri (3rd edition), B.S. 1388, p. 56; Dharma Narayan Sarkar, *Rai Saheb Panchanan*, published in Bagura, Bangladesh, B.S. 1391, pp. 21-2; and A. K. Roy, 'Some Notes on the Kshatriya Movement in North Bengal' in *Journal of Asiatic Society of Bangladesh*, Vol. XX, No.1, p. 49. See also COI, *1891 Report*, Vol. 3, p. 268, para 357.

22 Cited in Barman, *Kshatriya Itihas*, p. 56.

23 The account is based on ibid., pp. 56-9; Sarkar, op.cit., pp. 21-2, and Roy, op.cit., pp. 49-57.

24 Barman, *Kshatriya Itihas*, pp. 59-60; and Roy, op.cit., pp. 52-3. E.A. Gait, Superintendent of Census Operations, Bengal for 1901 observes, "The Rajbansis of North Bengal wished to be styled Bhanga or Brata Kshatriya and to be classed among the twice-born castes" (COI, *1901 Report* Vol. 6, Pt.I, p. 382, para 617). In Subsidiary Table II, Chapter XI, p. 460 of the Report population figure for Rajbansis with Koch in bracket is given.

25 For a life sketch and activities of Panchanan Barman see U.N. Barman, *Thakur Panchanan Barmar Jivan Charit* (hereafter *Jivan Charit*), Jalpaiguri B.S. 1387; Sarkar, op.cit.; and also Sibendra Narayan Mandal, *Rajbansi Kshatriya Jatir Sankshipta Itibritta*, Gouripur, Assam, n.d., pp. 48-51; and Roy, op.cit., 53 ff.

26 Ibid.

27 Barman, *Jivan Charit*, pp. 13-4.

28 For evidence put forward in support of the claim and relevant details see Barman, *Kshatriya Itihas*, pp. 4-24; and Roy, op.cit., pp. 54, 61-70.

29 *Kshatriya Samitir Karyabibarani* (a compilation of Proceedings of the annual conferences : hereafter briefly *Karyabibarani*), Pratham Sammilanee, Rangpur, B.S. 1317(1910); Barman, *Jivan Charit*, pp. 14-6; and Roy, op.cit., pp. 54-5.

30 Ibid., p. 55.

31 COI, *Report 1911*, p. 445.

270 *Jalpaiguri 1869–1947*

32 *Jalpaiguri SSR*, p. 10; Barman, *Jivan Charit*, pp. 20-3; and Roy; op.cit., pp. 56-7.
33 See the resolutions adopted at the different annual conferences; and also Roy, op.cit., pp. 57-8.
34 Thus, a resolution adopted at the seventh annual conference held in B.S. 1323(1916) stated : 'Bride-price is bad. The custom of giving dowry to the bridegroom is a heinous crime'.
35 The journal brought out from Rangpur was first published in B.S. 1328(1921).
36 Barman, *Jivan Charit*, pp. 23-5.
37 Ibid., pp. 30-44, 86.
38 See the memorandum on constitutional reforms submitted by the Kshatriya Samiti to the Chief Secretary, Government of Bengal in December, 1917 published in full in Kshatriya Samiti's Ninth Annual Proceedings.
39 *Karyabibaranee*, fourth annual conference, B.S.1320, p. 18.
40 Ibid.
41 See the memorandum referred to in n. 38 above.
42 Ibid.
43 See Kshatriya Samiti, Ninth Annual Circle Report, B.S.1325.
44 See *Karyabibaranee*, eighteenth annual conference, B.S. 1335.
45 See Rosalind O'Hanlon, *Caste, Conflict and Ideology*, CUP, 1985.
46 Sumit Sarkar, *Modern India : 1885-1947* (hereafter *Modern India*), Macmillan, Delhi, 1983.
47 *Duars SSR*, p. 106.
48 *Arbuthnot Report*, p. 9, para 17.
49 Ibid., p. 9, para 17.
50 *Jalpaiguri DG*, pp. 109-10.
51 Ibid., p. 110.
52 For a more detailed account and analysis of the movement than what is presented here see the present author's 'The Oraon Labour Agitation: Duars in Jalpaiguri District, 1915-16' in *EPW*, 30 September 1989, pp. 2197-2202.
53 For Tana Bhagat movement see Sarat Chandra Roy, *Oraon Religion and Customs*, Calcutta, 1928 (1985 reprint), pp. 339-405; Nirmal Kumar Bose, *Some Indian Tribes*, National Book Trust, New Delhi, 1972, pp. 140-1; Stephen Fuchs, *Rebellious Prophets: A Study of Messianic Movements in Indian Religions*, Bombay,. 1965, pp. 38-42; K. Suresh Singh, 'Tribal Peasantry, Millenarianism, Anarchism and Nationalism: A Case Study of the Tana Bhagat in Chotanagpur, 1914-25' in *Social Scientist*, November 1988, pp. 36-50; and Benoy Chaudhuri, 'The Story of a Tribal Revolt in the Bengal Presidency : The Religion and Politics of the Oraons : 1900-1926' in Adhir Chakravarti, *Aspects of Socio-Economic Changes and Political Awakening in Bengal*, GOWB, 1989. However, except Chaudhuri none of these authors makes any reference to the Duars movement.
54 Cf. Fuchs, op.cit.; and also David Hardiman, *The Coming of the Devi: Adivasi Assertion in Western India*, OUP, Delhi, 1987, pp. 153-4.

55 S.C. Roy, op.cit., p. 342; N.K. Bose, op.cit., p. 141; and Singh, op.cit.
56 *DPA Report* for 1916, p. vii.
57 *BAR* for 1916-17, p. 17.
58 *DPA Report* for 1916 p. xi.
59 NAI. Home. Political. A. Nos. 280-81 of June 1916. 'Oraon Unrest in Bengal and Bihar Orissa. Judgement of the Special Tribunal appointed under the Defence of India Act in the Oraon Case' (hereafter NAI. Oraon Unrest), p. 5.
60 Ibid., p. 5.
61 Ibid.
62 *DPA Report* for 1916, p. ix.
63 Ibid., pp. 285-6.
64 Ibid., p. 286.
65 NAI. 'Oraon Unrest', p. 6.
66 An account of this incident was given in the *Amrita Bazar Patrika*, 10 May 1916 editorial entitled 'The Oraon Unrest : The Second Case'. The editorial sharply criticized the government's attitude. *Amrita Bazar Patrika* wrote another editorial in its issue of 2 May 1916. Both the editorials were considered "objectionable" by the Criminal Intelligence Office and there was a move for prosecuting the *Patrika* under the Defence of India Act. See NAI. Home. Political. Deposit No. 12 of June 1916.
67 Ibid.
68 Cited in NAI. 'Oraon Unrest', p. 7.
69 Ibid., p. 7.
70 This citation and the next one are from Nai. 'Oraon Unrest', p. 7.
71 *DPA Report* for 1916, pp. viii-ix.
72 See Ranajit Guha, *Elementary Aspects of Peasant Insurgency in Colonial India*, OUP, Delhi, 1983, p. 226.
73 *DPA Report* for 1916, p. 286.
74 Ibid., p. viii.
75 Ibid., pp. ix, 287-8.
76 We have come across a list of names of twenty-nine tribals—both Oraon and non-Oraons—convicted in Jalpaiguri Duars between June and December 1916 (*DPA Report* for 1917, pp. 426-7). See Appendix I below.
77 Ibid., pp. 422-7. See also the correspondence between the DPA Chairman and several garden managers on the one hand and the Superintendent of Police on the other.
78 NAI. Home. Political. Deposit. No.68 of June 1917. FR, 1 May 1917.
79 NAI. 'Oraon Unrest', p. 3.
80 Ibid.
81 Ibid., p. 2.
82 The Judgement read: "One characteristic of the movement is that all Christian Oraons were excluded from the meetings. So it cannot have been deliberately organized by any German missionary". Yet the Special Tribunal gave the verdict... 'it seems clear that it must have been started either by some German agent on by some agitator or by some imposter'. (NAI. 'Oraon Unrest', p. 8, para 5).

83 Cf. Guha, *Elementary Aspects of Peasant Insurgency,* pp. 169-70.
84 See *DPA Report* for 1917, pp. 426-7.
85 See Fuchs, op.cit.
86 K.N. Das Gupta, op.cit., p. 4, Jalpaiguri, 1976.

CHAPTER 6

1 For a penetrating analysis of these movements see Sumit Sarkar, *'Popular' Movements and 'Middle Class' Leadership in Colonial India : Perspectives and Problems of a 'History from Below'* (hereafter *Popular Movements*), Centre for Studies in Social Sciences, Calcutta, 1983, pp. 38-47.

2 For a study of the Non-Cooperation movement in Bengal see Rajat K. Ray, 'Masses in Politics: The Non-Cooperation Movement in Bengal 1920-22', *IESHR*, Vol. XI(4), December 1974.

3 Sarkar, *Popular Movements*, p. 40.

4 In an interview with the author on 27 December 1980 Khagendra Nath Das Gupta said, 'Mahatmaji's speech had an electrifying impact on me'.

5 Among them names of Purna Chandra Bagchi and Sitanath Pramanik deserve particular mention. See Das Gupta, 'Swadhinata Sangrame Jalpaiguri Zilla', *Jalpaiguri Zilla School Shatabarsikee Smarak Patrika,* Jalpaiguri, 1976, pp. 4,5.

6 Interview with Samarendra Deb Raikat.

7 *Amirta Bazar Patrika,* 21 April 1921. For Durga Charan Sanyal see the preceding chapter, Sec.1.

8 *The Mussalman,* 22 April 1921.

9 *Amrita Bazar Patrika,* 7 March 1922.

10 Anil Gangopadhyay, 'Swadhinata Sangrame Alipur Duar', *Centenary Souvenir,* p. 335.

11 Das Gupta, op.cit., p. 5; and also interview with him on 27 December 1980.

12 For the phenomenon of Gandhi see, among others, Ravinder Kumar(ed.), *Essays on Gandhian Politics: The Rowlatt Satyagraha of 1919,* OUP, Oxford, 1971; Judith Brown, *Gandhi's Rise to Power—Indian Politics 1915-1922,* Cambridge, 1972; and Sarkar, *Modern India 1885-1947* (hereafter *Modern India*), Macmillan, Delhi, 1983, particularly pp. 178-98, 204-28, 281-4, 294-5, 328-31.

13 *The Mussalman,* 29 April 1921.

14 *Amrita Bazar Patrika,* 2 June 1921.

15 Das Gupta, op.cit., p. 5.

16 Interview with Das Gupta on 27 December 1980.

17 Among them Manmatha Dutta, Elahi Baksh and Darajuddin Ahmed of Boda, Nagendra Nath Roy, Ganesh Chakraborty and Mani Bagchi of Debigunj, Debananda Roy and Suren Banerjee of Pachagar, Keshab Datta and Trailokyanath Chakraborty of Patgram, Chandia Das of Dhupguri, Mahendra Basunia of Amguri, Tarini Basunia of Maynaguri and Chandradip Singh and Magha Dewania of Alipur Duars deserve particular mention.

18 These are the major points, as reported by a police Sub-Inspector, of a speech made by Trailokyanath Chakraborty at a meeting held at Patgram Bazar on 24 June 1921. WBSA. Political Dept. Poll Br. Confidential. No.39 of February 1921.

19 Interview with Das Gupta on 27 December 1980.

20 These aspects are most perceptively captured in Satinath Bhaduri's novel *Dhorai Charit Manas* in *Satinath Granthabali*, Vol. II, Calcutta, 1973. The locale is a village in Purnea (north-eastern Bihar) situated on Kosi–Siliguri Road and inhabited by Tatmas, a very low-caste people. See also Shahid Amin, 'Gandhi as Mahatma: Gorakhpur District, Eastern UP, 1921-2' in Ranajit Guha(ed.), *Subaltern Studies III*, OUP, Delhi, 1984, pp. 1-61.

21 *Ananda Bazar Patrika*, 7 June 1922.

22 Das Gupta, op.cit., p. 6; and Gangopadhyay, op.cit., pp. 335-6.

23 Gangopadhyay, a leading lawyer of Alipur Duar, writes: 'I was introduced to the three R's at a national school' (His communication to the author.)

24 *Ananda Bazar Patrika*, 7 June 1922; and Das Gupta, op.cit., p. 6.

25 *Ananda Bazar Patrika*, 19 April 1922.

26 Das Gupta, *op. cit.*, p. 6.

27 This was a feature found in widely separated parts of the country. See Sarkar, *Popular Movements*.

28 *DPA Report*, p. vi.

29 WBSA. Political Dept. Confidential. S.C.395/1924 'History of the Non-Cooperation Movement and Khilafat Agitation in Bengal', p. 10.

30 Op. cit., p. vi.

31 NAI. Home. Poll No.18 FR 1, January 1922.

32 FR 1, February 1922.

33 FR 2, February 1922.

34 FR 1, February 1922.

35 Gangopadhyay, op.cit., p. 337.

36 GOB. *Report on the Land Revenue Administration in Bengal* for relevant years.

37 FR 1, February 1922.

38 FR 2, February 1922; and *The Mussalman*, 10 March 1922.

39 FR 1, February 1922.

40 Gangopadhyay, op.cit., pp. 337-8; and Das Gupta, op.cit., p. 6.

41 FR 1, March 1922.

42 *Ananda Bazar Patrika*, 12 and 18 July 1922.

43 Ibid., 26 and 29 July 1922.

44 *The Mussalman*, 23 April 1923.
45 See Sarkar, *Modern India*, pp. 209-26 *passim*; also Gyan Pandey, *Ascendency of the Congress in Uttar Pradesh 1926-34: A Study in Imperfect Mobilization*, OUP, Delhi, 1978.
46 Das Gupta, op. cit., p. 6; and Mukulesh Sanyal, 'Swadhinata Andolane Jalpaiguri', *Centenary Souvenir*, pp. 325-6.
47 For an account and analysis of the activities of the rural Gandhians see Hitesh Ranjan Sanyal, 'Dakshin-paschim Banglay Jatiyatabadi Andolan', *Chaturanga*, Baisakh-Asar B.S.1383, Aswin-Agrahayan B.S. 1383, Baisakh-Asar B.S.1384; and Tanika Sarkar, National Movement and Popular Protest in Bengal 1928-34, (Delhi University Ph.D. Thesis).
48 Das Gupta, op.cit., p. 6.
49 *The Mussalman*, 23 February 1923; and 4 May 1923.
50 *Amrita Bazar Patrika*, 2, 11 and 12 June 1923.
51 Nirmal Chandra Chaudhury, 'Abismaraniya Sangbadik Jyotish Chandra Sanyal', *Saradiya Janamat*, B.S. 1386, p. 3.
52 Bhabaranjan Ganguly, 'Jalpaiguri Jelar Sambadpatrer Sankshipta Itihas', *Centenary Souvenir*, pp. 196-7.
53 See, among others, G. Adhikari, 'Politics and Ideology of National Revolutionaries', *Mainstream*, 25 April 1981.
54 Benoy Chaudhury, 'Agrarian Movements in Bengal and Bihar, 1919-39' in A.R. Desai (ed.), *Peasant Struggles in India*, OUP, 1979.
55 See, among others, Tanika Sarkar, op. cit.
56 Gautam Chattopadhyay, *Swadhinata Sangrame Banglar Chhatra Samaj*, Charuprakash, Calcutta, 1980, pp. 26-7.
57 Satyendra Narayan Mazumdar hailing from Siliguri, a neighbouring town of Jalpaiguri, and a well-known Communist leader in his later life was in his teens in the 1920s. He has given an authentic account of this impact in his *Amar Biplab Jignasa*, Manisha Granthalay, Calcutta, 1973.
58 Interview with Bijoy Kumar Hoare on 7 October 1981.
59 Mazumdar, op.cit., pp. 62-78.
60 Interview with Hoare.
61 *Amrita Bazar Patrika*, 24 and 25 September 1929.
62 FR 2, September 1929; and *BAR* for 1928-29, p. xiii.
63 Interview with Hoare; and FPR 1, March 1929.
64 Interview with Hoare.
65 See Chap. 4 above.
66 This and the preceding three citations unless otherwise stated are from WBSA. Home. Pol. Confidential. File No.403 (Sl.Nos.1-10) of 1929.
67 See in this connexion Upendranath Barman, *Uttarbanglar Sekal O Amar Jivan-Smriti* (hereafter briefly 'Jivan-Smriti'), Jalpaiguri, B.S.1392 (1985), pp. 46-9.
68 For the movement's attitude towards the *bhadraloks* see 'Titbits About Bhadraloks', *Kshatriya*, Falgun B.S. 1332(February-March 1925), pp. 251-2.

69 WBSA. Pol. Confidential. S.C.395/1924. 'History of the Non-Coop-
    eration Movement and the Khilafat Agitation in Bengal'. See also
    Rajat Kanta Ray, *Social Conflict and Political Unrest in Bengal 1875-
    1927*, OUP, Delhi, 1984, p. 306.
70 Barman, *Jivan-Smriti*, pp. 31-5.
71 Barman, *Thakur Panchanan Barmar Jivancharit* (hereafter *Jivan-
    charit*), Prasannanagar, Jalpaiguri, B.S. 1387, pp. 67-75.
72 A resolution adopted in the seventeenth annual conference of the
    Samiti held in Asar B.S. 1333 (May 1926) stated, "We ... Kshatriyas
    are expressing our sincere and firm devotion and loyalty to the
    [British] Raj" (*Kshatriya*, Vol. 6, No. 4, Sraban 1333, p. 91).
73 See, for example, the resolutions adopted in the seventeenth con-
    ference and published in ibid., pp. 91-7.
74 See Abinash Chandra Biswas, 'Bharate Ingrez Sasaner Falafal',
    Kshatriya, Chaitra, B.S. 1332 (March-April, 1925), pp. 267-70.
75 Barman, *Jivancharit*, pp. 23-5.
76 See the Proceedings of the eighteenth annual conference of the
    Kshatriya Samiti held in Patgram (Jalpaiguri) in mid-Asar, B.S.
    1335 (June-July 1928); and also Dharma Narayan Sarkar, *Rai Saheb
    Panchanan*, pp. 73-81.
77 See 'Hindu Sangathan and Hindu Sabha', *Kshatriya*, Jyaistha, B.S.
    1331 (May-June, 1924), p. 24; and the resolution on 'Hindu San-
    gathan' adopted in the fifteenth conference, *Kshatriya*, Asar B.S.
    1331.
78 *Kshatriya*, Sraban B.S. 1332, p. 96.
79 WBSA. Revenue. Land Revenue. F.No. 2-A-I, Pr. No.11-19 of
    February 1923. (I owe this reference to Swaraj Bose). See also D.N.
    Sarkar, op.cit., p. 97.
80 *BLCP*, Vol. XXX, 2, 13th session, 1928-9, Proceedings of 14 and 15
    August, particularly pp. 76-82, 96-107.
81 *BLCP*, 14th session, 12-14 March 1924, Vol. XIV, No.4, pp. 66-7.
82 Ibid., p. 69.
83 See Sir Abdur Rahim's Minute dt. 14 June 1924. WBSA Home.
    Appointment. F.No. 411-12(1-3) Pros. A, Nos. 70-71, November
    1925; and also Shila Sen, *Muslim Politics in Bengal*, Impex, Delhi,
    1976, p. 56.
84 *BLCP*, 16th session, Vol. XVI, August 1924, pp. 68-9.
85 WBSA. Home. Poll. 8A-1. Nos. B 393-406 of August 1925.
86 *Trisrota*, 17 July 1927; see also 14 August 1927.

CHAPTER 7

1 See, among others, Bagchi, *Private Investment in India 1900-1939*,;
   B.B. Chaudhuri, 'The Process of Depeasantisation in Bengal and
   Bihar 1885-1947'(hereafter 'Process of Depeasantisation'), *IHR*,

Vol. II, No.1, July 1975, pp. 105-65; Sarkar, *Modern India*, pp. 257-8; Adrienne Cooper, *Sharecropping and Sharecroppers' Struggles in Bengal 1930-1950*, K.P. Bagchi, Calcutta, 1988, pp. 37-48.

2 *ITPA Report* for 1930, p. 30.

3 *DPA Report* for 1931, p. vi.

4 Griffiths, *The History of the Indian Tea Industry*, p.190, also pp.188-9.

5 See *ITPA Report* for 1932, 1933 and 1934.

6 The DPA Chairman addressing the annual general meeting held in early 1932 reported: '... the earnings of our labour have had to be reduced considerably during the year...' (*DPA Report* for 1931, p. vii).

7 Omkar Goswami, 'Agriculture in slump: the peasant economy of East and North Bengal in the 1930s', *IESHR*, Vol. 21, No.3, July-September 1984, p. 347, Table 5.

8 Saugata Mukherjee, 'The Jute Industry in Eastern India during the Depression and its Influence on the Domestic Economy of the Region', *Occasional Paper* No.44, CSSSC, 1981, pp. 24-34.

9 See *Deshabandhu*, Vol. 1,No.1, 6 Falgun, B.S.1344, pp. 10-1.

10 Cf. Partha Chatterjee, 'Agrarian Structure in Pre-partition Bengal' in Sen, Chatterjee and Mukherjee, *Perspectives in Social Sciences* 2, pp. 113-224; Chaudhuri, 'Process of Depeasantisation', pp. 113-24, 137-9, 145-6; and Cooper, op.cit., p. 38.

11 *BLAP*, 6th session, Vol. IV, Nos.2-3, December 1939, pp. 11-4, Questions put by Niharendu Datta Mazumdar and Khagendra Nath Das Gupta; and Upendranath Barman, p. 52.

12 Op.cit.; and cf. Sugata Bose, *Agrarian Bengal: Economy, social structure and politics, 1919-1947*, CUP in association with Orient Longman, Bombay, 1986, pp. 65-7, 96-7, 140-3.

13 Cf. Chaudhuri, "Process of Depeasantisation"; Chatterjee, *Bengal 1920-1947*, pp. 142-57; Goswami, op.cit., pp.353, 356; Cooper, op.cit., pp. 41-4.

14 GOB, *Report of the Bengal Land Revenue* [Floud] *Commission*, Vol. 2, Alipore, 1940, pp. 120-1.

15 Ibid., pp. 118-19.

16 See Goswami, op.cit., pp. 358-9.

17 John Gallagher, 'Congress in Decline' in Gallagher, Gordon Johnson and Anil Seal (eds.), *Locality, Province and Nation*, Cambridge, 1973.

18 See, for example, Tanika Sarkar, *Bengal 1928-1934 : The Politics of Protest*, OUP, Delhi, 1987, Chs. 2 and 3.

19 *Bangabani*, 28 January 1930.

20 Ibid., 2 April 1930.

21 Rabindra Nath Sikdar, 'Jelaye Jatiya Andolaner Dhara', *Madhuparni, Jalpaiguri Jela Sankhya*, B.S. 1943, p. 262.

22 Nehru Memorial Museum and Library(NMML). *AICC Papers*, File No.G-86/1930.

23 *Bangabani*, 17 July 1930; *Trisrota*, 27 July 1930.

24 *Bangabani* of 24 July 1930 reported one such *hartal* at Domohani.

25 Ibid., 17, 19, 23, 24, 26 and 31 July 1930; and 'Banglay Swadhinata Sangram', *Ananda Bazar Patrika*, Autumn Special No., B.S. 1338 (1931), pp. 113-14.
26 Ibid.
27 Ibid.
28 NMML. *AICC Papers*, File No.G-86/1930.
29 *Trisrota*, 29 September 1930.
30 Ibid., 10 January 1932.
31 Ibid., 10, 17 and 31 January 1932.
32 Interview with Birendra Kumar Neogy.
33 *Bangabani*, 1, 22 and 29 February, 14, 17, and 26 March, 8, 17 and 20 April, 2 and 26 May, 20 June, 13 July, 17 September 1932.
34 Ibid., 8 April 1932. For a slightly different version see Khagendra Nath Das Gupta, op.cit.
35 *Bangabani*, 17 April 1932.
36 *Trisrota*, 5 February 1933.
37 WBSA. Home. Poll. Confidential. No.162. Pros. Nos. 1-12 of 1932. Allocations for some other districts were the following: Midnapore—Rs 300, Dacca—Rs 300, Hooghly—Rs 150, Rangpur—Rs 250, Dinajpur—Rs 200, and Mymensingh—Rs 100.
38 *Bangabani*, 20 June 1932.
39 Ibid., 11 October 1932.
40 Tanika Sarkar, op.cit., pp. 97-104, 120-3, 126-34.
41 *Bangabani*, 11 October and 15 November 1932.
42 Interview with Bijoy K. Hoare on 7 October 1981.
43 *Trisrota*, 12, 19 April 1931.
44 Ibid., 21 December 1930.
45 Chatterjee, *Bengal 1920-1947*, pp. 166-7; and Tanika Sarkar, op.cit., pp. 129-34, 155-64.
46 Among other districts thus affected were Faridpur, Bakarganj, Chittagong, Noakhali, Rangpur and Pabna. See Chatterjee, *Bengal 1920-1947*, p. 166.
47 NMML. AICC Papers, File No.935/1932. Special AICC Bulletin No.1, 30 March 1932. I owe this reference to Tanika Sarkar.
48 GOB. Annual Land Revenue Administration Reports for the relevant years.
49 *Trisrota*, 19 July 1931.
50 See R. Das Gupta, 'Ambiguities of Class Formation: Plantation Capitalism, Workers and Collective Action in the Duars 1890s-1947', *Working Paper Series*, Indian Institute of Management, Calcutta, p. 42.
51 WBSA. Home. Poll. Confidential. 1936. FCR 1, April, FCR 2, May, and FCR 1 June 1936.
52 WBSA. Home. Poll. Confidential. FCR 2, September 1936.
53 See Tanika Sarkar, op.cit., pp. 26-33.
54 The following persons were the office bearers of the Jalpaiguri DCC. Their social background is given in brackets. President: Sreenath Horae (lawyer-cum-planter); Vice-Presidents: Rajendra

Kumar Neogy (planter), Satish Chandra Lahiri (ayurveda physician) and Khagendra Nath Das Gupta (political worker); Secretary: Sasadhar Kar (political worker); and Assistant Secretaries: Pritinidhan Roy (lawyer), Rabindra Nath Sikdar (teacher turned into political worker), Dhiraj Mohan Sen Gupta (doctor), and Jatindra Nath Roy (khadi shopkeeper). Only one Muslim, Jaharatullah Ahmad (pleader), a few Rajbansis, one of them Debananda Roy (formerly a village *dafadar*) and a few women like Subhasini Ghosh, Aruna Das Gupta and Heeraprabha Sen Gupta were among the twenty-eight members of the Committee. (*Trisrota*, 2 August 1931).

55 *Deshabandhu*, Vol. 1, No.1, 6 Falgun, B.S.1344(1937).
56 Ibid., 'Khasmahale ki bhave andolan chalaite haibe'.
57 Such an understanding was indicated by K.N. Das Gupta in his interview with the author on 27 December 1980.
58 Prafulla Kumar Tripathi, 'Pallite Congresser Prabhab', *Deshabandhu*, Vol. 1, No.8, 17 Jyaistha, B.S.1345.
59 *Trisrota*, 18 January and 2 August 1931.
60 Ibid., 18 January 1931.
61 Ibid., 2 February 1935; and WBSA. FCR 1, July 1936.
62 WBSA. Home. Poll. 8A-4 of 1931, B Nos. 394-406, December 1931; 8A-2 of 1932, B Nos.16-31, November 1932; and *Trisrota*, 12 February 1933.
63 Shila Sen, *Muslim Politics in Bengal 1937-1947*, pp. 74-7.
64 Cf. Ibid., p. 80.
65 See *Trisrota*, 31 March, 25 August 1935.
66 WBSA. FCR 1, May and FCR 2, July of 1936.
67 Op.cit., 1 Kartik 1345, p. 213.
68 Interviews with Sabed Ali Ahmad, an octogenarian, who was an office-bearer in the district Muslim League organization and also very close to Musharaff's establishment; and Birendra Kumar Neogy, also an octogenarian, who held important positions in Jalpaiguri DCC in late 1930s and early 1940s.
69 The preceding text is based on Barman, *Jivan-Smriti*, p. 64.
70 Ibid., pp. 64-5.
71 See Indian Franchise Committee, Vol. XVII, Pt. III, *Selections from Memoranda and Oral Evidence*, 'Memorandum submitted by the Bangiya Jana Sangha', p. 539.
72 Indian Statutory Commission (Simon Commission), *Selections from Memoranda and Oral Evidence by Non-Officials*, Vol. III, Pt. II, 'Deputation from the Bengal Depressed Classes Association and the All-Bengal Namasudra Association', pp. 98-103.
73 See the Oral Evidence given by Bhagirath Chandra Das and Panchanan Burma (Barman) before the Indian Franchise Committee on 16 February 1932, *Selections from Memoranda and Oral Evidence*, pp. 539-43.
74 See op.cit., p. 539. It is worthwhile to note that this position differed from the position of several other caste movements, particularly the

Namasudra movement which was agitating not only for seat reservation but also for separate electorate.

75 Barman, *Thakur Panchanan Barmar Jivancharit*, pp. 76-8.
76 Ibid., pp. 61-5.
77 Cf. Shekhar Bandyopadhyay, 'Towards a Corporate Pluralist Society: Caste and Colonial Policy of Protective Discrimination in Bengal, 1911-1937', *The Calcutta Historical Journal*, Vol. XI, Nos.1-2, July 1986 - June 1987.
78 *Trisrota*, 19 July 1935.
79 See Barman, *Jivan-Smriti*, pp. 70-2.
80 *Deshabandhu*, 1 Agrahayan B.S. 1345, p. 226.
81 Barman, *Jeevan-Smriti*, p. 69.
82 Musharraff had the reputation of manipulation (see Shila Sen, op.cit., p. 94, n.40) and it is not clear from available evidence whether he was elected unopposed through some sort of manoeouvre.

CHAPTER 8

1 R.P. Dutt, *India Today*, Bombay, 1949, pp. 477-9; and Sumit Sarkar, *Modern India*, pp. 343-4.
2 See, among others, Gautam Chottopadhyay, *Bengal: Freedom Struggle and Electoral Politics* (hereafter *Freedom Struggle*), Indian Council of Historical Research, New Delhi, 1984, pp. 138-9.
3 For Praja movement see Jatin De, 'The History of The Krishak Praja of Bengal, 1929-47: A Study of Changes in Class and Inter-Community Relations in the Agrarian Sector of Bengal', unpublished Ph.D. dissertation, Delhi University, 1977.
4 Shila Sen, *Muslim Politics in Bengal*, pp. 101-25.
5 Interview with Birendra Kumar Neogy, Kalyani on 28 December 1980. Neogy was Jalpaiguri DCC's Assistant Secretary in late 1937 and 1938 and Secretary from mid-1939 to 1942. Some time in 1941 he joined the CPI. *Deshabandhu*, a local fortnightly edited by Pritinidhan Roy, a prominent lawyer and a Congress leader who became the DCC President in 1939, too made an oblique hint at the leader or group-based nature of Congress activities in Jalpaiguri and its adverse impact (*Deshabandhu*, 15 Paush B.S.1345, January 1938, p. 262).
6 Partha Chatterjee, *Bengal 1920-1947*, Sec.13; and G. Chattopadhyay, op.cit.

7 Ibid., pp. 150-1, 156-7; and Chatterjee, *Bengal 1920-1947*, pp. 172-3.
8 *Neeti O Kaj*, pp. 1-23, and *Sammelan Report*, 1943.
9 Interview with Neogy on 28.12.1980. See also *Deshabandhu* 15 Chaitra B.S.1345,pp. 39-40 and 1 Jyaistha 1345,pp. 74-5. This was, however, not a feature of Jalpaiguri Congress alone. To quote from an official report, 'Congress activity showed a marked increase' throughout Bengal. NAI. Home. Poll. F66/40 of 1940.
10 *Deshabandhu*, 15 Chaitra 1345, p. 39.
11 See Datta's reminiscences entitled 'Jalpaiguri Jelar Krishak Andolaner Gorar Katha' published in a serialized form in *Jalpaiguri* (a fortnightly), in particular the issue of 1 July 1972.
12 Prafulla Tripathi, 'Pallite Congresser Prabhab', *Deshabandhu*, 17 Jyaistha 1345, p. 95. For reports on Congress meetings see ibid., 15 Chaitra 1344, pp. 39-40; 6 Baishakh 1345, p. 52; and 15 Baisakh 1345, p. 65. Amongst these who addressed these meetings were Khagendra Nath Das Gupta, Charu Chandra Sanyal, Prafulla Tripathi, Sasadhar Kar, Madhab Datta, Birendra Kumar Neogy, Keshab Datta, Debananda Roy, Piyus Kanti Mukherjee and Nalini Mohan Bhattacharya. The last two were leaders of the Alipur Duars Congress.
13 The Kshatriya Samiti had six MLAs: Puspajit Barma and Kshetra Nath Singha from Rangpur, Premhari Barma and Shyama Prasad Barman from Dinajpur, Tarini Charan Pramanik from Malda and Upendranath Barman from Jalpaiguri.
14 See *Deshabandhu*, 1 Chaitra 1344, pp. 29-30.
15 *Deshabandhu*, 1 Jyaistha 1345, p. 71.
16 Bengal Provincial Political Conference, Jalpaiguri Session, *Address of the Reception Committee Chairman* (hereafter Reception Committee Chairman's Address), 21 Magh 1345, p. 1.
17 *Deshabandhu*, 13 Paush 1345, pp. 261, 263.
18 Ibid., 1 Jyaishtha 1345, p. 73.
19 Interview with Neogy on 28 December 1980.
20 See the report of such a meeting in *Deshabandhu*, 1 Jyaishtha 1345.
21 Ibid., 15 Baishakh 1345, p. 65.
22 Ibid., 1 Chaitra 1344 (March 1937), pp. 31-2 and 6 Baishakh 1345, pp. 59-60.
23 Das Gupta, 'Jalpaigurite Bangla Sarkarer Khas Mahale Bangiya Praja Swatwa Aain', and 'Khas Mahale Nutan Jareep Anujayee Bardhita Khajna', ibid., 6 Falgun 1344, pp. 9-11.
24 'Duarbaseer Marmakatha', ibid., 15 Chaitra 1344, pp. 45-6, 15 Baishakh 1345, pp. 62-3.
25 'Jalpaiguri Zilla Board', ibid., 1 Sravan 1345, pp. 133-5.
26 Ibid., 15 Baishakh 1345, pp. 70-2.
27 Ibid., 1 Sravan 1345, pp. 127-30, 15 Sravan 1345, pp. 148, 157-60, 1 Bhadra 1345, pp. 165-7.
28 Chattopadhyay, *Banglar Chhatra Samaj*, p. 40.
29 *Deshabandhu*, 15 Chaitra 1344, p. 39.
30 Ibid., 15 Sravan 1345, p. 157.

31 Ibid., 1 Agrahayan 1345, p. 239.
32 Ibid., 15 Poush 1345, p. 261.
33 BLA Proceedings, 6th Session, Vol. LV, No.2, 5-8, 11 December 1939.
34 Baradanath Bhowmik, 'Krishaker Abastha', *Deshabandhu*, 1 Agrahayan 1345, p. 231.
35 The following is the relevant extract from Charu Chandra's address: ...In the *khas mahal* [area] the tenant has virtually no right. Even for construction of a homestead government permission is necessary and it is not easy to get it. For transferring land the government will have to be informed of the name and address of the [prospective] buyer and, if the government considers the person as a desirable one, only in that case he is allowed to make the purchase. As the *jotedars* or *talukdars* are unable to bear the burden of revenue their lands are being auctioned and in their place big modern peasant zamindars [landholders] are being created. Each of them is owner of 5 or 6 thousand *bighas* of land and many *adhiars* or *bargadars* work under them as agricultural labour. The consequence is that there is on the one hand a few handful of monied modern zamindars and numerous poor agricultural workers on the other and that the flame of discontent among these agricultural workers can already be seen. Under the Permanent Settlement too an increase in the number of agricultural workers can be witnessed. It is the perception of the *jotedar* that the *adhiar* leads a happy life, for he has no worry about rent. At the same time, the *adhiar* thinks that the *jotedar* is more happy, for the latter's gain is greater. Seeing all this it seems that a gigantic change is inevitable". (*Reception Committee Chairman's Address*, pp. 12-13).
36 *Deshabandhu*, 15 Agrahayan 1345, pp. 250-1.
37 *Reception Committee Chairman's Address*, p. 8.
38 *Deshabandhu*, 15 Agrahayan 1345, p. 254.
39 *Trisrota*, 18 December 1938.
40 Ibid., 22 January 1939.
41 *Deshabandhu*, 6 Falgun 1345, pp. 6-8.
42 Ibid., 1 Chaitra, pp. 33-6, and 15 Chaitra 1345, pp. 47-8.
43 Op.cit., pp. 13-14. The Address, however, did not make any mention of the Kshatriya Samiti's political position.
44 *Deshabandhu*, 1 Chaitra 1345, pp. 29-30.
45 'Kshatriya Samajer Rajnaitik Karmadharar Paribartan' in ibid., 15 Poush 1345, pp. 258-60.
46 Barman, *Jivan-Smriti*, pp. 73-5.
47 Ibid., p. 75. According to Mandal's version Hem Chandra Naskar was elected as leader of the ISCP. (Jagadish Chandra Mandal, *Mahapran Jogendranath* (Vol. 1), Calcutta, 1382, p. 43.
48 *Deshabandhu*, 1 Bhadra 1345, pp. 162-3; see also Gautam Chattopadhyay, *Freedom Struggle*, pp. 151-5.
49 See the reference in note 45 above.
50 It should be mentioned here that the data sources for Muslim politics in Jalpaiguri are extremely scanty. Almost all the Muslim

families who were active in the social and political life of Jalpaiguri migrated to the erstwhile East Pakistan in the 1950s and 1960s. Not a single issue of *Nishan*, a weekly edited by Muslim League-minded Kazi Abdul Khalek, could be traced. The account presented here is based on scattered references to Muslim politics in *Deshabandhu* and *Trisrota* and interviews with the late Habibar Rahman, Sabed Ali Ahmad and Abul Huda Sultan Alam, and also Hindu political workers who were active in the 1930s and 1940s.

51 Several references to activities of Jaharatullah have been made in the preceding two chapters.

52 See *Trisrota*, 27 January, 26 February, 5 March and 16 July 1939.

53 Interview with late Habibar Rahman (younger brother of Shukurullah) and Sabed Ali; and *Trisrota*, 20 and 27 August 1939.

54 Ibid., 25 June and 9 July 1939.

55 *Deshabandhu*, 6 Falgun 1344, p. 5.

56 *Trisrota*, 27 August 1939.

57 *Deshabandhu*, 1 Agrahayan 1345, p. 234.

58 Ibid., 1 Kartik 1345, pp. 213-4.

59 In the author's interview with Sabed Ali Ahmad the latter used the term *kath-mullah*.

60 Shila Sen, op.cit., p. 123.

61 A.M.L. Rahman was a brother-in-law of Musharraff.

62 *Deshabandhu*, 15 Agrahayan 1345, p. 245.

63 *Trisrota*, 26 February 1939.

64 Ibid., 25 June 1939.

65 See G. Chattopadhyay, *Freedom Struggle*, Chapter VIII.

66 In a note entitled 'Swatantra Krishak Sangher Abashyakata', *Deshabandhu*, 1 Sravan 1345, pp. 131-3. Birendra Nath Dutta explicitly referred to these ideas.

67 Das Gupta's letter to the author, dt. 13.11.1981.

68 Interview with Bijoy Hoare.

69 Interview with Neogy on 28.12.1980.

70 Interview with Biswanath Mukherjee.

71 Interview with Mukherjee and Bimal Hoare.

72 Datta, 'Jalpaiguri Jelar Krishak Andolaner Godar Katha', *Jalpaiguri*, 1 July 1972.

73 *Deshabandhu*, 1 Jyaistha 1345, p. 73.

74 Ibid., pp. 95-6.

75 Ibid., pp. 131-3.

76 Interview with Bimal Hoare on 28 June 1982.

77 *Deshabandhu*, 17 Jyaistha 1345, p. 86.

78 Ibid., 16 Asar 1345, pp. 118-19.

79 *Trisrota*, 28 December 1938.

80 Op.cit, p. 261.

81 Ibid., pp. 261-2.

82 *Trisrota*, 8 January 1939.

83 For much of the details about the Krishak Samiti and early peasant movement in Jalpaiguri district I have relied on Sachin Das Gupta's reminiscences entitled 'Krishak Andolane Jader

Dekhechi' published in *Trisrota*, 25 February, 4, 11, 18, 25 March and 1 April 1979 and *Janamat*, 29 Magh, 27 Falgun, 5, 12 Chaitra 1386.
84 The biographical details are from Das Gupta, *Trisrota*, 25 February 1979.
85 The main sources of the information presented here are *Hindusthan Standard*, 9 and 15 December 1938, interviews with Bimal Das Gupta who was an Assistant Station Master at Domohani and an important leader of the Union from its early days, and communication from Amrita Lal Mukherjee, dated 4 September 1982.
86 S. Das Gupta, *op. cit.*, *Trisrota*, 25 February 1979.
87 S. Das Gupta in ibid., 4 March 1979, and communication from Neogy to the author.
88 S. Das Gupta in *Trisrota*, 4 March 1979.
89 Ibid and Neogy's communication.
90 M. Datta, op.cit.
91 24 February and 9 March 1939. *Hindusthan Standard* of 6 February 1939 too carried a long report under the caption 'Huge Peasants Rally—Procession with Red Flags'.
92 *Ananda Bazar Patrika*, 6 February 1939 and *Trisrota*, February 1939.
93 S. Das Gupta in ibid., 4 March 1939.
94 *National Front*, 9 March 1939.
95 Chatterjee, *Bengal 1920-1947*.
96 Interview with S. Das Gupta.

CHAPTER 9

1 Interview with Birendra Kumar Neogy, Kalyani, 28 December 1980.
2 Madhab Datta's private communication to the author. The impact of these stories and of the interpretation given to them are, however, not known.
3 The term middle *jotedar* is used here only to give a rough indication of the socio-economic position.
4 Bachcha Munshi, a peasant activist of those years, in his interview with the author (15 March 1981) made a distinction between *purana swadeshi babus*, that is, those who spoke only of the anti-British movement and *naya swadeshi babus* who spoke also of anti-zamindar, anti-*jotedar* and anti-mahajan struggle.
5 *Trisrota*, 4 June 1939.

6 Ibid., 18 June 1939.
7 Ibid.
8 Ibid., 25 June 1939.
9 This citation and the two following ones are from *Ananda Bazar Patrika*, 29 June 1939.
10 This goes against the position of Andre Beteille in *Studies in Agrarian Social Structure*, Delhi, 1974, pp. 137-8. Beteille asserts, '... the *jotedars* came to be perceived as an important component of the agrarian class structure for the first time in the context of the tebhaga movement in 1946-7' (p. 138).
11 The full text of all the resolutions were published in *Ananda Bazar Patrika*, 2 July 1939.
12 Ibid., 16 July 1939. Among other members of the Executive Committee were Pramada Chakrabarty, Mahinath Jha, Dolgobinda Barman, Sirajuddin Sarkar, Machhiruddin Sarkar, Sasanka Bose, a Jalpaiguri town-based young doctor, Parimal Mitra, Secretary of the District Students Association, Sudhin Moitra, a medical student and a few others. The conference also elected a fifteen member Subdivisional Committee with Chakrabarty as President and Jha as Secretary.
13 *Trisrota*, 30 July 1939.
14 Ibid., 13 August 1939.
15 Ibid., 3 September 1939.
16 Ibid., 30 July 1939.
17 All the three women activists belonged to the family of Haripada Roy, a substantial landholder and cloth merchant of Boda. He had been associated with the Congress-led activities since 1921. Madhab Datta used to stay in his house and had a radicalizing influence on his family. He induced Sulekha, wife of Haripada's younger brother, to read Gorky's *Mother*. While they remained sympathetic to Krishak Samiti's activities in later years too, they did not remain active for long. (Communication from Datta, dt.16 June 1982.)
18 *Trisrota*, 13 August 1939.
19 See Sugata Bose, *Agrarian Bengal: Economy, Social Structure and Politics, 1919-1947*, pp. 74-5.
20 The account is based on Sachin Das Gupta, 'Jalpaigurir Adhiar Andolan', *Madhuparni*, Jalpaiguri Jela Sankhya, Balurghat, B.S.1394, p. 282.
21 Ibid., pp. 282-3; and Madhab Datta, 'Krishak Andolaner Gorar Katha', *Jalpaiguri*, 15 July 1972, p. 6.
22 Das Gupta, op.cit., p. 283.
23 Datta, op.cit., p. 6
24 Das Gupta, op.cit., p. 283; and Datta, op.cit., p. 5.
25 S. Das Gupta, op.cit., p. 283
26 *Ananda Bazar Patrika*, 2 December 1939.
27 Das Gupta, op.cit., pp. 283-4; Datta, *Jalpaiguri*, 5 July 1972. See also Satyen Sen, *Gram Banglar Pathe Pathe*, 1971, pp. 72-6; and Kali

Sarkar, 'Dinajpur Jelar Krishak Andolan' in Dhananjay Roy(ed.), *Uttarbanger Adhiar Vidroha O Tebhaga Andolan*, Malda, 1984, pp. 86-8. For an official account see WBSA. Home. Poll. 19/39. FCR 1, December 1939.
28 NAI. Home. Poll. 18/12/1939 FR 2, December.
29 BPKS Conference Report, p. 10.
30 Ibid., p. 11.
31 Ibid., p. 10. See also *Annual Report of AIKS, 1939-40*, Appendix D, Report on the Bengal Kisan Movement, 1939-40.
32 Ibid.
33 Das Gupta, 'Krishak Andolane Jader Dekhechhi', *Trisrota*, 25 March 1979.
34 *BPKS Conference Report*, Panjia, 1940, p. 10.
35 A list of these levies was published in *Ananda Bazar Patrika*, 7 February 1940. See also WBSA. Home. Poll. 19/39. FCR 2, December.
36 *Ananda Bazar Patrika*, 7 February 1940.
37 FR 1, December 1939.
38 FR 2, December.
39 Das Gupta, 'Jalpaigurir Adhiar Andolan', p. 285; WBSA. Home. Poll. No.19/39. FCR 2 December. See also *Ananda Bazar Patrika*, 7 February 1940; BPKS Report placed before the 1940 Panjia Conference and *AIKS Report 1939-40*. GOB's *Annual Report on the Administration of Land Revenue in Bengal* for 1939-40 stated, 'In the district of Jalpaiguri there was agrarian agitation which after aiming at inequities in Union Board assessments found its outlet in real grievances of adhiars and in objection to the levy of heavy bazar tolls by zamindars' (p. 14).
40 For an account of the movement in Dinajpur see Ajit Roy, 'Smritite Dinajpur Jelar Krishak Sangram' in Dhananjoy Roy (ed.), op.cit., pp. 48-5; and Sunil Sen, op.cit., pp. 46-7.
41 Datta, Unpublished Reminiscences, Bk.II and III.
42 FR 2, January 1940.
43 Das Gupta, *Madhuparni*, pp. 285-6, and also interviews with Das Gupta. See also *BPKS Coference Report*, p. 10; and *Ananda Bazar Patrika*, 3, 6, 7 and 10 February 1940.
44 M. Datta, Unpublished Reminiscences.
45 *Ananda Bazar Patrika*, 3, 6, 7 and 10 February 1946; and also FR 1 and 2, February 1940.
46 FR 2, February 1940, Appendix II.
47 Op.cit., p. 10. With reference to the movement in Dinajpur the Report stated that there the peasants rose against the opponents and resisted their attacks. As a result, a settlement was arrived at the initiative of the administration.
48 Datta, Unpublished Reminiscences, Bk.III, pp. 13,17.
49 FR 2, January 1940.
50 *Janayuddha*, 12 August 1942. See also next chapter.
51 Interview with S. Das Gupta.

52 For details of the *nankar* and *bhaoali* movement see Pramatha Gupta, *Mukti Yuddhe Adibasi*, Calcutta, 1964, pp. 47-51, and *Je Sangramer Shesh Nai*, Kalantar Prakashani, Calcutta, B.S.1378, pp. 56-61.
53 B.B. Chaudhuri, 'Agrarian Movements in Bengal and Bihar, 1919-39' in Desai(ed), op.cit., pp. 356-7.
54 Ibid., p. 338.
55 FR pertaining to different fortnights in 1938 and 1939.
56 BLRC. Vol. VI, p. 47. Sunil Sen is wrong in his observation that 'no specific demand for bargadars was formulated' (op.cit., p. 26). With regard to the *bargadars* the BPKS Memorandum stated, 'As far as this class [bargadars] is concerned, the main object of legislation should be to give back to them a definite legal status. It is clear that the main task is to confer on the vast mass of peasantry the status of 'peasant owner' and that wherever a cultivator has recently been driven off the land by force of economic pressure and has become a *bargadar*, he should be allowed the option and given the privilege to gain the status' (op.cit., p. 47).
57 Op.cit., pp. 10-1.
58 Private communication from Datta, dt. 26 July 1982.
59 It deserves mention that later on Anath Saran and Pramada joined Hindu Mahasabha. It is particularly interesting that in the early 1940s two members of the District Krishak Samiti Presidium and also of CSP Executive Committee—Satish Lahiri and Jogesh Datta—became very active in the Mahasabha. Both of them had strong Hindu nationalist inclination even in earlier years, and perhaps they developed strong reservations about the *adhiar* movement and its pronounced militant tone.
60 *Ananda Bazar Patrika*, 28 June 1939.
61 Ibid., 13 August 1939.
62 FR 2, January 1940.
63 WBSA. Home. Poll. Confidential No.134/41.
64 Rabindranath Sikdar, 'Jelaye Jatiya Andolaner Dhara' in *Madhuparni*, Jalpaiguri Jela Sankhya, p. 264.

CHAPTER 10

1 NAI. Home. Political. Confidential. FR 2, October 1942, FR 1, November 1942. Also interviews with Piyus Mukherjee, Badal Sarkar, Prabhat Bose, Deben Sarkar and Bidhan Sinha, all of whom were associated with the movement in Jalpaiguri in varying extent. Mukherjee was involved in the Kumargram *thana* raid.

Here a few words on the absence of any Quit India upsurge in Jalpaiguri district are in order. This is partly explained by the feature that, though the district lay in the zone of military activity, the socially and economically dislocating impact of the War was much less than in many east Bengal districts and a district like Midnapore. Men, materials and land were mobilized with active help from the planters, and Baikunthapur zamindars and big *jotedars*. But because of availability of vast stretches of sparsely populated tracts in the Duars the impact was perhaps less harsh than in many other districts and so the grievances against and hostility towards the British were perhaps less. A political feature was that Jalpaiguri, unlike other centres of the Quit India movement, did not have a tradition of vigorous nationalist politics and a powerful peasant base.

2 Of them Prabhat, Badal and Ghanashyam joined the Congress Socialists, Anil Roy, Sinha and Mazumdar RSP and Lahiri and Roy Forward Bloc. Deben Sarkar joined the PSP in early 1950s.

3 *Janamat*, 23 and 30 April 1945.

4 Among them were Sachin Das Gupta, Guruadas Roy, Madhab Datta, Naresh Chakraborty, Hara Ghosh, Manoranjan Das Gupta, Biren Neogy, Parimal Mitra, Anil Mukherjee, Paresh Mitra. The two Mitras were student leaders.

5 *Trisrota*, 19 July 1942 and *Janayuddha* (CPI's provincial weekly), 12 August 1942. For impact of *adhiar* agitation on official approach see Sugata Bose, *Agrarian Bengal : Economy, Social Structure and Politics, 1919-47*, pp. 259-60.

6 *Census of India* 1951. Vol. VI. *West Bengal, Sikkim and Chandernagore*. Pt.IA–*Report*, p. 263. For famine mortality data Amartya Sen, 'A Study of the Bengal Famine of 1943', in E.J. Hobsbawm *et al* (eds.), *Peasants in History*, OUP, 1980 p. 207, Table IV.

7 For empirical evidence on distress in Jalpaiguri see reports published in *Janayuddha*, 1 December 1943.

8 For reports on de-hoarding, relief campaign and related activities see *Trisrota* and *Janayuddha*, 1 December 1943.

9 For full list of members of the People's Food Committee see *Trisrota*, 14 November 1943.

10 Interviews with Biren Neogy.

11 *Trisrota*, 27 February 1944.

12 Bimal Das Gupta, 'Duarser Rail Shramikra Jaglo', *Bichinta* Vol. 4, No.4, pp. 212-4. Also several communications from Das Gupta to the author and interview with Parimal Mitra.

13 FR 2, September, 1943; FR 1 & 2, March 1943; FR 1 & 2, May 1945, FR 1, June 1943 and FR 2, October 1943 make specific references to Jalpaiguri Communists.

14 Bengal. Home. Political. Rajshahi Divisional Commissioner's Fortnightly Confidential Report (FCR) for March 1945.

15 For an account of how Barman became a minister see Barman, *Jivan-Smriti*, p. 82.

16 *Trisrota*, 21 December 1941.
17 Ibid., 11 January 1942.
18 Interview with Abul Huda.
19 For reports on participation of Dr Sulaiman in Communist–sponsored activities see *Trisrota*, 27 February 1944 and *Janamat*, 7 May 1945. For reports on joint programme of the Communist, non-Communist/and Muslim League students *Janamat*, 5 February 1945.
20 For reports on Mahasbha activities see *Trisrota*, 12 December 1940, 10 March and 14 December 1941, 8 and 9 August, 17 May 1942.
21 *Janamat*, 24 February and 5 March 1945.
22 *Amrita Bazar Patrika*, 26, 28, 30 August and 1 September 1945. Also Gautam Chattopadhyay, *Swadhinata Sangrame Banglar Chhatra Samaj*, Calcutta, 1980, p. 66; and FR 2, August 1945.
23 FCR 2, September 1945.
24 For the Dalgaon incident FCR 1, October 1945, and for the Rangamati one FCR 2, November 1945.
25 At the time of this arrest K.N. Das Gupta and other leaders had been members of Forward Bloc. But soon after their release most of them including Das Gupta switched over to the Congress.
26 Written note from Dilip Ghosh who was a leader of the CPI-led Jalpaiguri Students Federation and also interview with Bidhan Sinha, a RSP leader in the mid-1940s.
27 It should be mentioned here that the CSP committee formed earlier in late 1938 had become defunct by early 1940. It was in 1946 that with some young participants of the 1942 movement a Socialist Workers' Council was formed with Ghanashyam Misra as the convenor and some time later a regular CSP Committee was formed with Prabhat Bose as Secretary. (Source : Written note from Nikil Ghatak.)
28 FCR 1, September 1945.
29 FR 1, September 1945.
30 Ibid.
31 Notes of the CPI's Jalpaiguri District Committee meeting held from 13 October to 19 October 1945 to and preserved by Biren Neogy. One member observed, 'We tried to turn the tide, but failed'.
32 Neogy's Notes.
33 See Sumit Sarkar, *Modern India 1885-1947*, pp. 418-28, Gautam Chattopadhyay, op.cit. pp. 67-72, and 'The Almost Revolution', *Essays in honour of S.C. Sarkar*, PPH, New Delhi, 1976, pp. 427-50.
34 'Note' from Dilip Ghosh and interviews with Abul Huda, Sinha, Badal Sarkar and Prabhat Bose.
35 Interviews with Neogy.
36 *Swadhinata*, 9 January, 7 and 10 February 1946.
37 Ibid., 9 January and 8 February 1946.
38 Ibid., 9 January and 8 February 1946.
39 Communication from Nikhil Ghatak.
40 *The Statesman*, 29 March 1946.

41 *Amrita Bazar Patrika*, 31 March 1946.
42 Barman, *Jivan-Smriti*, pp. 98-9.
43 *The Statesman*, 31 January 1946.
44 See the report of such a meeting published in *Swadhinata*, 15 February 1946.
45 Reports on election meetings addressed by Bhowani Sen published in *Swadhinata*, 8 January, 4, 14 February and 16 March 1946.
46 *Swadhinata*, 14 February 1946.
47 Ibid.
48 Chattopadhyay, *Swadhinata Sangrame Banglar Chhatra Samaj*, pp. 73-4; and *Ananda Bazar Patrika*, 22, 23, 24 January 1947.
49 See following passages for Duars unrest and also Appendix II.
50 Note from Ghosh and interview with Sinha.
51 *Swadhinata*, 30 April, 7 May, 14 and 24 June, 14 August, 30 September 1947.
52 Bimal Das Gupta, op.cit., and interview with Parimal Mitra.
53 The data presented in the text are from *Rege Committee Report*, pp. 85-6. For a fairly detailed Communist account of the conditions of Duars plantation labour in the mid-1940s see Nani Bhowmik's report entitled 'Bikshubdha Duars: Cha-Bagan Sramiker Jivan O Sangram'. *Swadhinata*, 4 May 1947; and also Sachin Das Gupta, *Cha-Bagan Jatiyakaran Chai*, a Jalpaiguri CPI publication, 1947. Quoting figures published in *Capital*, 14 November 1946 Das Gupta shows that in the year 1945 some tea companies distributed dividend ranging between 65 per cent to 110 per cent. Rege Committee reported distribution of dividend by many Duars companies in 1942 at such high rates as 135 per cent to 200 per cent. (*Rege Committee Report*, p. 202).
54 *Detailed Report of the General Committee of the Indian Tea Planters' Association for 1945* (hereafter ITPA Report) Honorary Secretary B.C. Ghose's Report pp. 21, 25-6.
55 Ibid., 1945, p. 26.
56 *Detailed Report of the General Committee of the Dooars Planters Association for 1946* (hereafter DPA Report), p. viii.
57 *ITPA Report* for 1946, p. 26-7.
58 *DPA Report* for 1946, p. xxiv.
59 Ibid., 1946, p. viii; *ITPA Report* for 1945, pp. 20-1; and *Rege Committee Report*, p.74.
60 FR 1, June, 1946.
61 Raj. Div. Commissioner K.A. Hill's address to DPA Annual Meeting, *DPA Report* for 1946, p. xxx.
62 Ibid., 1946, xxiv.
63 ITPA Chairman's Address in *ITPA Report* for 1946, p. 15.
64 *DPA Report* for 1946, p. xxx.
65 B. Das Gupta, 'Duarser Antarele' in *Bichinta*, Vol. 3, No.11, pp. 32-3; also interview with Parimal Mitra.
66 B. Das Gupta 'Duarser Tebhaga Andolan Prasange', in *Bichinta*, Vol. 4, No.2, pp. 102-03. Also interview with Jamuna Oraoni.

67 Interview with Jagannath Oraon.
68 *Swadhinata*, 14 August 1946; and DPA Labour Officer's and Labour Adviser's Confidential Monthly Reports (unpublished), January 1948 to December 1948. (I am grateful to Ranjit Das, former DPA Secretary, for allowing me to consult these reports.)
69 FR 1, July 1946.
70 FR 2, July 1946.
71 FR 1 and 2, August 1946.
72 FR 2, September 1946.
73 FR 2, October 1946.
74 FR 2, November 1946.
75 *Ananda Bazar Patrika*, 14 November 1946 and 8 January 1947.
76 FR 1, November 1946.
77 *Ananda Bazar Patrika*, 23 November 1946.
78 FR 2, February 1947.
79 Interview with Bira Dhwaj Rai (popularly known as B.D. Rai).
80 Interview with Piyus Mukherjee.
81 Interview with Badal Sarkar. I have, however, failed to get any corroboration of this claim of the launching of CSP-led labour organization in 1946.
82 Nani Bhattacharya, *Chai Bagichar Mazdur Andolan Ka Itihas*, Duars Cha Bagan Workers Union, Kalchini, Jalpaiguri; and also communications from Tushar Bandyopadhyay.
83 *DPA Report for 1946*, p. 104.
84 Interview with Deben Sarkar; and Sachin Das Gupta, 'Cha Bagan Anchalke Bangla Haite Prithak Karibar Prachesta', *Swadhinata*, 3 October 1947, and S. Das Gupta, *Cha Bagan Jatiyakaran Chai*. For certain complexities of Gurkha League position see B. De and P. Ray, op.cit., pp. 29-30; and Satyendra Narayan Mazumdar, *Patabhumi Kanchanjangha*, Calcutta 1983.
85 Proceedings of the meeting of the DPA Committee and different Sub-District Committees held on 4 and 23 February, 1 March, 16 and 22 May, 2 and 9 June and 22 July 1947 published in *DPA Report* for 1947. See in particular proceedings of the Emergency General Meeting attended by the Superintendent of Police, Jalpaiguri held on 19 February 1947 in ibid.
86 This role of the Communists was impicitly admitted by Deben Sarkar (Jalpaiguri Congress labour leader in the years 1946-50) who told the present writer that the CPI did not enter the tea gardens as a trade union but primarily as a political party.
87 For post-War labour movement in Darjeeling see S. N. Majumdar, op.cit., and that in Assam see Amalendu Guha, *Planter Raj to Swaraj*, New Delhi and also R. P. Behal, 'Forms of Labour Protests in Assam Valley Tea Gardens 1900-1947' (mimeo).
88 NAI. Home Poll (I) F.No.18/7/46.
89 Proceedings of the Emergency General Meeting held on 19 February 1947 in *DPA Report* for 1947, p. 148.
90 See Appendix I below.

91 FR 2, September 1946.
92 *DPA Report* for 1946; and S. K. Haldar, op.cit., pp. 9-10 For the adverse reaction of the planters to wage revision and also Rege Committee Report see *ITPA Report* for 1946, p. 13.
93 Proceedings of the Emergency General Meeting in *DPA Report* for 1947, p. 148.
94 See Intelligence Branch, Weekly Confidential Report, D.I.B., Jalpaiguri (hereafter briefly Jalpaiguri WCR) for week ending 1 March 1947. It reported spread of labour agitation to new gardens: Lakhipara, Banarhat, Bandhapani, Soongachhi and Toonbari. (I am grateful to Arun Prasad Mukherjee, former Special I.G. Police, Intelligence Branch, Govt. of West Bengal for allowing me to consult I.B. records.)
95 The resolution entitled 'For the Final Assault. Tasks of the Indian People in the Present Phase of the Indian Revolution' was published in full in *People's Age*, 18 August 18 1946.
96 FR 2, November 1946.
97 Interviews with Abani Lahiri, Sachin Das Gupta, Biren Neogy and Biren Pal.
98 See the report of a Pachagar meeting addressed by K.B. Roy published in *Swadhinata*, 28 November 1946.
99 Interviews with Das Gupta, Neogy and Pal.
100 *Swadhinata*, 29 November 1946.
101 Interview with Neogy; and *Swadhinata*, 25 December 1946.
102 Interview with Neogy.
103 WBSA Land Revenue Department. Land Revenue Branch. F.No.6M-38/47 B of Dec.-/48 15-107 of which 105 para 4(b).
104 *The Statesman*, 9 March 1947.
105 As in note 103 above, para 4(e).
106 Interviews with Pal and Neogy; and *Swadhinata*, 19 December 1946, 1 and 29 January 1947.
107 *The Statesman*, 9 March 1947.
108 Op.cit., para 4(e). See also *Swadhinata*, 31 December 1946.
109 Ibid; and FR 2, February,1947.
110 See I.B. Report entitled 'An Appreciation on the Tebhaga agitation in Jalpaiguri district', dt. 23.4.47.
111 For SDO's report op.cit., para 4(c); and *The Statesman*, 9 March 1947.
112 For details of repression in Debiganj-Pachagar area see *Swadhinata*, 10 April 1947.
113 See in this connection, among others, Ranajit Guha, *Elementary Aspects of Peasant Insurgency in Colonial India*, OUP, 1983.
114 Cf. Sunil Sen, *Agrarian Struggles in Bengal, 1946-47*, PPH, New Delhi, 1972, p. 56, and also Guha, op.cit., 169-70.
115 Jadunath Singh, Lal Bahadur Chhetri, Man Singh, Budhan, Guhi and Mahabir Mistri were some of such railway workers.
116 Quoted in B. Das Gupta, 'Duarser Rail Sramikra Jaglo', op.cit., p. 215.

117 See Das Gupta, 'Tebhaga Andolaner Prasange', op.cit..
118 Interview with Jagannath Oraon.
119 Jalpaiguri WCR for week ending 22 February 1947.
120 Interviews with Ganguly; also Jalpaiguri WCR for week ending 1 March 1947.
121 Interviews with S. Ganguly and Jagannath Oraon.
122 Interviews with Buni Oraon, Deocharan Nayek and others at Oodlabari; and also Jalpaiguri WCR for week ending 12 April 1947.
123 *ITA Report* for 1947, p. 41.
125 Nani Bhowmik's report in *Swadhinata*, 4 May 1947.
126 Interviews with Jagannath Oraon and Arjun Oraon.
127 Interviews with Jagannath Oraon and Ganguly.
128 *DPA Report* for 1947, p. 142.
129 Ibid., p. 148.
130 *The Statesman*, 3 March 1947; *People's Age*, 23 March 1947; *Swadhinata*, 7 March 1947; *Nationalist*, 3 March 1947; and interviews with Ganguly and Parimal Mitra.
131 Interviews with Ganguly and Mitra.
132 Interviews with Sachin Das Gupta and Ganguly.
133 For details see *Swadhinata*, 11 April 1947. According to the police version, the crowd had attacked police and the latter had to open fire in self-defence. (Jalpaiguri WCR, 12 April 1947.)
134 *The Statesman*, 3 March 1947.
135 *Swadhinata*, 1 and 2 May 1947.
136 The team was composed of Dr Sailesh Chandra Bhowmik, Dr Mohammad Sulaiman, Dr Sukumar Sen Gupta, Dr Haren Hoare and Professor Santosh Batabyal; *Swadhinata*, 13 April 1947. Of them Bhowmik was a Congressman, Sulaiman belonged to Muslim League and Batabyal was a non-Communist Leftist.
137 The students' team consisted of Bidhan Sinha and Prabhat Bose (Students Congress), Golam Rahman (District Muslim Students League), Abul Huda (SF) and a medical student Nikhilesh Roy Choudhury.
138 The report submitted by K. N. Das Gupta, P. Tripathi and A.C. Guha to the Jalpaiguri DCC contained amongst others the following: 'We are satisfied that the mob did not attack anybody nor show any display of their arms. There was no clash' (*Amrita Bazar Patrika*, 21 April 1947.)
139 Note from Dilip Ghose.
140 In connexion with the geographical spread and involvement of different social groups in the *tebhaga* struggle in the province as a whole see, among others, Cooper, *Sharecropping and Sharecroppers' Struggles in Bengal 1930-1950*, pp. 180-96, 244-60; and Sugata Bose, op.cit., pp. 270-2.
141 For reports on the North Bengal Jatiya Mahasabha see *Amrita Bazar Patrika*, 17, 18, 20 May 1947 and *Swadhinata*, 24, 28 May 1947. With regard to the Bose-Suhrawardy plan see, among others, Sarat Bose,

I Warned My Countrymen, Netaji Research Bureau, Calcutta, 1968, pp. 183-94; Abul Hashim, *In Retrospect*, Dacca, 1974, pp. 134-7; Kalipada Biswas, *Yukta Banglar Shesh Adhyay*, Orient Book Co., Calcutta, 1966, pp. 402-3, 407, 410; and Amalendu Sen Gupta, *Uttal Challish:Asamapta Biplab*, Pearl Publishers, 1989, pp. 223-36.

142 *Swadhinata*, 18 June 1947.

143 *Swadhinata*, 18, 20 June 1947; and Jagdish Chandra Mandal, *Mahapran Jogendranath*, Pt. 2, Calcutta, 1979, pp. 22-4.

144 See Sachin Das Gupta, *Cha-Bagan Jatiyakaran Chai*.

Interviews and Correspondence

(The biographical information given below refers only to activities during the period under study in this volume.)

Ahmad, Sabed Ali. Octogenarian observer. Employee in Nawab Musharraff Hossian's tea companies. Muslim League organizer in 1940s.

Alam, Abul Huda Sultan. Students Federation leader and CPI member in 1940s.

Bagchi, Nirendranath. Septuagenarian tea planter and observer of socio-economic changes.

Banerjee, Amar. Advocate and observer from a family having close connexions with European planters and officials.

Banerjee, Late Narayan Mal. Doctor. Active in Congress.

Barman, Upendranath (1897-1988). Had Anushilan Samiti connexion in school days. Rajbansi Kshatriya Samiti activist and leader during early 1920s. Minister Progressive Coalition ministry, 1941-43. Joined Congress in late 1946. Constituent Assembly member. Writer and scholar.

Batabyal, Santosh. College teacher with Radical Democratic Party connexion in 1940s.

Bhattacharya, Chittaranjan (-1985). Political activist. Externed from Koch Bihar State in 1945 for participation in agitation against Koch Bihar Raj. Involved in peasant agitation in Alipur Duars area in 1946-7.

Bhattacharya, Nani. RSP organizer engaged in organizing plantation labour in the Alipur Duars area since late 1946.

Bose, Biren (1917-88). Advocate. CPI member active in cultural front and legal defence of peasant and worker movement activists.

Bose, Nirmal. Forward Blocist student leader.

Bose, Prabhat (-1987). Congress student activist; Convenor, Socialist Workers Council (SWC), 1946. Later on joined Congress Socialist Party (CSP).

Chakrabarty, Kamakhya. Long-time connexion with the tea industry.

Chaudhury, Taiyab. Sexagenarian homeopath doctor of local origin.

Das Gupta, Bimal (1919-). Bengal Duars Railway (BDR) employee. Assistant Station Master in 1946. Joined CPI in 1941. Organizer of railway workers and plantation labour.

Das Gupta, Jagadish. Forward Blocist student activist.

Das Gupta, Kalyani (1922-). Involved in political activities in student days. Secretary, Mahila Atma Raksha Samiti, Jalpaiguri (1942-52). Joined CPI in 1943. Associated with peasant and worker movement, 1946-47.

Das Gupta, Khagendranath (-1985). Revolutionary terrorist connexion in 1910s. Came under the influence of Gandhi in 1920 and devoted himself to building up of Congress in Jalpaiguri. Elected to Bengal Legislative Assembly in 1937 and 1946.

Das Gupta, Sachin (1913-91). Doctor. Participated in C.D. Movement. Member Jalpaiguri District Congress Committe, late 1930s-early 1940s. Organized CSP in 1938. Co-founder and Secretary of Jalpaiguri CPI, 1939-48. Associated with peasant organization and movement in 1938-48 and with tea garden worker struggle in 1946-8.

Dutta, Madhab (1912-85). Hailed from Barisal. Had terrorist connexions. Became involved in Jalpaiguri Congress in 1938 and associated with Krishak Samiti in early 1939. Joined CPI in early 1940s. One of the main organizers of anti-*tola* (tolls) and adhiar agitation (1939-40) and tebhaga struggle (1946-7).

Gangopadhyay, Anil. Advocate. Born into the nationalist family of Rasikilal Ganguly of Alipur Duars. Active in Congress and Forward Bloc.

Ganguly, Samar (-1989). Involved in Congress and CSP in late 1930s. Came into CPI contact in 1939. Fulltime Krishak Samiti organizer in Debiganj from early 1940s. Given the responsibility of assisting labour movement and organizing *tebhaga* in Duars in early 1947.

Ghatak, Nikhil. Advocate. Belongs to one of the earliest settler families of Jalpaiguri town. Involved in Congress, SWC and later on CSP.

Ghose, Dilip. Students Federation leader and CPI member.

Ghose, Hara. Fulltime CPI activist in peasant front and one of the organizers of *tebhaga* in Boda.

Guha, Late Bibhuti. One of the early organizers of Krishak Samiti and CPI in Dinajpur. Joint Secretary, BPKS, 1944-6.

Guha Neogy, Anil. Till August 1942 active in Students Federation. Joined SWC and CSP.

Hoare, Bijoy Kumar. Born into the nationalist family of Sreenath Hoare, a lawyer and planter. Revolutionary terrorist connexions in late 1920s-early 1930s. One of the earliest propagators of socialist ideas in Jalpaiguri and a CSP member in 1938-9. In early 1940s joined Hindu Mahasabha.

Hoare, Bimal Kumar. Advocate. Younger brother of Bijoy Hoare. Active in student movement in 1938-41. CPI member since early 1940s. A leading organizer of the food campaign in 1943-4 and legal defence for peasant and worker activists in 1946-7.

Hoare, Haren. Doctor. Member, Enquiry team on police firing on peasants and workers near Mahabari on 4 April 1947.

Hossain, Akram. Advocate.

Kerr, F.M. Retired manager of different gardens belonging to the Macneill group.

Kundu, Govinda. Doctor. Students Federation leader in 1940-44. Active in peasant agitation. CPI District Committee member.

Lahiri, Abani. Joint Secretary, BPKS, 1945-7. Had been given the responsibility of coordinating peasant movement and *tebhaga* struggles in north Bengal districts, particularly Dinajpur.

Mazumdar, Late Satyendranarayan. Siliguri. Revolutionary terrorist. Joined Communist Consolidation in jail. On release in 1946 became involved in plantation labour movement in Darjeeling district and also Duars.

Mitra, Late Parimal. Jalpaiguri Students Federation leader in 1939-40. Fulltime CPI activist since early 1940s. Organizer of railway labour, tea garden workers and peasants in Duars.

Mukherjee, Amrita Lal. CPI activist from Rangpur entrusted with the responsibility of organizing BDR workers in 1938-40.

Mukherjee, Anil. CPI member, Jalpaiguri since early 1940s.

Mukherjee, Biswanath. CPI leader.

Munshi, Bachcha. Middle peasant. Congress volunteer in Boda. Joined Krishak Samiti and became associated with CPI in 1939.

Nayek, Deocharan. Oodlabari. Tea garden worker militant and participant in *tebhaga* struggle.

Neogy, Birendra Kumar (1909-). Belongs to one of the earliest settler families of Jalpaiguri town. Assistant Secretary, Jalpaiguri DCC, 1937-9 and Secretary 1939-42. Became involved in Krishak Samiti activities in early 1940s and CPI member around 1941. Member, CPI District Committee and Secretary, District Krishak Samiti in 1945-7.

Neogy, Kalpana. Sister of Birendra Neogy. Mahila Atma Raksha Samiti leader and CPI member, 1940s.

Oraon, Buni (-1988). Oodlabari. *Adhiar* peasant organizer of *tebhaga* struggle in Oodlabari-Mal-Matialy area in 1947. CPI member till death.

Oraon, Jagannath. Mal. Tea garden worker dismissed for participation in worker agitation in 1946. Organizer of worker and peasant agitation and fulltime activist.

Oraon, Lawrence Sukra, Mal. Dismissed tea garden worker. Organizer of worker organization and agitation.

Oraon, Sukra, Neoramajhiali. Adhiar peasant activist and composer of militant songs. (Earlier CPI and later on CPI-M leader.) Because of his militancy came to be known as 'Lal Sukra'.

Oraon, Turi, Oodlabari. Participant in 1947 *tebhaga* struggle and injured in police firing on 4 April 1947. (CPI member).

Oraoni, Jamuna. Woman worker in Diana T.E. A militant activist and long-time CPI Member.

Oraoni, Mangri, Mal. Militant woman worker.

Oraoni, Poko. Neoramajhiali. A young girl during the 1947 *tebhaga* struggle and displayed remarkable militancy.

Pal, Biren. Fulltime CPI activist placed in Pachagar in 1942-7.

Rahman, Md. Habibar (-1985). Tea planter belonging to a Bihari family settled in Jalpaiguri town. Close observer with wide interests.

Rai, Bira Dhwaj. Nepali worker in a Bagrakot coal mine who

became involved in a labour agitation in Dumchipara T.E. in 1946. Later on emerged as a major leader of Socialist-led trade union.

Raikat, Samarendra Deb (Taru). Advocate. Belonging to one of the most respected Rajbansi families of Jalpaiguri town and grandson of Jagadindra Deb Raikat, adopted son of Jogindra Deb Raikat and also Baikunthapur Zamindar for some time.

Rasul, Md. Abdullah. Leader, BPKS and AIKS.

Roy, Dukiram. Rajbansi middle peasant Krishak Samiti activist in Pachagar in 1945-7. (Later on associated with CPI, CPI-M and CPI-ML).

Roy, Late Krishna Binode. President, BPKS, 1945-7.

Roy, Monoranjan. Communist labour leader.

Roy, Ranjit, I.C.S. Jalpaiguri Deputy Commissioner, 1946-7.

Roy, Rathin. Forward Blocist student leader.

Sarkar, Badal. Congress activist during 1941-5. Joined SWC in 1946 and soon CSP.

Sarkar, Late Deben. Secretary, DCC, 1946-7.

Sen, Subodh (-1989). Till mid-1940s active in Labour Party. Joined CPI around 1945. Organized Civil Liberties Committee in Jalpaiguri in 1946-7 and became involved in plantation labour movement.

Sen, Sunil. Played a leading role in peasant movement, particularly *tebhaga* struggle and CPI in Dinajpur in 1940s.

Sikdar, Rabindranath (1908-). Political activist since college days in 1920s. Initial involvement in Anushilan Samiti. Participant in C.D. movement. Secretary, DCC, 1937-8. Joined Forward Bloc in 1940. Imprisoned during 1942-5. Re-joined official Congress in 1946.

Sinha, Bidhan. Till August 1942 active in Students Federation. Later on active in non-Communist SF. RSP organizer in 1945-7.

Talukdar, Suresh. RSP trade union leader in Duars since 1947.

Select Bibliography

A. UNPUBLISHED OFFICIAL RECORDS

National Archives of India
Home. Political.
West Bengal State Archives
Revenue Department. Land Revenue Branch.
Home. Confidential. Political Department. Political Branch.

B. OFFICIAL PUBLICATIONS

1. *Government of UK*
   Indian Statutory Commission (Simon Commission), *Selections from Memoranda and Oral Evidence*, 1929.
   Indian Franchise Committee, *Report of the Indian Franchise Committee*, Vol. XVII, Pt. III, 1932.
   N. Mansergh (ed.), The Transfer of Power, Vol, IX, London, 1970-74.

2. *Government of India*
   Census of India, relevant volumes on Bengal.
   Imperial Gazeteers of India, Vol. XIV.
   Report on an Enquiry into Conditions of Labour in Plantations in India (Labour Investigation Committee, Chairman: D.V. Rege, 1946).

3. *Government of Bengal*
   Census Report of the District of Jalpaiguri 1891.
   F.O. Bell, *Final Report on the Survey and Settlement Operations in the District of Dinajpur 1934-40*, Bengal Government Press, Alipur, 1941.

A.C. Hartley, *Final Report on the Survey and Settlement Operations in the District of Rangpur 1931-38*, Bengal Government Press, Alipur, 1940.

J.A. Milligan, *Final Report on the Survey and Settlement Operations in the Jalpaiguri District 1906-16*, Bengal Secretariat Book Depot, Calcutta, 1919.

D.H.E. Sunder, *Survey and Settlement of the Western Dooars in the Jalpaiguri District 1889-95.*

J.F. Grunning, *Eastern Bengal and Assam District Gazetteers : Jalpaiguri*, Allahabad, 1911.

Proceedings of Bengal Legislative Council (select years).

Proceedings of Bengal Legislative Assembly (select years).

Report on the Administration of Bengal, Calcutta, annual (select years).

Report of the Land Revenue Administration of the Presidency of Bengal, Calcutta, annual (select years).

Report of the Land Revenue Commission, Bengal 1938-40 (Chairman Sir Francis Floud), 6 Vols., Alipur, 1940.

Report of the Labour Enquiry Commission, 1896.

4. *Government of Assam*

J.C. Arbuthnot, *Report on the Conditions of Tea Garden Labour in the Dooars of Bengal, in Madras and in Ceylon*, Shillong, 1904.

5. *Government of West Bengal*

Census 1951 : West Bengal : District Handbooks : Jalpaiguri by A. Mitra, Calcutta, 1954.

Durgadas Majumdar, *West Bengal District Gazetteers : Koch Bihar*, Calcutta, 1977.

Barun De *et al.*, *West Bengal District Gazetteers : Jalpaiguri*, Calcutta, 1981.

Report on an Enquiry into the Living Condition of Plantation Workers in Jalpaiguri District (Dooars), West Bengal by S.K. Haldar, Alipore, 1951.

C. RECORDS OF POLITICAL AND BUSINESS ORGANIZATIONS

All India Congress Committee Papers [Only those relating to Jalpaiguri].

Bangiya Pradeshik Krishak Sabha Papers [having relevance for Jalpaiguri].
Dooars Planters Association. Annual Reports. [Reports prior to 1908 could not be traced].
Indian Tea Planters Association. Annual Reports. [Reports for only a few years could be traced].
Kshatriya Samiti. Proceedings of annual conferences. [Proceedings of only a few conferences could be located].

D. UNPUBLISHED UNOFFICIAL RECORDS

Indian Tea Association. Labour Department (Dooars Planters Association). *Confidential Report of the ITA Labour Officer, Dooars, 1948.*
Nehru Memorial Museum and Library. B.P. Singha Roy Papers.

E. CONTEMPORARY NEWSPAPERS AND JOURNALS

Amrita Bazar Patrika, Calcutta.
Ananda Bazar Patrika, Calcutta.
Bangabani, Calcutta.
Deshbandhu, Fortnightly, Jalpaiguri, B.S.1344-5.
Hindusthan Standard, Calcutta 1938.
Indian Annual Register, Calcutta, 1929-33, 1937-47.
Janamat, Weekly, Jalpaiguri, 1944.
Janayuddha, Weekly, Calcutta, 1943, 1944.
Kshatriya, Monthly, Rangpur, BS. 1331,1332,1333.
The Mussalman, Weekly, Calcutta.
National Front, Weekly, Bombay, 1938.
People's Age, Weekly, Bombay.
The Statesman, Calcutta.
Swadhinata, Calcutta, 1946,1947.
Trisrota, Weekly, Jalpaiguri, 1927, 1930-36, 1938-45.

F. UNPUBLISHED THESES AND RESEARCH PAPERS

De, Jatindranath, 'The History of Krishak Praja Party in Bengal, 1929-47' (Delhi University Ph. D. thesis).

De, Barun and Roy, Pranabranjan, *'Notes for the History of Darjee-
    ling District'*, mimeo (Presented to Modern India History
    Section, Indian History Congress, Waltair Session, 1979.)
Kamtekar, Indivar, 'The End of the Colonial State in India, 1942-
    1947' (Cambridge University Ph. D. thesis.)
Mukherjee, Shib Sankar, 'Emergence of Bengali Entrepreneurship
    in Tea Plantations in Jalpaiguri Duars (1879-1933)' (North
    Bengal University Ph.D.thesis.)
Sarkar, Tanika, 'National Movement and Popular Protest in Ben-
    gal 1928-34' (Delhi University Ph.D. Thesis).

G. BOOKS, ARTICLES AND PAPERS

Adhikari, G. 'Politics and Ideology of National Revolutionaries', in
    Mainstream, 25 April 1981.
Ahmad, Abul Mansur. *Amar Dekha Rajnitir Panchas Bachhar*, Dacca,
    1970.
Ahmed, Rafiuddin. *The Bengal Muslims 1871-1906: A Quest for
    Identity*, Delhi, 1981.
Alavi, Hamza. 'Peasant Classes and Primordial Loyalties' *Journal
    of Peasant Studies*, Vol. 1. No.1, October 1973.
Andrew Yule and Co. *Andrew Yule and Co. Ltd.*, Printed in Great
    Britain, 1963.
Arya Natya Samaj. *Arya Natya Samaj, Jalpaiguri, 1904-1979, Plati-
    num Jubilee*, 1979.
————. *Akalanka Shashi* [A biographical booklet on Shashi Kumar
    Neogi], Jalpaiguri, n.d.
Bagchi, Amiya Kumar. *Private Investment in India 1900-1939*, Cam-
    bridge, 1972.
————. 'Capitalism and the Nature of 'Capitalist' Enterprise in
    India', *EPW*, 30 July 1988, pp. 38-50.
Bandyopadhyay, Sekhar. 'Towards a Corporate Pluralist
    Society:Caste and Colonial Policy of Protective Discrimi-
    nation in Bengal, 1911-1937', *Calcutta Historical Journal*,
    Vol. XI, Nos. 1-2, July 1986-June 1987.
————. . 'Social Protest or Politics of Backwardness? The Na-
    masudra Movement in Bengal, 1872-1911' in Basudeb
    Chattopadhyay, H.S. Vasudevan and Rajat K. Ray (eds.).

Dissent and Consensus : Social Protest in Pre-Industrial Socie-ties, Calcutta, 1989.

Bangiya Pradeshik Krishak Sabha. *Krishaker Laraier Kaida*, Calcutta, 1947.

————. *Zamidari Pratha Dhansa Karo*, Calcutta, 1947.

————. *Phasal O Jamir Larai*, Calcutta, 1947.

Bangiya Pradeshik Rashtriya Sammelan. Jalpaiguri Adhibesan, B.S.1345 (1939), Charu Chandra Sanyal, *Reception Committee Chairman's Address,* Jalpaiguri.

Barman, Upendranath. *Rajbansi Kshatriya Jatir Itihas*, 3rd edition, Jalpaiguri, B.S.1388 (1981).

————. *Thakur Panchanan Barmar Jivan Charit*, Jalpaiguri, B.S.1387 (1980).

Uttar-Banglar Sekal O Amar Jivan-Smriti, Jalpaiguri, B.S.1392 (1985).

————. *Rajbansi Bhasay Prabad, Prabachhhan O Henyali,* Jalpaiguri, 1385.

Basu, Sauren. *Charu Majumdarer Katha*, Calcutta, 1989.

Beckford, G.L. *Persistent Poverty:Underdevelopment in Plantation Economies of the Third World*, 1972.

Behal, Rana Pratap. 'Forms of Labour Protest in Tea Plantations in Assam Valley', *EPW*, Vol. XX, No.4, 26 January 1985.

Beteille, Andre. *Class Structure in an Agrarian Society: Studies in Agrarian Social Structure*, New Delhi.

Bhattacharya, Jnanabrata. 'An Examination of Leadership Entry in Bengal Peasant Revolts, 1937-1947', *Journal of Asian Studies*, Vol. 37, No.4, 1978.

Bhattacharya, Nani. *Chai Bagicha Mazdur Andolan Ka Itihas aur Chai Mazdur Ko Samasya* (Hindi), Duars Chai Bagan Workers Union, Kalchini, Jalpaiguri.

Bhowmick, Sharit. *Class formation in the Plantation System*, People's Publishing House, New Delhi. 1981.

————. 'Tebhaga Movement in Dooars: Some Issues Regarding Ethnicity and Class Formation', in *EPW*, Vol. XXI, No. 22. 31 May 1986.

Biswas, Kalipada. *Yukta Banglar Shesh Adhyay*, Calcutta, 1966.

Bose, Saugata. *Agrarian Bengal: Economy, Social Structure and Politics, 1919-1947*, 1986, Indian edition, Bombay, 1987.

Bose, Sanat Kumar. *Capital and Labour in the Indian Tea Industry*, Bombay, 1954.

Broomfield, J.H. 'The Social and Institutional Bases of Politics in Bengal, 1906-1947' in Rachael Van M. Baumer (ed.), *Aspects of Bengali History and Society*, New Delhi, 1976.

Chakraborty, Bhaskar. 'From Sub-Nation to Subaltern: Experiments in the Writing of Indian History' in Basudeb Chattopadhyay, H.S. Vasudevan & Rajat K. Ray (eds.), *Dissent and Consensus: Social Protest in Pre-Industrial Societies*, Calcutta, 1989.

Chakraborty, Sumit (ed.) *Tebhaga Sangram*, Calcutta, 1973.

Chandra, Bipan, Mukherjee, Mridula, Mukherjee, Aditya, Mahajan, Sucheta and Panikkar, K.N. *India's Struggle for Independence 1857-1947*, New Delhi, 1988.

Chattopadhyay, Kunal. *Tebhaga Andolaner Itihas*, Calcutta, 1987.

Chattopadhyay, Gautam, 'The Almost Revolution', in B. De (ed.), *Essays in Honour of Prof. S.C. Sarkar*, New Delhi, 1976, pp. 427-52.

——— . *Swadhinata Sangrame Banglar Chhatra Samaj*, Calcutta, 1980.

——— . *Bengal Freedom Struggle and Electoral Politics*, New Delhi, 1984.

Chatterjee, Partha. 'Agrarian Structure in Pre-Partition Bengal' in Asok Sen, Partha Chatterjee and Saugata Mukherjee, *Perspectives in Social Sciences 2 : Three Studies on the Agrarian Structure in Bengal 1850-1947*, Delhi, 1982.

——— . 'Agrarian Relations and Communalism in Bengal, 1926-1935', in Ranajit Guha (ed.), *Subaltern Studies I: Writings on South Asian History and Society*, Delhi, 1982, pp. 9-38.

——— . *Bengal 1920-1947 : The Land Question*, Calcutta, 1984.

——— . 'The Colonial State and Peasant Resistance in Bengal 1920-1947', *Past And Present*, No. 110, February 1986.

Chatterji, Suniti Kumar. *Kirata-Jana-Kirti*, 1951, Revised edition, Calcutta, 1974.

Chaudhuri, Asim. 'Development, Urbanization and Rural-Urban Relationship in Plantation Dominated Economy—Myth and Reality: The Case of Jalpaiguri District in North Bengal' in Biplab Das Gupta (ed.), *Urbanization, migration and rural change: a study of West Bengal*, A. Mukherjee, Calcutta, 1988.

Chaudhuri, Binoy Bhusan. 'The Process of Depeasantization in

Bengal and Bihar, 1885-1947', *Indian Historical Review*, Vol. 2, No.1, July 1975.

Chaudhuri, Binoy Bhusan. Agrarian Movements in Bengal and Bihar, 1919-39' in A.R. Desai (ed.), *Peasant Struggles in India*, Delhi, 1979.

————. 'The Story of a Tribal Revolt in the Bengal Presidency: The Religion and Politics of the Oraons : 1900-1926' in Adhir Chakravarti (ed.), *Aspects of Socio-Economic Changes and Political Awakening in Bengal*, Calcutta, 1989.

Chaudhuri, Nirmal Chandra. *Swadhinate Sangrame Rajbansi Sampraday*, Jalpaiguri, n.d.

Communist Party of India. *Tapashili Andolaner Dhara* (Bengali translation of an English collection of articles on Scheduled Caste Movement), Calcutta, n.d. (1946?)

Cooper, Adrienne.'Sharecroppers and Landlords in Bengal 1930-50 : The Dependency Web and Its Implications', *Journal of Peasant Studies*, Vol. 10, Nos.2 & 3, January/March 1983.

————. *Sharecropping and Sharecroppers Struggles in Bengal 1930-1950*, Calcutta, 1988.

Custers, Peter. *Women in the Tebhaga Uprising : rural poor, women and revolutionary leadership (1946-47)*, Calcutta, 1987.

Dalton, E.T. *Descriptive Ethnology of Bengal*, 1872, Reprint, Calcutta, 1960.

Das Gupta, Bimal. 'Duarser Tebhaga Andolan Prasange', *Bichinta*, Vol. 4, No.2, Kartik, B.S.1381.

————. 'Duarser Rail Shramikra Jaglo', *Bichinta*, Vol. 4. No.4, Poush, B.S.1381.

————. 'Jalpaiguri Duars Shramik-Krishaker Rakter Rakhibandhan' in Sumit Chakraborty (ed.), *Tebhaga Sangram*, Calcutta, 1973.

Das Gupta, Kanu (ed.). *Ateet-Smarakgrantha*, Jalpaiguri, 1980.

Das Gupta Khagendranath. 'Jalpaiguri Zilla Board' in *Desha Bandhu*, Vol. I, No.11.

————. 'Swadhinata Sangrame Jalpaiguri Jela', in *Jalpaiguri Zila School Satabarshiki Smarak Patrika*, Jalpaiguri, 1976.

Das Gupta, Ranajit. 'Structure of Labour Market in Colonial India', EPW, 1981, Special No.

————. 'Krishak O Rajneeti : Jalpaiguri 1938-1940', *Parichaya*, November 1983.

Das Gupta, Ranajit. 'Popular Movements in Jalpaiguri District', in *EPW* , Vol. XXI, No.47, 22 November 1986.

———. 'Peasants, Workers and Freedom Struggle : Jalpaiguri, 1945-47' in Amit Kumar Gupta (ed.), *Myth and Reality: The Struggle for Freedom in India, 1945-47*, Manohar, 1987.

———. 'The Oraon Labour Agitation: Duars in Jalpaiguri District, 1915-16', in EPW, 30 September 1989.

Das Gupta, Sachin. 'Jalpaigurir Adhiar Andolan' in *Madhuparni*, Jalpaiguri Jela Sankhya, B.S.1394, pp. 277-87.

———. 'Cha Bagan Anchalke Bangla Haite Prithak Karibar Prachesta'. *Swadhinata*, 3 October 1947.

———. *Cha Bagan Jatiyakaran Chai*, CPI, Jalpaiguri, 1947.

———. 'Krishak Andolane Jader Dekhechhi', *Trisrota*, 25 February, 4, 11, 18, 25 March, 1 April 1979, and *Janamat*, 29 Magh, 27 Falgun, 5, 12 Chaita, B.S. 1366.

Dasgupta, Satyajit. 'The Tebhaga Movement in Bengal 1946-47', Occasional Paper No. 89, Centre for Studies in Social Sciences, Calcutta, 1988.

Datta, Birendranath. 'Swatantra Krishak Sangher Abasyakata', Deshabandhu, 1 Sravan, B.S. 1345.

Datta, Madhab. 'Jalpaiguri Jelar Krishak Andolaner Gorar Katha', *Jalpaiguri* (fortnightly), various issues of 1972.

Datta Roy, Suranjan. 'Sahar Alipurduarer Ateet Ebong Bartaman' in *Jalpaiguri Centenary Souvenir*, Jalpaiguri, 1970.

De, Barun. 'Complexities in the Relationships between Nationalism, Capitalism and Colonialism' in Debiprosad Chattopadhyay (ed.) *History and Society:Essays in Honour of Prof. Nihar Ranjan Ray*, Calcutta, 1978.

———. 'Nationalism as a Binding Force:The Dialetics of the Historical Course of Nationalism I', Occasional Paper No. 93, CSSSC, 1987.

Desai, A.R.(ed.). *Peasant Struggles in India*, Delhi, 1979.

Devi, Gayatri and Rau, Santha Rama. *A Princess Remembers: The Memoirs of the Maharani of Jaipur*, 1976, 5th edition, New Delhi, 1989.

Dhanagare, D.N. 'The Tebhaga Movement in Bengal, 1946-47' in Dhanagare, *Peasant Movements in India*, Delhi, 1983.

Dooars Branch, Indian Tea Association 1878-1978, *Centenary Souvenir*, 1978.

The Duncan Group, *Being a Short History of Duncan Brothers & Co.*

Ltd., *Calcutta and Walter Duncan Goodricke Ltd., London, 1859-1959*, London, 1959.

Dutta, Paritosh. 'Jalpaigurir Nam-Rahasya' in *Madhuparni*, Jalpaiguri Jela Sankhya, Balurghat, B.S.1394.

Dutt, R.P. *India Today*, Bombay, 1949.

Gangapadhyay, Anil. 'Swadinata Sangrame Alipur Duar', *Jalpaiguri District Centenary Souvenir*, Jalpaiguri.

Ghosal, S.C. *A History of Cooch Behar* (tr. from original Bengali work *Kooch Biharer Itihas* by Khan Chowdhuri Amanatulla Ahmed), Cooch Behar, 1942.

Ghose, B.C. *The Development of Tea Industry in the District of Jalpaiguri 1869-1968*, Jalpaiguri.

Ghosh, Anandagopal. 'Jalpaiguri Jelar Musalman Samaj' in *Madhuparni* : Jalpaiguri Jela Sankhya, Balurghat, B.S.1394.

——— . 'Kochbihar Rajyer Bharatiya Unione Jogdaner Patabhumika' in Gautam Chottopadhyay (ed.), *Ithihas-Anusandhan* 2, Calcutta, 1987.

Goswami, Omkar. 'Agriculture in Slump : the peasant economy of East and North Bengal in the 1930s', in *IESHR*, Vol. XXI, No.3, July-September 1984.

Griffiths, Percival. *The History of Tea Industry in India*, London, 1967.

Guha, Amalendu. *Planter Raj to Swaraj*, New Delhi, 1977.

Gupta, Amit Kumar (ed.). *Myth and Reality : The Struggle for Freedom in India 1945-47*, New Delhi, 1987.

Gupta, Amit Kumar. 'The Leftists and the Rural Poor in India, 1934-39', *Occasional Papers on Indian Society*, Second Series, Nehru Memorial Museum and Library, New Delhi, 1989.

Gurjangjhora Tea Industries Ltd., Jalpaiguri, 1882-1982, *Souvenir: A Century of Progress*, Jalpaiguri, 1962.

Hamilton, Dr Francis Buchanan. *An Account of the District of Rangpur*, 1810. Extracts in *Jalpaiguri D.H.*

Hashim, Abul. *In Retrospection*, Dacca, 1974.

Hooker, J.D. *Himalayan Journals*, 1849. Extracts in Census 1951 *West Bengal District Handbooks : Jalpaiguri* by A. Mitra.

Hoare, Somenath 'Tebhagar Diary', *Ekshan*, Autumn Number, B.S. 1388, Supplement.

Hunter, W.W. *A Statistical Account of Bengal*, Vol. X, *Darjeeling, Jalpaiguri and Cooch Behar State*.

Indian Tea Planters Association, Jalpaiguri, *Golden Jubilee Souvenir*, 1965.

Jalpaiguri Jela Shata-Barshiki Smarak Grantha. Jalpaiguri District Centenary Souvenir 1869-1968, eds. C.C. Sanyal, K.K. Chakravarty, |Pritinidhan Roy and R.M. Lahiri, Jalpaiguri 1970.

Khan Chowdhuri, Amanatulla Ahmed. *Koch Biharer Itihas*, 1st Part, Cooch Behar, B.S.1342.

Lahiri, Chandidas, 'Jalpaiguri Jelar Byabsa-Banijya' in *Madhuparni*, Jalpaiguri Jela Sankhya, Balurghat, B.S.1394.

Lahiri, Abani. 'Last Battle of Bengal Peasants under British Rule' in Nisith Ranjan Ray & others (ed.), *Challenge : A Saga of India's Struggle for Freedom*, New Delhi, 1984.

Lahiri, Rebati Mohan. 'Jalpaiguri Jelar Itihas' in *Jalpaiguri District Centenary Souvenir*, Jalpaiguri, 1970.

Madhuparni: Jalpaiguri Jela Sankhya, Balurghat, B.S.1394.

Mandal, Jagadish Chandra. *Mahapran Jogendranath*, Vol. I, Calcutta, 1975.

————. *Mahapran Jogendranath*, Vol. II, Calcutta, 1979.

Mandal, Sibendra Narayan, *Rajbansi Kshatriya Jatir Sankshipta Itibritta*, Gouripur, Assam, n.d.

Mazumdar, Bhusan Arun, 'Oonabingsha Satabdir Baikunthapur' in *Jalpaiguri District Centenary Souvenir*, Jalpaiguri, 1970.

Majumdar, Bimalendu. 'Toto Janajatir Artha-Samajik Bibartan' in *Madhuparni, Jalpaiguri Jela Sankhya*, Balurghat, B.S.1394.

Mazumdar, Satyendranarain. *Amar Biplab Jingasa*, Calcutta, 1973.

————. *Patabhumi Kanchanjangha*, Calcutta, 1983.

Mukherjee, S. 'Emergence of Bengalee Entrepreneurship in Tea Plantation in a Bengal District, 1879-1933', *IESHR*, Vol. XIII, No.4, October-December 1976.

Mukhopadhyay, Saroj, *Bharater Communist Party O Amra*, Pt. I, 1930-41, Calcutta, 1985.

————. Pt.II, 1942-1947, Calcutta, 1986.

Mukhopadhyay, Sudhir and Ghose, Nripen. *Rangpur Jelar Krishak Andolaner Itihas O Party*, Serampore, Hooghly, 1985.

Munshi, Surendra. 'Tribal absorption and Sanskritisation in Hindu society', *Contributions to Indian Sociology*, New Series, Vol. 13, No. 2, July-December 1979, pp. 293-317.

Namboodiripad, E.M.S. *A History of Indian Freedom Struggle*, Trivandrum, n.d.

Narjinari, Hiracharan. 'Jelar Mech Samaj O Sanskriti' in *Madhuparni: Jalpaiguri Jela Sankhya*, Balurghat, B.S.1394.

O'Hanlon, Rosalind. *Caste, Conflict and Ideology: Mahatma Jotirao*

Phule and Low Caste Protest in Nineteenth Century Western India, Cambridge, 1985.

Pandey, Gyanendra. *The Ascendency of the Congress in Uttar Pradesh 1926-34*, Delhi, 1978.

Raikat, Jagadrinda Deb. *Raikat Bansa O Tahader Rajyer Sankshipta Bibaran* (Nirmal Chandra Chaudhuri, ed.), Jalpaiguri, B.S. 1389 (?).

Rahman, Md. Habibar. 'Danbir Vidyotsahi Mahammad Sonaullah', in *Sonaullah Uchcha Madhyamik Jayanati Smaranika* 1984.

Rao, M.B. (ed.). *Documents on the History of the Communist Party of India*, Vol. VII, N.D., 1976.

Rasul, Muhammad Abdullah. *Krishak Sabhar Itihas*, Calcutta, 1969.

Ray, Rajat K. 'Masses in Politics : The Non-Cooperation Movement in Bengal 1920-22', *IESHR* Vol. XI, No.4, ——— October-December 1974.

——— . *Social Conflict and Political Unrest in Bengal 1875-1927*, Delhi, 1984.

——— . *Grame Gramantare*, Calcutta, 1985.

Ray, Ratnalekha, *Change in Bengal Agrarian Society 1750-1850*, New Delhi, 1979.

Risley, H.H. *The Tribes and Castes of Bengal, Ethnographic Glossary*, Vol. I, 1891, Reprint, Calcutta, 1981.

Roy, A.K. 'Some Notes on the Ksatriya, Movement in North Bengal' in *Journal of Asiatic Society of Bangladesh*, Vol. XX, No.1, April 1975.

Roy, Debesh (ed.). *Dhaner Gaye Rakter Dag*, Jalpaiguri, 1967.

——— . *Tista-parer Brittanta*, Calcutta, 1988.

Roy, Dhananjoy (ed.). *Uttarbanger Adhiar Bidroha O Tebhaga Andolan*, Calcutta, 1984.

——— . *Rangpurer Adhiar Bidroha O Tebhaga Andolan*, Calcutta, 1986.

Roychaudhury, Tapas Kumar. 'Duarse Bhumi-Rajaswa Byabasthar Bibartan', in *Madhuparni, Jalpaiguri Jela Sankhya*, B.S. 1394, pp. 155-72.

Sanyal, Charu Chandra. *Reception Committee Chairman's Address*, Bangiya Pradeshik Rashtriya Sammelan, Jalpaiguri Adhibesan, B.S. 1345.

——— . *The Rajbansis of North Bengal (A Study of a Hindu Social Group)*, Calcutta, 1965.

Sanyal, Charu Chandra. Jalpaiguri Saharer Eksha Bachhar, *Jalpaiguri District Centenary Souvenir*, Jalpaiguri, 1970.

Sanyal, Hitesranjan. 'Arambager Jatiyatabadi Andolan (1921-1942)' *Anya Artha*, 6 (September–October 1974); 7 (November–December 1974).

——. 'Dakshin-paschim Banglay Jatiyatabadi Andolan', *Chaturanga*, Vol. 38 (1976-7), 1, 3 and Vol. 39 (1977-8)1.

——. *Social Mobility in Bengal*, Calcutta, 1981.

Sanyal, Mukulesh. 'Swadhinata Andolane Jalpaiguri', *Centenary Souvenir*, Jalpaiguri, 1970.

Saha, Rebatimohan. 'Jalpaiguri Jelar Koch-Rabha Samaj' in *Madhuparni: Jalpaiguri Jela Sankhya*, Balurghat, B.S. 1394.

Sarkar, Dharma Narayan. *Rai Saheb Panchanan*, Bagura, Bangladesh, B.S. 1391.

——. *Uttarbangiya Rajbansi Kshatriya Jatir Itihas*, Rangpur.

Sarkar, Sumit. *The Swadeshi Movement in Bengal 1903-1908*, New Delhi, 1973.

——. *Popular Movements and Middle Class Leadership in Colonial India: Perspectives and Problems of a History from Below*, Calcutta, 1983.

——. *Modern India 1885-1947*, New Delhi, 1983.

Sarkar, Tanika. *Bengal 1928-1934: The Politics of Protest*, Delhi, 1987.

Sen, Asok. 'Agrarian Structure and Tenancy Laws in Bengal 1850-1900' in Asok Sen, Partha Chatterjee and Saugata Mukherjee, *Perspectives of Social Sciences 2 : Three Studies on the Agrarian Structure in Bengal 1850-1947*, Delhi, 1982.

——. 'Subaltern Studies: Capital, Class and Community' in Ranajit Guha (ed.) *Subaltern Studies V*, Delhi, 1987, pp. 202-35.

Sen, Bhowani. 'Banglay Tebhaga Andolan' in Sibsankar Mitra (ed.), *Bhowani Sen Nirbachita Rachanasangraha*, Vol. 2, Bharater Communist Party, Calcutta, 1977,

——. 'Bangadeshe Communist Partyr Itihas', in Sibsankar Mitra (ed.), op. cit.

Sen, Manikuntala. *Sediner Katha*, Calcutta, 1982.

Sen, Satyen. *Gram Banglar Patha Pathe*, 1970, Reprint, Calcutta, 1971.

Sen, Shila. *Muslim Politics in Bengal 1937-1947*, Impex India, New Delhi, 1976.

Sen, Sunil. *Agrarian Struggle in Bengal 1946-47*, New Delhi, 1972.

Sen, Sunil. *The Working Women and Popular Movements in Bengal : From the Gandhi era to the present day*, Calcutta, 1985.

Sen Gupta, Amalendu. *Uttal Challish : Asampta Biplab*, Calcutta, 1989.

Sikdar, Rabindranath. 'Jelaye Jatiya Andolaner Dhara', *Madhuparni, Jalpaiguri Jela Sankhya*, B.S. 1394.

Singh, Bhai Nahar and Singh, Bhai Kispal. *History of All India Gurkha League 1943-1949*, New Delhi, 1987.

Sinha, Surajit. 'Bhumij-Kshatriya Social Movement in South Manbhum' in *Bulletin of the Department of Anthropology*, Vol. VII, No.2, July 1959.

Sonaullah Uchcha Madhyamik Vidyalay Jalpaiguri Hirak Jayanti Smaranika, Jalpaiguri, 1984.

Umar, Badruddin. *Chirasthaee Bandobaste Bangladesher Krishak*, B.S. 1381, Reprint, Calcutta, 1978.

Xaxa, Virginia. 'Colonial Capitalism and Underdevelopment in North Bengal' *EPW*, Vol. XX, No. 39, 28 September 1985, pp. 1659-65.

Index

and Civil Disobedience, 134-7; constructive programme and social reforms, 119, 137; in mid-1930s, 149; in 1937-8, 151-7; radical stirring within, 138, 164, 167; and 1937 election, 146-7; Provincial Conference (1939), 152-3, 156, 172, 173; and Gandhi vs. Bose controversy, 201; in 1939-40, 201; and Quit India movement, 202; and 1946 election, 208, 209, 211, 212, 213; socio-economic composition and background of District Congress Committees (DCC) leadership, 113, 123, 141-2, 241; in Alipur Duars, 109, 219, 220; and upper castes, 85, 102,123, 141, 158; links with planters and *jotedars*, 113, 241; and rural Congressmen, 141-2; and Rajbansi Hindus, 111, 126, 141; and Rajbansi Kshatriya movement (Samiti), 111, 126, 141, 156, 157-9; and Muslims, 111, 139, 141, 151, 156-7, 160; and Hindu nationalism, 130, 142-3, 157, 237; and partition, 237; attitude to agrarian issues, 115, 141, 142, 150, 151, 153-4, 155-6, 211; and police firing on *tebhaga* peasants, 236; attitude to labour, 105, 113, 125, 141, 154, 156, 218, 219, 222. *See also* nationalist politics, no-rent (no-revenue) movements, Krishak Samiti

Congress Socialist Party (CSP), 149-50, 154, 168-70, 172, 174-5, 206, 208, 210, 214, 221, 236, 239, 305

Constituent Assembly, 212

constitutional reforms, 148

Cooch Behar State Railways, 72

Cultural Institute, 213

Dacca, 195, 249

Dalton, E.T., 13

Darjeeling, 11, 28, 48, 60, 62, 65, 216, 222

Das, Chitta Ranjan, 110, 119, 137

Das, Dhepai, 135

Das, Dr Sundari Mohan, 120

Das, Kharga Narayan, 135

Das, Laxmikanta, 61

Das, Pramatha, 134

Das, Rabi, 134

Das Gupta, Bimal, 204, 218, 257

Das Gupta, Birendra Nath, 83, 108, 170, 200

Das Gupta, Jagadish, 257

Das Gupta, Kalyani, 257

Das Gupta, Khagendra Nath, 108-9, 120-1, 125, 130, 134-5, 141, 146, 149, 152-3, 172, 182, 201-2, 208-11, 236-7, 257

Das Gupta, Manoranjan, 119, 193, 225

Das Gupta, Sachindra Nath, 135, 165, 168-71, 174-5, 178, 181-2, 225, 257

Datta, Birendra Nath, 122-3, 135, 165, 168, 174, 181

Datta, Dr Bhupendra Nath, 122, 138, 165

Datta, Jogesh Chandra, 136-7, 168, 181

Datta, Keshab, 136

Datta, Madhab, 151, 154, 166, 171, 175, 181, 185-6, 192-3, 225, 257

Datta, Manmatha, 117

Datta, Swaprakash, 123, 135

Datta Gupta, Birendra Nath, 84, 165

Deb Singha, Amar Chandra, 158

Debiganj–Pachagar–Boda area, 90, 117, 175, 176, 181, 182, 184-5, 188, 190, 191-2, 203, 210, 212, 224-9, 236

debt *see* indebtedness

Debt Conciliation Board, 153

Depression, 164; impact on plantation industry, 131-2; and plantation workers, 132, 140; and agricultural economy, 132; and peasantry, 132-3, 138-9; rice and jute prices, 132; *adhiar-jotedar* relationships, 133; and Congress, 142

Deshabandhu, 133, 141, 144, 151-3, 155-7, 159, 167-8

dewania, 47-8

Dewania, Aftaruddin, 205

Dinajpur, 8, 12, 18-20, 28, 38, 44, 48, 76, 83, 87, 91, 157, 180, 184-8, 191, 194, 196, 224, 227-9

District Board, 72, 153, 160, 161

District Mohammedan Association, *see* Mohammedan Association

District Muslim Students League, *see* Muslim Students League

District Road Cess Committe, 78

District Students Association, *see* Students Association

Doms (Scavengers), 119

Duars, 5, 7, 31; annexation from Bhutan,